COLLECTED POEMS

Micheal O'Siadhail was born in 1947. He was educated at Clongowes Wood College, Trinity College Dublin, and the University of Oslo. A full-time writer, he was awarded an Irish American Cultural Institute prize for poetry in 1982, and the Marten Toonder Prize for Literature in 1998. His poem suites, *The Naked Flame*, *Summerfest*, *Crosslight*, *Dublin Spring* and *At Night a Song is with Me* were commissioned and set to music for performance and broadcasting.

His *Collected Poems* (Bloodaxe Books, 2013) includes the contents of thirteen collections: *The Leap Year* (1978), *Rungs of Time* (1980), *Belonging* (1982), *Springnight* (1983), *The Image Wheel* (1985), *The Chosen Garden* (1990), *The Middle Voice* (1992), *A Fragile City* (1995), *Our Double Time* (1998), *The Gossamer Wall: poems in witness to the Holocaust* (2002), *Love Life* (2005), *Globe* (2007) and *Tongues* (2010). He has previously published two other compilations with Bloodaxe Books, *Hail! Madam Jazz: New and Selected Poems* (1992) and *Poems 1975-1995* (1999).

He has given poetry readings and broadcast extensively in Ireland, Britain, Europe, North America and Japan. In 1985 he was invited to give the Vernam Hull Lecture at Harvard and the Trumbull Lecture at Yale University. He represented Ireland at the Poetry Society's European Poetry Festival in London in 1981. He was writer-in-residence at the Yeats Summer School in 1991 and read at the Frankfurt Bookfair in 1997.

He has been a lecturer at Trinity College Dublin and a professor at the Dublin Institute for Advanced Studies. Among his many academic works are *Learning Irish* (Yale University Press, 1988) and *Modern Irish* (Cambridge University Press, 1989). He was a member of the Arts Council of the Republic of Ireland (1988-93) and of the Advisory Committee on Cultural Relations (1989-97), a founder member of Aosdána (Academy of distinguished Irish artists) and a former editor of *Poetry Ireland Review*. He was the founding chairman of ILE (Ireland Literature Exchange), and was a judge for *The Irish Times* ESB 1998 Theatre Awards and the 1998 *Sunday Tribune*/Hennessy Cognac Literary Awards.

Micheal O'Siadhail's website: www.osiadhail.com

Micheal O'Siadhail

COLLECTED POEMS

BLOODAXE BOOKS

ISBN: 978 1 85224 981 6 hardback edition with CD
          978 1 85224 982 3 paperback edition with CD

First published 2013 by
Bloodaxe Books Ltd,
Highgreen,
Tarset,
Northumberland NE48 1RP.

www.bloodaxebooks.com
For further information about Bloodaxe titles
please visit our website or write to
the above address for a catalogue

Supported by
**ARTS COUNCIL
ENGLAND**

CD manufactured by Sound Performance, Telford.

Cover design: Neil Astley & Pamela Robertson-Pearce.

Printed in Great Britain by Bell & Bain Limited, Glasgow, Scotland,
on acid-free paper sourced from mills with FSC chain of custody certification.

In memoriam
Bríd

ACKNOWLEDGEMENTS

Collected Poems includes the contents of thirteen collections: *The Leap Year* (1978), *Rungs of Time* (1980) and *Belonging* (1982), first published by An Clóchomhar; *Springnight* (1983) and *The Image Wheel* (1985), first published by Bluett; *The Chosen Garden* (1990), first published by Dedalus Press; and *The Middle Voice* (1992), *A Fragile City* (1995), *Our Double Time* (1998), *The Gossamer Wall: poems in witness to the Holocaust* (2002), *Love Life* (2005), *Globe* (2007) and *Tongues* (2010), all first published by Bloodaxe Books, *The Middle Voice* as part of *Hail! Madam Jazz: New and Selected Poems* (1992).

The readings on the accompanying CD were recorded at Westland Studios and Sonic Studios (2009-13), production and sound by Ross Martin.

I would also like to thank Phyllis Ford for her help in making earlier poems available electronically, Hester Higton for her copy editing, Aaron Edwards for his indexing work, Phil Dunne for his help in checking the proofs, and Paul Waldron at All Write Media Ltd for editing the recordings for the CD.

CONTENTS

Rungs of Time (1980)

III *Rungs*

Belonging (1982)

Springnight (1983)

The Image Wheel (1985)

The Chosen Garden (1990)

I *Departure*

II *A Blurred Music*

The Middle Voice (1992)

A Fragile City (1995)

FILTERED LIGHT

VEILS AND MASKS

Our Double Time (1998)

The Gossamer Wall: poems in witness to the Holocaust (2002)

REFUSALS

PRISONERS OF HOPE

Love Life (2005)

CRIMSON THREAD

COVENANTS

Globe (2007)

Tongues (2010)

FOREWORD

People love to assign poets a line of country, to pin things down and sum them up. Sometimes it is the contents, more often the form. There are the modernists, the imagists, the language poets, the new formalists and so on. I have never felt any temptation to align myself with any given school. Others have a passion for tracing a kind of poetic lineage: so and so is influenced by such and such a poet. Of course, I know we are all shaped by those poets we have read who have moved us. I belong to several traditions at once, so to trace a lineage would involve some complex criss-crossing.

It is forty-five years since I was a student in Oslo. When I revisited Norway recently, a friend quoted two lines to me from a poem by the Swedish-language Finnish poet Edith Södergran:

Jäg går på sol, jag står på sol	I walk on sun, I stand in sun;
jag vet ingenting annat än sol	I know nothing else but sun.
(*'Triumf att finnas till...'*)	('Triumph to exist...')

Suddenly it all came back to me – the thrilling bare honesty of those Scandinavian women Edith Södergran, Karin Boye and Halldis Moren Vesaas. Was it shaped by Scandinavia or was it as women they could risk this? I wonder are they still ringing in me when I chronicle in *The Leap Year* a growth towards daring to live in the sun:

> Here I am. I walk the earth,
> One lovely morning in eternity.
>
> ('Mirror')

A roofer once warned me when he saw me climbing a ladder to slide my hands up the rails on each side as I took another step up onto the next rung and not just to grab the next rung up with a free hand. It's risky – you're a second or two without a grip. It is temperament, I suppose, but all my life I have loved the excitement of that airy moment.

I was thirty-two when I was writing *Rungs of Time*:

> Already that's one year you have on Schubert,
> A whole year to bloom before Christ's torture.
>
> ('A Birthday')

My age is reflected in my concerns. Like many in their early thirties I am grappling with the first intimations of how quickly time passes, and of the humility required for slow work and spiritual growth, reassuring myself of the worth and sustainability of what I felt called to do. I am mulling over the spark of delight that made any plodding stoicism seem so dull, while conscious of how so many are tied to repetitive drudgery. At this time too, sheer carnal joy and deepening of love are held in play:

> A living space for a separate passion.
> A roof is framing our slanted intimacy.
>
> ('Roofing')

By *Belonging*, it seems the themes take a further societal turn. I am taken up with relationships and reconciliations, with forebears, family, friends new and old, children, former teachers and lovers, the marginalised:

> Parts we play prepared for us
> In the grand ensemble of humanity.
>
> ('Clerk')

The next two collections, *Springnight* and *The Image Wheel*, which followed closely on *Belonging*, continue in a similar thematic vein. But here I think I wanted a feel of greater ordinariness, to revel in detailed portraiture and mood. These were to be the last 'collections' inasmuch as soon afterwards I was able to devote all my time to my work as a poet, and from then on I wanted to write books which circled around and meditated on aspects of a single theme.

In *The Chosen Garden* I try to sketch the emotional trajectory from the garden chosen for me to the garden I chose. I am forty and living in a suburban three-up-two-down built around the same time as a similar house a mile or so away where I spent my early childhood. I have made the move, declared my hand as a poet and nothing else, and am working at a window overlooking a garden. Have I come full circle, or has this been a spiral upward? I had left for boarding school, for the exuberance of the 1960s, the clenched fist of ideologies, the desolation of failure, the second chance of love, and now the sense of return to a witting innocence:

> Double nature of nurture, of damage.
> There's no undoing all our knowledge.

> *Bon voyage!* Where will you choose
> another garden, another innocence?
>> ('Child')

When Bloodaxe published *Hail! Madam Jazz: New and Selected Poems*, the new part was a shorter book called *The Middle Voice*. I am forty-five and conscious of being middle-aged and in all probability well into the second moiety of life. The generation ahead is fading and I am a tradition-bearer, a memory-passer and a welcomer. In this baton change between two generations there is a poignant responsibility:

> ...here I am saying it's good
> to stand in between our coming
> and our going. Hinge and middleman...
>
> Receiver and sender. A signal boosted
> onwards. Pride and humility of a medium.
>> ('Three Rock')

In the early 1990s my close friend the theologian David Ford introduced me to the work of the philosopher Emmanuel Levinas, whose emphasis on the face of the other as the ground for ethics fascinated me, and I began *A Fragile City*. I was thinking about trust as the core of all good human and societal relationships. Trust is so open-faced, but its abuses veil and mask the face. While there are necessary boundaries to maintain otherness, the great celebration of trust is the face-to-faceness of feasting and dancing together:

> I feed on such courtesy.
> These guests keep countenancing me.
> Mine always mine. This complicity
> Of faces, companions, breadbreakers.
> You and you and you. My fragile city.
>> ('Courtesy')

I do not know why I was for many years haunted by the idea of death. I suspect I am not alone in this. *Our Double Time* starts as an attempt to come to terms with death. Yet it is much more. In some ways the whole of life is a preparation for its end. To embrace our finitude frees us from the compulsion for escapism whether through drugs, alcohol, overwork or constant entertainment, and allows us to live in the intensity of the moment. We not only taste each moment but also savour it so that time is doubled:

> A nagging unease, a thought I'd tried to shirk,
> Some hazy dread. At last I think I'll dare
> To face it squarely; even to trust its work.
> Such release! To care more and not to care!
> Twin intensity of knowing that now is now.
> All time is borrowed, borrowed and double.
> Two-sided, it both belongs and transcends.
>
> ('Our Double Time')

The Gossamer Wall: poems in witness to the Holocaust is structured as a mirror image, a chiasm. At the core of the book are the concentration camps. The cycle begins with the build-up of prejudice over almost two thousand years, and it ends with the long aftermath. On either side of the core are, first, the collapse of the town Northeim to Nazism and the hardening of ordinary men to violent killings in Battalion 101; and, second, the resistance of the village of Le Chambon and of brave individuals to Nazism. All of this is based on researched historical evidence.

Why a book of poems in witness to the Holocaust? I can try to say, but the reasons may be retrospective. I was reading Etty Hillesum. A friend showed me the tattooed camp number on her arm. I was menaced by neo-Nazis in Norway. On a different level, I felt the Holocaust had not really been confronted and that my post-war generation needed to face up to it. Whatever, I simply had to bear witness and see if I could come through with hope intact, still believing that to engage with the full richness of life is the only way to avoid such tragedies recurring:

> A raucous glory and the whole jazz of things...
> We feast to keep our promise of never again.
>
> ('Never')

What a delight it was in *Love Life* to turn to pay homage to a woman I had loved then for thirty-six years. To re-capture after three dozen years the first flush, the courtship, the promises, the ordinariness, the intimacy and growth in commitment, the mutual transformation and ageing together.

After a reading from *Love Life* at a conference in Scotland I sat to take a breather in an alcove. Two women sat within earshot, but didn't see me. 'What did you make of that?' asked one woman. 'I hated it,' replied the second. 'It brought me all the places I didn't want to go.' Ah, the power of poetry. I learned to begin such a reading by saying that I know how blessed I was:

> The longer we long, the further on beyond,
> Desire homing towards where desire began
>
> As though from its beginning a tune returns;
> Glory of our music how our music yearns.
>
> ('Caprice')

Then comes *Globe*, a meditation on history, process and vision in a time of restless change. Who shapes history? How do we remember the scars of tragedy and loss? Is there in all the criss-cross of cultures with their blurred boundaries a jazz of new and endless possibilities?

> Shared space
> Holding what we hold and not to fear
> Those bars
> Where our history clashes or jars,
> And in lines unsymmetrical to the ear
>
> Still hear
> Deep reasonings of a different lore.
> No map
> Of any middle ground or overlap,
> Yet listening as never before –
>
> ('Session')

I trained as a linguist and have always loved language. How could a poet not love language? In *Tongues* I give explicit expression to my lifelong delight in the word. Clearly every poem I have written implicitly rejoices in language, but here I want to revel in how words shift and change, how they are interrelated across languages and echo in us with the history of three or four thousand years:

> A hidden image lurks behind each word,
> Some secret cargo stored below my mind:
> A resonance, a coloured first-time heard,
> Recalled frisson never quite defined.
>
> ('Overlap')

I want to show in a playful way the extraordinary variety and inventiveness of the human imagination in the workings of language, in conveying meaning through visual signs, in proverbs which store wisdom. Then there is also my deep sense of gratitude to those who initiated me into other languages and their cultures.

But all this is hindsight. Collected poems are a kind of retrospective symphony. There was no grand plan. Different phases of growth, the various exigencies in the theatre of living call up the movements.

So much for the themes and movements. The classical Greek idea of the perfect marriage of content and form is probably every artist's dream. I have always tried to let a theme find its own form; often things just fall into a form:

> Delicious liberty of notes to rove
> Extempore
> *Con amore*
> As in between the lines we wove
> Inaudible noise
> Of a middle voice
> Underwrites our undersong,
> *Cantus firmus*
> Holding us
> In melodic progression, headstrong
> Silent tenor,
> Our rapport.
>
>   ('Caprice')

I am sure if you could scan a world of poetry somebody has used a similar form before. Who knows? But then there are many classical forms and variations on classical forms: the sonnet, blank verse, villanelles, couplets, tercets, quatrains and many more. There is both syllabic verse and free verse.

There are combinations of classic rhyming and syllabic verse. One I like to call a saiku (which means 'craftmanship', 'a piece of work' in Japanese) and is for me a portmanteau word to describe alternating the great classical form of Japan, the haiku, with the great classical form of the west, the sonnet. 'Crimson Thread', the final poem in *Love Life*, is a saiku.

Another favourite is the zigzag rhyme, where a word in each line rhymes (or occasionally half-rhymes) with one word anywhere in the following line. I use this frequently in *The Gossamer Wall* to chain together a deliberately sober account:

32

Company platoons surround the village.
Fugitives are shot. The others round
them up in the market. Anyone gives
trouble, gun them with infants or feeble
or any who hide. Able-bodied men
set aside for camps as 'work Jews'.

    ('A Polish Village')

The rhymes or half-rhymes *surround/round, fugitives/gives, anyone/gun, feeble/able, hide/aside* bind the description with echoes.

I also love to alternate an eight-syllable line with a six-syllable line. I found myself tumbling towards this in *Tongues* when meditating on characters:

Earlier three birds on a tree
But now only the one.
Imagine swoops of homing rooks
As evening tumbles in...

    ('Collection')

It is an honour to be a channel for our cries for meaning, for our desire to be part of some greater coherence. I spend my life in this 'ministry of meaning' which is poetry. I so often receive messages of response that hearten me and remind me of the privilege it is to word for others.

There are trends, fashions, pieties and politics in poetry, as in all else. I have always taken the long-term perspective on things. The Bengali poet Rabindranath Tagore was on to this:

Day by day I float my paper boats
One by one down the running stream....
I hope that someone in some strange
Land will find them and know who I am.

    ('Paper Boats')

I am grateful to critics who gave time and energy to discovering who I am. The poet and novelist Mary O'Donnell ended an extraordinarily perceptive piece on *Tongues* by asking: 'Whither now?'[1] As I write I am coping with the most difficult circumstances in my life so far. At the same time I am trying to contemplate how the modern world of thought, imagination and action is shaped. Things personal and things societal. God only knows where all this will take me.

I am deeply grateful to my publishers, to my translators, to those who have invited me to read and to all who have supported me in so many ways. But in the end the circle of meaning is completed by readers:

> Guests all
> At Madam Jazz's beck and call.
> For nothing but the music's sake.
>
> ('Session')

[1] *Studies Irish Review* (Autumn 2012), vol. 101, no. 403, pp. 335–41, www. studiesirishreview.ie. Mary O'Donnell also contributed a chapter to *Musics of Belonging: The Poetry of Micheal O'Siadhail*, edited by Marc Caball and David F. Ford (Carysfort Press, Dublin, 2007). Among a number of works, this book and David C. Mahan, *An Unexpected Light: Theology and Witness in the Poetry and Thought of Charles Williams, Micheal O'Siadhail and Geoffrey Hill* (Wipf and Stock Publishers, Eugene, OR, 2009), have been for me particular sources of insight into my own work.

Hail! Madam Jazz

Worship, hold her a moment in thought.
Femme fatale, she shapes another face,
unveils an idol. O Never-To-Be-Caught,

O Minx beyond this mind's embrace,
Hider-Go-Seeker, Miss Unfathomable,
Demurring Lady playing at the chase.

As stars or atoms we turn, fall
towards each other's gravity. I spin
in your love's nexus, Mistress All.

Once a child of Newton's fallen
apple, I'd the measure of your ways.
My stars, my atoms, are we one?

Mischievous Strategy, Madam Jazz!
Old tunes die in metamorphosis.
Rise, fall, reawakening. I praise.

The Leap Year

(1978)

Motion of Thanks

To that delightful woman,
Who gave to Micheal one year's pension
To sit on a bench in Stephen's Green,
A thousand thanks!

And if I seemed a layabout,
Muse and darling of Parnassus,
This indolence it was that shaped me.
All rights reserved.

Mirror

This morning of all mornings
Ask the mirror what I become
Or count for in the scheme of things
In millennia gone or still to come.

Mirror, mirror on the wall,
Humbly I accept today
Whatever now you chose to say –
Tell me all!

Go on! Who from Adam down
Stands in front and says to me:
Here I am, I walk the earth,
One lovely morning in eternity.

Surely!

You who'd loved her beforehand
Or found her in my aftermath,
Surely we'd understand each other,
You and me.

One day we'd sat face to face
Naked on a train,
But were we blind to one another,
You and me?

We thought we'd take each other's hand
Before we'd leave the train –
Out of hand we'd left each other,
You and me.

Among the shades, have no doubt,
These lives of ours we'll talk through;
Guardian angels for each other,
You and me.

Temptation

In this park, lead us not into temptation.
Does an evil angel walk in Stephen's Green?

'Please, just good sense,' he says respectfully.
'I plead with you to stop all this immediately.

'Who'd mind? but look at those old women feeding
Ducks. And, friend, that's where you're heading.'

Then after a billion years of pure anticipation,
That moment especially for me the sun had risen.

There and then, I knew them by their beauty
Those three eternal goddesses of our story,

Bending to feast a world of ducks on a crust.
Do they weave for us our threads of fate from dust?

Of Course

Of course, it's only reasonable:
This journey was incomprehensible;
At every glance's end, winter waited.

But today I saw the spring, my friend.
A whole wide world has germinated.
Hail and welcome!

Just today winter flung off its coat
And humbly stood outside the womb,
Begging again a world without end.

Stairs

Such talk, my love, of any stairhead,
A rumour for our heirs in every tread.

At the top of a stairs what would you do?
Written here is what we always knew,

This old mystery in steps of stairways:
The ascent itself is what we praise.

Upwards and with you, tread by tread.
Could it be we're near the stairhead?

Spring

I saw one morning at nine,
A bird on the run for all its worth
From tree No. 1,
A public servant moving heaven and earth
To see his master's will is done
In tree No. 2,

And almost unbeknownst to me
If I hadn't heard on the grapevine
That he'd a wire from his minister
To tell us how another year
Returns. Nothing amiss.
Just as everything should be –
It is.

Call

Set your course and let's depart –
Moonbound now but don't lose heart –
Take leave of sense!

Long fed up with holding back,
It's skyward for everyman Jack –
And Jack means you!

No, begrudgers can't hold sway,
If you Jack don't lose your way;
Stay the course.

In this valley robbers all,
In each thief's cross and call
His own deliverance.

Dizziness

A giddy spool keeps on turning
Images of bliss that wheel about,
Wide and dancing ample ring,
Mind your head, look out! Look out!

Southward of Stephen's Green,
Blue, red, yellow and white,
North around and back to south,
Light and life, clay and light.

Long and lovely, so true a ring,
Flawless circle, true and long,
Beguiling ever and ever ring,
In whose hub you lived a while.

Grace Before Drink

Come to my aid, dear Father,
In giving humbly in to dissipation
That I may come before you
And ask forgiveness.

Solstice

She conceals from us what she intends,
The slow return to winter she desires,
But today is spoken in the present tense,
So what if Midas has his secret ears.

Sun, ease us as we disclose the hidden,
Gently tell your secret to the forest
That bows to the sun, bends with the wind,
In the sheerest joy, the sheerest trust.

Regrets

When March first came in, I'd thought
I'd concentrate on nothing but my tree;
Slowly as a child, slowly so slowly,
It would germinate, shoot by shoot.

Talk of a war, a worry, a distraction;
Then, one small thing after another
Somehow smudged my best intention,
Drawing me from the business of a father.

Now, over again the need for autumn,
For three secret seasons in the womb
Before I'm born to re-attend my tree's
Slow, precise unfolding of a history.

Graffiti

The warmest summer in a hundred years;
The toughest work, the sweetest wine;
As usual the women were even finer
Than ever before.

This was the summer I at last conceded
The unfathomables, even pleasures I'd miss.
Was this ageing or a glimpse of paradise
Through the needle's eye?

Like the monk who chronicled a dread of wintery
Vikings, I felt the need to mention
One good season. For the annals my entry:
This was summer.

Report

Friends, countrymen and so on...
At long and longer last,
An end to angst and doubt,
To growth in dark.

Here the wind, here the sun,
You may dance or cry your heart out;
Seeds delighted in dark;
Here's the light.

Bench

Come and sit here on a bench.
Lovely, more lovely girls become,
A parade of beauty's rivalries –
Infinite comparative degrees –
O God, there's generations yet to come!

Come and sit here on a bench.
Still to the good, still we count
The one we won,
The long-lost one,
The one whose brand your heart has burnt.

To hearten you I ask you to come
To say on this bench a man once sat
Who knew the grief you know too
And thought a moment just of you.
Brother, this bench is no comedown.

Red-letter Day

This is a red-letter day, my friend,
Ten thousand, two hundred and sixteen
Already spent
Of this life's bloom and merriment –
Its brevity the fault I find.

Eve should have left the apple alone
And sat tight in that easy garden,
But I think she'd understood
In fallenness and worldly mud
All saints are honed.

So out of that bed, come on!
Grab this shaft of sun today.
The world and its mother know
To let no moment slip,
On this lovely trip we undergo
South and out of Babylon.

The Bridge

For years I puzzled over those words of the Curé d'Ars
About that Frenchman who threw himself into the water;
He'd said in the moments between the bridge and river
A man prepares his soul.

For years I couldn't understand his strange pilgrimage
Until I too had walked to the edge of that bridge
And there staring into the dark had caught a glimpse
Of light in the bridge's eye.

For years I puzzled over those words of the Curé d'Ars.
We accept, he said, even what an ill-wind has blown.
In that space between the arch and the river's foam
Am I made whole?

Stephen's Green

You've been listening so long now
I understand your need to know
Who am I?

You were right all the while,
I'm the bronze head you passed by
This morning in the Green.

The famed patriot condemned to death?
Poet from the last century I've seen?
I can't decide!

At your ease keep about your business.
Pillared among bushes your spirit's guide
Watches over you.

Picture

Although all night it poured rain
Any second the sun will rise again
When she's chosen a mirror she fancies
Among these puddles.

Already one dog on his grassy round
From barrel to barrel on sodden ground,
Tail in the air, sniffs out the latest
Global news.

Soon it's nine a.m. or so.
Office girls head to a Dublin bureau
With Renoir's loveliest umbrellas
Borrowed for the day,

And round a corner here you are
Who'd managed yesterday to mar
The scene – but that's for historians,
Let them do as they may –

A fortnight ago when weather was dry,
As sea vapours rose, their spirits high,
Molecules worked their subtle miracle
On water and warmth in love.

As you were deep asleep last night
Rainclouds devised plans to put it right,
To clean the canvas from side to side.
Now is another story.

Over Again

Over again a formula for the ineffable,
Still fresh line of sinner and rebirth,
The sun and a tree it raised from earth,
A season's new barley as old as the hills.

You're no sensitive Athlone youth
Discussing the social themes of our time,
Expert in Malinowski's efficient paradigm
For human beings and their milieu.

But between ourselves (and tell the truth!)
Didn't you always travel my touch and go,
Between the allegro and grieving largo,
Here between our heavens and our earth?

Birdsong

My God it's well for us I know –
Fol de rol derido.

We're the blessed ones, we birds,
No sooner fed to the teeth with worms

Than off on a caper to a chapel spire,
Up to the high heavens of our desire.

O look at our man measuring his earth
A thousand, thousand miles below.

We are the chosen, we are the birds.
Fol de rol derido.

Sonatina

First announce a true note,
Then, of course, the theme:
That the likes of you and me
Were here a while.

Easy now! Hear my story.
I was that father to your father,
Who cried one evening at the gate –
I am Adam.

Stepwise raise the tune again.
Light is seen on the horizon –
Didn't I lay my hand on your shoulder?
Come along.

Louder now and banish misfortune,
It's the March of the King of Laois in state,
In slow and sweet triumph to retake
His lost uplands.

Compliment

Were those women meek and humble
Who once whispered in a man's ear
That a god was a dominant male?
Then tell me that we know better.

Among the bright women of the world
There have always been those goddesses,
As we crossed our makeshift scaffold,
A universe built in time and space.

Did some of these women think it through,
That few who drifted through my youth;
The two or three, who somehow drew
My threads together, wove my cloth?

A wonderful cloth, my shirt of linen,
My chequered gift, a self they've woven,
This shirt that's closer than the bone,
The bright women of my world have given.

Chanson

Should it be
I'm not there
To walk with her
As autumn falls
And winds officially declare
The festival of leaves is open,
The annual commotion
In the city of God.

Should it be
My tree has toppled,
Walk here with my heir,
Walk with your playful air,
And here's to your health,
A toast to you both
As autumn falls
In the city of God.

Sunflower

The danger of tautening towards the sun:
To lose is to lose all.
Too much gravity and I'm undone;
If I bend, I fall.

Tell me it's all worth this venture,
Just the slightest reassurance,
And I'll open a bloom, I'll flower
At every chance.

Then praise me all the way to the sky,
Praise me with light, lover,
Oh, praise me, praise me, praise me,
And I live forever.

Cradle Song

The Queen of Sheba's questions done,
For all the wisdom, lore weighs down,
Poor Solomon begins to doze;
Maybe now you'll nod, who knows?

Hushaby, no need for angst,
Tomorrow no holiday or feast,
The gods are wearing everyday clothes,
Footling away on tippy toes.

Long lashes gather around the daisy,
Round and round its yellow eye,
The eyes ahead and behind we keep,
While you my child are fast asleep.

Watches

Sometimes in the watches of night
My heart begins to pound
For fear I'd wake
In the land of snow,
Storied and travelled stranger,
Who lost his youth along the way.

Sometimes in small hours I think
I've spent my bag of wishes
As randomly as Faust or Séana
Tying demons and devils
To apple trees.

Surely in the depths of any bag
Lies the thrift of a heart's desire –
You only ever had one wish –
To flourish under the sun,
This deliberate second sowing
That now by stealth is growing
To ripeness.

Fable

When autumns spark
Their tongues of fire
Through the trees in Leeson Park,
Turn this street into a fable

And tell of all before us,
War or peace, stroke or ruse,
In each brick a reminiscence,
Novels folded in a countenance.

You zone in on one visage
And there it is, your own image:
Autumn's tongues of fire retell
Stories wound within your story.

Night Song

Loves and desires,
The burn and tears,
Our human contrarieties
Of frosts and fires,
Almighties inveigling you
Into their weave.

Which reminds me of the sun –
I need just to be certain –
Is what they tell me true,
That yellow purse too must end?
O that quandary, old conundrum,
Cock that will tomorrow wake you.
Tonight, comrade, feel at home,
Here in the house of your friend.

Souvenir

Recall a leaf still in its prime
A wind had bought as a souvenir
It throws on trees and leaves to sear,
So it will turn to gold with time.

Don't cry for autumn, don't cry although
Such riches seem to scatter in vain,
Our last year's snow will fall again,
Just given another season or so.

Sometimes

Mother, I thought the world of you,
The skies above, the ground below;
Lodestar, my childhood's say-so,
Until that universe unhinged,
A star in my high heavens plunged.

At other hearths on autumn nights,
Sometimes when I begin to laugh,
Half aware, half wittingly,
You're still that angel of light
Travelling for ever deep within.

Dispossessed

At a rally, standing on a bench, I saw that woman;
A heart on her sleeve seemed to flinch as she began:

'Don't tell me it's over, we're an extinct breed,
The hand that planted lives, the tree is dead.

I'm resolved to save those leaves, come what may,
If it means I'll be nailed onto this passion tree.'

I once saw a woman standing on a park bench
Gluing a yellowed leaf back onto a branch.

Was the tree stretching down a naked limb,
Lifting that woman quietly up into its bosom,

To cradle her gently, then rock and soothe her,
Tucking her into a long sweet sleep of winter?

Wanderlust

Lift up that cross, a stranger to your own,
Ignore the drill from all the schools of life.

Gather up your luggage, then straight off,
Both eager and afraid set sail alone.

As west you go and wandering off course,
Your aim still *terra firma* though you sail

To carefree lands where all may fail,
The lonely isle where endless food still grows.

Season

A season ago these trees had flung a libraryful
Of ochre leaflets in a crosswind's free-for-all,

As if determined to pose for months in the nude,
To allow the low sun warm their leafless blood.

And still it's winter. Still this twentieth century.
What news item will we run today? What's the story

To break? The naked trees, a bird's plaintive sound
Asking whether a world still breathes underground.

The hard-crusted soil turns in its sleep and cries:
'Just live, man, I'm busy pushing up the daisies.'

Something young and dangerous stirs in the marrowbone
Of earth. Await the leap and resurrection of a season.

Rungs of Time

(1980)

Preface

Here I'm back again
Just by my teeth's skin
Yet under your thumb,
Ninth muse that's mine.

For a while I retreated
From you, up the creek,
Seeking the quick kick –
Gone to the dogs instead.

Adultery wasn't for me;
Too long now we belong,
Too long interwoven,
And so accordingly

Here once more I come,
Your lapdog and yes-man,
Forever under your thumb,
O ninth muse of mine!

I. ROPES

Only the Dance

Out of sight and mind,
As much as I can do
Once again to wind
Back into the dance.

The dance all I crave –
To amplify the refrain
My only need for gain.
For want of that, you thief,

Only your comic number,
Every night a *petite mort*,
Morning a Lazarus – no more,
You, brother of slumber!

I slip out of mind.
Bending over backwards
I wind again to the swords
At the dance's core.

Moment

My lovely aimless moment
Surely you'll linger a little,
You link in my chain's middle,
Summer girl's carefree ribbon
Blown in the wind.

Please just a second or so
Allowing me this interim;
No heroics or bravado,
Let me recollect one gem
Through life's window.

Are you a winking mirage?
I sit as the moment goes
Like summer ribbons' badinage
Or instant grass that grows
Over our memory.

You made this bed of mine
Which I'm now lying on,
Each child a father of the man
On your wide window, aimless moment,
Already smiling from beyond.

A Birthday

Already that's one year you have on Schubert,
A whole year to bloom before Christ's torture.

Strange how, after a frantic decade of imprudence,
These thirties seem almost nearer to our teens.

Is this gravity at last bending us to its rule
Or a fertile ring of history turned in the skull?

Is it age the thief plotting against our will
Or an auxiliary circle curved within a circle?

A cock kicking the wind, determined to fight;
Another light-year moving towards the infinite?

Then tell me first which pure truth is truer –
Riddle me that today, my wise old codger!

Definition

Father my own, what should I say to you?
There was father after father after you,
As many fathers as a youth shed skins.

Good father, by stealth you seemed to fix
My boundaries. *Alter ego*, yardstick,
Needle's eye I pass through into a world.

Is a shell defined by its need to unshell?
A subtle fragility, breakthrough and bustle,
A scurrying from one prototype to another,

Doubt after doubt unhusking to the kernel.
At last, this ease between modelled and model.
Father, comrade, what should I say to you?

So-and-So

For this awkward son of a gun
Nothing but his own sweet ways,
Who once spent his days dithering,
Hithering first, then thithering,
Too long considering all doorways –
Already is what's done so done?
Sonny boy, where's your confidence
To board this exile ship of time
Sailing straight before the wind,
A cargo carrying no crown prince?

Look! Here Caoimhín comes to you
Who eluded you that time by a gene
Or two. And Anna's growing too.
But that young man a child of Caitlín's?
Could that be? Time sneaks away
A half-lifetime just while you drift
From yesterday towards another day,

A sorry mess and still no side-kick,
Who somehow let the moment go –
Aren't you the contrary so-and-so?

But aren't you the unlucky get,
Never content with one generation,
Who had to deal in legerdemain
And leap beyond every limit –
Six ages before and six ago –
You that too headstrong navigator,
Playing your games of hide and seek,
Some dozen lines and leaps of lineage,
Those piggybacks you've promised later
Down the line of Mister So-and-so.

Circus Rider

Astride two loping haltered horses
He circles the arena, a *tour de force*
Astraddle a skittish gap. Watch him
Holding those barebacks in tandem.

A deft balance. They seem to want
To veer apart as though two different
Voices called. We clap to the music;
A rhythm curbs the tension of his risk.

'Please more rope,' begs a right hand,
'Allow your nature the scope and bond
Of its affections. Don't rein me in.
I'm the cry of your children's children.'

'Stay the course!' whispers a left hand,
'It doesn't matter what others demand,
I'm your ecstasy, queen single-mindedness
Chafing a dream with pure-bred giddiness.'

At last the rider's moment of applause,
A smiling lap in his red-striped blouse
Astride our joy and wonder. Who'd remember
All the halter's sweated fray and tear?

Sand

Time is sand
On a river's bed,
Beyond blustering men
Boast and whistle;
Over here women whisper,
Their silk skirts rustle
Across the water.

Such unfathomable understanding,
a well that can't be sounded,
until the sloe will bloom white,
and yesterday returns.

Woman's will to love
is a well of abundance;
a waterlily on its surface
the shallow share of a male.

We tried to sound it once
but were far too selfish;
we saw our own poor image –
the well itself is bottomless.

Time is sand
In a lover's mind,
Age and childhood recycle,
Form and substance are one;
The world is a youth again
And sand is time.

Becoming

What's infinite and female in a circle
Eludes me. Always that hub of room,
A roundedness arcing behind the angle
Of my vision. I'm yearning at the rim.

A juttedness seems to fawn and dither,
The moth of my desire angling at every
Candle butt that flickers a come-hither,
A fickleness roving near the periphery.

Ah, women. Insiders, bearers of the womb
That shaped us, it's as though you dwell
Within a turning, somehow always at home
And there beyond me, your being a circle.

Whatever's in a ring can never arrive,
Just keeps on bringing its curve full
Circle, a figure certain and receptive.
This eternal becoming, this making whole.

How Those Ants

How those ants don't tire or pause,
Bustling around a low-pitched nest,
Eternally expiring for the cause,
All their revolutions second-best.

See how not a star has roved
Or even danced in death's embrace,
Forever holus-bolus they still move
Across their wide and milky ways.

Our stars and insects all mother-wit –
But spare a thought for others' loss,
Who taste the apple's acrid bite,
Weigh themselves on reason's cross.

Never Ever

Never ever go asking why
Or question joy's tearful eye,
When in your mind friends gather
From years each better than another,
All in your callow prime.

Friend, don't ask the why or wherefore.
Both frost and fire will burn as well,
Hankering after ships to Valparaiso,
Wistful for where you'll never sail,
All in your youth and prime.

Never ever demand to know
If it's your father's tears that flow
In willy-nilly soft remembrance
With its eternal beguiling dance,
All in your fading prime.

Need

Fed to the teeth I'm sick and tired!
This monkish rule, matins and nones!
Here I am a prompter snared,
Crooked side-stage and incognito.
Where now all the exotic zones,
Where now those once lands of snow?
Where's Cleopatra and her asp?
My need to grasp at life.

And still I want to break harder earth,
Digging out my own inscape;
Each time again just back and forth,
The same old tracts I need to bless
To understand what curve of lineage
Turned in wombs when we took shape,
To see a child in old men's eyes
As in the child the eye of age.

Cleft Stick

Not that they didn't always know
The cleft stick of urge and skill;
Philosopher, saint or politico,
Every artisan knows it still.

Philosophers who under full sail
Chose the deep and ventured out,
But coasting now too much by skill
Without the undertow of doubt.

The politico who whipped a crowd
And held their anger in his sway,
His expectations too slipshod
For the same revolution day by day.

The day of honour the *dies irae*
For saints who once blazed with zeal;
When all is said become too blasé
Their credo now an easy spiel.

For any deeds or words or thought
Desire decides the pulse's rate;
Mind and skill and scheme blot out
The hungry pang, the heart in spate.

Hangover

We regret a break in service –
One wheedling piper carries the can,
Who's taken a short cut like this
Through the door to seventh heaven.

Pleasure's bailiff knocks to serve you –
The skull pounding out its warrant,
A charge for drones, instalment due,
His final red admonishment.

A morning shaft of light will dazzle,
A wall-to-wall sparkling rake;
As fanlike breezes worn to a frazzle
Blowing this lazybones awake.

Is wind of word today enough
To give these bagpipes' drone a blow?
Is this a piper slacking off –
Between two bulletins a scherzo?

So soon we can restore provision
Service will return to normal
With all the sounding out and vision;
For now forgive my gospel's lull.

Rest

Since the Holy Ghost's on strike –
All work's against the constitution –
Since fate's wheels are so erratic,
Best to bend with each temptation.

Rhythmless tunes just rigmarole,
a stalling line pure tedium:
My polkas, rumbas, sambas all
Little more than pandemonium.

In the end if that's how it is,
This dilly-dally too may heal,
So hoop yourself in idle bliss –
To try no use despite your zeal.

Bad and all as rest may seem,
The more somehow you try the more
You find your clumsy foot off-beam –
Rhythm's still the dance's core.

A block overcome again I tread
The sparking rhythm. A pulse caressed
Ups once more the blood to my head
And soon I won't recall this rest.

Banishing Demons

Out, I say, my dark memory,
Devil a bit of your concern
To tease me here. Secret heartburn.
Hidden spleen. A cul-de-sac
Darkening out all fantasy.
White is black.

Come in my one bright memory
Shaped as this butterfly soul of mine.
Éadaoin born to a king from wine,
Token of my garden's right
Mellowing all Gethsemane.
Black is white.

All We Have

Spare a thought for lives that hinge
So much on chance, on hit-or-miss
Of random words we tweak or twinge,
As cosying up we must caress
And stroke them till our dalliance
Can slip behind all common sense.

Word by word as you trade off,
Syllable by syllable you'd give,
Every living phrase you'd slough
For just some bars of music's drive
That pulsing in the vein beguile
And lead you to the Blessed Isle.

Feel for us – we're so dependent
On each slip-sliding statement.
Are actions louder than what's uttered
In words we know no parsnips buttered?
Yet all we have. And seeing it's so:
This madcap fling, our only throw.

Pioneers

Without forerunners sailing on ahead,
Would we whom they encourage and stall
Too long ago have run our course instead?
Without our pilots would we sail at all?

Unless they voyaged far on their longships,
If others hadn't berthed in the straits,
How could we've ever ridden out whitecaps;
As in their wake our boat still navigates?

Sick and tired of following in tow,
Always veering to track those gone before –
Sink or swim, whatever, here I go;
Self-reliant now I take my chance.

Our slow advance the common debt we owe,
All in this fickle cockboat tossed and thrown;
Our line each turn united in a row –
No generation ever on its own.

Craft

Much use this song to me –
In a flirt's purse a kiss,
No more a poem's envoy
Than any angel's hubris,
A pin in a scholar's cushion,
Frail dream of landless men,
A pillow-talking lover.

What's a strain or verse,
Pound, pincushion or kiss?
Whatever I can do
To finger-bones and nerves,
With all my main and might
Unclasping sloth, I unlatch
My gable window's light.

Striptease

You think this work is only fun?
Strip off and stand there in your buff!
Deep still watchers' waters run.

'And what he thinks he is, this guy?'
They'll say, the sly and cunning ones,
In draughty mansions high and dry.

'Aren't you the gullible Simple Simon,
Exposing all, your heart in mouth,
Such hullabaloo, your rattling on?

'Sonny boy! I call that cheeky,
A holy show around the town
With fiddle-faddles about your psyche.'

So hesitate then just enough,
This hogwash doesn't suit you –
It's fasting for lopsided love.

The silent ones beside each other
But busy still they haven't seen
You're standing in the altogether.

Somehow you're owned by them as well,
Their offhandedness and bias,
Just like their silence their credential.

Their disregard a scale of your success,
Your cake you keep and eat by stealth –
This unrequited love your business.

Declining

'Is living so alert not deadly,
That vigil for what's best for me –
Better to live a while outside,
A free-wheeler?

'What would you do with trophies,
Your mind too still, too much at ease,
Perched there on the world's top,
The slippery peak?

'Perhaps it's noble to fall behind,
As long as you go when you're inclined' –
So many at my heels advise me.
Thank you all for the thought!

Mind

No point in going fully out of it,
My stratagem to stay there hanging on;
Best indulge its roundabout dull wit,
Crying from within like Baptist John.

Let's not even abandon common sense
But rather tend the sudden inner ray
Of suffering that if we ever betray
Our absent minds unravel into nonsense.

The frenzied mind too *à la carte*,
Only thought's hands-on restraint will do,
Every half-wit is like his counterpart,
And all must say 'I depend on you,'

For no one measures empty space alone.
But still we need John's wilderness
To zone in on those we call our own;
Lying low we serve our circle best.

Footsteps

To grope around a tiresome carry-on,
To feel your slow and deviating ways,
Gesturing airs and graces here and yon,
Chalked mark to mark within the honey maze.

A maze that's honeyless without the chalk,
Which by our yearning's light alone is seen,
As making tracks in others' steps we walk
In secret places where they too had been.

Back to wall or cornered in dead ends,
Their insisting compass our encouragement,
Footsteps of disciples, the chalk of friends,
A needle's proof we aren't off the scent.

Frustrating stuff this rummaging about
As step by step we make our upward way,
The further off the beat, the more remote,
The sweeter in the comb the breeze's play.

Their narrow needle still your guarantee
That in this labyrinth there's honeydew;
More or less you'd always find unworthy,
Their faithful compass needle warrants you.

Unless

All too well I know
Both calm and storm;
My worry the sudden blow,
Payments I can't afford.

How to fill my well
Of pleasure to its lip;
Store of fun topped up
Which doesn't brim or spill.

Two things both half done:
To deepen and fill my well
So I bask in joyful sun
And not to fear a drought.

The better the well can last,
The worse in the end your thirst;
Unless by other measures
Pleasure's memory is longer.

Work

You insatiable bitch you!
Even still I can't quit you,
never flit from your manger.

Again and again, you slut.
So cruelly you've looted
my meagre legacy of years.

You're the merciless whore,
a wantonness still scourging me,
agony of desire in the loin

I'll never want to do without.
Rather you than your counterpart:
a tediousness turning all to dust.

You're the ghost of an old lover,
you're there at my bed's four corners;
even sweetness palls without you.

Pleasure

Lucifer's worst arrogance
The thin flattering hand
He once insinuated
Under the skirts of chance.

Let-go now and leisure
Between me and myself,
Voluptuousness and ease,
Nothing for me but pleasure.

Lenience for my bones
As I tauten both vein
And flesh to break and enter
God's amorous zones,

As mad for linen and lace
I twitch at the flicker
Of a thigh and skill
With skill-lessness replace.

Earthen vessel at play,
Flamboyant on the precipice –
Because or in spite of this,
How lovely now our clay!

Rope

Pleasure's taut and slack we'd tested
And either way it kinked and twisted,
As though it must be wound enough
To hold in check our rope of love;
That long-haired strand of lust,
That hempen strand of lack,
And joy the third well woven in.

No ease or glib let-up in sight,
Long-haul slog of passion or rebuff
Our growth. And no looking for pity.
Just name the prouder gift of grace,
Declaim the secret inner delight
That's ours. Pleasure is not enough;
Our love a triple-stranded rope.

II. RUMOURS

An Oslo Brewery

Seven a.m. sharp. Right on the button
electric life is recreated. A shuddering
back into action of greased and sleepy
machinery. The steam whinges and rises.
A first arrival from the locker dodges
past iron girders, climbs to his post.
A clang and blare louden. It's hell
for leather. A conveyer shakes a *joie
de vivre*, a huge quaking expectancy,
a world in suspense awaits its morning's
bottles. A quarter of an hour. Hurry!
Stack up those labels; snug and ready,
give those containers a fix of glue.
A move on, mate! A gooey bucket tilts
and spills. Someone swears. A messer!
A few minutes yet. The rush and pitch,
rattle of fellowship and tempered steel,
camaraderie of cog for tooth. Solidarity.
The steam clouds the ceiling's lights
blotting out the dome of work's temple.
Every mother's son and daughter bends,
priming, tuning, fixing, bringing a house
to order. The daily advent of the bottle.

And there she goes. A first bottle
up to its neck in ale. Thousands more
behind, driven by their gods, urgent,
relentless, skittling on to the conveyor,
hiss and jostle for position on the belt.
Clack and rat-a-tat, rattle and whirr.
For every bottle the cap that fits.
Clack and rat-a-tat, rattle and whirr.
Two labels per bottle, belly and neck.
Clack and rat-a-tat, rattle and whirr.
A brand for every bottle, a personality;
for every bottle its body and soul,

as it squeezes towards the carton machine
tended by its acolyte labellers and packers.
And still seven endless hours to go.

How else can all this time be thought of?
Electric light doesn't rise or set,
heavens don't fill and darken with rain,
no chance break to shelter in a ditch.
Still seven hours of wilderness to go.
Imagine a taskmaster, any pleasured sultan
measured or ruthless as the clock's dial
putting such a face on inner intensities,
a holy of holies of crystal oscillations.
Clack and rat-a-tat, rattle and whirr.
Well, what time do you reckon it's now?
Numb slowly, fall into a day's reverie.

Look out! Numbskull. Nitwit. *Tosk!*
A bottle trips, stumbles along the belt
unlabelled. Droves of bottles fumble
one another, climb and jam in clusters.
For God's sake, stop that conveyor!
A stupid idiot. And it's time lost!
Remember the bonus. A sudden squabbling.
Recall the creed. A Serb is taking off
gloves to wipe his forehead and dream
a fortnight at home. He smiles his motto:
The more bottles, the more money.

Outside a day is lengthening in its sky.
These bottles live out their inner life
by time and motion, a sacred predestination
from top to label, to pack and fork-lift.
A loud whoosh! Some newly filled bottle
collides and bursts. And nobody startles
or heeds a blow-out. Half-asleep, half-awake.
A Turk is relighting his cigarette butt;
a packer pulls her rubber apron tighter,
stooping that grey and wasting chassis.
The more bottles, the more our money.
Read here a winding litany of unlanced
heart-sores, a long sigh of forebearance.
Something will never find itself in words.
The more bottles, the more our bonus.

According to the Act: so-so many minutes
break per hour allowed for self-repair.
Somebody is sitting on an upturned crate,
a mind is ungearing itself into neutral.
Closeted in the john, an ochre-skinned
addict swills a lukewarm beer on the sly.
A young bearded radical preaches the day
when every inhuman clock is torn down,
but his dream is a nightmare even stranger
than the daily abyss of clocked-up hours.
'Is this then the inferno?' his youth asks.
Across the belt Turkish women joke and laugh.
A world always hung between a hell and heaven.

So slowly the time is stealing forward.
How is it certain this day has happened?
Who arrives in dark, leaves in dark.
Lowry's brittle figures ashen and pink
file to the exit. Press the random button.
Red: frisk for any smuggled bottles;
Green: pass unsearched through the gate.
'A good weekend,' someone says. 'And you too.'
Behind the red bulb's buzzer sounds. Frames
veer into the street. A strange inalienable
dignity flushes those sombre homing faces.

Nugent

Eye-catching flash, thin air,
a moment on the evening news
leaps across a television's
magic lamp. The prisoner.
After two years and nine months
prisoner Nugent released today
from Long Kesh prison.
                    My God,
was it the glare that lit his eye
unhinged us?
                    History resumes:
another story from Nicaragua,

Final race of the day from Naas.
So little time for news or history?

And that's it. Tomorrow his picture
seen on half a million papers:
prisoner Nugent yesterday released.
Tomorrow the backroom's clean-up.
In fact his image got covered
By some stray spattering of paint.
What cause is worth a blood drop,
To say nothing of youth's bloom.
The soul's current affairs our music.

Well then who was that Nugent?
Another martyr from netherlands,
all wound up with cause and rights
and stooping under forty years.
Again in Nugent's fearing eyes
a last private soldier walks
starved and broken behind Napoleon
or any camp-follower trudging
through frozen land of history
to recompense our cosiness.
Is it his own glittering eyes
That now in ours ignites a glare?

Escape

Today by just one of those chances
I met a thinker completely rational
And yet consistently out of his senses.

A crackpot maybe but no simpleton,
With all his sharp and complex thought,
So following the tortured line he'd spun

All my wit had seemed to dissipate
As though I'd bowed to his hair-splitting,
A hair's-breadth from swallowing his bait,

Until suddenly I'd laughed again
And breaking loose unravelled a way
From such a sad consistent brain.

Stony Patch

The crowd move on and leave
after them remnants of history's blunder,
to mimic them in mind and manner;
their welfare, they say, to be like them.
A peculiar fish, the philosopher in exile,
an orphan of time held in the balance,
without bowed head or head on high,
scratching his story in the wax of his soul.

But maybe many's the time before
a thin beam of insight flashed from the blue
on some posse of Egypt's hermits long ago,
on a lay monk gathering dungcakes in the west
on a cold stony patch in Aran or Skellig Rock.
How can we know a fine needle of light didn't catch
in their soul's wax the music playing?
Sheet to shroud the crowd sailed on.

Unquenched

Surely not in vain
our whole life stowed
on microfilms that contain
the book of the world.
Long years ago
Our candle quenched
but for that hole
we bored
in the bushel's side.
We abide
one winter to another,

from master to master
on a candle's memory
that nearly went out.
Our revolution a dream,
our dream a revolution –
in every thought
eternity
incarnates.

The Game

Down you come and off the ditch!
Since the morning sun has risen,
since the ball was thrown in
to our match's final strike,
our doing the beginning and end,
the *sliotar*'s alpha and omega.
But what kind of hurling is that?
Down you come and off the ditch!

So you faithful yet to come,
you who urge us from behind
you so long gone on ahead,
door-closers for the bolted horse,
we hear you here inciting us
yet somehow we too make no move
and can't get off our knowing ditch.
Be patient now all you faithful,
no moment grander than the next
and every generation's purpose unknown
until we listen.
The twentieth century's last quarter
well begun. Here in Dublin,
come from every province and county,
every nook and chimney corner,
a half million gathered now
to take our turn in the hurly-burly
of the game.
A half million of this generation
abandoning our forebears' world

in all our knowingness.
Sweet temptation, forbidden fruit!
We left the tilled field turn fallow,
shut the last half-door behind,
made our way to the decider
in our urban labyrinth.
Such luck!
Such fortune that we should be the ones
tasting from this tree of knowledge,
gobbling all forbidden fruit,
coming to such knowingness.
Here now in our city's maze,
fierce, lavish and rebellious,
we spend the best years of our bloom
in this turmoil. Another feather to pick
from life's shimmering peacock –
all our joy is young and pagan
in Rathmines and Ranelagh pubs.
Here's to life! Long life!

We spend and are spent by time
as one by one by one
a generation ahead bend their knee
to the course of things and sneak away.
Are we these merry soldiers still
marching?
Left, right, left, right.
Here's to life! Long life!
We spend and are spent by time.
Here we are as always knowing
hung from a tree we grew ourselves
since Durkheim made his god of gloom.
If a faithful mind counts no more
and roles line up in our drama,
so many buttons on a narrow thread;
if what matures from older thought
is no more than a ruse we benefit from,
what redemption for us now
sliding on and towards our fate?
If this game of ours is meaningless,
no rule, result or referee,
little wonder we perch on the ditch.

Are we the merry soldiers still
Marching, marching? Who are we?
Sadhbhín's Máirtín's offshoots,
Jimí Neansaí's aftercomer?
When Morse was sending his first wires
Colm was busy back on his plot
preparing the ground.
Neansaí and Sadhbhín there on the slope
played jackstones. And unbeknownst
Morse and Nietzsche overshadow them,
laugh their dark and withered laugh.
When Kafka was in his death throes,
Máirtín was about to take the plunge.
We with our surnames and numbers
on a silicon chip
will write the history of our times.
We can't retreat to a nook in some valley
no more than we return to the womb.

We spend and are spent by time.
In this our urban labyrinth
as sourly we still huff and sulk
and toss our pints down the hatch.
Order a half-one as a chaser!
Left, right, left, right.
Here's to long life! Long life!
We talk again about old Kafka
in Rathmines and Ranelagh pubs,
announcing to the world *non serviam*.
We're content, we're satisfied,
we're replete and at our ease
on our ditch of knowingness.

Drunk
with cleverness
did we stumble in love
with the tedium of gloom?
Bearers of terrible news
grown fond of our burden.
Is water lost
in vinegar's self-importance?
Did we somehow run out
of humour?

Where's the court jester,
the clown who'll wink
at the king of knowing?
Of course the mighty emperor
swaps his crown for a joke.
The knowing king will rule the ditch –
The jest still will make the cut.
In Rathmines and Ranelagh a rumour
Some inbred hope is breaking through.

Our despair was more a nightmare.
We'll wake again and light the lamp.
Hush, my child how could I lie?
Tomorrow will be another tomorrow.
Left, right, left, right,
we're not soldiers but children playing
all over Rathmines and Ranelagh
this leap beyond our time's parenthesis
as through such humour we re-awaken
here and now in our city's maze.

So you faithful yet to come
and you so long gone on ahead,
time on purpose made such use
of the pain and privilege of this knowing.
Ours then not to question why
we were sin-binned off the pitch.
And no gainsaying the referee,
the law and rule of any game.
No generation nearer the All-wise
than the next; a God of glory needs
no tick in the tally-stick of time
when counting hairs of every head.

Down, down from off the ditch!
Since the morning sun has risen,
since the ball was thrown in
until the final stroke of the game,
our doing the beginning and the end.
Alpha and omega of our being.

Affliction

More than the pain, the anticipation,
That long anxiety before the travail.
Is suffering this low November sun
Slanting a mean and narrowed angle,
A subtle stinging glint of affliction
Touching this face against my will?
Caress me. Even a hint of solace.
Oh, empty then the fullest chalice.

More than the affliction, the aftermath.
The will indulged or the will checked
Are beams of a cross, a length and breadth
Where desire and fragility intersect.
Can patience heal or must the sun
Hoist again my light? Or is it both,
Process and outcome kneaded into one?
My heart struggles with a crux of growth.

Signals

The truth bare-boned and plain,
You're searching now for news in vain;
A million times ago or two,
All this had happened the likes of you.

What else have you to say?
The whole lot happened anyway!
The way a tantrum child will plunder,
Must we tear our toys asunder?

A plaything only, a knick-knack,
Without truth's magic only lack;
Is heat no more than cold's thief,
And light our dark's short relief?

Our deepest wish a whined despair,
Murmur and grumble in our prayer;
Have our forebears' gifts been replaced,
A heritance now we only waste?

The final grief if we should lose
Or miss the signals, hints and clues
That for us alone this grand encore
Of all that ever happened before.

Though You're Not Nero

Though you're not Nero
Carefree and violining
His vigil as Rome
Was burning, yet prowling
You rummage a backroom,
Where despite yourself, you plunder
A spacious house of wonder.

Beware ideologues of gloom
Who walk under burdens
Of all the world's concerns;
By grind and sweat you've wrung
Out of the binge of song
Your parable's passion,
An enduring fashion.

Clear of pompous nonsense
Lance all self-indulgence
And humbly name the sins
That from your soul you rinse;
For some loner you're a match,
Your secrets all a lifted latch –
Your life just another instance.

III. RUNGS

Morning Prayer

Now into this heap of bones
Sound again a soul's reveille;
O gods don't abandon us,
You who made us all from clay.

Save us from our reason's plot
That lures us down a specious track
And traps us in its basket cot
Of rods we made for our own back.

Spare us please from any tedium,
That layabout, that lazybones,
Who smears and binds our wings with gum
While turning all our blood to tar.

Deep within this heap of bones,
Light our magic lamp today;
Lord do not abandon us,
You who made us all from clay.

Indian Summer

What about that for a sun!
What would you say to that minx!
Three months unfaithful to summer,
here she is the shameless hussy,
having it off with autumn.

This old woman still game.
What else is there to say?
Certainly not before its time!
But still, my lady, all hail!
My Indian summer at Michaelmas.

News Flash

Yet another day to fill
My hunch with gladness –
Greased lightening thrill,
My lap of the cosmos.

One daisy in a chain
Of time's catenations –
Me that link again
Between two generations.

Since Adam passion's
Trough sustained us,
Between our rations
Of gleam and dust.

News and cameramen
(Free drinks for you!)
Just write it up again
How we've pulled through,

Revelling in one theme,
We the smooth linkers –
No dance ever as game
As the one-tune piper's.

The Umbrella

Again he overtakes me. Who is that fellow
Stepping out past me along a morning street,
So polished, so clean-shaven, dapper and fit,
A single stride behind his furled umbrella?

I know I've sometimes felt, as he outpaced me,
a knife of envy. Am I too diffident or callow?
My Bohemian soul covets such swish authority,
A sureness striding behind a furled umbrella.

But is it a calm and genial walking stick?
I see a crop lashing a haunch in its sweat,
A baton with an orchestra breathing its beat,
A cane poised to thrash or hold in check.

But that tie! I recognise an old school emblem.
It might well be his seat was once worn thin
By a bench that years later left a countersign
In mine as I fidget *Ad Majorem Dei Gloriam.*

I glimpse his face through a childhood's lens.
What's a furled umbrella so anxious to swat?
Today as he passed, I wondered if we'd caught
A giddiness flickering in each other's glance.

Lame Dog

He's lame but won't go away,
This dog will have his raving day,
A madcap chance to dream again
One perfect moment he'll attain.

Look! This dog is doing his best
And yet both plot and telling contest,
So all this give and take's a slight
Bit off the mark, as though despite

Himself his nature seeks recall,
But over moments his shadows fall
And caught in themes of all and each
Beyond its own our eye can't reach.

Sharper the eye, the more disturbance
Between ourselves and radiance,
Heisenberg and this poor cur,
One eye here and the other there!

For ages we try to find such laws
As nature long before us knows,
We can only trust our hunch may fit –
If dogs are lame, then so be it!

Song without Tune

Grand flakes of blown snow,
Those moments our likes can spend,
Flake pennywise,
Pound-foolish flake,
Old snows we let unnoticed go.

Each question greater than its reply
As though our gods we now defy,
Higgledy-piggledy
The cat with the cream,
Grasping shadows we reach for the sky.

Your sea days small fry and fugitive
That bubble in a sailor's dream,
Helter-skelter,
Pitter-patter,
We're fetching water with a sieve.

All our years a grain of sand,
So many grains across a strand,
Mixty-maxty,
Topsy-turvy,
Watch how we weave each rope of sand.

Visions

This still a million leap years
Before that fall from light of Lucifer's,
Before all those sellers gathered
Around the temple's dealing table,
Before our joy went into exile,
Before the journey of the cross.

Let's let ourselves go again!
A magic wand now every instant
So darker memories are brightened
As we gather round a table of friends
Without even a Judas in our midst.
Is tomorrow that day that never comes?

For Me

But for me always the mermaid –
I keep her hood well out of sight
Or she'll have slipped off on the quiet
As I stand here on land dismayed.

Always iron for the life of me,
Metal always my constant share;
Yet leaking drops, a puff of air
Could turn to rust such density.

In this kingdom desire is all,
Our proof we do or don't endure;
Fate's tent a balloon we puncture,
Your business just to find the hole.

Endless praise for sky and air –
In celebration we're remade –
Honour iron, praise the mermaid,
From doubt I make my perfect prayer.

Here's To You!

After three dozen years of dissipation,
Brim again another heart glass,
The fatted calf get ready now at once,
We scattered pearls for half a generation
But now re-meeting we're prodigal sons.

Two right pearls we're fallen to flesh
And sin. Brother, who'd put us to the blush,
Like gamey women at their mirror we sit
Counting wrinkles and crow's-feet,
A wisdom earned, a sprinkle of sense.

Childhood friend what misfortune took us?
Was every moment spent apart betrayal?
So what that all those years were jealous,
On each other's mind a mark and trail;
Our mapped return across a honeycomb.

Unfree Verse

Fickle March winds aren't enough.
Between caprice and sun, steady
She goes. There's ballast in sobriety
When the sheets are slackened off.

As frost and fire both can burn,
In music's joy the music's cries;
Behind even the brightest eyes,
Concealed sorrows still can yearn.

Care can't break the care of tunes,
Desire always exigent,
The drones' meticulous lament
Hides in music's undertones.

At the Height of the Snow

At the height of the snow,
Brazen-faced and grey,
Here she comes – one stray
Arriving out of the blue.

Petite grey stranger!
Of fellow human love
I've barely got enough,
My uninvited ranger!

Caressing my anklebone
And cosying up to me,
O temptress without pity
Of origins unknown!

You ridge of arching fur –
But I'm no soft touch –
Cupboard-loving smooch,
But she has begun to purr.

You say our will is free,
As if we really chose!
To best you she can schmooze
Better to stand than flee...

I yield to you and bend,
You know the lips you kiss;
Without self-love you'd miss
The other you comprehend.

The day it began to thaw
My cat took off elsewhere,
With no forebear or heir,
A bolt back into the blue.

Rondo

On a lake's underside
As new moons rise
This worm will glide
And tinier even
Than you, it turns
Clockwise, sunwise,
Until the full moon.

No sooner in wane,
Off it will shift
Anti-clockwise again,
In tune with the moon,
Like a screw that turns
Either right or left –
I'm telling you!

The moon may languish
And won't it grow tired
Of lowlife anguish
Or under spring moons
Is a worm that fit?
Maybe to tour or retire
To the depths of the lake,

Just swim with the flow
And who'd mind a fortnight
On Costa Brava below?
But on the lake's floor
In a moon's first phase,
Still day and night
The spiral vigil.

Around it's fate
An internal pilgrim
Can concentrate
On forever turning.
Is such faithfulness
Worth even a straw?
Yet the worm will gyrate.

Where it learned all this
No one knows;
In a mind's bliss
The unknown known dream;
If inborn instinct goes,
Our secret's forgotten.

Friendship

No wonder we're happy just to meet,
As the spirit moves us, on and off;
An easy support of nothing to prove
As we unwind, stretch in the light of
Each other's sun.

Little wonder we're content to meet
Once in a while, just as it suits.
Such concurrence never frets or doubts;
We've shot our long wedge-shaped roots
To the water plane.

No wonder a fluid runs from root
To root, a conduit of *eau de vie*,
An underground, our liquid conspiracy
The cherishings and waterings of intimacy
For a feast or drought.

Lead Us Not Into

On a sweet edge of wind
All the huff and whistle
Forever call your kind
Until the breeze is fair
Go easy now. Go easy.

The ripples of cat's-paws
Beckon and blandish,
Watching their chance because
They want you among them.
Go easy now. Go easy.

Those ants still lie in wait,
Mute hucksters of time
Who hedge you and bait
Their traps to catch you.
Go easy now. Go easy.

A line of blooded poppies,
Heads on sacrificial blocks,
Quarrel, revolution, unease –
Yours is mine, mine my own.
Go easy now. Go easy.

Ringed moons in spring
Wait in every lunatic,
Who made of this elusive ring
A stubble field sown fallow.
Go easy now. Go easy.

Since the start of humankind,
Our best move our courage
In the haggard of love's grind,
Here in this our meanwhile.
Go easy now. Go easy.

Casting Off

Long since all our lading done,
The marriage vessel full and weighed
And now aboard she heels with fun
As by each other we get laid!

Ma belle for us the roaring main
Where every sun each day has died.
And any regrets for ever remain
With those we leave tied up quayside.

With every tidal wave we eke
A yard yet nearer the horizon;
Let any gloomy bible-thumper speak
Of falls from grace, shipwrecks anon.

Sufficient unto the day and swell
Until the pirate moment when
We must wish or take farewell –
Then part, my love, without chagrin.

Roofing

A lifelong day, a night's secrecies:
Only the rafters themselves must know
The beams' strains and stresses, slow
Givings and takings, the touch and go
Of our attunements and compromise, how
we raise the roof or make our peace.

A timber's head nestles in another's,
A mitred joint, this bevelled match,
Two beams and their collar-beam which
Shape a triangle, the tie and apex
Of togetherness. So easily one forgets
Couples are a liaison of two rafters.

And always under us or in between
That dangerous breach we never close,
A zone for household gods we choose
Or need. Here, then, allow some room
For unlike memories, dreams to dream,
A living space for a separate passion.

A roof is framing our slanted intimacy.
Unless each of these matching couples
Beds snugly down into opposite walls,
The timbers sag. Somehow we're stronger
In separateness, this sloping encounter
Our braced ridge, our tie of ecstasy.

And Again

Go easy on, my love, a little
I wouldn't mind but trying to kindle
A male who's done what he's good for;
Just forty winks, *la petite mort*,
Another opiate stab of sleep.

See if you'll soft-talk me then,
Frenzied woman coaxing again –
Still too easy-osy for my part,
Of course no fault of yours sweetheart;
Your bed's lazybones now revives.

Ready, steady are you all set?
I'm wide awake, no sleeping yet
Prepared again for the tidal wave,
In swoons of joy this rush and wave
Gather around our earth-fed shores.

What Worthwhile Did I Possess?

What worthwhile did I possess
That you should make a play for me,
What innate come-hitherness,
What flatteries unwittingly
Awoke desires to interweave
Me in your realm? Bear with me
Woman, just a spell of grace,
A rebate in debts of our delight
The satiated can't see –
Now it's fasting overnight,
A call aside so we abstain
In deserts where we grow again.

Woman, tell me what's now wrong,
What's this angst or talk of fasting?
Stamp my licence here once more
In your realm and even casting
Off your kit don't ever leave
In place a single stitch you wore
To curb a man who envies dress.
Our fever now its own relief
As in fathoms of your embrace
All my measures of this cosmos;
In frozen pleasures now belong
The hidden *envoies* of this song.

So Long This Day

So long this day tomorrow re-dawns,
This smith's content with stock-in-trade,
His hoard of less or precious stones;
He'll choose the light before the shade.

Is everything already said,
All words and talk in verse now caught
And any other syllable instead
A strange and sudden busybody's cut?

Or is the smith's tongue too downright
Lazy to unlatch whatever's blurred,
To open doors, augment the light
That forebears hide within each word?

Such words are gems, his promise hints,
For you tonight this smith will hoard;
His playful mind spellbound by glints,
Those stones remembered word for word.

Goblin

My goblin ruiner of blackberries,
Though we read each other as such,
Was I for you an easy touch?
What about my learned degrees,
All that college gloss and polish
(Not even to speak of Jesuit finish!).

Some talents too I'd been granted,
Could pick and choose all I wanted,
Doctor, professor, even lawyer,
Lance, learning or red seal.
What posturing! Such a spiel!
Come off it, barefaced liar!

All right. Yes, that first desire,
Heedless blaze, capricious fire;
Headstrong now until you find
Unravelling a goblin's mind
How nothing else would ever do,
Nothing less than all of you.

My goblin ruiner of blackberries,
Aide-mémoire, autumnal sign,
Don't fail me now my pooka please,
Don't ever dim the berry's shine.
Already this song's historical.
Mañana the best blackberry of all!

Sleeplessness

Angst for fear I wake,
Afraid I'll grow anxious
That the day may never break
Or the sun too soon will rise
And find my bones too weak.

Restless I groan and complain,
Each step as I regress
More foolish. To refrain
Impossible – I give in
Altogether to my madness.

A thousand ghostly figures
That pass and wheel and veer,
Circling me with whirrs
Of mischief-makers who jeer
And call me interloper.

Outside is still my bailiwick,
My trouble I can't mix
With them. The crowd's rubric
Won't allow you speak of gifts,
That solitary mother wit.

Such hubbub and alarm.
Do they still fear your aplomb
And struggling lose their way,
Adrift and hazily astray?
Do I near sleep's charm?

Saint

House of joy a place I needn't fear?
Did demons die unexpectedly?
Or will Ignatius's skull come mocking me,
Allowing all and sundry their last jeer?

Are spurs of terror still a necessity
To tense us up? Or must we undergo
Every cringe and every humbling blow,
A lifetime's sticks and stones, or can we

Enjoying this quick and brittle span,
Somehow let it glow and still not burn
As even a sodden boat will yearn
Drunkenly to sail out on an ocean.

What drug do I need or what restraints
To whip me from the pleasures of despair,
Apprentice who makes it, surviving probationer
Ashore in the fretted purlieus of the saints.

Fluid now as a music-maker's finger,
Rung by rung I climb this giddy ladder;
At last we spin and growing even madder
On cloud nine's flightiness we want to linger.

O right-hand thief how did your tête-à-tête
Make you so certain of that feasting cup,
So sure at least you'd get that final leg-up,
Late gatecrasher arriving at the banquet?

Musical Stave

Musical stave of a song
The step ladder of gods,
The gap between the lines,
The space between each rung.

The space so blue as I strode
My youth and climbed the ladder,
My veins furious and jealous
Of the god's bright abode.

All I'd achieve, an upstart,
Full of action and swagger –
What's wrong with the gods
Their rungs so far apart?

While we complain and whine
The rungs stretch from each other,
Below further from above,
Between the top and bottom line.

Our blood cools and thins out,
Our clay and vein will harden;
The vault of sky is space
And space an abyss of doubt.

All our youth's thrill and high
That knew no worm or patience,
Thinner, paler and languid
Under the gods' grand eye.

Just the stave of a song,
The gods' fragile ladder,
An abyss between the lines –
Our end between each rung.

Night Prayer

Wipe me with honey from your comb
And turn my blood to opium;
Rake the ashes on my heart's fire,
All my rush of thought and desire;
A chance to edit what I become,
A little grace in the mind's newsroom.

Forgive us tonight every trespass
And with your potion of forgetfulness
Clear my debt and mortgage. And also, God,
Please don't forget my morning prod!
No disrespect for your shebeen as such,
Just things of this world I love so much.

Belonging

(1982)

Line

A table three foot by five of knotted pine,
Prowling ground for prophet and harbinger;
Here set down this dreaming bowl of mine,
Defiant micro-world where I beat air.

Realms and empires in the world outside
Fade from sight; like ages long outworn
Our own lifetimes now drift and slide –
We fall in love, a child's child is born.

Still about my kingdom here in splendour
On daily warps of knowledge, love's design,
Each teased-out moment seems so similar –
We tend a point, a point becomes a line.

The Patient

It is, we whispered,
lightening the unlightenment,
it is the crab!

He's past the paltry skill
of vein and muddy reason
we name the mind.

Fathoming the unsaid,
we scan terror in his eye.
Do you think he knows?

Knows amidst the bevies
of nurses with light laughter,
gay and white as linen?

Knows these guarding angels
are no paradise messengers
but gate-keepers of Gethsemane?

Knows hearts moved to pity
harden before cockcrow?
Gethsemane is a lonely garden.

One summer will melt
Memories of winter dark;
Our sorrow drowns in luck

As pain must thaw to joy.
Brave in the jaws of terror,
We worship the overall.

Moving House

Pride, covetousness, lust, anger, envy,
Gluttony and sloth – our gable and wall,
Precise bookkeepers, count our deadly sins
As spall and brick watch every move and bend.
Too long a house's silent beams and purlins
Have straddled us – half and hollow friend,
Who feeds on you a while then sucks you dry;
This gloomy house of ours entraps the soul.

Surely stones would never have the nerve?
Go on! Which gable spoke to me like that?
These walls defying me – it can't be true!
Listen! Which impudent brick, what brat
Said no one ever on the face of the globe
Dared tell us better. The likes of us deserve
No lasting shelter or to evade our web;
We decamp to find again ourselves anew.

Little enough I care for gables, God knows!
The joys of newness flowing in advance
Now banish demons. A sinner's second chance!
No sin's arrears, no debts or such restraints;
Maybe there at last the abode of saints?
All that gable's passing talk imagined,
We wake tomorrow out of boredom's doze.
With no remorse I close the door behind.

Petition

Less substance I'm afraid, more show and gloss –
A craven soldier still this body of mine,
Fickle and under daily burdens bowing down.
I won't defy You nor do I want to whine;
My one petition: Spare the thorny crown.
High enough for me our human cross.

Clerk

Eight clear-cut one pound notes
And a handful of coins together
He'd laid on the counter with care,
Speaking politely about the weather;
His tuneful voice so competent,
Everything bit by bit by rote,
A clerk's courtesy and savoir-faire,
Everything correct and decent.

Suddenly we'd change the tune we play;
A moment's spur, out of the blue
The counter would spin and turn about
And there I'd stand a clerk spruce,
Pleasant, confident and punctilious
As sure as night would follow day,
As sure as something carried through,
But for the way it all turned out.

But for the way it all happened
Would our eyes give away the show,
Our faltering hearts betray us?
In my stead an ex-clerk would stand,
Diffident, secretive and dubious,
His memory fingering strange notions,
As sure as there's no bill on a crow,
As sure as thimbles empty oceans.

In accordance with some law and order

Whose inception we don't remember,
Many moons ago we'd fulfil
All we imagined we might be.
Each other's dreams still harmonious
We'd chosen of our own freewill;
Parts we play prepared for us
In the grand ensemble of humanity.

Brother

That's how it was. No blame or any reproach.
Enough that I'd once overshadowed you
To make you need at least to change approach,
To turn your back on what I dreamt I'd do.

And so we're men. Here's the field of play.
King now in your kingdom, potentate
Fenced well in with wealth and holding sway,
In charge of all and master of your fate.

No manger dog that speaks – and yet and yet,
Although in love I plough a furrowed dream,
I still admit sometimes I must regret
That this is how it was, though there's no blame.

I only ask you please don't choose to harden
Or leave behind that boy that once was you;
Though what we set our hearts on we've done,
O say a child within could still come through.

Temperament

Morning. Into seething water
oatmeal thrown anew
to dance the whirlpool.
All eagerness, tending it
I watch again creation.

Damn my consuming fire!
A gift or a derangement?
Taut as a fiddle's bow,
anxiety hardens my veins.

Come now, why the panic?
Unless a day is spent to the full,
unless a moment catches courage,
all is a duck's trace in water.

Half-eternity at least, it's said,
to aim at the target; another
half-eternity to be nonchalant
the instant the arrow is fired.

Damn this endless ardour!
My cravings are a millstone.
Under the sway of some urge,
I burn on a griddle of fervour.

The oatmeal spins a storm.
A million granules rise;
fuddling, whizzing, rivalling
truths. What's to be done?
Patience. Wait for the thickening.

Letting Go

An old stab of your keen-edged knife,
The pain of an insult darts through me:
My need again for revenge and strife.

But surely that wound is long since bled,
It's maimings forgiven? Why this sting?
Has a crutch become a sugar stick instead?

With favours returned did I compensate
Or think I'd snuff you with forbearance?
Again my wound begins to suppurate.

The producer's lance is what it needs.
To cut and splice my memory's tape.
And yes! the price of words still deeds.

Nest

Marvel at the work of this nest:
love-straws kneaded into kin;
still the nest's law is to scatter
feather and wing, one and all.

We're born to betray the nest,
to quit the brood, flutter alone:
brothers no longer of a feather,
sisters already lone travellers.

And so it is. In spite of ourselves,
no sooner now the tribe together
than all the nestling sores lurk;
we're rivals in the peck and chatter.

Star-guided or even by chance,
blank strangers gathered this nest;
its fragility still its own fail-safe:
daring to gather is daring to scatter.

Ingebjörg

Just imagine not knowing
the likes of you existed –
but here you spring on us,
a beautiful plump child.
Still a sovereign mistress,
careless of place or time –
I name and bless you roly-poly.
Are you my lovely Ingebjörg!

In your eyes I gaze a crystal,
the same once seen in mine;
what lands will you travel –
how often fall in love?
Ingebjörg I speak with you
a language you won't understand,
with only this to tell you:
your mother was a gentle friend.

Deal

Comrade, partner in every sport,
Mother, daughter, sister, consort,
Siren to each mood and bent,
All promise, all fulfilment.

My attention-seeking need,
My petty envies please don't heed;
Your company I couldn't share,
Divide your love, your light or care.

To strike a deal it takes two –
But can the like of me give you
Or bring on all of this to bear
Even the bargain's softest share?

Is what's said true or not?
Or can I even trust the thought
That full and lack offset each other,
The whole imagined in these together?

But in my questions I'm betrayed,
My fault such thoughts of gauge or grade;
Our deal the deal, no more or less,
My original sin to double guess.

Salute

So tell me how are things going?
But I hear a stranger's unconcern
lurk in syllables of our greeting.

I've no regrets. Why should I?
What seems best was done;
once that way, this way now.

Still such easy greetings don't fit.
This trivial chatter on a street
could broach our memory's cache.

Doesn't it now seem bizarre
that we're more than strangers –
as if old intimacies come between us?

But watch my eye for the clue.
Neither of us has grounds to rue
that our purposes once crossed.

No, not regret, more a chagrin
that a street's chance salute contains
all of what was once affection.

Tracing

So now, like so many more,
My crowd scattered all over;
My sum of hereditary lore
Some vague recall of a father.

A father's father wandered
From Devlin in Westmeath,
A journey north and upward
As clerk to town's auctioneer.

Is it the same high season
That handsome shop apprentice
Delia Garvin travels east
From close to Ballyhaunis?

How they fall for each other,
No business of mine at all;
How outsiders get together
To climb the worldly pole.

Now their son's son's leisure
On the back of all such sweat
Can write their epigraph here
To pay arrears of fate.

But what do we care for a forebear
Or whatever genes we own –
All friendships surely closer
Than brittle ties of bone?

Unless though unbeknownst
We still must sometimes follow
A track they beat before us,
Their plan inscribed in marrow.

This mix of chance and will
In anything I claim;
My thanks for how it fell,
That here's the way I came.

Senses

My eye dwells on such a shapely sway,
But soon its hankerings fade and give away
To other jealous senses. Blushed and eager
I want to savour you. Your voice I hear;
My touch becomes a touch that soon incenses
All desire between us. Oglings now
Turn a laughing stock as clowns that bow
Before the lusting faction of my senses.

Once your body's fragrance seizes me
I'm unhinged. No quarter please or mercy,
My every fibre fallen for that spell
Of first instinct, my abbess sense of smell
That answers any doubts with subtle echoes
To sharpen now all four so I'm undone;
I see, I hear, I taste, I touch in one.

Waiting

Under the meagrest of sparks
a random blast of wind
turns fuel to fire.

In every game one tough move,
a startling turn from underdog
to a winning upper hand.

Intimacy and a split second;
a glance of an eye can turn
affection's day-by-day to love.

Grace is less than an instant.
On the spur of a day's moment
we wait. On this alone

Hinges our statement of progress;
balanced between profit and loss,
an accountant's right hand raised.

Aside

For all the years we've spent together,
again I want to summon myself aside
to mull over that falling for you,
gather up an image of this double-life.

In some haze of workaday mystery
we're ferried across the abyss;
drop by drop our time elopes
and still I can't trap its image.

I've no sooner focused a memory,
no sooner fixed a picture of you,
than you flee the frame I've managed;
a fluid image drifts away from me.

Somehow a glimpse is never more
than a plan by which we manoeuvre;
do I imagine some distant eternity,
a skylight onto a travelling image?

From the daily dream of your company
(sunny water running over shingle)
this is my yearly summons aside,
an overview of all between us.

Terror

I see them in gardens of paradise,
The professors of appleologies;
I hear their laughter splitting their side,
Behind pillars of salt others hide.

As top and bottom millstones grinding
I hear their voices still fault-finding;
I feel them in my veins and know
How their reason envies brio.

I tell them what they want to hear
But, my level-headedness insincere,
Such flattery seems an affront to them,
All this sweet-talk out of bedlam.

I feel my inner mettle flinch
As soon as I just sense their approach,
So carefully gauged and hidebound,
Their footfall on much firmer ground.

Tell me – I really don't think I care,
Nothing will break my spirit or flair.
A daring turns all worlds about:
The scoffer scoffed, the mocking caught.

Ladder

More than the end, if the ladder is desirable –
Any wielded power has made you fickle;
Lacking purpose, the ladder's top will wobble,
Soon or late what's uppermost will topple.

That sucking up in awe to the strong,
If the lower rungs we find we despise,
Or among our rivals we bear malice,
The shame of falls when all goes wrong.

Lower down, but content despite
The risks, here too we must admit
That season every human plight,
Framing all our watches of delight.

Postman

Here comes my whistling dunce –
So heedless, an air of indifference!
You'd think he's unaware of being
Official bootlegger of our belonging.

Easy for him such light-mindedness –
I think I hear the squeaking gate?
His slung bag my dangling fate
And he need only pick and chose.

Off with you then, my clumsy lout!
As if you're someone I'd care about;
Bad luck, you thieving scoundrel –
To count on you is courting trouble.

I'd never want to trust in you –
Why'd I bother with your bundle?
My friends assemble round my table,
Smiling, waiting on what's new.

If I succumb or lose my courage
They'll still move within my memory;
There above my table their luminary –
For them every thought I'll forage.

Off cheat! postmaster of pretence –
But please tomorrow come once more
And plump a communion through my door
For fear I'd lose my self-reliance.

A Woman

I see the charm, I know how striking,
Your magic gathered its truth around me
From first acquaintance on to liking.

Not that I didn't think it worthwhile
To journey between the hint and glance,
On edge between delight and will.

But another lovely woman cast
And shaped this male you stand before;
I carry that heart on a pane of glass.

Kiss me. This boundary line so thin.
Knowing you a grain of malt
That growing richer ferments within.

An East Wind

(for prisoners of conscience)

The wind's blowing its scruple,
a long pleading of oppression
eddying from gable to gable
around this Maytime Dublin.
Like rounded fists of confetti
blossoms cluster on cherry trees,
handfuls of memories to scatter.
What does the wind's voice say?

Did you hear the policeman's tap?
They knocked nearby last night.
Did you feel Siberia's frost
Turning bitter, a heart tightening?
Scared, I still stood my ground;
my fears were stitched with trust
until terror froze in my mind;
even my cry for pity dries up.

I hear it whispered in my ear.
Does anyone heed the wind's rustle?
A daily round, a circle of friends
through a train's window veer
and steal away. No returning.
Believe, in the teeth of the wind,
it's for you, my friend, I whistle.

Carol

There's life in the old dogs after all –
Let the globe dance round its ring –
Why tonight do we wait on healing?
So soon our sleep without recall.

Alone we children of Israel's land,
What ages we wait for some respite,
From out the yoke, for the upper hand.
Proudly we look for a prophet tonight.

The torn rags of triumph we disown,
Coup after coup and yet the grindstone;
Compassion still the unshared right –
Humbly we watch Bethlehem tonight.

Eoin

I don't demand it every way –
I go with the flow of silent beats,
Soundless notes that still complete
The breezy rhythms, a music's sway.

I'm not asking for it every way –
I'm taken at once by Eoin's face,
So light the arms of fancy's embrace,
This countersign of hope I praise.

In a moment years would have flown,
If only I could bear the joy;
No time at all and he'd have grown,
On my shoulder's age the hand of that boy.

But my children's children everyone –
To have it both ways I can't demand –
On a child's forehead I lay a hand
In the name of his father and his son.

The Shouting Man

His like still walk our global city street;
Every second footfall in measured feet
He shouts again, then off before we can
Even ask how all of this began?
Perhaps in some recall an old blown fuse
Or small misprints within his script of fate,
Some mad longwinded half-untold excuse;
With words to the wise, you'll disassociate:
Wink and pass to show you're no one's fool.

If all his torment gathered in one yell
Or if one scream released him from his hell,
Just some relief that we might recognise –
But all that metered pain inside his cries
Demanding no respite. Already he's gone,
And shout by shout escapes the ridicule
Of some abuse as full of common sense.
And grinning broadly you must hurry on:
Wink and pass to show you're no one's fool.

Pacifist

Rebellion's flag hoisted,
my heartbeats flooded
and the crowds tramp by.

Hearing the drum-thump,
my bones remember betrayal,
rekindle in me a pagan.

So, are you hero or a whimperer,
soldier or chicken-heart?
Who'd suffer such indignity?

I hear the drummed question.
My pulse loves its answer;
my mind is checking my foot.

Grappling an enemy, I'd see
everything through his eye,
desire only his world.

Empires are seeds in the snow,
Roman, Turkish, Saxon,
every reign an eel's back.

Though no lover of wrongs,
my soul frosts with fear.
Let the drummer pass by.

Three Charms

1 *Against Jealousy*

Even if aggression whets the knife,
a calm mastery has a keener edge.
Consume me in searching out the golden apple
but don't urge the prick of jealousy;
tame in me that wildest beast.

2 *Against Loneliness*

Though I relish action,
on purpose I've chosen a quarantine
to try to reach the core of things.
Don't let it be a friendless renown,
a bait on the hook of loneliness.

3 *Against Despair*

Yesterday's gladness tore me
asunder. Today I pay the reckoning.
The grapnel of despair won't catch me.
I refuse a smooth answer of self-misery.
Well, maybe. Another SOS from MO'S.

Approaches

Almost familiar but still vigilant,
we zigzag. A gentle dig, a careful hint.
We watch the other's words. Will or won't?
A child once burnt will dread a fire,
a terror nestle deep in the flesh.
Come a storm, will we recall fair weather?

Will I, won't I? We soften each other up
with floods of talk. Now warily we swap
old secrecies. And is there no end
to all we share? Years of one temperament
have plotted for us a common pilgrimage,
shaping us into each other's image.

Anxious still, we're probing one another.
Oh, let's not waste this precious time.
I won't mince words. You're my brother!
I will. I yield. Manoeuvre as you like.
Without you – I'm alone, bare-shouldered.
A friendship thickens water into blood.

Lament

In heat of youth lifetimes from where we are
We fancied each other. Recall our whim and will
Gadding about Spiddal, Enniskillen, Castlebar –
Just those names and I begin to well.

But it could never last. A dizzy encounter,
Our ardent caprice. Too flighty and thin-skinned,
We scorch each other, flaring undisciplined
And sultry fires, then drift with no rancour

Our own sweet ways. No passion without rewards.
What's gained still lingers in my thankfulness.
Your race now run, a grief refuses words.
So once lover, God requite such lavishness.

Journal

Daybreak:
Up with the morning star. On her heels
a rumour of sallow light now spreads
over our horizon. A master hands down
the theme: the sun's trip westwards,
topic for our song, plot for a psalm.

A blind of unconcern night had drawn
over the mind now lifts. Gradually,
we prepare for another journey.
Truth or fable, feast or abstinence –
how is the journal chequered today?

Day's End:
Today the tiniest pretext was enough
to slip away: a telephone's ring,
a letter to answer, a coffee cup,
hubbub; so many matters to attend,
any distraction to evade ourselves,
anything but the price of unbusyness.

Night is falling. We're called once
again to our aloneness. We wonder
which merits most, bustle or repose,
fuss and action or a cloister's rigours?
A heaven's desolate star lights up.
To both their due, hermit and hustler.

In Memory of a Teacher

His laughter still subverts our solemnity.
A baron of knowing. No hint of crabbed professor,
Ample bodied, a prince in voice and calibre,
Under his sway the young swam in lavishness.
A teacher's lot to yield the key to a palace
He may not see. Of course, he was disappointed

As his indifference hurt, until beyond it –
A learner's fate to touch a teacher's loneness.
In breaking loose still some sense of loss,
A wall's part broken. Remembering his generosity
I'll shut the gap and mend again the breach.
You were my patron, youth's sheltering ditch.

Ghetto

My ardour is no longer enough.
A prophet in a land with no heir,
a left-behind without a faithful.

If full could understand lean...
Weight of numbers menaces our want,
every thought a surrounding threat.

I plead guilty. Slyly I scheme
to throw off rags of drought,
tatters and patches of famine.

I stand accused. So charge,
not with arrogance or ambition,
just a refusal to die in a cavern.

Leaving is treason for the zealous,
a trespass for the powerful; I understand
Paul, neither Jew nor Gentile.

Yet he didn't shrink. Farewell
to dark. I'm coming to grips
with a world. I hunger for life.

Psalm in the Night

What kind of turmoil has come
between me and my night's sleep?
Such foolishness! Wake up!

Damn and double damn him,
the funk, the lousy turncoat,
skulking from all I stand for.

But what's the point of my anger,
this belligerent chatter that didn't
snuff the hanger-on, there and then.

Why did I let him away with it?
That swindler. Now alone I examine
twists of my conscience's loudmouth.

Was it lack of spunk, what-it-takes,
or my own too courteous backbone
that made me bend for that louse?

Which was better? To back off
or view the world with his eye?
Lie with a dog, rise with a flea.

A night's trouble throws me between
secrets of two testaments: the old,
the new? But look! already a sun

in darling humour is opening a rift
in my tomb of dark. Mover of light,
lure my eye to where well-being lies.

Laurels

And then at last the sides emerge,
Whoops and cries for teams we urge,
For forty minutes or so each side –
Who'll play with the wind, hit their stride?

Bundled up in comfort's herd,
Live a while on guess and watchword.
Look! Already the ball's thrown in!
See again how worlds begin.

Our meat and drink each hero's feat –
Will he lash it into the net?
In such frenzy are we satisfied?
O yes, but just a fraction wide.

All ambition's dreams can thrive
In this enchanted whistled life,
And hope runs so madly astray
Out there on that field of play.

Off on a solo to take aim
In this the senior final game.
How much more time before the end?
So is it now or never, friend?

Heroes carried high around
And around what was a battleground
With cup and flag overhead.
Three cheers for a team defeated!

For us now three cheers allowed,
For us among the scattering crowd,
For this our human gift of eking out
On fables of an evergreen shoot.

Forebear

Delia Garvan, it's you I accuse.
The deck stacked, I was dealt
a five of trumps, a flighty hand.

You're to blame for the wild abandon;
at your door my Connacht contrariness,
aceless robber of insanity's trump.

In the throes of the game you snapped,
broke our mind's lobsided bargain
between frail wisdoms and a giddiness;

threw in your hand. And still traces
of your deranged years whisper
conspiracy, hide in genes of my game.

Yet it's you I always have to thank:
madness and song are the same suit.
I praise your name. I play your trump.

Will

Hearsay only, but yet I set my course;
A running tide and I felt the swell within.

I ploughed the sea. No need now for remorse –
True to nature, I sailed close to the wind.

Loner out ahead, I sighted a newer world,
As at the sacred streak I stared wide-eyed.

For the gloomy their throw. For me, all sails unfurled,
I leave my bright and bidding prayer behind.

Springnight

(1983)

Aubade

The sun has outdated darkness, another morning
pacemakes history, man the word-bearer re-awakes
and dares to praise. Begging my tongue of fire,

I proclaim a motto theme, naming in ecstasy
mysteries of time. Always I crave the centre –
serenity suffused by passion, endless and complete.

Although I celebrate, I still hear the metronome's
remorseless beat. No rubato here or emancipation;
accomplices in the scheme, each day is our biography.

It's January. Secretly a season turns its rondo.
In the clue of our rhythm flickers an incarnation,
time and timelessness counter-subjects in this fugue.

Streetscene

The aim fidelity, a perfect wide-angled focus.
But the frames slide into a movie, reality
blurring under a metaphysical Midas touch.
Is this the perpetual street? Spring says yes

as sporting a soft indigo cambray blouse,
a cinnamon suede skirt, a plum-coloured
underskirt jutting below, a young office girl
passes on some mid-morning postal mission.

A lorry driver's mate winks, wolf-whistles
an easy-going admiration; then stoops to lower
through an opened pavement grill another
squat beer cylinder, trundling to the underworld.

Hell must be dumb, a terrible dank cellar
of wonder bottled up, shuttered from the sun,
tight-lipped, tongue-tied, the word slips memory.
Unexposed to worship, we wither in darkroom silence.

Blinking in the sun, this viewfinder rescans
the non-stop synergy of a street. A child chases
a coin pirouetting over a gutter; touching each other
two greying men swap hush-hush information.

A flower-seller highlights, proclaims her titles:
freesia, tulip, anemone. A Whitsun gift.
Crouched, the sound-man records the sacred words;
open-sesames unlock again the gate of Babel's Tower.

Four Verses for Midlife Lovers

Watch a gossamer's nervous growth,
Network thrown against the odds,
Flown in face of bygone loss,
Blown in spite of broken trust,
Flimsy thread of golden dust.

Shorter span, the more the need –
Briefer space, the dearer spell;
Lust now tamer holds its head,
Weighs up lack and gain until
Life the weaver sways the will.

Wooers share a web of bliss –
Tell what gladness you recall
Swells with thanks or that regret
Paid with sorrow, dulled by pain;
Spin your cosmos, self-contain.

Love a self-sustaining world
Nurtures its own sweet habitat,
Equilibrated lake where foster
Rays inflow the sun's floodlight,
Life re-chains within a birthright.

Another Flat

Old faithfuls rallied, pitched in. But now the van
unloaded, we're alone with the old inventory
of *homo sapiens* and pitiless unshaded bulbs
sketch unlived-in rooms. We're bone weary

among these blankets slung with kitchen gear,
boxes crammed with books as bewildered plants
mock the wisdom of our move. A touch of irony
manages a laugh: were we mad to shift afresh?

Breaking laws of thrift, trailers not climbers,
we strayed, followed our own sweet pilgrimage,
always believing we'd found the one dream home
where all must thrive. And so it had to be.

Embedded, we adapt. A month's plunging period
and former quarters forgotten, our rehabilitated,
busy Lizzie declares a shocking pink manifesto,
wandering Jews hang out their mauve flowerets.

A partnership the invariant as meshed we trust
some strategy still charts our inmost rationale.

A Resignation

Time has it every way. Changeful,
a moment mirrors the ultimate chance
or multiplies an endless monotony.

Apostles lost in ecstasy don't fret
as terms play follow-the-leader,
each year dispatching another student

generation. Unabashed, the missioner persists –
no lack-lustre, no common-room chitchat
erodes his dream. A teacher, he senses

in each disciple the dateless epiphany.
The less blessed, ensnared by fluke or default,
endure the trammels of a chalky despair.

Was it a muse or a gene programmed
to non-conform, a dare-devil compulsion
to waver – then plunging, free-fall alone?

The genuine said 'Good luck with whatever.'
Threatened, the would-be quitter mocks:
'Tell us, what will you do for bread?'

No fanfare. Saunter through a cobbled quad,
an arch, a wicker-gate half-open to the light.
Tug the ripcord. Faith mushrooms overhead.

Setting Out

Nagging again the starter switch,
I hope the battery cells have hoarded
their fill of ergs and amps.

The choke serves a pick-me-up;
giddily, a current jumps the electrode
gap, begets the holy spark

that fires the inspired mixture
of petrol mist. The pedal gingered,
the chassis shudders in resurrection.

A flutter or two before cams and cranks
co-operate. Pivoting on neutral, we modulate
from gear to gear, from mood to mood.

Engines have their moments and memories.
Now the pistons in their four-stroke cycle
pump, excited as knees on a tandem.

Name the brake linings, the oil sump –
it's Saturday, father in a greasy gaberdine
is sprawled in state, busy under the body.

Mention the spell of a butterfly throttle –
the future opens. A man lives figuratively.
Internally combusting, I lever into overdrive.

Recital

His profile nods in tempo, unbelievable
nerve-centre issuing myriads of recalled
orders as forearms and wrists measure
to check a flow of fingers bubbling

over the keyboard. Lulled by the sound,
body and piano move in symbiosis,
from brain to string; loyal but uninhibited,
presenter not creator recasts the immutable.

Under troubled upper-voiced leaps
and mile-a-minutes *canto fermo* gains
ground, keeps faith. Fluid and spontaneous.
unity and diversity together. Let go,

Better sorry than sure, better chance
the glad-sad gene; a roaming harmony
teeters uneasily in its minor key,
resolves and seeps to its tonic chord.

Heaven's no sinecure. A lone grind
before the twinge, the exquisite note,
moment when a work curving homeward
floods, relieves, then bathes in pleasure.

He tos and fros, bows acknowledgment
to our admiration. Away from the grand
a tableau figure, a dampered leave-taking
lover waves goodbyes to our applause.

Portrait

Taut frame and wide quizzical forehead,
a trigger happy intensity that spells
danger. Once a pre-med he had flunked.

So a stint abroad, then he took to the law.
Rumbustious as ever, he drank, philosophised –
boxing the cards, never quite ready to play.

Exams slide. Years flick through a daybook –
troubled entries include one runaway wife.
Friends prosper, reproduce. Drunk on dole day

he ruminates on life's enigma variations:
must a man solidify, pillar up stability,
embrace their measure, strains and stress?

Maybe the have-nots will hatch revolution,
upturn and spread all the loot. Then what?
Whirl again the zealots' vicious circle!

Why not knuckle under, live only for perks,
Adjust to the system, feather a Pharisee nest?
Nobbled by his unsolved puzzle, he dozes.

Swivelling hair-breadths from a rare sanctity,
his daily shuffle hunts the ace of trumps.
A chronic exegete, this beggar and chooser.

Early Irish Lyric

Once again picture him near St Gall,
a monk in exile. Cinctured, diligent,
he is glossing, paving a Latin grammar.

'There are persons in the noun and particle,
though they are infinite!' He annotates a text
with his cryptic memory aids. Today's

lesson prepared, he unbends, daydreams.
It is early morning. Suddenly fired,
high on the elixir of spring, he declares:

'A hedge of trees overlooks me; for me
a blackbird sings – news I won't conceal...'
Febrile, meticulous, he chronicled the astoundment

a thousand years ago on the lower edge
of a vellum folio. This is another spring
and we are brothers conjugate in ecstasy.

Something ignites. Possessed by the flame
the psyche hums. On a jag of ink
a nib travels in delirium tremens.

Late Beethoven Quartet

Proud brainowner, once a Napoleon fan,
he pounded heaven's door. Those drum rolls
now acquiesce in a throb of equanimity.

Quadruple beauty: a risqué violin trend-sets
the cello's ruminant assent; prudent fiddle,
work-a-day viola interject a casual symmetry.

Motifs then fragment, configurations interweave,
mix, shapeshift with maniacal precision –
a reckless accelerando of distilled simplicity.

A poise not a posture; no truculent stance
toys here with despair. The word is praise,
the theme a scale of infinite permutation.

A Note with Flowers

Another day stirs in me
marred by the recollection
of yesterday's mean-mindedness.

Acquit me of malice. A flaw
in the make-up, a split second
throwback to juvenility

prevailed. Gallant flowers
must chance a rebuff –
bowing, ask for pardon:

The *I* acknowledges the *thou*.
Self-forgetting, the flowers submit –
each inch now a mile.

Words too contentious, only
mute repentance can redeem
our intimacy. So let

this bunch, final resource
of one contrite male,
make silent amendment.

Father

After Sunday lunch, gentle with wine and garlic,
snuggled in a fug of cigarsmoke, he nods, drops
into ritual doze. Anxious about draughts, tiptoeing,
gingerly protective, we spread a rug on his lap.

That sleep-mask fascinates. His features belie his age
though the hair is now wisps. 'I declare to God,'
he reported lately, fingering the crown of his head,
'given another year, I'll be as bald as a coot.'

Asleep, a frame so fragile denies a presence
encompassing my childhood until the push and pull
of growth unravelled its cocoon. Secret recollections
sneak across the room, savouring moods of afternoon.

Awake again. Sharpening a congenital zest for language,
craftsmen, we tackle the deadly serious business
of a crossword. Synonyms, cognates pun, criss-cross
in double-meanings. Nonplussed I turn apprentice.

In the evening a ceremonial drink, then music.
Pleading age, he recoils from the wistful; so Strauss's
Perpetual Motion spins on the turntable as father
reminisces, summons mythologies of memory; a favourite

the night he danced the Lambeth Walk in Casablanca.
Listening, I reflect on our comradeship. It isn't
who follows or fathers whom; infinitely more subtle,
our courses parallel, plot to converge on a horizon.

High Fidelity

A kid I telecommed by thread and tin lid
over gardens with a tomboy. Tonight, a prefix
selected, the wave signal is auto-switched,
exchanged and beamed aerial dish to dish
as leapfrogging satellites it sets its sights on me.

All in an eye-blink. No wonder Bell's contraption
bewildered Brazil's emperor. 'Quick from home' –
a jiff and in the earpiece your voice evokes
the whole of our life together as novelty unseams
and fidelity cheats across our time and space.

Hemmed by company, guarded, we speak our words
blandly as though a commoner local call.
Unscrambled, the intonation's messages caress
my inner ear. So glad to defraud such distance,
love's revs and vibes now dart across the sky.

In a New York Shoe-shop

Canned blues rhythms hum the background.
Air-conditioned from the swelter, a choosy
clientele vets the canted wall-racks

of new-look summer shoes. Unbargained for,
a handsome inky coloured man catching
the snappy syncopation, jazzes across the floor

to proofdance a pair of cream loafers.
Beaming, he bobs and foot-taps; pleased
with his purchase, he jives a short magnificat.

A friend from Maryland had once described
seeing in grandfather's cellar rusted irons
that had fettered a chain gang of black slaves.

Behind the polyrhythm, the scoops, the sliding
pitches and turns, I hear the long liquid line
of transcended affliction; women with gay

kerchiefs are prayer-hot in the praise house
or whoop in Alabama's cotton fields. Life ad libs
with a jug and washboard; sublimity forgives.

In submission to the pulse, the customer lets go,
swings low to the bitter-sweet quadruple
time, unmuzzled, human and magnificent.

Solidarity

In early afternoon mizzle, men in orange jackets
scooping a gully, shovel broken asphalt
onto a truck. The uplift, the spade's flick and lob,
chunks of gravel arching the tailboard fetch
from memory a summer's navvying near Bayswater.
Overcoming misgivings, I shut my sanctum's door.

Fulfilment unhurried, contemplation drips and trickles
as sand filters down an hourglass chamber;
last grains unloaded, sifted through the channel,
a hand again upturns the glass. Time recedes
as mind and heart co-radiate, the anchorite's laser
scans, then focussing, burns to an invisible core.

Tarmac steams and brews in an oven-trailer.
Urgent mixtures barrowed, tipped in the trench.
Hot black ooze slops and settles. On their knees
two push rough wooden floats, others skin-slap
with shovels. A signal, tools clattered, tossed on a lorry.
Twin-tracking now, two energies fuse in pleasure.

Fashion Show

Out in the daylight green is the rage,
chlorophyll the mode. Trees let it all
hang out while indoors poor leafless
sophisticates of shape and dye present
a spring collection. Quietly sensational
in magenta, lilac, beige or stone,
high-stepping ladies arm for summer.

Models turn our heads with readymade
come-hither smiles, lope in their spotlight
circle, splash their favours of layering
and fabric, whisk past in giddy colours;
a final bout, then swishing down the steps,
unbuttoning, they breakneck for a cubicle.
We await another creation. Meantime

three new mannequins swirl on stage,
ambush the eye, the compère patters on:
'Now a summer dress in china blue
with a scalloped hem.' How can they dream
up such stratagems, the tuck and cut
To self-assure, frazzle the male to ask
no whys or wherefores. O lovely woman!

No! Stop! The tease will unman me –
if only they would speak, say something
unreasonable to slow desire, but those
body linguists will show no leniency.
Beaming all the more they swoop
across the platform. Bewitched again,
fall a little for these frame-dames!

Get-together

In an alcove a school-leavers' get-together
grows boisterous, erupts in colt laughter,
noisy flashbacks, ebullient reminiscence
jar conviviality. A barman looks askance.
Their chatter is cyclonic and never hears
its silent centre where every bond
is breaking, each career now a catalyst
to sunder the tie, change the orbit.

Plans abound. The moment is nescient,
guffaws a filibuster, every laugh
an overdraft on a common kitty
asks 'Do you remember when....?'
Already the shared ground shifting,
soon camaraderie turns to reticence,
a wish to backtrack on a faded image –
shier than strangers they'll pass by.

Drink up! It's away over time!
No big farewells, emotion eschewed –
sure, we'll bump into one another –
bets hedged, options oiled and open.
Gentlemen please! Hardy nightlies slope
to the doorway. Well lit up, wobbling
with neighbourliness they bungle
loud goodbyes. A night is a millennium.

Upheaval

I gaze at a wired photograph of a revolutionary council.
Overwrought young men in fatigues outstare me back.
Months on end, hiding out, deep in hinterland,
teenage guerrillas in dugouts lopsided their youth.
A life-chain broken; wrenched out of childhood,
stunted, no time to settle, ripen unknowingly.

Their glance too jagged, sultry dissonance unresolved.
Generations of thinkers muddled with this conundrum
of power, to calm or swirl upheaval. But now,
the action over, we gamble on life's own chemistry
to self-correct. An acid snaps the secondary links;
determined to re-bond, an essence floats and curdles.

Homeward

After climbing, we level out. Tuned to a ground-station
our yaw self-adjusts while, trusting to the whirl
and pitch of turbo-props, we move by inspiration.

Streamlined, believing in magnetic flux, we navigate.
Over these months, I have indulged freedoms of a man
in love to admire the beauty of every woman I met.

Yet mindful of Icarus, I'm glad each pivoted needle
in the cockpit's angled maze of switch and dial
swings homeward. All thoughts now focus on you.

It has been a long continence. Love knows
feast and fast. Parted only by an hour
I dream, unfasten a little long-distance libido.

The first frenzy of unison over, we'll bask
in a routine, relearning the daily shuttle
of union and separation, love's drag and thrust.

So the approach. Our undercarriage untucked,
flaps curved, windward we surge then sink;
closed throttle, nose up, we touch down.

The Doctor

An altar boy at boarding school, wiry and serious
in a pleated linen surplice and poppy soutane,
at evening benediction he carried a sentinel's candle.

His thatch is now a shade thinner as he arrives
punctually, picking his way shyly past patients
to the sanctuary of a down-to-earth consulting room.

His surgery a tumble-down one-storey wedged
on a centre-city street. Each evening at six
cross-sections of inner citizenry line the waiting room.

Gainsaying mission, he alleges professional fascination
for the mixed bag disorders of have-nots: 'You see,'
he self-deprecates, 'I'm the end of the line!' Gashed

hardened winos from a close-by hospice spice the queue.
Whispering, pushing up a pew of rickety chairs they near
his door. Each diagnosed with sober bifocal compassion.

Simply, as a story plots out the mutual heartland
of fact and fiction, his mind seems to double thrust –
pinpoints and overviews. Sometimes a sidelong smile,

a slow slanted humour uncovers his midland
mixture of gravity and surprise; the sentient self
relaxes, content with a steady flame of chosen naivety.

Once Lovers

At first, I know this change asked most of you.
Bruised, suffering loss of face, you might well
ignore me. Sublime, we tactfully modulate;
happy in trust of other partners, we confide,
prize each other's company. Playfully, we mention
old flames; like work, a crisis smoothes in hindsight.

Once lovers, we could not meet as strangers.
Why should we? Grateful that our intimacy
endures as friendship, reunion binds us closer.
We had to choose. Following an inner must,
one only seems to lose. We stood the hazard,
came out on top – winners on every count.

Springnight

Framed by our window, trunks and branches
of chestnut trees are handbook illustrations
of arteries, veins charcoaled on a frosty sky.

Unnoticed, tee-shaped shoots fuzz the outline.
After a winter's wait an increment is sprung
in slow motion, growth catching us unawares.

Night is falling. The foreground darkens.
A trail of mauve clouds along the skyline
tones into the murk. A change of scene.

I gaze. You, my love, are tucked in sleep.
On edge, I begin the loneness of a night;
all eyes and ears I'm keeping this watch.

Starlight throws a window oblong on our wall,
a screen where homing cars project the trees –
slowly, then rushing back in previews of dawn.

The night will never stay. A half-refrain
from the primary reader unreels in my mind
like a mantra. Will a bird come in on cue?

A distant lemon streak. The trees blush.
In my vigil a world is disclosing its meaning:
wonderful terror, terrifying wonder of waiting.

Breakdown

Intent, the forebrain frets, misses
the beat. Jittery, we scumble
our vision, inhibit the pulse.

Struggling too much, a rhythm limps.
Deaf to the thrum, can we relax
in humility, will again to be chosen?

Caring less, we self-accept. Fallible,
juxtaposing the sacred and the ordinary,
I re-begin, pick up the tune.

Impassioned momentum of a germ motive
twists and turns as a plan abandoned,
yields to a dream, then gels.

Too conscious, I jam or jangle.
Unclamped the fingers run free.
The notes alone strum and sing.

Wounds

Who wasn't wounded on the way, doesn't ferry
Scattered in the flesh shrapnel memories of a failure,
Grapple with fears that, fed on, a fragment buried
In the self, could sour the blood, infect the brain?
You planned the scalpel's cool careful incision;
Then, cutting briskly through the scar skin excised
Dead tissue of those old sores. That eagle vision,
Lady-hand and lion-heart. A pain is exorcised.
Transplanted thoughts restore the damaged cells;
Skin-grafting pocks and scars you facelift sorrow,
Implant the mind with germs of bliss. A presence
Tones my morning, each evening fulfils a promise.
Nursed by affection, slowly I choose to grow;
Removing lesions, your love is surgeon to the soul.

Schoolboy Final

At each corner flag-sellers double-deal.
Colour-parties of schoolboys stump, file
through turnstiles, bustle to the stands.

A hub-bub swells while banners, mascots
swirl and vie: already togged cheerleaders
megaphone their slogans. One commissar

glancing towards the field, eyes someone's
sister among the schoolgirl camp-followers;
concentration wavers, resumes as a battle-cry.

Huddled between factions, inwardly fluttering
parents affect a sangfroid: 'Let's hope they're
evenly matched.' A warrior-priest chain-smokes.

Furore. Two squads erupt into the arena,
flexing, limbering. A pent-up frenzy
steadies, runs up, kicks. Life in parenthesis.

The sun raids the pitch, angling spring-light
past a grandstand gable; the crowd's chant
surges and slumps as chance twirls the volume.

Loose ruck, the ball tunnelled back, picked
up, a long looping pass, well-gathered, chipped
forward. On the attack. Commenting in the lingo

the old-timers' adrenalin empathises; reruns,
inklings of cosmos within cosmos reconnoitre
life as an enthusiasm. The world turns seventeen.

For a Teacher

A burly man, a fraction larger than life,
his presence declared by cannonades of laughter;
a branched beard, vivid shirt over tapered
cord trousers lent an air of pirate king.
Encyclopaedic, some a lecture confined him;
unfussed by footnotes, a compulsive teacher,
persuasive, sweeping, thrived at the centre
of tavern kingmakers. Those were his moments.

Praised burdened him. So paying the ultimate
disciple's compliment, I moved on. Although
blind to my lodestar, generous and unshakable
he'd wished me his stoic's *bon voyage*.
We create our fathers as needs may be,
to tease the latent; but finding uniqueness
we still trace something of their lineaments,
muster their memory. He was a father of mine.

Lady at Cocktail Party

Somewhere in a middle distance
I'm your admirer. The overall
tonal key, the emotive texture
evolves around your presence;
my childlike perspective conceptual,
every movement aspires,
all lines and curves allude
to you; honeypot of attention,
epicentre of our foreground.

Woozy, a little out of sync,
stills reel, the movie takes,
a whole assemblage of images,
successive changes of form
reposition, pass by, leave
elusive impressions on the eye;
walk-on parts are bleared
second-bests, extras unfocused
by you, the leading lady.

Freeze again the party scene
so I can revel in one frame
with you my lovely centre-piece
in black stilettos and stockings,
a blouse and low-crowned
hat to match, with red
ribbons reflecting a mid-calf
culotte; a thoughtful
study in red and black.

Lovers

Infatuation the first sweet kick. In compulsive
pain-pleasure each aches for an obverse; as lifetimes
file through the flow chart of our daily evolution,
we choose to love. The mundane burns white not red.

This is the intricate riddle, life's strangest incongruity:
as jigsawed counterparts we become ourselves;
yet once complete, new entities we face each other –
the surer each selfhood, the more we give we gain.

For a Child

Strange, how I feel I've a stake in you,
starting another lap. A few years his senior
I was commandeered by neighbours to chaperon
their son to school. That son is your father.

No blood relation, my intentions only spiritual,
but in reckoning your career, you'll forgive
one secular question: is speed inherited?
Your father was an athlete, sprinter and wing.

I wonder what masterplan chromosomes submit
what information unloads, messages transmit,
self-replicating, relaying a human marathon;
aeons of genes culminate, uncode in you.

Such possibilities converge! Yet you take
the fuss in your stride. Already I have seen
you flash your mother's smile; catching
the gist of living, you stow your memories.

Someway I think you know we're fêting
your entry to the race. Reassured, quickened
by your incarnation, the absurd recedes.
A baton passed, our thoughts turn forward.

April Soliloquy

Give just an omen, the merest sign
the word is not ill-spent. But a subtle
all-wise unfolds the birch's larva bud,
a token to endorse a winter of thought.

Along Dublin's suburban roads, cherry
trees market their blossoms; the late
April breezes are throwing fistfuls
of confetti to sway and freak and fall.

Syllables of a soliloquy, planned obsolescence.
Something overspills, flows in a eulogy.
Part of this nature, I accumulate in delight
a sinking fund against a reckoning day.

Gainful as a hermit's centripetal thought
or a pick-up needle skating the grooves
to a great finale, spellbound in perfect
concentration, everything is new to say.

A plectrum plucks the nerve of joy.
Nothing but the word contains the intensity.
A profusion. Sudden headiness of being.
Is life itself the burning bush?

A Diary

A memory machine, the playroom press's
jamjars of marbles and lead soldiers pensioned
among first-phase debris, and a rummage in a back
corner discloses a dog-eared diary with ribbon.

A scrawled ten-year-old's minuscule pencilled
these shaky world events: *Friday January 4th:
to Dundalk by train; Sunday January 12th:
my birthday*. February peters out, an annal fails.

Memoirs tap the keyboard, feeding their input,
words to speed highways and flip the gates,
to retrieve a trillion after-images etched,
childhood's data, safe in a lightening back-up.

Plumbing a past heartens me, though I blundered
into a close-mouthed March. But a muse admits
no self-reproach – no regrets to her invitation!
So inventing high-level language, key in

to a master program. Coyness, a grudging accolade –
our choice is binary. Only the yes-impulse can plus
instinct's magnetic core. In deliberate trance
I switch the sequence, play April fool with time.

Child in a Swimming Pool

Rejoice in wetness,
weightless plash
and gargle, watch
water sway, break
over the scum trough.

You aboard let's
breaststroke a width,
gasp to the side-rail
under your glee-cling
which is, gives faith.

Further up worlds
butterfly, belly-flop in
spluttered laugher; deep-
end gaiety beckons.
So, smile amazed.

Gulping fun you
still grip but begin
to loosen, bent on under-
taking some giggling
makeshift adventure. Then!

womb-memory awake,
palms shoved sideways,
downwards, leg kicking
you float alone. Breathless
your years tread water!

Break Up

The glow dwindled. We registered the danger signals:
an invisible schism, a sullenness, notes that jarred.
But was it imagination? Should we pass it over,
a temporary reverse, just symptoms best ignored?

Six months on, the word of their break-up broke,
burst like a stun bomb. Incredulous, blotting out
intuition, fudging misgivings we'd managed
to forget. In camera their estrangement festered!

Neither had wanted it so. Yet it had happened!
Bonded by closed chains of swapped recrimination,
they bickered, cold-warred, brainstormed in remorse,
faltered in souring labyrinths of fractured love.

In their coming together, we'd gained a friend.
Every conversation now bicentric, our symmetries
fear two-facing either. Worrying on both fronts
risks double loss. Falling back on hope, we redeploy.

Easter

Dizzy with joy, the Easter morning
sun trembles in the heavens;
the tacky buds unclenched, release
an appropriate festschrift of leaves.

Unsuspected, in their micro-world
tiny cells teem, crossplay,
rich networks of twisted strings
interlace, relate to the concord

of history re-begun. A starling mimics
Bravura, wood-pigeons whoop it up,
the orchestra purrs, tunes into
a master craftsman. Life da capo,

as riding our whirling earth-ship
we zip around the sun;
umpteen billion miles apart
stars both giant and dwarf

are suns that tug their planets,
constellate, take their partners
to dance the zillion-handed reel,
pinwheel outwards to eternity.

Glimpsing infinities of perfection,
awestruck, half-enlightened man
refracts the marvel, magnifies
an all-inclusive Easter thought.

Leslie

Mentioning him will nudge our memories
to fumble reminiscence, piece the pebble mosaic
of those four years. Undergraduate incarnate,
he conjured up some never-ending world
of talk. Every subject a fascination, he juggled!
with life, sorcerer of friendship, impresario of fun.

Something urged a scurry of experience:
episodes epic and birthdays turned festivals
of spring. Every day condensed a symphony
as nightly he kept vigil with an insomniac friend.
When after college he drowned, we wondered if
A mission accomplished, he'd moved to higher things?

Or did he? Here we still tread the boards,
growing older all the more tempted to trim
and shirk love's limelight. If ever we now falter,
or reaching blindly for props go solemn as sin –
timeless he still waits in the wings, guardian
jester of laughter that never can transgress.

Post-operative

Green-blue medicos in bakers' hats
mazed about the ante-theatre –
friends, my fear was measureless!

Limp, by ward sisters rewoken,
shaken back from semi-dead,
grateful, I welcome reincarnation.

Lazarus, this is wonderful! Though
tell me did you, like me, look back
on faithless moments before the dark;

feel forgiveness lagged with linen,
touch this sheet or hear in hints
far-off laughter guest a neighbour?

A shade surreal beyond a towel,
flimsily glance flowers and grapes,
taste another sensational chance?

Body-weak but glad to be
heed anew the hand of joy.
Can even this still-life laud?

Dún Laoghaire Pier

Shivering, I often stood on deck to watch these arms
greeting us as the ferry slid between the cutstone
fists on into the bosom. But lazing on a Mayday noon,
suntrapped in the elbow of the west pier, I luxuriate
in its enormous repose. Occasional joggers lumber past,
a lady calls a wayward dog; the wind jingles shrouds
of a moored yacht, a blue-jibbed dinghy dawdles by.

Make-believe. Slip a century back, daydream a fleet
of brown-sailed trawlers, coal-boats with grimy deckhands
like minstrels blacked for a show. Clean-stone lighthouses
on the pier-ends are thumbs-up to passing merchant ships,
cruisers, frigates. Grey-coated, red-cuffed constables
with glazed hats patrol busy quays. Sea-captains intrigue
in power-houses, tussle for the berth of harbour master.

The pier-wall, a crazy pavement of granite and sandstone
glistens: now along its base dandelions clump in garlands
for those unnamed, who slaved with caissons, shunted
wagonloads of boulders. The fittest survived outbreaks
of cholera, riots, strikes; a thousand plus they reckon
squatted on Dalkey Common, bullied rocks from the quarry.
In their embrace I consecrate a morning to their memory.

Water Lily

As per plan, fleshy underwater stems
now stretch upwards to announce
a perennial publication. Relaxed they surface,

then launch the season's latest titles.
No blurbs required. Plum and green
notched, blades float a sovereign serenity.

Over the shiny waxed texture of a leaf,
careering like a thrill-seeking schoolboy,
one fancy-free fly! The time is ripe.

Prepare for revelation! Discreet, unnoticed,
hidden in the prophetic shade of leaves,
a bud breaks water, noses up to summer.

A day's mystery. Towards evening she segments
her oilcloth cape, throws off her seven veils.
Buoyant in worship, she dances in the sun.

Two Evening Songs

1

Not venturing to tally credit with debit
I tender these words, my worldly wares –

For as love atones for the daily deficit,
commerce balances in this evening leisure.

The memory turns over a fresh ledger leaf,
another subvention, a pledge of credence.

Compounding our interest, together we grow;
hope our compost, love the mould.

2

Tomorrow dig a deeper channel,
sink a keener joy to fathom
me or even sound me out
on sorrow. Keep the sap in flow
lest careless the juices clot.
Move me! Permit this player's middle
ear to monitor his part, record
Endless adventures of emotion, make
me telltale each escapade, share
my zest, break what's new or bust.
Rhymesters serve in self-exposure.
Tomorrow dig the channel deeper,
fill it so its seams will burble,
blurt a secret bliss or sadness.

Birch

When winter darkens the urge
I've wavered. Losing my verve,
I doubt even a nudging mover.
What is it nerves again the sap?

Discreetly, buds bring out a year's
debutantes. Curious as mouse-ears,
vivacious, petite, see-through
leaves spring into the life-light.

Barely condoning such frivolity,
a stoic, this narrow white tree
indulges its limbs, though its trunk
wears a black belt all through summer

in spoil-sport memory of a fall.
The ascetic birch now waits
for autumn's curtain call to remove
its make-up, throw off the frippery.

Another year curves to completion,
signing a circle deep in the stock;
reason is cyclical – while upwards
love swerves seasons in a spiral.

After-image

Curious, rubber-necking through landing banisters,
we sneaked glimpses, in suspense waited or snooped
by the drawing-room door to overhear a mumble
of conclave as mother detailed the portfolio:
the bedroom would be off the scullery; duties
entailed the daily haul of our home affairs.

Night out Tuesday, half-day Thursday and Sunday.
Those strange times when girls from the country
in a pinafore uniform kept halfway house,
chored for their board. The fortunate, dancing
on their evening out or the August holiday find
a husband, bow themselves out. Children,

all nuances blunted, we borrow an older sister.
Mary, Molly, Kathleen – the names return
even if the faces smudge a little, trick
recollection. Incredible how lives once woven
inexorably slip and drift. Still they survive –

Distant figures in the fretwork of the memory,
scatter-hoarded after-images of our affection.

Elegy for a Singer

Fevered woman too quick afire;
song-queen too giving glowed
over, fuelled a chiller world.

Heady days ago we played
love together; two limelighters
mood-changed, flamed and quenched.

That was then not now; so why
self-condemn, regret delight –
No how nineteen years could fathom

slower growths of fondness; but
know that always after parting
I cherished you. Now, girl, goodbye!

Mastermind demands you leave,
quit the dance in swing and drive,
lonely take the last route home.

Still a little my once sweetheart,
rest a while and then farewell;
travel gently the forever zone.

Epithalamion

A fresh page one. Two concurrent
tales have met, so begins another
volume of this forever thriller.
Purring in predestined pews, guests

key up to celebrate; whispered
tête-à-têtes guess a who's who
across the aisle as cameras blitz
the bride's arrival. A season ago

these were strangers. Some ingenious
author unslipped themes, contrived
the plot, scene-shifted to rendez-
vous these lovers. Already an era

colours the interleaves of memory's
scrapbook; the novel wins its own
momentum until it feels no other
end could be, each instant edging

to an irresistible this. Strangers
born of one-time strangers, we
yearn to trust. A season's a kiss,
a lover's glance to vouch his credit.

Now she streams to the altar. Sustained
by ceremony a congregation murmurs
prayers. A July morning is musing
through the chancel windows: how

will a narrative decipher its epigraph?
Enough solemnity. Unbreakfasted guests
gurgle for the temporal; make water wine,
clink our glasses for life in flesh.

Grey-groomed brothers, former ushers
shower confetti, sprinkle the grain.
Time let this story roll and catch
their passion in the glare of living.

Seepage

Eight painstaking years we'd strained to cheat
Mistrust, to fill this sea, to take the plunge –
Swim in each other's confidence; with one deceit
The ocean floor is porous, bedrock again a sponge.
Who'd have thought the sea could leak? Naïve,
We took no soundings, dismissed all our fears,
But shallowing us, you siphoned our will to believe
And sieved away the sum of both our years.
So I'm your fall-guy, high and dry. Yet younger
By half, I watch you growing frailer, thinner-faced.
Afraid that time may ache with retrospective hunger,
I covet this chance. We've no time to waste!
Beginning the slow penance of a seeped devotion,
We spoon-feed trust, thimble back the ocean.

Patrons

Separately, they nursed my growth
Medicis who sunned a spring.

Before my time their affairs had been
A city's gossip; a generation later
The fable dims – a romance remaindered,

A handful of tempestuous poems;
Only cognoscenti recall the muse –
Is this all or is there more?

Self-flattery aside, I believe each
Touches the other in me; uncannily
I weave between their memories.

Though they parted, moved their ways,
Love by its nature has gushed
Into my mould. Now I their son –

Unseeded, but nurtured by the equal
Wonder of water turned to blood
Tap the pigment of their imagination.

Thank-you Note

Thank you for walking at Enniskerry. Rhododendrons,
a copper stream supplied the mobile backdrop
for our wonderland of thought. Those currents
of talk and silence seem to gather and pattern
the logic of a year's biography. Splicing experience,
we catch the astonishment in a sunburst of laughter.
Friendships know no genealogy, yet carefully grafted
knit like bones strengthened, braced by the mend.
Still we behave oddly. For four leap years
we've seldom met to layer our common ground;
content with heartwood, annual rings surround us
in brotherhood. Is time only of the essence?

Implicated in each other's story, the sap is mutual.
Long after meetings, hints, strange underplots,
asides, hunches in an interrogative mood re-emerge
as subterfuges of growth, burgeon by remote control.
Alone I chuckle. Infinity is the root of friendship.
Amazed remembrance explodes in an endless thank-you.

The Image Wheel

(1985)

Invocation

The nerve-threads are strings
on a violin, out of the heart
winds the ribbon of melody.

Round and round the potter's lathe,
life lurches in a spinning wheel,
the giddy ghost of the trinity.

Let me dance, let me dance,
give me the madness for the waltz –
three great beats of eternity.

Somewhere

A cluster of girls, busy
with gossip, are laughing;
hearing what's new, they
whisper names, dropping
hints of a timeless land.

Deft in their sleep
lovers turn in the night,
nudge back together,
sovereign in this kingdom,
no-man's-land of trust.

Suddenly, waking in the strange
borderland of darkness,
a child is crying. The mother-
hand relights the lamp,
kindles the hum of sleep.

Slack in an October sun
the calm of old stagers
again seems to say:
time is no fast-land,
measure only by light.

Somewhere in the outlands
a man listens. All history
fidgets in this heart, aching
to uncode a word
hidden in the moment's pathos.

Magellan

How could I know if I dreamt or raved?
Night after night in Oporto's taverns
I ran my finger around a globe
of wine, caressing the lure of a curve.

Loud in the torchlight beggared veterans
talked of gold; my thoughts drifted west,
below the Line, then through a strait,
probing a thread of South Sea islands.

Monsoons blow through the palm leaves,
canoes race over a deep lagoon;
fame is where the orange-tree blossoms.
Shipless mariner, did you dream or rave?

Still I believed it all would happen.
Months of sodden hope against chance,
combing the mutinous reefs and shallows.
Magellan, Magellan, are you mad?

Follow the flagship, ask no questions!
El Paso – I wept when we passed
The Lands of Fire and fled for summer.
Soon the sky had turned to brass.

We drained butts of yellowed water.
The watch changed, the sand-glass ran –
the mind is the most capricious ocean –
Magellan, where's your land of spice?

Memory shrinks those days to one.
A late March morning, over the horizon
a canoe glided; among their gifts
I saw a Chinese jar. All my life

surrenders to the subtlety of its sphere.
'Men,' I shout, 'the world is measured –
as these figures painted around a jar
our names etched on the curve of time!'

I never doubted the signs and wonders.
Yet, like Thomas, I needed the wound.
I wrapped my hands around that jar –
then I knew I dreamt, not raved.

New Year's Eve

In some neighbour's flat
a party sways, chained
hands conduct the ritual,
midnight clamour backed
by the late streets'
hoot and blare – gaily
the year glides in.

Time deepens; a canvas
widens hue and volume;
life's sweep and reach
glance through the mind,
wonder where and how
scattered friends watch,
wake the sliding year

hazed by good fellowship
or alone in prayerfulness
edge to the unplumbed,
each consciousness midmost
hub to a wheel of hopes
that recalled an instant
crowd again around.

Eliding years of absence
in split-second intensity,
jets from the frame-trap
of remembrance gleam
as tenses slur all
warm in the sacrament
of friendship's thanks.

And thanks for the party!
Doors slam. A girl
squeals, giggles shyly
on the landing; mind-
blown someone garbles
a song's refrain, then
sputters into the noiseless

frostbound night. Sap
lies low in the limbs.
Solstice past, secret
orders given, we bed
snug in new resolve;
underworlds turn over,
sleep homesick for spring.

Burdens

Instantly, we meet at your request –
old resentments you wish to unload.
Dreading this transfer of burdens,

Head-hung, helpless, I must listen
as every sentence wrings from me
business long dismissed. Unflinching,

trembling, you insist I recall
words once lipped too lightly,
never dreaming they might weigh

years of hidden trespass. Frightened,
I risk your welling eye, watch
anguish simmering. 'Everybody said

You'd jilt me, shed a skin' –
blenching, I fumble idioms of sorrow,
hesitant words to anoint a scar.

Ill-balanced against so deep a wound,
talk adds injury, regretful
phrases ring hollow, hopeless.

Walking you home through the drizzle,
jet hair glistens in the streetlight.
Stricken, I search each glance,

begging some signal of forgiveness,
selfless gift to loosen this
bundle of shame. Hint of a tender

look and we are slipping back
sixteen years. Again I throw
late-night pebbles at your window –

younger yet older, more afraid,
awestruck by the sting and splendour,
terrible delicacy of woman's heart.

A Fall

Late one night we found him in a drunken doze,
curled up on the frozen pavement, his full-moon
face and stub-nose shining snugly in fuddlement.

We knew him to see; by all accounts a stage genius
bound for the summit – yet somehow he slithered, blew
his chance, bungled, stood great impresarios up.

A mountaineer keen on the climb, the low trail,
the long hike, steady tedious uphill trek,
till sheer handhold over foothold, ledge by ledge

he peaks – then scanning the grandeur of his vista,
senses guilt, misses the hazard of ascent; dizzy,
feeling the odds creep up against him, he slips.

We dragged him to his feet. Gathering a rugged dignity
he managed comrades! – mounted the steps to his door.
Anxious below, we watched the windows for light.

Spring

Time again from the word go,
dark in the soil seed stirs
wills to spring. Forever the same
joy to tingle, need the surge
upward, yet always self-doubt.

Each separate seed must brood,
sweat a single destiny, mooch,
wonder where the itch leads.
Every bulb stalls and asks
what is this that buzzes me?

Sit tight, leave well alone,
cosy deep, dim in earth;
why risk the forecast light,
a far-fetched heat or chill –
what is this that frightens me?

All might fail, any move
amiss blights, brands me
a seedbed dud; yet
shame stagnates. Go get!
What is this that urges me?

Each seed dreams itself
overground, sees a dewy white
surprise, an upstart flower
nodding under February sun.
No sooner dreamt than done.

Doubt dispelled, a bulb unzips
the thrill-sting of upswell,
the purpose-push, breakthrough
spurt, budsnap and bloom.
One snowdrop; so a spring.

Letters from Assisi

1 *Francis to his Father*

Father, if only you'd understood
I craved to be the man of every hour –
All your ambition slept deep in my blood.

I loved the touch of silk, the feel of power,
To gossip, joke, outshine Assisi's cavaliers;
For all that talk of bird or flower

I'd your merchant's will to vie. Two years
Caught a prisoner in Perugia, I was still
Half-aware I'd fought for a town's profiteers.

A ransom. Then, the homecoming. 'Is Francis ill
Or in love?' people asked, wondered why
I looked so distant. I did the parties until

Something snapped. Every stricken passer-by
Now fixed his stare on me, saying 'Francis,
All turns on you; Francis, look me in the eye!'

There were riches in Apulia; I'd lances,
Troubadours' songs to sing. I could forget.
But haunted daily by those strangers' glances,

I sold your bale of cloth to let
Some paupers eat. Father, you whipped me,
Branded me a madman; each time we met

You cursed me, so I paid a down-and-out a fee
To bless me as his father, taunt your sorrow –
I wanted to outdo, best the world in poverty.

I was so young and life was tomorrow.
Already my followers scheme for a benefice.
The road seemed short – I could beg or borrow

Rags of humility, call your care avarice.
Time unlocks compassion's garden-gate.
Father, can you forgive my Judas kiss?

2 *Francis to Clare*

My Clare, in years to come they'll
puzzle over us! *Francesco e Chiara.*
I can almost hear them chuckle.
Let them wonder! If they don't know
that love's first sight can seal
a lifetime, how will they understand?
You came to me when I already
was sworn to Mistress Poverty.
Saints carry their souls in lovely
vessels; only iron wills have made
our rule. There's a thousand ways
to know another; we may not share
the daily buzz and flittings of a mind.
Each alone in prayer acclaims this love,
still in the cell of its first perfection.

3 *Francis to his Followers*

You know the joy and stigma we the prophets wear?
Bat just an eyelid and the splinter newness of another
Reborn wisdom dims. Only a while, my brothers!
Although I didn't see each knot in the net of time,

As any visionary tiptoeing the fringes of his sanity
I glimpsed an image-god hiding in the mind of man;
As every mender of history takes up his strand,
I tied a love-knot, hitched my thread to the work.

Morning on Grafton Street

Grafton Street is yawning, waking
limb by limb; jewellers' steel
shutters clatter upwards; the sweet
doughy smells from hot-bread

shops steam the frosty morning,
warm our passing; disc-stores'
sudden rhythms blare an introit,
launch the busy liturgy of day.

Look! Two breakfast wooers
fallen in love with farewells
smooch, soul-kiss on the kerb.
Gently, my street puts on her face.

Grafton Street, witness of my time,
seer, watcher of every mood,
traps me the grandeur, the melancholy,
ever-new carnival of man.

Walk here alone in broodiness,
inwoven, anonymous, swept along;
stroll here infatuated, self-communing,
lost in the lyric flow of street.

Self-portrait

Intense, set stooped, he walks as though weighted
Down by unfinished thought ablaze in the rubble
Of his mind; this poet of Donnybrook has made
His song and dance of every joy or trouble.
God knows who chose him for the job. A strange call,
Unbidden moods honed along the marrowbone,
Alone assured him that something of the overall
Tune had stirred to lift a single undertone.
It happens unwittingly; one man's epic becomes
The soundboard for his time. So once more
Falling for the pulse-music, a dreamer succumbs
To the mind-expanding frenzy of word and metaphor
Light rays fuse the perpetual in the transitory,
In the lover's lens through which he views the story.

Memoir

Thoughts lain years
untouched stir and so
find courage to recall
her. At last I dare
burgle childhood's archive,
gather up the collage,
knowingly now probe,
search in thanks to word
the marvel of a woman
once this man's globe.

Watch her again,
mistress of her bureau,
thick in wire-filed
dockets, monthly tots,
tallies – there sits
a wasted Kaiserin.
Look deeper. Alone
a silent novelist
unreels in commonplace
another otherworld.

Herself an only child,
hours she spellbound,
traced in her father's
line the tangle-saga
of his dozen siblings –
how Bill ran away,
took the king's shilling,
died young. This
lonely epic still
marches my middle brain.

Prayers down to earth –
beadless fingers tapped
aloud a rhythm litany:
St Anthony, Pius the Tenth,
Blessed Martin de Porres,
protect us from infectious
diseases. Poems mystified;
she laughed: a pity
to keep a man idle,
so little keeps busy.

One winter evening
breathtook, struck
terror when pulling
open the tallboy's
bottom drawer she
uncovered business-like
winding-sheet and candles –
once her mother's, next
her own – we children
should know in case.

Black-haired, oily-skinned
crown prince to those
genes, grateful heir
to many-mooded raptures,
quivers in the dance –
in daily brinkmanship
every twitch, gesture
remembers her in me.
All blunted whetted,
what smouldered burns.

Ode to a Juggler

Such style! The incredible untroubled
Faraway look of twice-doubled
Concentration: one, two, three, four.

One ball caught by the crook of the neck,
She steadies a little to countercheck
The rhythm, tosses it back into orbit.

Five. There's a long career ahead;
A genius called Rastelli once fed
The air with ten at a time. But there

Among the primroses, in on the grass,
This juggler entertains us as we pass
On more urgent business. Short-cutting

Through the park most must adhere
To the narrow path of errand; for a mere
Moment we stop to watch, wonder if

Her playfulness mocks our humdrum worth.
The balls roll in mesmeric mirth,
jokes told with flawless timing,

Or are they stars held in motion,
Not by gravity but by devotion
To a great god of fun? Seemingly

Unaware of our admiration, she enthrals.
The endless edgeless tennis balls
Move in the abandon of her serenity.

Nocturne

Life burns low. Lounging,
relishing the movement and repose,
balanced ease of late evening,
lazy eyes freelance. There
orbed in lamplight you browse.

Occasional comments log a day.
No statement, merely venerate
detail: bright red plant-pot,
blue-pattern covered cushions,
softly lit in your sphere.

Thriving in the outglow of the hour,
calm globe of wellbeing,
we bed the seed, incubate
thoughts, warm tomorrow's theme.
Hazy, ready to grow in sleep,

sorrow's long shadows fall
beyond the nimbus of our lamp.
We huddle in the kernel. Cares
drown outside love's circle,
blurs well-flooded out by light.

Notes in the mind treasure up
this moment's tune; a melody
finds words to wrap the night,
hoard a measureless memory,
gather our instant into eternity.

Scruples

or the day's vanity, the night's remorse
YEATS

Comrade, pilot of my travels,
You have given generous light –
Yet an inner voice cavils;

Prophet-poet by what right?
Self-doubt and scruples hover,
Conscience cries by night.

How can I now recover,
Redeem your years spent
Loving the bemused half-lover?

Double-mated, I never meant
To fail, to shortfall you;
The mood-changer muse has leant

On me, squeezed more than due;
Untrue, undertakings broken,
I forfeit my claims on you.

Excuses too smooth-spoken,
Words shallow at source,
Comforts too soft to token

Divided pain or to endorse
My shame, that counter-theme
Matching your sorrow with remorse.

Can nothing I do or dream
Charge a cell of resurrection,
Bring again love on stream?

Amazed at such introspection,
'Love,' you whisper, 'why remorse?
Am I not queen of my affection?'

Loss

The last summer he walked slower, chose to linger.
Pausing in a laneway, he ran a thumb along the seam
of an old garden wall – 'Those joints need pointing,'
he warned; attentive, we saw in his face some strange
play of inward movement. On request we drove to Meath;
those fields a dozen times the size of his own
pleasured his eye. At Christmas leaning on the window sill,
lovingly he gazed over a few loamy acres towards Gola.
In mid-January, cutting back briars, he fell with his scythe.

Several years later, I waken deep into the night,
hear you sobbing to yourself. It's Patrick's Eve,
that evening your father used return after
his winter exile, a labourer in Scotland; three
eager children watch the dark beyond Dunlewy.
Now, at last, the bus's headlamps arc the sky
overjoyed you race the lights to meet him at Bunbeg.
Tonight, here by your side I listen, then kissing
your forehead, throw my arms around your sorrow.

Fathers and Sons

Time's an old man lifting his glass,
toasting life and saying, 'Son,

no one can sound another's depth,
alone, alone fathom the well-shaft –

the long clanging fall from the sun,
the draught upwards back to light.'

Time's a young man's swaying bucket
slapping water over its brink.

Daisies
(for Sinéad and Caoilinn)

The day's eye, little noon
Thousand joys, sunbeam bloom,
Margarita, beauty, pearl,
Litanied flower, many-named girl
Waiting out history for this accolade;
Fresh witnesses, you create
A daisy link for the litany chain,
In your newness christen again:
Lover's eyelashes, pirouetting tutu,
Frail ballerinas poised in the dew.

Cat on Garden Wall
(for Ciara)

Yesterday, playing hard to get,
he came and went between the railing,
pushing through his nose and whiskers,
then withdrawing. Today I fancy

he watched for you, hunched, pretending
he just happened here to lap
up your affections. Lovely rogue,
he arches, mooches, dribbles pleasure;

following you along the wall-top
he dodges under branches to keep
pace, rubbing his cheek against
a gate pillar, sucks another goodbye.

At last, propriety makes you leave.
He cocks his wistful eye to say:
Life's a greeting and a parting,
yet I lived for such a meeting.

Homage

Nearly eighty, slow-paced,
stooped, he enters. Even his suit
has seen better days; but touching
that instrument, his face is chamois

which puckers, ripples each phrase;
a smile inscrutable, ears pricked
for an inward zing, heard deep
in the calm of age. This virtuoso

Vlado Perlemuter a half-century
ago, Ravel's apprentice, played
these pieces for the maître whom
in his turn Fauré had fostered.

Lineage of love, strange dynasty
beyond the blood, every succession
wills on the gift; a current
skips from fingertip to tip

along life-giving lines, as once,
suddenly, thumbing through a treasury
we find ourselves, stumble on
forerunners who forefather us.

Warmed by homage, a melody resung
reddens again the afterglow;
son to many far-flung fathers,
there are sons who watch for you.

Fly-by

Bone-weary, my nerves played out,
nothing in the mind turns over, takes off.

Seated by the window I'm gaping,
praying for a happening to lift the soul.

Out of the blue, a coal-tit has splashed
down on the wet balcony railing.

His head twitters, his eye uneasy
follows a magpie who is hedge-hopping

menacingly below. Darting downwards
his spindle legs cling to a bar

like climbing irons. Still he jerks,
carries out this probe manoeuvre

then drops, docks in the flower-box.
Gobbling a crumb, his throat pouch

bulges and shrinks; a sudden invisible
signal from mission control orders

a dash to the edge, a quick check
before the lift-off. Refreshed, I'm

happy to broadcast the commentary,
privileged to be a flight-recorder.

Rebels

So once you wished to clean-sweep the world –
first outfling of hurt, fledgling's overreach.
In fuller flight we wheel an earth-shaking circle
of loyal friends, throw light or shadow,
soar or sweep, rebels within that sacred theatre.

Weather the knowing nod, the foolproof remark:
'So at last he's seen the light.' As if a youth-
long hope could pass blighted by a moment, bubble
blown, pebble skimmed over water. Believe me, brother,
mellowed we serve, lifetime comrades of a dream

harmony where each anguish shared soon resolves,
passing dissonance, spice-notes in sweeter melodies
of being. Gentler, we fly closer to the wind,
let life slip through logic's web until we glance
a scheme in the million-coloured spectrum of our praise.

Listening

Afraid for you, hastily I interfere,
Advising this or that to avert
Another danger and so appear

To chart your course. Salt in a hurt –
Though I would be Job's Elihu –
My words sting. In pain you blurt:

'Friends pick my sores, outdo
Each other in choosing the wisest plan
To mend my ways. Now it's you.

Easy for you, you chanty man,
To know the ropes by rhythm and song!
Words of wisdom scorn me. How can

You fathom my affliction? I belong
To those troubled who must grieve
Alone. The weak are a riddle for the strong.'

Humbly I concur; but the heart, naïve
In its listening, begs you to hear
The silent rhythm's call and heave.

For My Friends

Spendthrift friendships once ravelled and unravelled,
Carefree, leisurely as a journey without a plan;
Easy-come, easy-go, there was a while I travelled
Lightly, made my friends catch-as-catch-can.
Gradually, the casual twisted the precious weave,
This tissue of feeling in which I have grown;
Though I follow a single thread, I must believe
That bound to the whole we never drift alone.
Crossed, matted fibres long inwrought,
Friendships prove the fabric of a common story,
The web which takes the strain of every thought,
Shares the fray or stain, joys in our glory.
Interwoven, at last I dare to move without misgiving;
I touch the invisible, love this gauze of living.

A Short Biography

Tell me, friend, how this began.
Was it that morning you tricycled
up the slope along the path
to the woods; wheeling around,
pedalling frantically homewards,
snowflakes spun in the trees,
and passing through the garden gate,
you turned forever into Eden?

Or maybe one winter afternoon,
alone in the sitting room listening
to music on a radio left idling
after the news, you were staring
through the window, when suddenly
the trance-dance stirred? Then
all was transfigured. Again
you'd blundered into seventh heaven.

Or the autumn evening, carrying back
messages from the shop, you watched
a man stooping to bundle the last
sheaves? The yellow stooks ranked
sunwards, the damp seed-smell
of corn seized you; startled,
a half-dazed witness to the majesty,
you climbed over the narrow stile.

Meeting

We both chose to sphere another world,
To wheel and turn around a different sun;
So since when circles touched or curled
In tandem, meetings seemed a duty done.
An eye which flicks a mock surprise, a stab
Of doubt now mars your words, reveals a new
Control, a silted fear that I might blab –
In shedding former secrets unorbit you.
Our fields unlike, we spin on separate poles
But still are fuelled on memories shared by both;
Each fed on gravity, pulled by different goals –
Must we disown our commonwealth of growth?
I owe you too much to push such memories aside;
At every tangent, I long for our suns to coincide.

Einstein

Caught in the rhapsody, I watched a pipe's smoke
cloud and twist its thousand shapes of magic;
walking in shallow summer water, at each footfall
a puff of sand mushroomed and I was afraid.

Will a mind stretching to grope an essential statement
find that galaxies have followed the same equation?
Attentive as a man learning a language from his lover,
I heard amazing rules among sweet nothings.

Absence

On my own I swore I'd settle calmly down:
Hours later, plans threadbare, my mind hovers
Uneasily; again I wander the evening town,
My aloneness grazed by each pair of passing lovers.
Halved, my life is now unreal, as though,
Rootless, the everyday events are tossed
Around in uncompleted reverie; in mid-flow
You left a sentence, the conversation's theme is lost.
We too have myths, symbols, a world of our own,
A universe of tangled memories, hopes and schemes;
Counterpoised within that dovetailed zone,
We share our chosen take-for-granted dreams.
Without you, my love, too many thoughts unspoken,
Words are babble, a sacred thread is broken.

Blue

When demons dance, even you must
Dare again the threat of dust;
Those days you too will falter.
Undone by rifts of self-distrust

You mope, try once more to persuade
Yourself, saying 'If only I'd made
Other choices; where now are all
My might-have-beens? I'm afraid.

I'm straying, losing my clue to the maze.
Surely I could find other ways
To serve?' No, it must be so!
Although you turn back to praise,

Only fools won't hear this rumble
Between the panegyric lines. A humble
Song manoeuvres in the hinterland
Of hope. You too must stumble.

Pardon yourself. Then feel the shove
Onward, a booster, until above
And beyond the image-wheel turns,
Spins from doubt fables of love.

That Woman

For me to even mention her
always casts an ego-shadow
across a spilling self-lost light.

Yet the old giddiness wells in me
the want to prize again this sun,
lavish giver, source of trust.

Often when watching that splash,
outpour of brightness, I feared warmth
might fall on thankless ground.

To spare needless waste, I stretched
unwieldy branches to ration the gleam,
begging her to measure slowly.

Jealous of those generous rays,
numbering out each giving,
unwittingly, I tamper with infinity.

Lunchtime in a London Café

Table by table the café fills
till talk and the clap of plates
bulge with well-being; a dark
waitress's patchwork skirt
hurries behind the counter;
every face under the sun peers
at the window menu; more
voices join the steamy pentecost.

Here in the metropolis nothing
shocks. Out of its huge anonymity
worlds of strange gossip crowd
this lunchtime café. And I'm in love
with its mystery, the peculiar rapture
of life à la carte. The window mists;
after wine, the Basque in the corner
turns his smoky eyes on the waitress.

Outside the door, the buses shriek,
rush and judder; a city's jamboree,
hope and haphazard, limitless
chances, choices wait. Sitting
here I know I've felt the throb
of Jerusalem or Rome or any city
yet to come, where there's a café
and we, citizens all, break bread.

Around the Bandstand

A brass band is giving vent
to something in our consistent
soul. Listen to the snare drum –
a tribesman is rapping the skull
of his prey as down the trumpet's
cylinder early man intones
his loves through a femoral bone.

But here at last we are
around a bandstand in a park,
our hearts beating a tempo
under the sway of a baton,
as strangers take each other's pulse –
we've never heard of alienation,
we're tapping our feet to civilisation.

Brass or bone I am certain
man from the beginning has heard
above the tuba's grumble
the gaiety of the unpredictable
rhythm run counter to his march
as through the force-house of a horn
blows the ragtime of our hopes.

Travellers

Recall the first outpourings
of excitement. Nothing unsaid,
we trusted the heart-swell,
the pitch of the moment,
to somehow find the word
to coincide. With the grace
of beginnings, we hurried
to match; yearning for oneness,
we dreaded all-aloneness.

Allowing love its life-room
with time we have begun
to value the unuttered, dealing
in hints and images,
we travel alongside –
never flush but letting
light slide at will
to fondle and caress
this awe of our uniqueness.

Midday Nap

A top upright in fretful spin,
a wheel lurching forward until
around its drowsy rims you whisper:

Wobble, fall! Stone-still the hub
dozes, marrow moves darkly
within, lullabies noon's misgivings.

Let this life-grammar leak;
tense, mood, aspect intermingle,
slack in semi-liquid ease.

Murky in the brainstems, ongoing
dreams mix, placid nerves
tranced, twitchless, seek and find

memory islands of ever-summer,
a maze of warm hindsights
drifting purposely through the mind.

Then thoughts re-dawn, up the tempo,
stretch to embrace recycled morning,
newborn wonderment of afternoon.

Romance in Couplets

The sober must decry the trust-leap of romance,
Ask who are we to bend loaded laws of chance?

Both lives will change in the warp of light and time,
Till lines of thought bulge at the seams of their rhyme.

Who then holds sway, knowing the other is bowing?
Which of us must listen to the sweetness of allowing?

There are many corners, strange labyrinths in the mind,
And I can only answer: how can a love be blind?

Heart-on-sleeve

Heart-on-sleeve, you seem too green –
You will learn to wear a mask –
Piecemeal then perfect the screen,
Masquerade for fear men ask

Leave to hear your hidden dream.
Thoughts unsealed live double lives –
Who forecasts what life will scheme –
Unforeseen they'll sharpen knives.

Still remember friends you made;
Touched by love you sensed the true
Tone of friendship, words unweighed
Showed a vision, shared your you.

Fuelled by them you flare again
Careless chances. Trust your task.
Half-clown, half-priest among the men
You must never wear that mask.

Autumn Report

Nel mezzo del cammin di nostra vita

DANTE ALIGHIERI

Autumn is touching us with a summer's afterthought.
The tilted sun hazes around the yellow-fringed
branches of maples, eking out our tapered season.
Soon an occasional dash of tangerine will singe
these leaves, as even now a few frizzled casualties
butterfly in the hint of a breeze. September, a chancy
friend, blows hot and cold, yet caution cramps us in –
fritters the grand event; so propped in this side-street
doorway, a gap on the pavement between two vans
affords a patio where sunlight swabs our regrets,
loosens the mind to osmose the indelible past,
balance its books. Let this sun-captured moment be
a throw-away line, a fly-leaf dedication that stretches
to reach the essence, snatch the tenor of the whole.

Hardheaded Vikings used to figure their age by winters,
but further south we may chance a count in summers.
I've lived a round three dozen – one over the half
of man's allotment; moving into the second moiety
I tender friends and shareholders an interim report:

Even in this fall, wholehearted life reverberates
some almighty gaiety, invites me to adore
the immense integrity; wines my veins until
I'm sure my frame will warp under such
exuberance. I've never felt so near the centre
of all that is.

There goes another rumpled
leaf, frisking and nose-diving in the draught
as if to ask what has the whippersnapper new
to say? Today's sun has never shone before,
never found me in this doorway; history has
accumulated this moment, now funnels through me
the urge to utter. In this instant I'm Adam
the first to mouth, to feel the garden overflow
in word and rhythm.

Yes, there were certain liabilities
to meet: mornings which would not wake, days
that moped and brooded on their failure until
shame, an unfed stomach, turned the acid fuel
to gnaw the lining. Dozing on, I recapped each collapse,
idly watched the digital clock matchstick
away my time, slip noiselessly into desperation.
Yet reaffirmed by woman's ardour, again allowed
untense, surrender afresh to laughter, I have
unjailed the self. Some all-embracing love
forgives my shortfall and I am glad to present
this reconciled account.

But a statement is current,
the entrepreneurial everyday rushes forward
to speculate all over again and we who traffic
in life must venture on. Why hedge our bets
or play too cool? Detached we might miss
the passion to broaden the bore, deepen the joy.

The wind freshens, risks another leaf or two,
floats some unbidden debenture. Please give me
a few moments more, just to exult in this
last reflux of summer, luxuriate in its praise.
Then gambling on, I'll bless the breeze and go.

The Chosen Garden

(1990)

I. DEPARTURE

Baciami sulla bocca, ultima estate.
Dimmi che non andrai tanto lontano.
Retorna con l'amore sulle spalle,
ed il tuo peso non sarà più vano.

Kiss me on the mouth, final summer
Tell me you will not go far away.
Come back with love on your shoulders,
and your weight will no longer be in vain.

SANDRO PENNA
(trs. Alessandro Gentili
& Catherine O'Brien)

Espousal

Days early, my trousseau lay in the hallway,
Mother's own school trunk newly hinged,
freighted as prescribed – all regalia
taped and numbered: rug, napkin ring,
tuck-box, laundry bags. Hour by hour
a dreamy September holds its breath.

Late evening, a scuffle of gravel as cars
brake on the castle's forecourt. Novices
reconnoitre, bustle of arrivals, goodbyes,
last advices, and already I fidget, eager
to embrace my venture; parting promises:
a visit in a fortnight; waves in the half-light.

Down the marble steps into the vast
corridor of wainscotting and notice boards,
lists of placings for study-hall and chapel;
chance meetings, the territory explored –
playrooms, libraries. The tug of a bell,
a hush and we file towards night-prayers.

So, this is the honeymoon of my fantasy,
a reverie of quads, pillow fights, decent
chaps with parcels and cads in Coventry...
My friend was coming, I begged to be sent.
'You're on your own', father has warned.
'You've made your bed, now lie in it.'

Ten twenty. Lights out in the Holy Angels,
we slide into iron beds; a skittish
silence falls; in earshot another dormitory,
same prayer, commanding flick of switch.
Neighbours whisper introductions: Michael
Walls, Roscommon; Flannery from Tipperary.

Snatches of a parlance, subliminal spells:
all out, lectio brevis, night-squares,
smoke in the mind; days to come
gleam, a jingling clump of mortise keys.
I espouse a new world, drop into sleep;
expectation whirrs in the tongues of bells.

Initiation

By hearsay beginners fear the passage rite:
dark talk of toilet dousing and shamings.
Watch your step. Last year's weaklings lord
a brief revenge – *old scout's preference.*
To endure is everything; so now bide time.
Day by day the hierarchical bluff is called.
Seats at table fixed by scramble, the head
holds sway, portions out the food at whim,
waylaying second helpings for his table-top
cronies. It's Monday. Roly-poly and custard
for dessert; O'Sullivan acts the tough, threatens
to confiscate my share...Outside I tackle him;
a flurry of punches, I fall in a stranglehold.
Days later another flare-up; again he wins.
His taboo endangered, we have settled down
to a sultry peace. Fantasy slips into reality.

Inmates of a world slowly, slowly enamoured
of our narrow purlieus, every rule and loophole,
bounds and out of bounds, little by little
we grow fond of our containment. After dinner
in the hamper-room cutting a slice of cake
One of *the hards* comes wheedling, menacing
Give us a scrounge! Swear at him loudly –
grinning, he moves on. The weeks pass,
the fittest thrive. No Joyce, no Stephen Dedalus –
your ghost may sulk on the Third Line crease,
baulk at our scramble, but your gaze is hindsight.
We think we dream of home and all the while
who got *sleeps* or a parcel, who made the team,
shifts of comradeship, rumours of a prefect's mood,
concerns, subterfuges map our hours and fill
an atlas of our living. We're in love with survival.
All other worlds are slipping out of reach.

Icons

I stir an entourage of ghosts, icons of youth.
On Sunday nights by turns a sermon. Curious
in the pews, watch the red pine sacristy doors.
Enter tonight's turn, stoled and surpliced,
a gladiator in this fastidious arena: Reverend
J. Burden, S.J., Father Procurator – head high,
manner aloof, he mounts the marble pulpit steps.
'My dear boys, I want to tell you how I recall
one vivid evening in a tent in India...'
I allow the dogged tones bring into focus
memory's image, hold up compassion's looking glass
to read the mirror-written agenda of his words.
It seems the chapel has emptied, I listen alone.
He slopes forward with the weight of utterance, then
tosses back his head as though withdrawing all.
'Smirk if you will. A padre I staunched souls'
forebodings, shared tent and table with my troops,
rough-hewn men, salt of the earth, the Empire's
marrow. Smile, yet it wasn't easy to settle
to age in a draughty castle. Here might have been

the seedbed of Home Rule, our country's Eton –
forgive me if I sour, a fruit beyond its season –
instead this your mix 'em gather 'em state...'

But we are streaming up the aisles, another Sunday:
a brief pause and the great varnished doors
open to release the Hooley to the lions. A titter
darts through the congregation; all agog we watch
Father C. Gilhooly, bespectacled, a self-defensive pout,
tilting his left shoulder to trace some invisible
wall of support, in sheer spite of himself
the unerring clown: 'I was once driving in a car – '
The Hoolahan in charge of a car? Loud chortles.
'Actually,' he falters, 'I was driven by a woman...'
I hear our ridicule still echo down the chapel.
Bleed for him now a miscast man, remember
his moments busy in the hobbyroom or watercolourist
taking his clutch of favourites on nature walks.

Who is this hurtling through the doors, a fierce
energy swirling in the full skirt of his soutane?
Bugs O'Leary, Rev. Father Organiser of Almost
Everything, charmer of boys' sisters and mothers,
guardian angel to the nurse, prefect of the study-
hall where his thick soles creak on the parquet
as he spins accusingly: 'O'Herlihy, shut up!' –
his strange adenoidal bark plays a little
to the gallery. Now and again, breviary in hand,
he exits (a smoke on the side in the nearby bookroom).
Why do I always imagine him a benign *pater familias*
walking up an aisle giving away bride after bride?
Now enter Jacko, a bluff poseur, his profile
a fixed scowl. I watch him twitching at his collar:
'Damn it man, if you found a bicycle in a desert
you'd assume some originator' – proof by design,
as if proof were needed. 'So you know I was
here in your father's time,' he bawls at my neighbour.
'That's why I sometimes call you Andy!' Nothing
or little had changed; a sort of proof by stolidity.
The upholder of our equilibrium was happy in his heaven.
He readjusts his collar, marches across the sanctuary.

Four ghosts of old certainties forsake that altar.

Visit

Sunday afternoon about three o'clock
('with prior permission from your prefect')
pewed in a car on the gravel forecourt,
our talk swivels between two worlds.
Angling herself in the passenger seat
my mother turns her face to me;
awkward behind a steering wheel, father's
eye catches mine in his rear-view mirror.

I rehearse this scene, trying to read
my mother's face, wondering if she sensed
I had left for good – son and emigré.
Four months' days ticked off a calendar,
at last I'd return a displaced guest
uneasy with neighbours, missing school-friends,
my eye proportioned to halls and arches
and home diminished as a doll's house.

Family doings, bulletins from a neighbourhood,
mention of names, small emissaries
of emotion from suburban roads, old
gravities draw me for a moment homeward.
And I resist. We are visitors for each other.
Unwittingly those weeks of initiation leave
a baffle between us. Our words fall short.
I am learning a new language, another lore.

Foster-figure

Even now there is some enigma
in that glance. Though long grown
beyond a first self-surrender
or cooler reappraisals, I prize
his affirmation, always revere him.

Odd how I had found favour.
Did he know I craved the nurture
of his words? I fall on my feet:
prodigy, prize-winner, captain,
a protegé moving in his slipstream.

Surely among my fosterers
he laid the lightest of hands;
strings until then silent
in a father's shortfall of sanction
stirred, trembling toward song.

I probe the essence of this energy;
no blandishments or blind approval,
his unblinking trust enticed me,
fingered some awareness of worth;
in his praise all is possible.

Though at first a copy-cat tremor,
after many storms I'll still
strum the chord of his assurance,
that music I'll make my own,
an old resonance I'll summon up.

Shoulder-high

An image shapes those winter afternoons:
our breath plumes the frost as we drill
scrumming down over the stud-pocked mud.

A sweaty rapture heaves and shoves,
furies of willpower rise moonlike
in the mind and we bullock inches forward.

Faith in flawless moves, elusive flashes,
clay feet as light as angels' wings you race
and race and dream immortal touch-downs.

'Run it !' the crowd urged, 'run with it!' –
around men's jostling shoulders you'd glimpsed
a winger arcing inwards to the corner flag;

whistles, rattles, horns, coloured scarfs
flung in loops of glory, we'd stamped
as a train rumbled under the stand.

A thumping bell: *wumba, wumba, wumba,*
ging, gang, shoulder-high down the marble steps
ride the conquerors. Three cheers for the captain!

Dusk. Like tap-dancers we clack the bootroom's
terrazzo, sit musing fleshy and happy
plucking soil from between the studs of our boots.

Fallen Angel

Returning another autumn we discover
a changed regime, a community reshuffled;
losing my sponsors in that shake-up,
roots too shallow, I fall from grace.

New brooms with fresh sweeps.
How easily we become how we're seen;
failure throws an oblong shadow,
I cover hurts with a jaunty humour,

pretend not to care, affect disdain,
harden the core to day-by-day
humiliations – tiny erosions of respect –
learn the slow rustings of shame.

And laugh a bitter laugh! while inside
discs of trust skew and warp.
Where can you turn? You've made your bed,
now lie there widower to your dream.

How many faces must a wound wear?
Iconoclast, windmill-tilter, self-saboteur,
stunted years of a poise too hard won;
yet in such moves the spiral turns...

Nothing. A squall in a child's cup!
But you're the child, this is your cup.
I own no master. My gods of innocence
fallen, I clench a fragile self-reliance.

Reverie

He must have seen in my make-up some countersign,
he must have seen me seeing him despising
demons of his childhood he needed to exorcise,
his own clumsy intensities mirrored in mine.

It seems he must have enjoyed my fall from grace;
a tap on the left shoulder 'Straighten that slouch!';
term reports: 'This boy daydreams far too much';
those constant small-time displays of O'Grady-says.

Friends stand by me. I bluster and swear
some day I'll tell him; we indulge the numb
reverie of revenge. In turn that day will come:
walking by a bus queue who should you see there...

There had been rumours of a breakdown. 'A hyper-active
temperament,' they said, 'poor Father Joe.' As I slip by
I catch that ageing man averting his nervous eye.
What ironies make a captor more victim than his captive?

Old Wine

Another October, middle-aged, black-dressed,
urbane. It will have been mid-June we last
shared refectory tables, years of crumbs
wedged in their grooves. Dream beyond terms,
hopes, fears, expectations. A quarter-century:
rub-a-dub and who do you think we'll be?

A stranger, a handshake, a name spoken.
Imagine swathes of hair, gawky enthusiasm.
Maybe it's the voice's fall I recognise?
How the mind plays tricks: mouth, eyes
begin to resemble memory turned hindsight;
this was the story to be, the face to fit

a brewer, a banker, a hotelkeeper. We swap
life-tales. (Will some shy away; black sheep,
the loners?) Five years apart for each year
I'd spent there. Some shaft sunk together
into our early earth, a corridor of fondness
moistens, wells. An old yearning openness.

'Are you happy?' I dare. 'Well maybe not
the way I'd dreamt, I just accept my lot.'
A face that suffered. Another recalls rivalry
others remember differently. Let it by:
nexus of myths, fictions to which we cling,
wine of fables spilt deftly on the tongue.

Blue cheese, swirls of cigar smoke and guffaws;
a toast, our madcap heckling, boisterous applause.
The past is present. Confirm me class-brother;
ghosts we tame and need or crave to lay together.
Addresses, promises and I'm full of at-one-ness,
of aloneness. Warmth flickers in a glass.

A Harsher Light

There we were, blazers and whites,
hands thrust in our pockets as we talked,
figures from a faded epoch that final
long summer term before the scattering.
Suddenly in the cram and grind of exams,
a hurried leavetaking and all was over.

Soon new realities are shaping.
Dumbfounded how readily we trusted,
took childhood's caste for granted.
We sort our memories, deftly rework
once certainties to mould conscious
visions of perfection, in hindsight

deplore that old man emptying slops,
our servant *Johnnies*, menial Brothers
(even in the graveyard serried *Paters*
and *Fraters* never mingled). At late-
night parties raising mugs of wine
we'll sing *There but for fortune*...

Bohemia, that counterworld is waiting,
unlatching its oyster of adventure; yet
entering the lonely labyrinth of choice,
for all the bravado, in spite of disavowal,
on the sly I rue the loss of an ordinance
open-and-shut, an inmate's bitter-sweet.

II. A BLURRED MUSIC

Come sarebbe belle il mondo
se ci fosse una regola
par girare nei labirinti.

How beautiful the world would be
if there were a procedure
for moving through labyrinths.

UMBERTO ECO

Youth

Break boyhood's taboo,
step on every line
to crack a devil's cup.
Hurts turn to arrogance.
We're naked and brazen
under the skies.

Our gods can wait.
No need to hurry.
Old wisdoms painfully unfold;
sooner or later
will we return, fumbling
from clue to clue?

Amazing how the gods
will choose to gamble,
hanging our destinies
on such flimsy plots
we stumble on a trail,
children on a paper chase.

Gestures, even intonations,
quirks of our childhood
heroes, once imitated
now become our own,
we stitch together
a patchwork of self.

Maybe some hints,
prompts from deities:
a word of praise,
spin-offs from mistakes,
strangers we met,
women who chose us.

Hearing the jazz of chance
we advance, making
headway by detour,
in such journeys subsist
the working of our karma,
the whirling of our stars.

Hesitation

The first awestruck flutter. To think
another cares! Promised phone calls,
letters in tinted envelopes, presents
swapped, delicacies of dress, faint
traces of *eau de Cologne*, a gentling
closeness; we nestled in such intimacies.

Meals *en famille*. A wealthy father
listens shyly to name-dropping, tiny
attempts at creditworthiness, while
mother bestows protective luxury,
allows a sort of ease by implication;
we are children playing house.

But something is sowing a doubtseed:
an instinct maybe or scapegrace need
to abandon shelter, stretch a wing,
perhaps a dream of an Eve *fatale*
who waits to bite a forbidden apple.
Must we lose the comfort of the garden?

Then those long spring evening walks;
wistful handholding, blushed words,
minor kisses in the porch, our dallied
goodnights. A last orchard tenderness
before passionate winds outside those walls
lift such timid blossoms towards pleasure.

Questing

A time for gaiety, a time to sunder
taken-for-granted gods, to flounder
or squander; a feckless valley-time
before we find a cause and climb
into the laps of countergods, a bizarre
time when in some Dublin bar,
arguing the toss as best one could,
we served our apprentice adulthood.

Till closing time we talked and talked;
the intellect now cock of the walk.
What does it mean? We interrogate
our upbringing, unravelling with apostate
zeal a web of code and token,
and court our guilty ecstasy of broken
symbols, a dance along the precipice,
new and giddy pull of the abyss.

We leave carrying our parcels of beer;
across a sidestreet; someone for the sheer
hell heaves a brick at a windowpane –
we scuttle out of trouble down a lane
back to our meagre Bohemia to expound

meanings of the universe. Above the sound
of our voices a bedsitter radio is playing;
between stations, a blurred music sways.

Manhood

Soap the butts of the fingers, back straight,
knees bent, the shovel does the stooping;
whatever you do, keep scratching. The sagging
cement bag heaved from a shoulder thumps
dead-weight on the dust, its layered paper
slit across the belly-bulge by angled
jabs of our shovels, each half then
tugged apart. *So you'll never
go back now mate!* A bucket
swung by its handle, slops of water
puddle through grey powder, shovels
knead in the gravel, scooping, slicing.

Student? – the Clare ganger menaced.
Jaysus no! Money, of course
(notes fanned and counted on a bed)
but more an expiation. Remember a first
shock hearing returned Araners
round on their children, shout in Cockney:
Shut your bloody mouths, wi' you!
Here they were in Pimlico. Blistered
palms atone for privilege, self-obliteration
mixing the powder with gravel. Back
straight, let the shovel do the bending;
scooping, slicing, working into one.

Out on top, you and the sledge –
orders from the ganger. Storeys up
jauntily astride a sheer wall
Blacks are billowing brick and dust.
One breaks this rhythm to watch
my unsteady hands measure timid
swings for the sledge. *Hey*, he hoots,
hey! You paleface is yella!

Below the ganger's arms beckon.
He rehearses a now ritual dismissal
(a nephew due next week from Clare)
You'll be finishing up tomorrow.

Friday at noon abandon duties,
search out another site, another
start. *Excuse me, could you
please tell me where...* a bowler-hatted
man cuts a silent half-circle,
passes in disdain. Stung an instant –
a desire to pull rank, to rail,
tell him who you really are...And
who may I ask are you, sir?
Smeared with gravel and limestone
(insignia of reparation), human and alone,
scan that London skyline for a crane.

Spilling

Should we regret
our rush towards light?
Belligerent shoots of elder,

pimpled and taut, sun-
hungry jabbed upwards
through an old canopy.

Should we regret
a youth spent spilling
our bonebred innocence?

First water runs
through dry clay
yet trails of its moisture

Clot the porous soil.
Earth thickens to trap
its second innocence.

Reflection

Surely we fell for the self in the other,
our sweet will a mirror admiration;
fellows in intensity, our volatile attraction,
quick countersigns of likeness.

Fringe and lashes gleamed in laughter;
with swoops of black hair shoulder-length
she jutted her head rebelliously; behind
her jerky gladness a frailty lurks.

She stood on a table, sang *O rise*
up lovely Sweeney, every note
a theft, a spilt life – her nerves
spinning out that spalpeen's odyssey.

Under her command the room quivers.
(Did we fear for the spendthrift spirit?)
All in my youth and prime we drift
together *from the clear daylight till dawn.*

How blindingly we travelled. Confess
hindsight: maybe less love more desire,
a sullenness uncoiling moist and grateful.
'All my men were lonely,' she said,

'all my men were driven' – her generous
mandate to caress the loner, to tempt,
to take, to rock, to slack, to lull
a moment in forgetfulness. How blindingly

at one, at odds, our humours shuttled –
loving or rowing – forever caught
in ironies of likeness; a self-recognition
drawing us together, pulling us apart.

III. FISTS OF STONE

Was there ever a cause too lost,
Ever a cause that was lost too long,
Or showed with the lapse of time too vain
For the generous tears of youth and song?

ROBERT FROST

Wanderers

*O saga of all that has happened
we know the tales and still
must we too be wanderers?*

*Gilgamesh strikes out for glory,
journeying to the Land of Cedars
to fight the giant Humbaba.*

*Redresser of wrongs, grasper
at golden shadows, Quixote
the knight is spurring his horse.*

*Is it then the same story:
a bid to shortcut history,
our scattergood craving for Eden?*

*Heroic or errant, do we loop
the loop or does goddess life
love the intensity of our tour?*

*Watch over us on our travels
o saga of all that has happened
if we must be such wanderers.*

Stranger

A youngster I came, pilgrim to the source;
fables of a native bliss stirred mottoes:
A land without a tongue, a land without a soul.
As the currachs drew alongside the steamer
men in dark blue shirts shouted exotic words.

In the kitchen a daughter returned on holiday
switches from her mother's tongue to chide
her London children. As I listen it seems
I am foreign to both, neither fish nor flesh.
Was I to be a stranger in this promised land?

I slip into a glove of language. But there's still
a vividness, an older mood, small courtesies
to fortune: the sea must have its own – to swim
is to challenge fate. Child of reason and will
I am at most a sojourner in that mind.

Talk then of the mainland as *the world outside*,
enter and become a citizen of this stony room:
handkerchief fields claimed from rocks, dung
dried for fuel, unmortared boulder walls,
calfskin shoes, stark artifices of survival.

A widower welcomes my visits, opens his sorrow
to the incomer. Gauchely, I mention his loneliness:
Hadn't he his turn? ask two neighbour women
swirling in their petticoats. *What ails him?*
they banter, standing in the sunshaft of a doorway.

One evening on the flags dancing starts up;
no music, island women summering from Boston
lilt reels, long to be courted. But men
shy of plaid skirts or lipstick don't dare
(still too boyish, subtleties pass me by).

Nudges and smothered laughter among the men.
Over again the word *stranger*. I bridle,
yearn to be an insider, unconsciously begin
a changeling life; turning a live-in lover
I wear my second nature, a grafted skin.

Folksong

The voice is the only music that says what it tells –
When I go to the Lonely Well I sit and anguish…
A message stretching its tendrils to memory calls,

summons up echoes, as if the bereft – the vanished
or absorbed – are naming their ghosts, a medley
of losers: Picts, Mayas, tribes of the Suquamish…

The singer quavers out that one love's agony,
cranks its rhythms out of a neighbour's hand:
the undertwang of the music keeps shifting the story.

The sap running in the pine carries the red man's
sacred meaning, the water's murmur is the voice
of his father's father; the white man takes this land

but all things share the one breath. The poise
of the dispossessed freights and lifts the turns,
tuning each line to the same plaintive noise.

Will the stones remember their feet? the seabirds
claw ogham epitaphs in the wriggled sand?
The singer winds down to the final spoken words.

A loneness in the shaft of the song refuses to end.

Coastlines

A temperament takes on the world. I chose bleak
slabs of limestone, lone outcrops, promontories
poking their stubborn arms against an Atlantic;
supple elbows of strand seemed like cowardice.
Lines will blur, a seaboard fret and shift,
waves spending and being spent into the silence
of endless sands, rhythms of challenge and drift
husbanding or yielding the jigsaw shore of an island.

It's best the blue-grey rocks know nothing of how
constant water wears, a coiling uncoiling motion
flushing each snag or edge, ebb and flow
scouring the grain, their work being worked by ocean;
clenched fists of will jutted in their prime,
tangs of stone daring a tide or time.

Leavetaking

A moment balancing on a thwart,
then aboard the mainland steamer;
an islandman shook my hand,
laughed 'When you land, hide
all that Gaelic under a stone!'

His words echoed. All over
the earth people are drifting
on this tide towards amber lights:
cities stretch out arms in greeting.
These were the giants we'd fight.

Was this Sancho Panza gainsaying?
Take care, your worship, they're
no giants but windmills, their arms
are sails whirled in the wind
to make the millstones turn.

But his worship could not hear;
zeal has its own defences: I knew
while in Boston fellow-countymen,
still too close to feel safe,
had scoffed at his broken English.

I clung mulishly to that world;
with the strange infatuation of rebuff –
that half-caste love – I claimed
my membership. (Leaving the school bus
someone jibes 'There goes the patriot.')

Older I'd plead the cause:
an inheritance was sliding away.
If only I had been a treasurer
of fragments but all my youngness
willed that life to survive...

It was enough to love. We thought
the giants would fold their arms
and yield, as though nothing
could beat our stripling will:
youth and death were strangers.

Decades after in a city hospital
I interpret for an islander. (At first
they'd thought him deaf: nurses
enunciate loudly; sign and gesture.)
The touring matron halting a moment

on rounds, speaks her *cupla focal*
and reverts. A face lightens and darkens
inwards. And how many days more?
Would he have to return? I hear
humiliation fall like a millstone.

The steamer cranks its anchor in,
swamping the last creaks of wooden
thole-pins. Black-tarred coracles
ride accusingly out of reach:
I wear the skin not the flesh.

Timepiece

Some gentleness seemed to mark her out among
the islanders. Days on end her talk mothered me.
Could I bring anything to thank her? I'd asked,
surely there was something she'd fancy? Childlike
in anticipation, pincering a thumb and forefinger
around her cuff, she'd mentioned a wristwatch.

I loved her toying delight as she watched
a golden arrow flicking its delicate seconds by.
A gift or a spoiling? Shudders of suburban grey,
the panic of clock-watching an unkillable time
counting down remorseless minutes, a millennium
of hours before a homecoming, turn of a latchkey.

There was, of course, the alarm with a yellowing face
and clumsy tick but mostly just her half-glance
at the angle of light in the door. Days tumble
into easy rituals, clearing of ashes, the thump
of sods in a bucket; even moments of gazing,
tiny flickers of meaning, fragments gathering.

I'd heard her tell the story of the sleeper's soul:
butterfly leaving his mouth to wander and return;
when he woke his dream had been the insect's journey.
Long afterwards a brain surgeon remarks how we explain
so narrowly, how maybe consciousness hovers beyond
the skull... Does history toss our loss and gain?

It will all happen so quickly, one decade
catching a few centuries of Europe's change.
Off-the-peg chequered jackets begin to break
the uniform bawneen; a new buzz of motorcycles,
electric light, a screen perched in the corner,
exiles with newcomer wives return to settle.

'To set the hands, pull and twist it here' –
I took for granted. Fingers never focused
on such smallness fumble about the winder.
Laughing aside the awkwardness, I take her wrist
where a tanned hand meets the white of arm
like a tide-mark, I tighten and buckle the strap.

In Memoriam Máirtín Ó Cadhain

Which face of many faces entranced
our fledgling time? Outsider
untamed and untamable, scorner of prudence,
blind and wide-eyed,
a hurt innocence striking out on every side.

Or was it a mirror-nature mothering
out stories to transcend
failure, lover of the blundering and the suffering
on this road without end,
a watching watchful eye stark and tender?

Those closing years, probing and embattled,
he sought somehow to wed
the avant garde with the vanishing, straddled
a destiny – a watershed,
new and old flirting and parting in that head.

Over Kirghiz, he broods as the engines swirled:
were high-haunched jets horses
riding to the Well at the End of the World? –
For no one knows
through what wild centuries roams back the rose.

The sweetsmelling heartbreaking rose.
He puzzles Oisín's tour to a zone
of youth, his touchdown to dust: 'Who knows
maybe they'd foreshown
Einstein's time moving in a chamber of its own.'

Or the gritty humour? When the hearse stalled
we hoisted you shoulder high
slowing a midday city to a crawl;
laughing nearby,
a spirit rode the white steed skyward.

I see you returning ten generations on,
defiant and full of youth,
demanding how three hundred years have gone.
Tighten the saddle-girth;
your foot must never touch our island's earth.

Visionary

What was it then, what commanded such ardour?
A scattering of lonely islands, a few gnarled
seaboard townlands, underworld of a language frail
as patches of snow hiding in the shadows of a garden.

But the dwindling were so living. In this wonderland
of might-have-been I fell for the rhythm, the undertone
of my father's speech, built a golden dream.
(As you dreamt that land was falling asunder.)

A world as it is or a world as we want it:
when to resist old fate's take-for-granted
or when to submit; had I known before I slid
into a snowy fantasy, a fairyland of squander...

Was it a lavishness, a hankering for self-sacrifice,
part arrogance, part the need of the twice
shy for a paradise of the ideal, pure and beyond,
where one man's will turns a hag to a princess?

Oh I was the fairy story's third son, the one
who, unlike his elder brothers would not shun
a hag by the roadside: surely I'd rub the ring,
summon a sword of light to slay the dragon.

Tell me now that land was a last outpost,
a straggling from another time no one's utmost
could save; the hungry beast of change roved
nearer, that vision was a ghost dance with the past.

Tell me now third brothers too have grown
older, have even learned to smile at highflown
dreams. Then tell me still somewhere in the thaw
a child is crying over a last island of snow.

Dark

When the God of childhood first fell
I tossed my hair over my shoulder;
there was a will, there was a way –
the sap rises, the tide fills,
flushed with dreams of its own motion.

Now there's a will but no way,
must the sky with all its stars
rest stoically on these shoulders?
Did Atlas, loser of a golden
apple, resign and turn to stone?

No, not stone. Most of all
I fear the half-measure of greyness.
I choose the dark (or does the dark
choose me?) I want to fall,
open a chasm black and deep.

I plunge into an anarchy of gloom.
Can it be that dark before it slumps
conceives a light, prepares in its ruin
the already and not yet, heaves
long rhythms of chaos and creation?

But dark is dark: saddle of nothing
riding black hogs to the abyss.
Travel velvet spaces of despair;
terror, like a dredge, is scooping
out a void for love's surrender.

IV. TURNS AND RETURNS

Dark dreams in the dead of night
And on the reckless brow
Bent to let chaos in,
Tell that they shall come down,
Be broken, and rise again.

EDWIN MUIR

History

And we keep beginning afresh
an endless history
as if this odyssey
had never happened before? Yes,

yes, ours was a spoiled generation
secure, even tepid
somehow untested –
no plague or war, torture or starvation.

Look how some were keeping faith
in a gulag while we
fumbled out our destiny,
walking our easy under-urban path.

So it wasn't their route (wince
at the thought). Still,
freedom was a crucible,
blundering chalkless tour in labyrinths.

Maybe we grope the same journey
scooping the oracular
in scandals of the particular
light we throw on some greater story.

Why does the word keep taking flesh?
O nameless dream,
wild stratagem
wanting to shape our venture. O Gilgamesh,

forever traveller, your myth brooding
in us, we grapple
with redemption's fable.
O Scheherazade, healing a cuckolded king.

Belonging

A child wanders
beyond his father's living-room,
timorous adventurer.
Suddenly, bearings lost, he has begun to roam
a lonely hallway of doors.

A young man flaunts
his loss of innocence, laughing off
the boy that once
didn't know a warm room was an alcove
walled in by his father's wants.

His years unwind.
A sceptic he scanned the doors and said
On the one hand
but then on the other. Lists of choices unmade.
What was it he didn't understand?

Was his wisdom
unlived in, second-hand experience
Of Peeping Tom
agog on every threshold, whipping his glance
between the frame and jamb?

Guarding his freedom
he shrugs if others pass through the door
of a chosen sanctum,
as though he doesn't know he's chosen a corridor,
this long and draughty room.

But still a question:
how, knowing every argument and angle,
to find a way in,
to tread wittingly over one door's saddle
into a room of belonging?

Underworld

Mid-morning. Beyond my blinded window
a day of creation is playing its show,
its theatre of noise. After elevenses
roofers hoist metal ladders against
a nearby gable, down a lane
children are chanting *Cowardy cowardy
custard*; my neighbour must by now
be pegging her rainbow of towels on a line.

All day to do it and nothing done.
Three other books opened, begun
and abandoned; days of no purpose,
blank canvases, nadir of choices
unmade or deferred, nagging self-pity,
endless wavering and analysis. A scan
of newspaper columns fancies 'An Arabian
company requires a dynamic...(only

under twenty-fives need apply).'
Clock-watched hours weigh a century,
All day to do it and nothing done.
Is there nothing new under the sun?
Here is spiral of dark irony:
a dread of transience begins a despair
which in turn makes time unbearable.
Chaucer named *a synne of accidie*

this see-saw anguish: a thwarted will,
a clotted mind struggling to a standstill.
And meaning seizes up. *Dip your bread*
in mustard the laneway children said.
Are our days just moments that appear
and disappear or is every act heir
to an act and time that gathering river
where histories run? Wake up, sleeper!

I turn over, glazing my mind
with fragments. My tongue begins to thicken.
All the flow has gone to earth.
Ground waters stir underneath,
between soil and rock through sandstones
and shales a spring gargles against
a flag's stern underside. I dream
I'm shifting slabs from over a source.

Probing

And there is no knowing
the weight that weighed, the agony that drove
a mind beyond its edges. Although disavowing
daylight, was he still begging love
by that dark going?

A child, a vague
signal of trouble – a threat inbred –
his name had seemed charged with guilt by lineage:
'The eyes and temperament' they said,
'his spitting image!'

A little older
I recall a visitor warm with charm:
'Remember I am both uncle and godfather'
he laughed, stretching a gentle arm
around my shoulder.

For years the same
lavishness: a windfall cheque 'just a token
of affection!' I'd almost forgotten the capricious gleam
in his eye when suddenly a broken
man came

flamboyant in despair.
I knew his moods, his jerky semaphores
of warning, struggled to answer 'What does it matter?',
strove vainly to hold doors
of trust ajar.

At first the narrow
seed of terror, a tribesman's fear,
such an end might coax their kin into a burrow
of dark; I'm afraid his ghost might steer
too near the marrow.

That blotting out
I search again, summon his generosity –
uncle and godfather remember! And did I doubt
the gentle arm stirring pity
like water in a drought?

An arm now cleaning
shafts, unclogging disused conduits,
compassion at such an exit probes an opening
in old wells; shared genes and spirits
cry out for meaning.

Our lives reverberate.
As though by proxy beyond the frontiers
I have visited the blackness of his forever night
and now return to double-live arrears
of fragile sunlight.

Vision

Hollowness of eyes with no
more tears; brittle vessel
that won't weep from its clay.

Imprints, traces, shadows
of all who suffered summon
my crying. Need into need.

Breakdown of self,
cleansing of sight,
watering to the roots:
oneness with everything.

High Tide

O goddess life, gather me into your flow!
White horses ride high into the taking shore –
who's winner, who's loser in such a love-making?
The mind resists a moment, hanging like a bird
caught in crosswinds. So this is high tide.
I wonder as I walk Bull Island's ribbon of sand
is this the morning Gilgamesh wept because a world
held back its secret? *But be merry and make your bride*
happy in your embrace, this too is the lot of man.
A chaos of foam recedes, look an archipelago,
islands of froth dividing, a genesis in water,
creation's second day, a world reshaping!

Dunlins wheel in unison, fledgling consortium
snatching in their span plays of light's mystery,
they tilt out of dark undersides of splendour.
And still the earth melodeoned by the moon's
gravities moves a tide. Near the waterside
an old man sits to watch the sun's climb

to another summer; tumbling, tumbling in the dunes
tip and tig children still laugh and hide
in their laughter. *Is everything marvellous in its time?*
So who then can number the clouds in wisdom?
Goddess life sighs dizzily in her ecstasy –
'Love me!' I heave sweetly into our surrender.

Freedom

Enough was enough. We flew
nets of old certainties,
all that crabbed grammar
of the predictable. Unentangled,
we'd soar to a language
      of our own.

Freedom. We sang of freedom
(travel lightly, anything goes)
and somehow became strangers
to each other, like gabblers
at cross purposes, builders
      of Babel.

Slowly I relearn a *lingua*,
shared overlays of rule,
lattice of memory and meaning,
our latent images, a tongue
at large in an endlessness
      of sentences unsaid.

Those We Follow

The best said little, yet enough to signal praise;
the best said least, never laid too heavy a hand –
just a glance of light, a path I might find,
but I followed false signs, stumbled into byways.

At last I retrace, begin the haul again –
the double task that probes the double faith of loss
before gain. And then a patient glow of progress.
I so wanted them to know, to call to them:

Oh, look what I have done! But they have gone
beyond the bend and out of sight. I sway
an instant, peering ahead; a voice resonates:
steady as you go, you carry someone's beacon.

Touchstone

Surely I'm not alone in this? Everyone
remembers some first fragrance – or was it
a colour or sound strumming the cranium?

My parents sat up night after night
to vigil my fever. Delirium and eternity
smudged into weeks I'd lie and wait,

gathering nerve for an August afternoon,
when at last I'm promised a whole hour
by my window, where the days still shone.

The curtains breathe an aroma of autumn.
The latticed speaker of a big orange-dialled
wireless croons and fills the bedroom.

Red gladioli rage busily in the garden,
blooming their loud swords, pickets
on paradise. It must have happened then.

And nothing else would ever do again:
blaze of an instant, infallible gauge
before we'd given it a meaning or name.

Or do some forget? Do some skate
easily along the rims of gloom?
Dark is darker after the light.

I crave take-off, long flights inward,
a glowing, height after height, hum
of a moment flown Icarusly near the sun.

Return

O river, indomitable woman
unearthing a course, a stubborn
momentum looping, your shovel
gouging by stealth; determined,
you scoop your bed – a lover
leaving no stone unturned.

I knew a half-bend of this river,
a slow arching of the Dodder
alongside a park-path between
two busy bridges, an elbow
of adventure where my Captain
Imagination sailed the Shenandoah.

School children had we begun
to gauge the swerve of wonder?
Who said truth was a fact?
The longest reach is the Nile:
somehow my Dodder contracted,
like a love not quite to scale.

Perhaps to know is to regain
the loss of gain, as when
he knew each loop and eyot
Twain mourned for mystery:
turning master and pilot,
had he lost his Mississippi?

In the same September sun
I skim a sliver of stone,
to count in water ricochets
decades now worn older:
I unwind into come-what-may,
an Atlas untensing his shoulders.

Is this then the return?
But the river hurries on.
No regrets. Wherever a curve
wanders at large, her waters
close up a hoop, cutting off
ingrown meanders of remorse.

O mover, driver of water,
channel of unplanned demeanour,
beautiful rover, you wriggle
of river, my Dodder of youth,
endless hunger for the possible
living from source to mouth.

V. REROOTING

This is travelling out to where

a curved adventure
splashes on planes of sunlight to become
one perfectly remembered room...

ANNE STEVENSON

Journeys

Does something mischievous scheme to leave
an infinity in each face of a single muse?
Does a man know every woman since Eve
travelling the ring of one lover's moods?
Maybe we choose a point to enter
the circle; then slant our painstaking
angle, a slope to the flaring centre,
a focused abandon, a slow love-making.
Strange, at the rim it seemed we left
a whirl of choices beyond recall;
in the hub's flush all angles met,
a needle-point where winner takes all;
a wheel is the rim of many ways,
spokes of intensity, journeys to the blaze.

Beginnings

A wing stirs in its sheath. Now it seems
all the fumblings of the larva years prophesied
this moment; under a crust our dreams
uncurl, eager again to dart and glide.
Still the giddy phase before the flight
when the gravity of self holds a little back;
once bitten, twice shy, we just might
dally in our shell, a last-minute back-track.
All or nothing. We shed our last alibi
as when the insect nymph dares to prize
open unwanted skins, love's dragonfly
stretches its veinlike wings into the sunrise.
Two wings interlocked, the flight begun,
a speck of news flickers under the sun.

A Presence

Idle with pleasure, I let my misty gaze
find its slow way through the subdued
light to where the contour of a porcelain vase,
busy in silent meditation, alludes to you.
Along the dressing table a ceramic bazaar
of creams, moistures, lotions, ointments,
an exotic row of shapely pots and jars
stoppers the scents and vapours of a presence.
Your spirit travels in such lovely earthenware,
at ease in its clay, a vessel well turned,
cajoling the mind down from a castle in the air
back to the sweeter givenness of your world.
Still, like a wooer on his first sightseeing,
I relish the emblems, your haberdashery of being.

An Unfolding

An eager new shoot, I brimmed with sunkissed
boyish dreams of where my years might glide,
little knowing how a bitter frost could decide
the date of flowering, our story's turn and twist.
Damage done, the self – that secret strategist –
staunched its wound, anguished out of bruised pride
visions of Utopias, worlds cut and dried.
The heart, a frosted bud, tightened like a fist.
Your love – though it disclaims what it achieves –
unclenches me, keeping a watch, loyal yet unblinking,
full of yeses, fresh starts or that silent act
of merely being easy and ample as a mid-spring
coaxing open the horse chestnut's sweet smelling bract
to lodge sunlight deep in the fabric of its leaves.

Squall

A misunderstanding we should but didn't broach
rankles, then flares; one loaded remark
rocks our world. Strangers, we stand stark
and alone as words sweep us in whirlwinds of reproach.
Old sores glare. Once more the soul's search:
why did we risk the naked light or embark
on this journey? Yet why forestall dark with dark?
Buffeted we ride the storm's pitch and lurch.
A squall clears, the sky lifts – our kisses
timid tokens of amnesty as the purged air
breathes its sweet aftermath. Diffident, we pledge
never again like fledgling lovers still aware
how the great fluke of love poises on a knife-edge;
even the turning earth trembles on its axis.

The Other Voice

You came lean and taut, a barrage of innocence.
I remember a bluster of haughtiness hiding a boy
still dazed with childhood hurts, a man tense
with desire; slowly I thawed and rocked you in joy.
You mocked our speck of being, I showed instead
of dust a galaxy whirling in the sunbeam's eye;
you cried at the size of eternity, I hushed and said
eons count as kisses under a lover's sky.
No half-measures then. I have made this island
of life a kingdom. Have I stinted your ease
or pleasure? No, how could a woman understand
that men still talk of freedom to go as they please?
My love is your freedom. Do or die or downfall,
it's all or nothing and I have chosen all.

Out of the Blue

Nothing can explain this adventure – let's say a quirk
of fortune steered us together – we made our covenants,
began this odyssey of ours, by hunch and guesswork,
a blind date where foolish love consented in advance.
No, my beloved, neither knew what lay behind the frontiers.
You told me once you hesitated: *A needle can waver,
then fix on its pole*; I am still after many years
baffled that the needle's gift dipped in my favour.
Should I dare to be so lucky? Is this a dream?
Suddenly in the commonplace that first amazement seizes
me all over again – a freak twist to the theme,
subtle jazz of the new familiar, trip of surprises.
Gratuitous, beyond our fathom, both binding and freeing,
this love re-invades us, shifts the boundaries of our being.

St Brigid's Cross

All business, a sheaf of rushes cradled carefully
in your arms, a culotte swaying daylight in your stride,
you hurry indoors to set about a February ceremony
shaping your namesake's token, flourish for Spring's bride.
A city child, I'd seen the crosses above doors but missed
this rite, so it always seemed that something in the stretch
of those curious jerky arms with bows on their wrists,
honey-coloured and brittle, beckoned to a world beyond reach.
Lank green stalks crisscross their sign language;
seasons of hands are working that saint's emblem,
a lineage moving in your fingers; instinctively you bridge
worlds kneeling on a Dublin floor to knot a rush stem.
I watch you weave as the rush twists and reappears
a fresh-cut badge of love, this nexus of our years.

While You Are Talking

While you are talking, though I seem all ears,
forgive me if you notice a stray see-through
look; on tiptoe behind the eyes' frontiers
I am spying, wondering at this mobile you.
Sometimes nurturer, praise-giver to the male,
caresser of failures, mother earth, breakwater
to my vessel, suddenly you'll appear frail –
in my arms I'll cradle you like a daughter.
Now soul-pilot and I confess redemptress,
turner of new leaves, reshaper of a history;
then the spirit turns flesh – playful temptress
I untie again ribbons of your mystery.
You shift and travel as only a lover can;
one woman and all things to this one man.

Hindsight

Though thankful, at first finding the glare too bright
I flinched – as when the long-sought sun comes,
shrivelled by too much winter, the core numbs;
timorous in the glow – a sudden bout of stage-fright.
But it's all summer now. Your lavish sunlight
wakes and stretches these Van Winkle limbs;
I nuzzle up to the warmth, the love-sap brims
over, plush with the freedom of second sight.
Yet sometimes across the moon sky a sullen
cloud laments those angry years – hauteur
of hurt – when spring slid without my noticing,
the willow covers its blossoms with silver fur,
as hedge-sparrows flirted and jerked their wings
and the east wind scattered the alder catkin's pollen.

A Circle

After lights out, weary from the long regime,
remember the dressing gowns, the illicit tiptoe
to whisper at the radiator hugging its last glow
until nabbed by the flashlight's accusing beam.
The first Christmas break passed in a daydream,
the rooms dwarfed, home become a side-show
to a cosmos of corridors and braggadocio, as though
the garment of childhood had slit along its seam.
Now I love to watch the lighthouse at Howth
flash its codes to steer ships past our gable,
to gossip in the dark with you my bed and boarder
and marvel at how, like tortoises in an Aesop fable,
our years have coiled their slow circles of growth;
a world brought back to scale, a house to order.

VI. OPENING OUT

The sun! The sun! And all we can become!
And the time for running to the moon
In the long fields, I leave my father's eye;
And shake the secrets from my deepest bones...

THEODORE ROETHKE

Disclosure

Remember how at school we folded and unfolded
sheets from a jotter, scissored chunky *m*s and *n*s,
a saw-edge,
a clump of paper squared, melodeoned.
Then delight as it reopens
a fullness of design, transfigured wounds
unfolding in a page
berries, acorns.

The moment's contours scatter in the light.
A crossbeam gathers in pattern and fringe,
traces of passion,
hologram of thought, memory's freight
until a beam re-throws the image,
an intensity unpacking stripe and whorl;
each fraction
an implicit all.

Acorns of memories, berries of dreams.
Does every pilgrim's tale sleep in one moment?
Some inbred
whole uncodes in a tree's limbs,
spreads in slow workings of environment.
Soil, air, water, sun quicken
a word in the seed.
Time thickens.

Grantchester Meadows

Across Grantchester Meadows, May has snowed
cow parsnip, hawthorn, chestnut; a stone's throw
from here the Cam grooves slowly towards King's.
An English heaven: 'My real life began since
I came to Grantchester. I eat strawberries and honey.
A perfectly glorious time. Think only this of me.'

I see you Rupert Brooke blazered, flannelled,
a strolling presence in this albescent funnel
of young summer or picnicking under an oak
with Darwin's granddaughters: 'We used to talk
wearily about art, suicide, the sex problem.'
Übermensch, libido, absinthe, fin de siècle.

A hundred rings in an oak which may have seen
George Herbert brooding by the *Came* or Milton
explaining the ways of God now Galileo's sun
no longer danced attendance on our world. Newton,
did you some midsummer hatch along this path
laws to bring our universe back to earth?

'Certainly I approve of war at any price,
it kills the unnecessary.' Evenings of tennis
and cricket. It's the Aegean 1913:
'My poem is to be about the existence of England.'
Dead before the Dardanelles. A circle closes;
the hawthorn almost in bloom, the oak leafless.

Wars. Disillusion. Certainty a fallen idol,
our daylight turns a dice-dance of potential.
Turmoil of change as an old order dies
into us. Herbert must have known the crux.
Does the slow-leafing oak trust without proof?
I know the ways of learning yet I love.

Ghost Brooke you could be my father's father,
yet I'm your elder. Ride my Aeneas shoulder
as Grantchester blooms a lover's carte-blanche,
another innocence. Do you remember how strange
the fullness of the riddle seemed? *The acorn can't
explain the oak, the oak explains the acorn.*

Motet

O my white-burdened Europe, across
so many maps greed zigzags. One voice
and the nightmare of a dominant chord:
defences, self-mirroring, echoings, myriad
overtones of shame. Never again one voice.
Out of malaise, out of need our vision cries.

Turmoil of change, our slow renaissance.
All things share one breath. We listen:
clash and resolve, webs and layers of voices.
And which voice dominates or is it chaos?
My doubting earthling, tiny among the planets,
does a lover of one voice hear more or less?

Infinities of space and time. Melody fragments;
a music of compassion, noise of enchantment.
Among the inner parts something open,
something wild, a long rumour of wisdom
keeps winding into each tune: *cantus firmus*,
fierce vigil of contingency, love's congruence.

Train Journey

As a boy I was sure that the track's anapaest
kept narrating each passenger's tale: like a charge
of experience, each face was a secret released.

Soon we rushed over a bridge's trestled brick-arch,
almost loving the dare and danger of a fall
till the train suddenly hurtled into shafts of dark.

Who would make it through this funnel
of night? Was it too long to believe
light might be waiting in the eye of the tunnel?

Some would go under in the dark. I grieve
for a fellow-traveller, a woman taut
as a violin, lavishing her girth of life

into song. Too near the edge and overwrought:
But how should I sing unless I burn?
Long afterwards I'd discover she'd fought

to the death her loneliness, flitting in turn
from friend's door to door. If I'd known
could I have comforted her? Was our sojourn

together a barrier to an inaccessible zone
of once intimacies? Always I remember
a voice spilling *from clear daylight till dawn.*

Like a child half awake on a morning in mid-summer
I'm rubbing the dark from my eyes. Unbelievable
how the light is dispatching its trees like ambassadors

that glide by our windows with an urgent epistle.
And I think I then knew that a train's undersong
began mourning the traveller whose story I'd tell.

Kinsmen

Father used to love to walk the block on Sunday;
skipping along a garden wall I found a slot
where our street met the road. 'The builder forgot
a brick' – my father shrugged but I insisted why?

Why? Why did that builder leave such a hole
just where our street met with the main road?
Why didn't Father know why? Through childhood
I am sure I puzzled over that slit in a wall.

Then I must have forgotten. Nearing the age
he begot me I think I heard someone explain
how the Hopi gathered their older children
in a hut to watch the gods' arrival in a village.

234

Painted ogres would circle, dance and howl,
then entering the hut they unmasked to expose
fathers and kinsmen playing at being gods.
I began remembering a peep-hole in childhood's wall

before the anger of disenchantment, before the flood
of our arrogance had swept both wall and garden.
So often since I have wanted to beg his pardon,
or at least to say how now I maybe understood.

Lately strolling the block again together
I asked nudgingly if he remembered that hole?
But he stares: 'Son, I am growing so forgetful!';
I fumble to link his arm, my ageing brother.

Matins

Segovia, guitarman, I know your prayer:
never mind, Lord, treasures laid up,
leave me this street where a greengrocer
draws a striped awning over his show
of yellow-buttocked melons and blowzy peaches.

I can idle here by the corner, watch
children busy chalking a hopscotch
on the pavement or eavesdrop on schoolboys
bragging and smoking by the railway
bridge where young executives scurry.

A very ordinary mortal I gaze
boyishly at women's turquoise rings
as their hands touch in talk, delight
in loose cottons, linen blazers,
perfumes hugging air as they pass.

O polyphony of being, doing, bliss.
My senses feast. I breathe and am.
O hankerer after the irrevocable.
O plucker at words, colours, chords.
Are they real? Do we dream it all?

Gilgamesh, Odysseus, Mad Quixote,
wanderers relive in us your daylight.
And hey! what stranger down the line
moves to this rhythm, whose moment
twangs in the blood? Good morning, Segovia.

Perspectives

1

Like pegs, our forearms held the skein's coil.
Arcs of the knitter's hand unloop
and ball by turn. Sweep and detail.
A feeling of beginning in childhood's wind-up
I keep on recalling. Somehow I'm between
a yarn uncoiling to a tight ball of destiny,
a ball unravelling back the promise of a skein.
Plain stitch and design, point and infinity.
Who changes the world? Oh, this and that,
strands as they happen to fall, tiny ligatures,
particular here-and-nows, vast loopings
of pattern, the ties and let-gos of a knot,
small X-shapes of history; our spoor and signature
a gauze of junctures, a nettedness of things.

2

Whose music? A quiver enters like a spirit,
a murmur of tension from and back
into space. A tune of trembles in catgut.
The pride of an instrument as at its beck
and call the heart vibrates: pulse-sway,
dominion of rhythm, power before the slack
and silence. 'Pride before a fall' we say,
sic transit...Should we've been puritans,
taut, untouchable, our unshakable self-mastery
a vacuum of muteness? O noise of existence
shake in me a tone you need; sweet
friction of rosin, play me limp or tense.
Possessor of everything, owner of nothing.
Whose bow shivers its music in my string?

3

Nineteen forty-three, Tegel prison, Berlin.
I picture a face superimposed on a grille:
first widening of a smile, the mooning hairline,
something plump and composed, relentless will.
Time-servers slide; many in their armchairs
rage. Call them opters-out or captives.
Success makes history, I hear him say. *There's*
no out. How will another generation live?
The question echoes on: yardstick of ambition,
our spirit-level. Hanged Flossenbürg camp,
April of forty-five. Dietrich Bonhoeffer,
Like an eavesdropper, I glean smuggled wisdom.
Sometimes, it was piano wire – slower than hemp.
Suffer them in the light of what they suffer.

4

Specky-four-eyes, carrots, fatso, dunce!
Jeer and name-call and how we changed it to sport,
swagger of couldn't-care-less: *Sticks and stones*
may break my bones, names'll never hurt.
But still he's there, that curly-headed boy
scrambling a pillar: *I'm the king of the castle*;
a shout of territory, the old pedestal cry
defining by rivalry. *Get down you dirty rascal.*
Always black and white. Why south, why north,
pale-face or nigger or prod? I, Paddy,
dream the schoolroom globe, a balloon viewed
with a spaceman's floating glance; my heady
vision a sea with tatters and patches of earth,
our odds and ends hung on a line of latitude.

Memory

Again a silent room.
Doubt bows the cello
of morning. A diminished chord.
Lord Shallot to his loom
spelled to watch the river
in a mirror?
Why? While people war?
While people famish?

All the suspicions, excuses.
Where's the extravagant stillness
of a lover's mind?
Alert as madness, fierce
sojourner in a small womb's
patience. Then slowness:
rhythmic openings and closings
of woof and heddle.

Warped threads of memory
dream a weft, a journey
of doing – triple interplay.
Am I warden of filigrees,
patterns, the colours and plot,
keeper of the cloth,
the bobbin's eye, a forethought
in the shuttle's long cast?

Not even to try. A texture
of knots and intersections,
a youth ravelling its fulness,
layered music of complexity.
Cypresses sway in their spring;
the lattice and web of things
a frail morning
eastering another garden.

And the river moves:
a light, a shape, a weave.
Someone was busy in a kitchen,
someone was patching a roof,
someone was sowing wheat
or hustling the market.
Who was it noticed and forgot?
For us I've remembered.

Child

It's evening as I pass the first garden,
a day's playthings scattered in the dew:
an upturned tractor yellow and forgotten
under lupins and London pride, a blue
rubber ball wobbled to a standstill.
Did someone call 'Come on, come on –
it's bedtime!' And did you stall
the lone moment of sleep, of abandon?

I know your player's garden in
and out. Behind a fence and walls
silent first growths are gathering
sap in the long uncurling falls
of a dusk. Innocent know-how
is not to know. Beyond this greenroom
there are ordeals of suspicion. I know
the rip, the pain before bloom.

This take-for-granted is your garden.
Sureness of path, stakes and wires
that hold the sweet-pea, our heaven
of invention, dream-castle of desire.
Doubts are jags of bottle glass
on an orchard wall-top. Bit by bit
you awaken, must learn to mistrust
these gates your father shuts at night.

An apple-bite and that garden vanishes
forever. You too will roam with Adam.
Sap in the trees' limbs still lavishes
memories. You grow to another millennium.
Is what we love what we find?
Is there somewhere a second garden,
an arbour where the quickened mind
soars between its knowing and abandon?

Will the stars you once thought your own
slide infinitely away; mischievous,
faster-than-light teams of subatoms
conspire beyond your common sense;
a universe of unfoldings and enfoldings
draw in its mystery? Part and parcel
as housekeeper not householder
will you dream, fumble with the possible?

A dangerous growth. Make or break,
a lupin slits its tight-lipped calyx,
London pride is living off its luck,
a rubber ball circles dark in itself.
Double-edge of nurture, of damage.
There's no undoing all our knowledge.
Bon voyage! Where will you choose
another garden, another innocence?

The Middle Voice

(1992)

Three Rock

1

I stare from a dormer into the morning.
A line of hip-roofs, trees and then
the smooth curves of Three Rock Mountain.

How did it all happen? For years
I carried a poem I thought would begin:
'Now that I'm young, I want to say...'

The last of our parents' crowd stoop.
Friends' daughters are almost women.
My jet hair flickers ribs of grey.

Instead here I am saying it's good
to stand in between, touching our coming
and our going. Hinge and middleman.

The mast on Three Rock glints in the sun.
Receiver and sender. A signal boosted
onwards. Pride and humility of a medium.

2

I open a window and there's a dandelion's
grey head, a seed-parachute drifting
to a future on small breezes of obedience.

How will it all happen? That strange
floating openness. A trust. A patience.
One weekend a laboratory assistant

forgets a window; a mould wafts
onto a plate of microbes and invents
Fleming's penicillin. A leap of chance.

On dull mornings Three Rock vanishes.
Is there a mast picking up our signals?
I cling to a moment seized in its glint.

Eleven leap years. I begin to grasp
what the stare of a greying psalmist meant:
I will lift mine eyes unto the hills.

Arrival

Sweet dreams, Rebecca!
Snug with milk, unfussed
by toys or tinsel, not yet
six weeks beyond the womb,
stranger, you still trust
the eastern star that beckons
towards the manger of sleep.

Goodnight, newcomer –
while all the merry gentle-
men romp about the town
to pack the smoky inns,
down the season's compliments,
sing and warm their bones
around the bowl of fellowship.

All's well, my baby!
Adam model two
swaddled in his stable
sleeps deeply, so you
breathe easy as the donkey
whose breath puts out
an angel's flaming sword.

Goodnight, my girl!
Somewhere in the small hours
years ago another child
uncurls, hurries to discover
at the bed-end wisemen's gifts,
frets and begs the light
unfurl a paradise of day.

Sleep long, my lovely!
It's December – Jerusalem
light years away. We bow
between our thanks and trust
and so re-enter what you
Rebecca still remember:
Eden of the eternal now.

Departure

(in memory of Máirtín Ó Direáin)

Autumn afternoons when time has weight
and shadows dip a balance towards the past,
now even you must use that wicket gate
through which a memory sometimes slips a ghost.
My friend, I know just the way you'll come;
mourning spring in the west, alone and glum.
Then coaxing I'll ask 'How goes the hereafter?'
Are the women as lovely? Stabbing at solemnities
until we manage to tease
from you a final and knowing flicker of laughter –

'See that coin: heads we're here,
tails we're gone!' Cureless and endured,
a stoical pride grey and forlorn
as endless crags of his childhood Aran.

Scars of poverty became a lifelong
doubt; poems gallant and headstrong
thrown like small feudal bridges
of distanced trust, a troubadour's message.

His balm was always words and women.
He'd told me once he was smitten
by a face in the street, how he made her
his muse. A last courtly lover.

– I'll remember on a dying countenance as we crouched
over a spirit sighing still in its shell;
near the end bereft of words we touched,
laying palms on your forehead, took farewell,
abandoned your room. Outside was spring in the east;
your brow of fever still clammy in my fist
as I gripped the hammer's haft, began to staple
a trellis to stay March's first caress;
fresh tendrils of clematis
unfurling trust in clefts of a pebble-dash gable.

Voices

1

From nowhere the Liffey estuary is spanned
by rainbow, a flyover of lensed sunlight
earthed in both its beginning and its end,
this voyage of a spectrum, arc of a flight

vivid and full. From where I stand
our house is in line with the bow's apogee.
It's almost as if I could stretch a hand
to either end. Shades of young Shelley.

I shrieked and clasped my hands in ecstasy.
The arch fades in the drizzle like a myth.
Dear, and yet dearer for its mystery.
This middleness. My watch under the zenith.

2

First a ring to my mother to ask what I'd like.
Then pigskin gloves, cuff-links, a tie-pin,
Anything a boy couldn't be seen dead wearing.

As I grew this would be our annual skirmish.
Finally, my twenty-first. A suitcase too big,
cumbersome and soon outmoded. 'Enough music

and books. He needs something solid to remember
his godmother with.' So maybe everything had
to be steady and tangible. A girl made good.

Grandfather treated her to holidays, a companion
for his only child. When she fell on her feet,
mother had bridled. Bittersweet. Love – hate.

'Who laid her out?' she demanded that morning,
rearranging mother's last coiffure. 'Now,
she looks herself. There's the Eileen I know.'

This afternoon a voice crackles down the line:
'No happy returns. Don't you know I'm eighty.
I thought you promised to come and see me?'

3

But I have another call to make. 'I'm six,'
a voice announces. Today is a birthday party.
Like names of reels, her blow-by-blow litany:
Hunt-the-slipper, Simon says, Hide-and-seek.
Out of nowhere a sunburst of breathless facts
about the colours and layers of her party frock.

We're talking long-distance. Timbres of each word
hoop through a satellite bowing the firmament
but we struggle with accents. I recall we scanned
favourite names guessing a gender in the womb.
And if it's a girl: *Rebecca Ford, Rebecca Ford.*
I'd imagined a strange intonation. 'I *am*, I *am*,

I *am* six,' she sings with delight. A conscientious
godfather, I've sent a gift-token but wonder still
should I have chosen. A god now doubting free will,
I hear her listing presents. Already she's anxious
to return to play. A nexus of imperatives and chance
await: *pass-the-parcel* and *ring a ring o' roses.*

4

Two voices on a November afternoon
draw me into their presence;
a strange vibrancy summons,
shatters the present into a time unknown.
A configuration of moments seems to gather:
an outreach of arms, an odyssey
transcending a handclasped ecstasy,
a self loosening to the voyage of another.
Beyond the bowed colours the raindrops disperse;
Do my outstretched hands tip the ends of a universe?

Blemish

How exactly it happened? Which generation?
Just something my parents seemed to mention
and veil again. A stain on the imagination,

a seeping of words: 'recluse', 'disfiguration'.
Brothers jostled with a sister who'll stumble
on the hearth. Then, a habit and wimple

to conceal her scars. Proud and humble,
via dolorosa of a girl's about-face.
A closed order. My tomboy and anchoress.

A life left hanging in an air of disgrace
plays with the fire of a child's mind.
So young a woman immured and disciplined.

I wonder if a slowness of time refined
a suffering, her long self-forgetfulness
travelling some infinite kingdom of service.

Her presence still dips and surfaces.
A doctor describes a congenital syndrome:
'murmur, high mouth and dimpled sternum,

that temperament.' I hear the giddy drum
of the heart as she fell. In a niece's goodbyes
some frailty again wakens the memories.

Our storyline: dowries of Xs and Ys.
Suddenly, from behind a cowl of years,
who knows who's blooming a gene of hers?

A flight becomes a call and the stairs
of retreat now wind our endless wish.
I tread perfections of a healing blemish.

The Builder's Men

Today the builder's men are scaffolding a gable.
Mortar has weathered, the brick might be unstable
And the whole frame begin to sag. Through
An open window the boom of their voices renews
A house's dominion. They climb a crib of iron bar
And space, chisel and trowel our wear and tear.

'Look, Baba, window!' prompts a mothering voice.
'Look!' he mimics and splutters arrays of noise
And wonder. 'Cooey!' calls the builder's man
Appearing and hiding at the window. 'Where's he gone?'
A little bewilderment before the sudden chortle,
Skips of delight. 'Where's the man with the trowel?'

Such amazing words! *the man, the trowel, the window* –
Namings unravelled from the past that echo and echo
Saxon serfs and Normans, the scribes, the courtiers,
Puritans and frontiersmen, all owners and heirs
To a house of meaning they built and so abandoned,
Its well-worn brick now pointed in a child's astoundment.

A playpen made of sounds, gift and encumbrance
Of the past. But look! he almost seems to dance
To rhythms of syllable and scraping trowel, to begin
A long gurgle of conversation with the self. Then
Distracted, he gazes at the window we've left ajar,
The light flushed down the builder's house of air.

Tradition

A feeling of passivity, of handing over.
All that was received I again deliver

by just being here. Available. No more.
A watch of dependence, complete exposure,

248

not even trying not to try to achieve.
This work is a waiting, almost as if

a host, his palms held up in supplication
between two guests, begins an introduction:

'For years I've wanted you two to meet.'
The middle voice fading as they greet

in the sweet nothingness of a go-between.

Nakedness

1 *Shying*

As I move towards the centre,
an old temptation to shelter,
a need to shirk any danger,
to close up, to shut down.

An unscorched wallflower I'd sit
tight. A clammed spirit.
And why should I step it
out in all my nakedness?

That unnerving gladness,
the dance swaying its labyrinths
so full of sweet promises.
Oh, the flaming sword at its hub!

2 *Hurt*

Your music took me by surprise; nothing
by halves, I matched you move for move,
I warmed, I opened, I yielded, I loved.
You of all people to double-cross!

Is it anger that stings or is it shame?
Intimacy cuts both ways: I'd mapped
your nakedness: do I pay you back
(that way you'd have called the tune)

or withdraw, wear an aggrieved look,
sullen air of those who finding the world
guilty seal off all the risks, turn
deaf ears to buffeting moods and rhythms?

Against the beat, between the throbs,
our moments leap and fall, jazz
notes of ecstasy, random arabesques
of anguish, a hazardous melody of being.

I reeled with pain, half anger, half shame;
reckless, over again, I gave everything.
Twice shy, I know I must curb the swing,
I know that I must watch my step.

But I know that I know nothing.
All that is certain is change. I plan
to gauge every footfall, but in the dance
my steps grow wide-hipped and lavish.

3 *Again*

The finesse of rebeginnings! Here like a novice
I seem to thrill at every spendthrift word
as we dispense ourselves in flares of newness.

We angle between a coyness of once intimates,
stiffness of half-strangers, allow our dead
image of each other quicken and become.

There have been so many dreams and stumbles,
infinitesimal shifts, inches of slow growth,
all our moves to make the same so different.

I hankered after you. Despite our separate
ways, our trade in coolness, somehow the flame
abides, sputters between desire and memory.

I confess my need to trim the blurred wick.
I love the thrift of shared ground, returns
to older trust, subtle closures of rift.

Hurt, jealousies, misunderstanding or drift?
Let's say it was a silence where we hoarded
the sealed years of business we now swap.

Wait! Supposing, how can we now be sure?
I shy from fire. You insist I drop veil
after veil; we stand before the naked flame.

A Toast on the Eve

Where is the star that winks in the east?
In this the nadir of the year, we sense
The drag of time. For a while deceased
Friends trouble us – a glum roundabout
Of memory. O beg a freshborn innocence,
Some star to blink beyond a doubt.

Where is the star that signals in the east?
Tonight I am both adult and child;
I shape and plan and still am an unleased
Tenant of my clay, never master of my history.
Ambitious and humble, I am reconciled
To bear this double witness to a mystery.

Where is the star that beckons to the east,
That God come down to bless the flesh
Of living? O give us the daily yeast
To burble through the veins and charm
Our sour grapes into wine. Find me the crèche
Where a god is cradled by woman's arm.

Where is the star that dances in the east?
Son of ghost and virgin forgive our meagre
Welcome. Busy in the inns, we feast
Your arrival cribbed between ox and ass.
O give us our innocence, all green and eager.
To a god of renewal, I raise this glass.

Rondo

Again that gangly earnestness,
'Actually here's another I drew'
as I admire, dreamily a question:
'You know that painter you knew,

had he a studio?' A quaver
in the tone triggers my subconscious:
I too am twelve, all eager;
a bearded artist primes a canvas.

I watch, gauche with enquiry.
'O no!' he said, 'my father
disapproved but when he died
I found my notices neatly folded

in his wallet, the good words
circled in red' – a posthumous
boost filling those voids,
years of unworded praise.

'Where was his studio?' A rondo;
now it's my turn to respond,
conscious that each syllable
may float a seed in the wind:

'On the seafront, so he saw
each morning a northern headland,
for years just kept drawing
that line in every weather.'

Is this the thrill of lineage?
I grow young in your ardour;
then crossing too soon your bridges,
fear those agonies in the garden.

You nod, frowning a little;
lightly the talk changes course.
I pretend not to notice the first
tremble of manhood in your voice.

Largesse

The generous sink into traces they leave in us,
In tiers of personality, gestures, words we use,

Flashbacks to small confirmations, that hand lain
On a shoulder. The generous are still a glow within.

Confident, they knew nothing diminished their glory,
As they nourished seeds to flower for a while in me.

The jealous I begin to forget, frightened spirits
Nipping the bud of younger and younger threats.

The turning-point and I face both ways like Janus.
Recall how terribly you needed praise. Then choose.

Wavering

What sort of a country! Damn it,
a man standing for his father's seat.
Objectivity – I fumed. His eyes glaze,
as he points to a few roods of clay:
'You see that field? When I'm gone,
even the worms belong to my son.'

I thought of our quarrel today as I strove
to countersign cheques identically above
as below. Too full of exuberance, I turn
my letters boldly; they sag when I'm down.
Sometimes I slant an efficient minuscule,
then the bank-girl smiles and I wobble.

So quickly our habit changes. A span
of school years and with ease children
talk in grams and metres. Dream
of screens and dials, charm of system,
hunger for a norm, passionate precision
of needle-points, touch-downs on the moon.

I become the generation between and want
it both ways. I envy the pilots, so vigilant
and clean-shaven in their take-offs. Oh yes,
the civic, the impersonal, policy, loftiness.
I still need inheritances of clay and worms,
measured in roods, in feet and even thumbs.

Hands

Moments of illumination, spirals of days,
pigments, washes, the evening satchel
hung and the nights woken in a cell
by vellum worlds creaking in the breeze.
A voyage their image: long-handed cruises
over scraped and pumiced calf-skin,
the steer and yaw of these quill-driven
crossings as a reed trails its juices.
Anonymous seafarers. Whose were the hands?
A copyist loose-limbed, calm; another
sedate and careful. Or there's Brother
Extrovert's black and violet flamboyance.

Publishers of the word, desktop wedge
and stroke; their being a hand just
hinted in a margin. The face is lost,
a traveller congeals in traces of voyage.
Christ's tempter a scrawny Byzantine,
Hebrew names, those Asia Minor faces,
Matthew a posed Osiris, pillar-bases
of Viking brooches, that Coptic Virgin.
A nothingness of ego. The hand worships
by work. And it seems the rim becomes
a hub gathering spokes, the scriptorium's
stillness a geography at its fingertips.

The harbour is a scribe's last verse.
Two centuries since Columba had quilled
to a standstill. A serpent asks its coiled
question: Is patience a trust to rehearse

such detail? Sail on seven centuries
to Gutenberg's book. Think of a lifetime
inked in a concordance. Did they dream
warm presses, the software of memories?
Just look at Lot's wife! And how venial
her about-face there, arched and faded
under an *M*. Who watches too far ahead,
or behind? Tell us the voyage is all.

A Broken Line

She tenses at every bend so you almost feel
her will touching the brake pedal. Her body gears
into a curve as she turns a phantom steering wheel.

Dual control. It had to be like that for years.
Two children silhouetted on a yellow school-sign
flash past. 'Watch out in case...' – she dares.

A tart silence. So thinly she oversteps a line
between concern and meddling. *Now mother, what is it?*
Hurt, she vanishes in reverie: the silhouette on a sign

is a child standing at the school door, her favourite;
a desire to part with and hold still not reconciled,
hers and not hers, a contour in that morning light.

The moody years of being both adult and child.
Now so, so independent – CAUTION CONCEALED BENDS –
now, leaning on her shoulder weepy and spoiled.

A drowsiness is falling, falling. Miles of patience,
those roundabouts of tact, byroads of submission,
the long climbing hills. HARD SHOULDER ENDS.

The broken line runs on and on and on,
centring a camber of road, langlauf of dashes,
Never-ending ski-strides of an abominable snowman.

She nods and jerks back to awareness. And yet
the road keeps gliding. She nods again. A whiplash
of vigilance. Down for the third time and out.

Sweet sleep of fecundity. The car speeds onwards.

Debonair

Against a tide of yawning suburbanites,
up the morning's street a homing débutante
links her dinner-jacketed cavalier, last night's
fling a carnation raffish in her ebony hair.

A down street commuter, out of the tail of my eye
I catch her recklessness, panache of such a beginning;
a rip-tide of energy, the home-goers pass by,
so debonair in that first circle of their laughter.

Feedback

Again this need to mend a world's mistakes.
For short-term gain,
Our fouled up shoreline, clogged lakes.
And sister earth is fretted: forest, air,
A waterflow, a breeze, a rain,
Intricate fragile web and net. A young
Man rages 'Greed and waste
Unravel nests we share.'

I love that fledgling lavishness as he
Explains the scope and sweep
Of nature's sharing: even fungi
Can live absorbing algae cells' excess,
In turn defend a fellowship
Of lichen. Stubborn harmonies of growth.
The more I ripen, the more
I fathom youthfulness.

So strange how first ideals flame a mind,
The glare and flash of thought
Too sharp, too edged and undefined.
'Select your dreams,' I warn, 'they may come true.'
But do we round each other out?
My narrowed concentration steals his fire;
The blaze I'd focus warms
In me its breadth of view.

Voyage

Then finally land dropped out of sight
and we were completely at sea. I thought
of Meno's puzzle *How can we seek*
if we don't know where the harbour is?
But if we knew how could we've sought?
We left the deck in the falling light,

swayed to a table at a restaurant window.
French loaf and a carafe of Chianti.
We bend to talk and our heads arc
intimacy under the lampshade, a glow
small and warm against the immensity.
A bright corridor sails the dark.

Fragile as swallows beating the air,
two earthlings cross a narrow water
on a minor planet of an average star
turning somewhere in an outer region
among a hundred thousand million
galaxies. Shall one swallow fall?

The lamp counts the glints of your hair
as we savour a meal, each moment
its own reward, absolute fulfilment.
Far from soil, we dally over grain
and grape, fondling our bread and wine.

Middle of nowhere. Middle of everywhere.

Cosmos

'All right?' booms the saxophone man.
'Everybody feeling chameleon?' The combo
expands the tune of a well-battered song.
An opulence of sound, clash and flow
as a spotlight tunnels dust in its beam,
glints the trumpet's bell and the hall
turns hot and hybrid, beery listeners
swaying and bobbing the mood of a theme.

From rainbows of timbre a strand of colour
floats into the air: the trumpet solo
burping one phrase of a melody, ripe
and brassy and buttoned down as though
a song is breathing over its origins,
those four hot-blooded notes weeping
their pleasure again on an old civil war
bugle. A sleazy backroom in New Orleans.

Sax and rhythm. The brightness of a reed,
winding tube and crook are working on
another hue of the tune that moves
into its own discourse: *Bud Freeman,
Johnny Hodges, Charlie Parker*. 'All right?'
he drawls, then scats a little as we clap
a tradition of subversions. But he's off again.
I watch swarms of dust in the spotlight,

swirls of galaxies, and imagine he's blowing
a huge balloon of space that's opening
our world of order. In a waft of creation
his being becomes a music's happening.
A red-shirted pianist now leans to seize
a gene of the song which seems to veer
and improvise, somehow catching a moment's
shifts and humours. Hail! Madam Jazz.

Let the theme return, its mutants echoing
as a tune balances against its freedom.
One key – so open-toned and open-stitched.

A beat poised, a cross-grained rhythm,
interplays, imbrications of voice over voice,
mutinies of living are rocking the steady
state of a theme; these riffs and overlappings
a love of deviance, our genesis in noise.

Is That?

Homing from a walk before turning in
we glance through someone's uncurtained window,
lights and shades of another life. But
look! ours too are lit. It seems as though
we stand outside ourselves or shed a skin,
turning our world a moment inside out.

So, there it is: a room in the universe.
Somewhere on a map an arrow is pointing down:
you are here. A booth of translucence between
two gardens, a lampshade like a full moon.
Is that where we eat and talk and play, nurse
our abrasions, wonder how else it might have been?

Or where we shift and wake in sunny weather,
spoors of desire scattered across a floor,
a stocking wriggled like an eel, an out of fashion
tie my careless lasso, then nearer the door
shoes – tongued holsters, biographers in leather,
their furrowed intensities footnotes to a passion.

So many questions. A breath's silver fur
floats into an immensity of night. Too lost
in thought could a Cartesian ghost begin
to doubt his footfalls on a pavement frost?
Where's the key? Turn its smallness. Undoor
our swarms of dream, a world of outside in.

Welcome

In early spring talk still young and high-flown
We laughed, there was an endless time to flirt
And toy with a fable of year. A snowdrop afloat
In an old wine glass on our table, already grown
Tumid with water, lifted the panels of her skirt
To show the pale green hem of her petticoat.

Soon we're strolling along the edge of a bay,
Kicking over the traces of an early swimmer.
It's deep into June: summer lush and unplanned
Rocks us in its lazy arms. In the blaze of day
We paddle in the shallows; I watch in a shimmer
Of water the sun doodling honeycombs in sand.

A year tilts into autumn; after its madcap
Race our Russian vine issues its manifesto,
A spray of flower. The sun sloping in humility
Smiles its frail approval as old men wrap
Against the chill. At last I think I know
Half of what we love is love's fragility.

A winter evening as I turn into our street
I hurry to see the rim of light that fingers
Around the curtain's edge to tell you're home.
You open the door and I sense as we meet
Our moment's wonder. A scent lingers.
I breathe deeply to feed memory's honeycomb.

Rhapsody

1 *Mid-points*

Nothing will stay still. You stretch to touch
but cannot catch, just graze it as it slips
out of reach. Yet savour it now it's passing,
at once an aftertaste that shakes the buds

of memory and foretaste of eternities to come.
Look, there is the marvel! But as you look,
You look behind, beside, between, beyond.
The lush sumac hides crimson and banana
hues, fragrances remind both of bygones
and tomorrow in the crow's foot and furrow,
dimpled children smile, genes bloom,
eons glide between your butter-fingers.
Have you so outgrown the age of time?
Prod of insight or knock on sanity's wall?
Scorch of wisdom's love or lure of madness?
A little quietude you ask, yet not
the balance that finds a point of equilibrium,
rather choose the tense delight that knows
tug of was, pull of will-be, that is
the calm of motion you desire. Always
all hovers in its changing, every instant's
gene pivots possibilities, mid-points,
diminished chords poised between tonalities.
You strike the moment's note, then overtone
over overtone ascends in fractions to where
all honest notes gather and are one.

2 *Flow*

This love that is forever is in motion,
a coiling stream of now and now and now.
Remember, remember a wistful time,
sunlit age, upstream once and long ago,
a paradise of past when all is well –
how things have changed! Or tomorrow you say,
tomorrow, maybe downstream soon and hilly
in the green far-away, if only when,
if only then you say – but it is now,
a world of happening forever is in motion,
now and here nothing will stand still,
our point of departure the actual; though
we search for footholds in what was or will be
or with a god's-eye view attempt detachment
to minimise our risks, human and fallible we
trust the love that is surrender to the flow.

In all this flux perhaps some patterns form:
eddies, rondos of experience, spirals, spheres
of remembrance, loops of history, forecast or guess;
yet you are never there, never have arrived,
for there is no *status quo*, moment by moment
like planets tense within our orbits, we trust,
we choose, we act and so become our story,
we do and tell our own once-upon-a-time.
Still there is room for surprise: we live
at the mercy of each new event, beck
and call of mystery, vulnerable to how it is.
Speak of glancing water or ever-fresh
configurations of a sky; flowing and mutable,
this love that is forever is in motion
and every here and now a widening ring.

Between

As we fall into step I ask a penny for your thoughts.
'Oh, nothing,' you say, 'well, nothing so easily bought.'

Sliding into the rhythm of your silence, I almost forget
how lonely I'd been until that autumn morning we met.

At bedtime up along my childhood's stairway, tongues
of fire cast shadows. Too earnest, too highstrung.

My desire is endless: others ended when I'd only started.
Then, there was you: so whole-hog, so wholehearted.

Think of the thousands of nights and the shadows fought.
And the mornings of light. I try to read your thought.

In the strange openness of your face, I'm powerless.
Always this love. Always this infinity between us.

Summerfest

1 *Open Air*

A first balmy evening and we've got together.
Chatter and music of a party seem to overflow
As we spill out into a sudden gift of weather,
Gathering around tables on a hot-bricked patio.
Even the solstice days were wet and overcast,
It was easy to lose faith when July fell away.
A season has held fire, kept best until last,
This must surely be the decade's hottest day.
The hostess is everywhere topping up glasses.
Miraculous as Cana's water, a courtesy and ease
Spreads among her chosen guests. She passes
By, her trace a slight hint of a warm breeze.
An August evening breathes its final sunshine;
This night will turn our summer back to wine.

2 *Shadows*

Dark. The hostess leans over our table to alter
The wick in a small coloured lantern she's lighting,
Her back sunned between the bows of a silk halter,
The curve of her shoulder blade a folded wing.
A mood seems to blur our lines of joy and sorrow,
In warm flutters of a candle, a wine-glass blushes.
Whose gentle shadows roam this garden we borrow,
Whose children once played among these bushes?
Through an open window a saxophone climbs a loud
Sad tune, pouring its soul and still unable
To tell why the fall of one late summer's night
Falters a moment over the loneness in a crowd.
An angel of memory has hovered near our table;
So many shades have loved this garden's sunlight.

3 *Sway*

The dance! the dance! everybody on their feet!
Move wine-loosened, quick-footed, rhythm-driven
And turn wild variations on what we're given;
Tilt and wheel, throb of the nodded upbeat.
Already we've become the dance; bodies and minds
A sweated ecstasy, a pulsing frenzy of control;
Our faces, vague and happy, merge into a whole
Delirium of summer. All that was wound unwinds.
A oneness of weaving and bobbing in the night air;
Again and again this play of check and freedom,
A jazz pulling against the sameness of the drum,
Our motion fallen in love with going nowhere.
Swirl, let-go, comeback. A flirtatious liaison.
Some dream in the dance's sway goes on and on.

A Fragile City

(1995)

Ὁ κόσμος οὗτος μία πόλις ἐστίν

This world of ours is one city.

EPICTETUS

FILTERED LIGHT

Euch kommt jeden Morgen das neue Licht
warm in die offene Wohnung.
Und ihr habt ein Gefühl von Gesicht zu Gesicht,
und das verleitet zur Schonung.

Every morning new light comes
warmly into the open house
and you have a feeling that moves from face to face
and that leads you astray to caring.

RAINER MARIA RILKE
translated by Robert Bly

Transit

Urgencies of language: check-in, stand-by, take-off.
Everything apace, businesslike. But I'm happy here
Gazing at all the meetings and farewells. I love
To see those strangers' faces quickened and bare.
A lost arrival is wandering. A moment on edge,
He pans a lounge for his countersign of welcome.
A flash of greeting, sudden lightening of baggage,
As though he journeyed out only to journey home.
I watch a parting couple in their embrace and freeing.
The woman turns, a Veronica with her handkerchief
Absorbing into herself a last stain of a countenance.
She dissolves in crowds. An aura of her leaving glance
Travels through the yearning air. Tell me we live
For those faces wiped into the folds of our being.

Folding

Our summer hide-out was the crotch of an old sumac,
A bole V-ing upwards into its light and pliancy,
Our feet in the fork, its boughs against our back;
A huddle of inclusiveness, first inkling of diversity.
Who was that strange child, that face at the rim
Demanding vision? It's as if our tree contracted,
Refusing the danger of renewal. A closing system.
That face returns and returns where never expected:
The Jewish woman in Chicago whose stare was rife
With memory or that Aran widower unfurling his story.
We seem to fold into each other, upsurges of a life
Drawing me into a seamless time, their past
A vibrancy of absence leaving its traces in me.
Is the child at the rim every stranger I've faced?

Beyond

Ask me then and I'm almost sure I'd say
A hand, a turn of shoulder, some voluptuous
Bend of playfulness kept inviting my caress.
Those days I talked of *truth* and *beauty*.
It was your expression. Those eyes that welcomed
Without reserve. Open-faced, so much a brother's
Keeper. It's as though we surrendered each other's
Freedom, freeing the other the more we succumbed.
It was years later I thought of Dante's Beatrice,
And how once you'd chided me for making fun
Of an old man. *Who knows what he's undergone?*
A face is filtering light from beyond a face.
You'd seen transparence in a stranger's infinite
Gaze. I moved in your light to see the light.

News

It was a struggle, but he arrived just after one.
Daniel George his father names him by telephone.
An unbroken line. And so he enters our universe,
God's my judge, Soil-worker as his grandfathers.
Who's he like? I try to imagine his countenance,
A little smudged, but finding its own structure
From genes and traces, incessant recommencements
Travelling towards a future. A recourse and rupture.
It's as though two separatenesses had come together
Blending their need with desire, a self and other,
Some kind of surplus in a lovers' touch and go.
Daniel George. One face of renewal and overflow.
Yours and not yours. You are and are not your son.
Fecundity's old riddle and a world moving on.

Quartet

These players nod and gleam as if they're seeing
And hearing the other's expression, each leaning
Into the fine-nerved strings, their whole being
Vested in this interplay, this gamble on meaning.
I remember a crescendo dream. We burned and burned.
Maybe it's age. I grow in this mutual succumbing:
Bow and pluck, phrase and breath of an earned
And watchful passion, our face to face becoming.
All shall be equal we'd said. But nothing matches.
Overlaps. Voice-overs. A sudden fertile digression
Loops into our rousing silence. Something over-reaches
Equality, a lived-in music shaping my compassion.
The conversation dips and wanders and tenses again.
A shining between faces, a listening inward and open.

Flare

There we were a cluster of twenty-year-olds.
A colour, a timbre fixes the sweep of that mood:
Cheap Chianti, candlelight, damp sugar-bowls,
A readiness to change a world half-understood.
No, nothing could ever again be the same.
Raise a mug of wine, a hymn to the proletariat.
The system's so damned unfair. But we had a dream.
We shall overcome. We'll sing our hearts out.
That chorus and I recall how our faces would blur
Into sameness. *Deep in my heart I still believe.*
Was it a cry for meaning we'd begun to squander,
Our well-meant vision turned faceless and assertive?
An energy flickers the untrimmed wick of a dream.
Our innocent anger keeps scattering the flame.

Focus

Our hurried need to flare and blaze both ends.
How slowly we'd grow, option by tiny option.
Catch us again, now that a fifth decade bends
Our lived-in dream, a jet of steadied vision.
Maybe I've learned to fear the sweeping chorus:
The masses, the system. Something cuts deeper.
Remember how young compassion first moved us:
A solo beseeching face calling me its keeper?
I reach across those years to re-focus a dream
Throwing its light again as our chorus fades;
My cupped hands sheltering the glow of a flame,
I see now in those eyes where their story leads.
Each life is thickening into its own fabric.
Every face so utterly itself. Alone. Unique.

Tension

The wrong voice, self-righteous, somehow out of tune:
Mr Chairman, I object to my colleague's actions.
One by one around the table we cast our stone.
He put a good face on it. Then, I saw he winced.
But where have I seen those hunted eyes before?
Frenchie, let's get Frenchie! The victim's glance
As he bolted hell for leather up a school corridor;
The patent shoes and corduroys, a swarthy difference.
I know the rules, but I want to halt this sacrifice.
My neighbour whispers: 'He's got to be taken to task,
A question of solidarity'. Does a fish squirm in a net?
I'm full of qualms. Was it just the tone of voice?
A face forgets a face breathing behind a mask.
The heart and the mind. Tensing poles of a magnet.

Casualty

She's at it again. Of course, she'll never learn.
Once she touches the stuff – well, that's that.
I read about it and know this classic pattern:
No insight and rock-bottom always too late.
We go on and on talking. All those far-fetched
Excuses, this ravelling of schemes and make-believe.
Am I the theory-man, trying to keep us detached?
History judges history and here's a write-off.
But her mother and sister are up again tonight.
The pancreas. Someone must drive her to casualty.
And besides there's the child; such a fright
Could bring his asthma on. In their fuss and care
I turn towards a countenance so alone and singular.
Something in her tragedy faces and outfaces me.

Revelation

Our train gains ground into the evening light.
Among the trees the sun catches in its fall
Glints and anglings of a stone in a distant gable,
A broadcast of facets, one and infinite.
I glance at you. There's so much unexplained.
Plays of your light keep provoking my infinity;
Already something in your presence overflows me,
A gleam of a face refusing to be contained.
How little I know of you. Again and again
I've resolved to be the giver and not the taker,
Somehow to surpass myself. Am I the mapmaker
So soon astray in this unknowable terrain?
Twenty-one years. And I'm journeying to discover
Only what your face reveals. Stranger and lover.

Translation

The tiler was deaf and dumb. He charmed all
With blue-eyed nods and signs until we forgot
His blemish. He pencilled needs on a bare wall:
2 ornamentals, 7 borders, ¹/₂ tub of grout.
One morning, his thumb and index shape a ring,
As he motions me aside to show a snapshot.
His face glows in this lover's mute naming
But a forefinger signals 'I'm slitting my throat'.
I smile at shyness, a sudden boyish withdrawal.
Is freedom our knowing that freedom is at stake?
He's young and hot in his leather. So I translate
Across trusting years into our male tick-tack.
My palms curve in the air a female figure 8.
I blow from my fingertips a kiss of approval.

Light

She tires easily, I'm warned, just a short while.
Well past ninety, a voyage fulfilled and intense.
I bend to kiss her. She smiles her girl's smile,
A presence begun absenting itself from a presence.
Surely she must be aware she's about to depart.
A strange translucence, an expression almost younger
And keener, as if she's taking the world to heart.
A boundless desire, a hunger nourished by hunger.
She has heard on the news of a newly discovered star,
A billion years it must journey our empty spaces;
The immensity of a conversation's flow and counterflow
Commands me with eyes I seem to answer to and for.
Beauty is truth, truth beauty. That is all ye know...
What is this light that falls between two faces?

Aversion

In fair Verona where we lay our scene. The theatre's
Warm as a festering London. Juliet and her banished
Romeo dally in the orchard, menders of their begetters'
Grudges. *Some shall be pardon'd and some punished.*
Another plot vibrates in me. A Norwegian ('The Slut'
She's called) flees with a German soldier, chooses
Her sweet, neutral days cooped in a Swedish hut.
They're found and shot. *A plague on both your houses.*
Cleansed and resolved, I exit headily to the street.
Of all people, look who's approaching! – a colleague
Who'd always done me down. I want our gaze to meet,
A single gesture. Enough dissembling and intrigue.
A glance averted and we've passed each other by.
Our long fallen history, one twinkling of an eye.

VEILS AND MASKS

Bortom era ord anade jag era ansikten.
De ansikten ni bär är inte era verkliga.
Ni var förklädda maskerade beslöjade.
Era obeslöjade ansikten är vakrare...

Beyond your words I sensed your faces.
The faces you bear are not your real ones.
You were disguised masked veiled.
Your unveiled faces are more beautiful...

MIRJAM TUOMINEN
translated by David McDuff

Intrusion

The glaze of loved and lover,
our amorous self-containment,
concentric and utterly present
to the other. Sweetest hour.

But what if between our gazes
shadows of the stricken fall,
the stares we seem to veil
keep on commanding us?

Our two-ness is never alone.
Whose is that intrusive face
that looms unseen between us
condemning all we haven't done?

The eclipsed. The destitute.
O sly worm of dominance
coiling its own discountenance,
our masks and blottings out.

Is love a threadbare blindfold?
'Yes,' say our shadows, 'unless
you turn to face the faceless.'
Who'll re-envisage the world?

274

How?

When the time comes, how will we have been:
giver or hoarder, sharers or sleek *gringos*?
Children of the barrio, how can I explain?

Silk I love: fall and flow and cocoon,
the worm's sheen, desire clinging and loose.
When the time comes, how will we have been?

And fruits: plums, tangerines, seedy moon
of a kiwi, yellow-orange flesh of mangoes.
Children of the barrio, how can I explain?

Or cheeses skinned with peppers, a stilton
waxy, wrinkle-rinded, my blue-veined gorgonzolas.
When the time comes, how will we have been?

Morning curtains, towels lilac and green
in the light, the pile of a rug scuffing toes.
Children of the barrio, how can I explain?

Something cries its grievance. A false coin
is spinning: heads I win, tails you lose.
When the time comes, how will we have been?
Children of the barrio, how can I explain?

Outsider

A sheltered arch or where underground
kitchens of an inn sent
through grids of pavement grating
the warmth of the ass's breath –
Where did last night's Christ lie down?

Every morning for months I watched
a man I might have been,
about my age and bearded too,
his face blotched crimson
with cheap wine and sleeping rough.

He walked the far side of the street
always hurrying somewhere;
a father who couldn't praise, I wondered,
or what had blurred his star?
For months our eyes never met,

though the street between us was narrow,
until that eve he crossed.
'Some help,' he said, but it must have been
my double's eyes that asked
where would He lie down tomorrow?

An old outsider within me winced,
shook him off and fled;
that street between was so narrow –
I chose the inn and was afraid.
I'm sure I've never seen him since –

but tomorrow when carafes go round
a lone presence will pass
tremors through our frail togetherness;
again those eyes will ask
where did last night's Christ lie down?

Tables

1

'You know yourself, nothing but money counts.'
I try my best to smile my knowing smile.
Nods to an age's spirit, a self-effacement.

So often he's the enabler, a hidden hand lent.
'On bread alone?' But any doubt is scandal.
I swallow mutinous words as the tables turn.

What did I ever know of deprivation? His scorn
whips me: shame, insecurity, angst that haunts
a body all its life. Nothing. I know nothing.

Self-made, yet so many taken under his wing.
Even innocence must sometimes wear a mask.
'That's talk for ascetics or the too well-off!'

2

An ascetic? No. A mortal who loves to eat
sharon fruits, blancmange, to sip iced rosé
or feel warm sand on the arches of his feet.

Young Keats dressed and quiffed for his table.
I bath early, grooming and scenting myself;
silked and rakish, I'm ready to love invisible

muses. Then everything cloys except the journey.
Endless desert. I feed on some hump of memory
and expectation. Ecstasy moving and stationary,

a delight fuelling itself. Unlimited supply
and demand. The end of desire is more desire.
My camel soul must travel the needle's eye.

3

He's sleeping rough. There but for a woman's praise
assuaging my temperament. (Who'll shelter my double?)
I tuck my knee-caps into the hollows of her knees.

And still he haunts me, my vagabond counterpart.
I know Thomas More brought beggars to his table.
Every loop of the mind I try keeps falling short.

So much dereliction I know I can't countenance.
Justice is a faceless scales. Tell me who'll be
the rich man sighting that prodigal in the distance

to fall on his neck and kiss him? The love cup
raised in celebration of a father's huge abandon;
the art of giving, the art of never giving up.

Hostel

Station of ease for the broken or frail.
A tear in an ocean. And yet that welcome
At face value, a roof and warmth, a meal.
Vague signals of angeldom.

So little. So short of grand revolution
We'll always want to dream of.
If only dreams could scoop or fill an ocean...
Thimbled gestures of a love,

Some gift of falling for endless tasks
Berth this moment's care;
The scarred visage of a down-and-out who asks
If an ocean starts with a tear?

Patient logs of strays and have-nots.
A youth stubborn and hurt
Uproots and wanders. No one knows his whereabouts,
Nomad and introvert.

Long headstrong years on the loose;
Now shattered and underfed,
A quarrelsome body yields nightly to delicious
Mercies of bath and bed.

One evening and again he's gone
Without trace. No mendings. No rebirth.
Tiny alleviations, something beautiful done.
A caress on the face of the earth.

Theft

Another wired photograph of an African woman
Holding a small girl with a pear-shaped head
And a shrivelled crowfooted face. Has someone
Thieved a child, left her this elf instead?

Drought. Failed crops. And the rains too late.
Hollows of famine rumble the bowels of the earth.
Look long and deep. Unable to clean forget,
I begin my day, busy in the lap of the north.

Little knoweth the fat what the lean doth mean.
I can't ghost-write a suffering. Only my guess
And leap, flickers of memory or the unforeseen.
I know how easily a world unsheathes my tinyness.

But nothing appeases her stare. Again I'll pore
Over this image of hunger. Is compassion a guilty
Fear of *there but for fortune* or is there more?
It's as though something in her gaze commands me.

A look both rapt and implacable. There's no wool
To pull over these eyes. Look long. Look deeper.
Cycles of dominance; a hemisphere's rise and fall.
She stares and stares. Am I my sister's keeper?

Two After Dark

1

I tuned in that night to a man's ageing voice:
'I'm fancy-free. I could have had my pick of them.'
An eavesdropper, had I already begun to pity him?

'Maybe if you're tethered young, you get used to it.
All you needed was the gab and a good way with you.
On the dance-floor I was as smart as any on my feet.

'Out there with a steady, if I saw a handsomer woman
I'd watch my chance. *But haven't you a girl with you?*
It's you I want, I'd say, *and sure don't mind anyone.'*

I stare at a wireless trying to envisage his face.
'And I did a great trade in women from far and near.'
An old notched gun smoking stubbornly in the corner.

2

I remembered sitting in half-light with an old friend
Stitching years we'd missed. But as night came on
I knew I'd heard her hearing my unasked question.

'I waited,' she laughed, 'for a prince to come riding
On a white horse.' Always one of us, she'd refused
To flatter or fawn; confidante and equal in everything.

A nature that had to give all. Why anything less?
She used to say 'Wait till I'm minister for fairness!'
Just wait. That was a time when we owned the world.

Men. Where will they all fade with their giddiness?
No prince. She rose, making her way across the dark
To a lamp, luminous and surefooted in her apartness.

Rowing Back

If she broached him near the bone, like his father
He'd abscond, then reappear in his boat to pout
For hours on end in the bay, sitting it out
Till she came beckoning guiltily from the shore.

I see him there shame-faced, glad of a let-out,
As hunching on his oars he turned and back-tracked,
Sullen but somehow holding his maleness intact,
Frail dignity balanced on the keel of a boat.

Come clean. What is it we've been so afraid of?
A fear of what we couldn't tame, wild otherness
Wobbling and ungraspable, a sway and completeness.
We row an unfathomable sea. Comber and trough.

Tumble and come-back. A filling tide's action
And passivity, slow logic of retreats and charges,
As wave into wave keeps gaining on itself, surges
Beyond our control and so full of direction.

But something in her expression is veiled and denied.
Those old patterns of huff, guilt and climb-down.
The ghosts of so many women are standing alone
Waving to an oarsman brooding on his phantom pride.

Is the boat in the bay cradling a dread of failure,
A bravado trying to face up to its loss of face?
Visible and invisible as children cribbing disgrace
Behind our fingers, forgive us as we row ashore.

At the Hairdresser's

My neck on the porcelain rim, a tautness unbends
Backwards into suds and rushes and squirts of water.
A teenage girl (she could easily be my daughter)
Gentles my head. Surely a world is safe in her hands?
Through the steamy towels and scissorings a radio
Blurts news from the East. Some million men dug in.
Our sly litany, old stealthy dream of domination:
Silkworm, jaguar, tomcat, hawkeye, sea-sparrow.
Her thumbs spiral deep into a skull of memory.
Sully's and Quinner's gangs fight for a school fort
With hedge-cuttings bound into whips. Lash and hurt
And threat of 'sissy' or 'coward'. Above all, don't cry.
My clogged maleness loosens in her determined fingers.
Those helmeted faces so boyish with their unspilt tears.

Embrace

The evening guests arrive, all flowers and wine
and loud hellos at the gate. *Come on, come in.*
Good to see you! Just a bottle for the kitchen.
I kiss the women's cheeks; between us, the men,
a handshake, our gesture and show of strength,
this double signal – hands-on and armslength.

I want to fling my limbs open and embrace.
A clumsy left hand glances a shoulder blade
and I know at once he's feeling some hand laid
to measure a deal's anxiety, nervous give-aways.
A hug is a dagger too close, a dealer's grope.
Something tightens at my touch and buttons up.

I'll take your coat. Flowers. You shouldn't have!
We shy from such receiving, a chink in the male
like a sideways revelation and a hurried withdrawal
or some blurted late-night confidence brushed off
in a morning-after silence or averted look.
Was I bad? I remembered nothing when I woke.

What have we done to ourselves? Years of tautness,
a gaucheness hiding its face behind our ritual,
a coil and wriggle in ourselves we want to veil.
Look! how those women caress and touch with ease.
Sisters, sisters, it's us you're trying to free;
more than your scorn, our dealer's grope needs pity.

And weren't you women once those mothers drying
up our tears? A face shown and withdrawn.
Slugs and snails and puppy dogs. *Stand like a man.*
Tell me, did you ever see your father crying?
A coin's faces, each a keeper for the other.
Woman and man, somehow we're in this together.

Tracks

1

How it sways in its tracks as it gathers speed!
We steady ourselves against any lurch of intimacy,
our deflected faces guarding invisible territory.

The jolted halt, the scurried terrazzo passage,
as elbow to elbow we show our tickets and wedge
towards morning. So much changed and unchanged.

Thousands of years, of mornings, of jostling men:
hunters, tool-users, ranchers, traders, explorers.
Defining. Redefining. Makers and crossers of borders.

Thousands of years, of mornings, of nourishing women,
protectors of inlands, rearers, nurturers, faithful
guardians of hearth, keepers of hive and churn.

We're shoulder to shoulder in this rush and scrum
of a morning. Subtler and more persistent, you wear
our masks and will outwit us. But was there a dream?

The train moves on, grumbling in the frame of a bridge
like a man moaning the linear premise of his station,
a zigzag of life swerving on its narrow gauge.

Our crush on living daylight tapers forwards.
When will you come bringing the milk and honey,
spilling a heartland over our rigid borders?

2

I'd waited all afternoon for her to return.
I glanced through a window at an empty road
of nunnish spruces, tall and dark and stern,
watching over asphalt where it had snowed
on and off, a vague but persistent caress
of muslin laid across a road's aloneness.

Hours delayed, she came laden with apologies:
a colleague ill – someone had to cover for him,
a report due tomorrow; then, halfway home,
the return to check in case pipes would freeze.

Her giving is so easily absorbed. A thermostat
of concern smoothes the air. Earth mother. Fail-safe.
Heavy-footed angel, I tread in with talk of
'staking out territory' and 'leaving it at that'.

Am I my mask? Our one-track compulsion to define
as a lavishness strives to expand our given space.
A sudden mantilla of doubt is shadowing her gaze:
'Why aren't we women as good at drawing the line?'

For a while, side by side, in the dusk we stood
and watched another shower, inhaling the slow
pervasion of a fall seizing on nothing, a mood
of persistence and letting be, its touch-and-go
decking spruces like brides, a mousse of zigzags
blurring and undoing the car's determined tracks.

La Différence

1 *Clash*

Suddenly you shrink – a carapace of pain.
Outsider I blunder further into protest.
Why? For heaven's sake try to explain.

Another wound. Hurt of a hurt unnoticed.
Can a man learn nothing but words? I bluster
clumsy half-sentences; thick-skinned, ham-fisted.

'If only you'd told me.' Instead you fester,
harbour a wordlessness that keeps trying to say
'to have to say is to fail'. My best filibuster

empties into silence. A mood leaves its highway
of huff-no-move stumbling towards self-reproach.
Am I the oafish male? And so we parley:

'If I were you I'd feel the same,' I approach
a sideways acknowledgement, a first breakthrough.
Words match words, the love-straws we clutch.

More the tomboy, more the sissy; atonement of two.
Dice of genes and *vive la différence.*
Woman me as I am manning you.

2 *Neighbour*

Me – possess you? See how I look
into your eye, human and similar.
I face a neighbour's face and talk
the common sense of common gender.

Much more the same than different:
fears, countless yearnings, our gauze
of meanings. So, by one consent
the welcome and appeal of face to face.

A delicate line of balance. But then
the rounds of your eyes grow murky,
the dark tips of your lashes lengthen,
a tremble in your aura caresses me.

Me – know you? So utterly more
different than the same. A modesty
absent in its presence, glory of desire;
something revealed, then drawn away.

3 *Nurses*

Staunch and calm in the dimmed light –
a charted pulse, a careful tuck –
I heed the dark sway of their bodies
as they keep watch, their rockabye
voices mothering towards sleep.

Where am I? Awareness sneaks
again to notice flushes of light,
lemon streaks of dawn re-establish
window-panes. I must have fallen off,
let ages slip through the sashes?

Allegro, full of good mornings
and how are we today Mr O'?
Girls with slender arms tidy
pillows, bring bowls of water
to swab and towel and daughter me.

Such young strides, such narrow waists!
They smile and know: born of women,
always theirs, they know beyond
my knowing. I yearn in their secret,
I sleep and wake in their wonder.

In the End

So I've confessed the cargo of my gender;
I know the subtle ways we've faced you down.
Maybe I've been more fortunate than others?

In the end I can only speak from experience.
I delight in womanhood. A marvel infinitely
refined. Nuances of strength. Their presence.

Together in everything, what veil of mystery
still falls between us? All I can't seize
seems to possess me. Comrade and mistress.

I love those tiny derailments of control
inviting me into the magnanimity of woman.
Unvisored. Somehow loosened in my role,

I wear a different mask, living and porous,
a delicious obedience to all my voices
allowing our musics their pitch and part.

Your freedom is our freedom. And I relearn
a forgotten register. Inward and airborne,
a soprano is gliding in my womanish heart.

Wisconsin

In May the Menomonie fishers show by the Lake
to spear some last treaty right in the shallows;
the local boys ride the water, jeer and smack
the waves, bucking their speedboat bronchos.

Someone, for God's sake, stop those bastards! Again
the absolute rage of youth: send back Mayflowers,
missioners with beads and guns, the frontiersmen,
caravels with their bellies full of conquistadores.

Our old indulgent dream of untouched races,
peace-pipe smokers, growers of squash and maize.
But they had drifted southward, married fur traders
and changed. Into the shifting muddle of what is

my anger blends. It's all too stitched in time,
the seams, the folds, the overlaps and patches.
Do you hear those outboard engines' scream?
We belong, we belong. Stop stabbing our conscience!

I think of Las Casas picking up the pieces
as regimes fall and one plan after another
sunders. He begins all over again; a business
unfinished, a ghost possessed by the word brother.

Doorway

I'd climbed the engineer's cabin steps, knocked
Like a schoolboy: Could I have a word with you?
There he stands in flannels, his navy blue
Blazer shining, framed by a door he's blocked.

'I'll give a man a hearing,' he says. I back
Downwards a little, still trying to glimpse
His face. It's London nineteen sixty-six.
Whoever he thinks he sees is probably black

Or at best a step beneath. And I'm effaced.
I stand under sentence: guilt by motherland,
Overseen by some blindness I won't understand.
A degradation: such pride and so much waste.

But I grow older, begin to wonder if he
Like Plato's tyrant stared at empty space,
Confronting nothing, and I was a shadow whose face
Had long turned away. I refuse this history.

I'm still climbing to a door, trying to retrace
Those steps. Tell me why you're afraid of me?
How lonely the eye in its majesty. See me.
Hold my gaze. I'm nothing but this naked face.

Shame

A mind already smitten;
rife and cloven cells,
alien vessels
of scorn doubling within.

In Pimlico Araners who shrank
when someone had spoken Irish,
a brand and blemish.
What would the Blacks think?

That African minister's rage;
his state-car blocked by a herdsman's
flock, he threatens
and shouts *Sauvage! Sauvage!*

Bitter moment of corrosion
when all that might have praised
turn to dust.
Iron eats into iron.

Progress

1

News of a truce broken. More shootings.
Young insurgents with sights fixed on square
one, some golden age about to rebegin.
A sweeping clean.
Always a flow in the flow of things,
will we ever start where we are?

Remember whose youth once fell for
loserdom, cragged faces of island people,
dream moment of a life standing still.
A glorious idol.
Or when it changed, how I'd begin to abhor
their cussedness, muddled and untameable.

Strange irony. Hairpin bend of fate.
The heart spawns our reason's overreach,
faces that moved us blur behind a veil
of pure ideal:
age-old lure of the clean slate,
of worlds begun from scratch.

2

The Suquamish kissing our earth as sister,
Antarchos the Greek centring the sun,
our Christ-Jew bannering the conquistador:
so much ravelled and then undone.

So many wisdoms won and suppressed
or the bitter foolishness of wisdom marred;
as if ground once gained is more than lost
and we keep returning in order to depart.

Something must love our rise, our lapses:
the contingent, the unforeseen, the fluent;
sideways and scrambled our tumbling process,
made or broken in the fullness of a moment.

Abel

I seem to follow the lure and flow of a story.
Then glimpses of a garden or a school dormitory
Shift and interchange. The frames begin to slip
Quicker than I understand. I'm losing my grip.
Why this crowd? And why are they hunting me?
Faster and faster. Suddenly I'm on a promontory,
The frenzy of chase closing its faceless threat.
Over the edge. I've woken in a snow of sweat.

Frenchie, let's get Frenchie. Again a tableau
Of schoolboy persecution sways in some undertow
Of memory. I hear the swishing wavelike noise
Of a mob in hot pursuit. Our ritual sacrifice.
A sallow and dapper stranger weaves and dodges
Down a corridor with a swarm of blurred visages
Close on his heels, whipping boy and scapegoat,
A swoon of oneness singling his difference out.

This evening in a country that I'd first come
To half a life ago, some blond youths loom
Up the platform, beer-cans glinting in the dark.
My suspicious swarthness. A Greek or even a Turk?
'Is it here we trounce foreigners?' sneers a voice,
Partly his show for the gang, partly his menace.
An ugly moment. I hurry on trying to pretend
I didn't understand, scanning exits for my friend.

Unbroken line of pogroms, this blindman's buff.
A planet now at stake, perhaps we know enough
To reveal even the slants and bias of our lens?
A stark figure transverses our shed millennia,
That first victim forever crying his innocence.
Stay the knife. Children of a jealous violence,
Fugitives on the earth, may we still ask his pardon?
Say to me, brother Abel, that I'm your guardian.

BOUNDARIES

Springbrunn är du, vars soligt glittrande stråle
skön i sin jämvikt, skön i sin formstränga båge,
skön i sin styrka, äger
makten att älska gränser och ädla mått.

A fountain you are, whose sunnily glittering beam,
beautiful in its equilibrium, beautiful in its form-strict arc,
beautiful in its strength, possesses
the power to love limits and noble dimensions.

KARIN BOYE
translated by David McDuff

Hopscotch

Our chalked figure of boxes squared
off and interlocked. Overlappings
of sides, T-shapes, half-shared
divides. A groundwork for high jinks.

'Your go!' And everyone hunkers to watch
if I toe the line. Footfall vigil.
Is this why the Germans call hopscotch
'playing a game of heaven and hell'?

Such passion for limits and thresholds.
Johnston's shop in Pettigo, its entrances
in both counties. A foot in two worlds.
Abutment and frontier. Old ambivalences.

Or the way sometimes exact same sounds
seemed to slide and play with words;
a child is riddling out how 'bounds'
means 'confines' and 'bounces forwards'.

Then, the pivot homewards. Our swift
about-face. Thrill and crisis of turning;
one ankle clasped, one hand aloft,
frail balance of gravity and yearning.

A skittish jump. Again our spreadeagle
heavy-footed landings astride a border.
Stop-go momentum of hop and straddle.
That need of lines. That leap's desire.

Noon

I've fallen in love again with gazing.
A lake is absorbing shimmered transfers
of grey alders and ripplings of leaves.

A hollow twig hesitates, then steers
outward, canoeing this ice-age maw.
Mountain eye. Basin of contemplation.

A skimmed stone tumbles and disappears.
Minutiae of an aeon. Noon is filling
the air with its riddles. Who am I?

Archaeologies of thought define me:
the words I use, phrases, gestures.
Is everything seen with an encoded eye?

Piecemeal layers of address and response.
Process of encounters: fall-out, settlings,
accruals, a womb of residues and ores.

Silent undertows. Still-living sediment.
A mountain lake swallows and endures
these slow, deep accumulations of sludge.

In the dark and light of every about-face
some beckoning aim, a hovering remembrance.
My spirit is watching over the waters.

Story

A man turns hostage for his friend's release:
It is a far, far better rest that I go to...
Abandon without return. Gratuity of sacrifice.

It is a far, far better thing that I do...
that cadenza of Dickens's *Tale of Two Cities*
and a child bursts in tears. Must it be so?

One story will haunt him all his living days.
The wartime girl with her German soldier flees
over the frontiers. Or tell him, now as he greys,

of an African spirit between one world and another
who stays around as a child just to make happy
the bruised face of a woman who'd become his mother.

My name is made illustrious in the light of his.
To break and enter another's brokenness and glory.

This is the story I'll touch in every caress.

Sunlight

Two children swimming out to the low tide rocks
and a woman watching. Breaststrokes. Headlong
aspirations of dips and bobs across the water.

Her lovely givenness a vigilance of substitution,
hostage to every breath and splash. Strange paradox:
the further they swim away, the nearer they are.

*'That's my place in the sun' is how the usurpation
of the whole world began.* And I fill with wonder
watching a woman watching. What is this reflex?

An abandon and weightlessness of concern. Pure
undergoing. Almost as if they float in the matrix
of her being, drifting in passivities of creation.

Some overflow of boundaries weaves its intrigues
of motherhood. A debt being payed before the loan,
as though she usurps herself in watching over

the whirl of their busy limbs oaring back water
in sunlight, the whole gown of her life turned
inside out. Her face glories in this reversal.

Some obsessive patience hears an ungiven order.
Does an echo somehow anticipate its sound?
She's so full of answers before they ever call.

Merging

Nursing your cold's fever I'm forever nine,
Worrying by my mother's bedside years ago.

A blind is drawn low to guard her eyes from sunshine,
Slowly I wipe her brow with a sponge. It's as though

Two women are merging into one. I swab her hairline,
Breathing and undergoing all she'll have to undergo.

A sudden exhaustion seizes me. Now I watch for a sign.
Maybe she's begun to doze. I leave. Sneaking. Tiptoe.

I wanted to be the Samaritan pouring my oils and wine.
But was I some skulking Levite abandoning her pillow?

I know to serve you better I need to hold the line,
Yet where that line should go, how can I ever know?

Here nursing your fever will I be forever nine?
You gaze a gaze that seems to say: 'To think it's so,

To think for someone else even this face of mine
Is the face of a certain man going down to Jericho.'

Dusk

Look! a pair courting against the mauve
Of evening. Silhouettes caress on a bandstand,
Fold in their oneness. (Was it so long ago?)
We draw close and pass their no-man's-land,
The first oblivion of kisses *quid pro quo*,
Those sweet trade-offs of *prima facie* love.

I glance their desire. Again a riddling elf
Of wisdom dances: are we only found in loss?
In going beyond our frontiers do we return?
Without reserve. Chosen even before I choose.
A first dalliance throws its nets of concern.
Matrices of care. Strange ecologies of self.

On a bench in fallen light that elderly couple
Tilt their bodies in a long mutual attention
Of nods and silence. Gestures seem to rehearse
Vigilant love-makings. Borders drawn or redrawn.
Drifts and siltings. All the brokerage of years.
A few strides apace and how far we travel.

Gull

An oilslick, jetsam of a tanker under
a flag of convenience, and here's another
wing filmy and sealed, that waddle
of shame on the rocks, a grounded gull
wide-eyed as a girl tarred and feathered.

Remember 'foe' and 'Erin' and 'liberty'?
The birds did whistle and sweetly sing
Changing their notes from tree to tree
The song they sang was old Ireland free.
Our innocence still a bird on the wing.

Who are we now? Our daily conspiracy
of mood and idioms, delta of memories,
names and quarrels of a shared place,
frail rootedness, complicities of ease,
womb of overlaps and shifting boundaries.

The rocks keep crumbling, trapping soil
in pioneer decays of lichen and moss;
some water-plant is netting in its root
the silt that clots a slobland. What
bird will nest its dream in our humus?

Sing the darker musics of complexity.

Image

Eighty miles or so from where I write
A divided house in love with an old hate
Feuds and kills. A ghostly tit for tat.
Bitter scores no one settles outright.

Even the terms are alien: 'Prod and Teague'.
Who are you neutral for and who against?
'Tar and featherings', 'kneecap punishments'.
Violence draws frontiers of a golden age.

World of black or white and perfect borders.
Verona or Belfast. It's brother on brother
In worlds long chequered into one another.
An X smeared on a wall. Evacuation orders.

Eighty miles I can't pretend to understand.
On screen tonight a woman mourns a childhood
Lover refound in middle age. Teague and Prod.
Eighty miles from here and still my island.

But I'm no Pilate. I can't now wash my hands,
For I too want these souring wounds to heal.
Those names! Drumshiel, Carn tSiadhail, Loch Shiel.
I'm mapped into landscapes of northern lands.

A woman's image is flying in the face of hate.
The lusts of eye for eye and blow for blow.
Somewhere let Capulet weep for fallen Romeo.
My Teague's hand reaches over a broken Juliet.

Parting

'I think of you often.' He nods
Knowingly. Parting he hugs me, pauses,
Then blurts 'alone in the woods
I've often seen
Your spirit darting among the spruces'.

I wanted to tell him before the train
Drew out how that morning I'd despaired
A wing rapped my window-pane,
A vehemence of friendship
Reaching out. And I wished I'd dared.

Radiance

Think of a black womb of nothingness.
An endless density. Then, it bursts.

A universe scatters through infinity.
The held momentum. The paced gravity.

As the helix tangles and grows complex,
Our feverish sun is a purse that leaks.

A knife-edge between chaos and leap.
Our running down and our building up.

At mutant rims, in my heart of confusion,
Some new and daring jumps of evolution.

Poem of becoming. Dance of detours.
Boundaries fall and a radiance endures.

The red giants die to zinc and carbon.
I grow with ashes of stars in my bone.

Music

Music, always music. And when the violins tumble
a thief has entered me.
Come and gone.
A sneaking anarchy
leaving spoors of memories I never had.

Incognito. Whimpers through crevices and pores,
quick bowings of a violin,
furious *pizzicato*
of what hasn't been,
whinnies and hops beyond a future I imagine.

My vigilance breaks down. Rupture of being.
This syncopation. Offbeat,
out of phase
with myself, I vibrate.
What's this breathlessness I can't catch up with?

That flight of thirds mincing up a treble
clef. Lines of joy.
Matrix of frontiers.
EVERY GOOD BOY
DESERVES FAVOUR. Silences are spelling FACE.

Endless glory of some muteness that eludes me.
Approach of another face,
tremolo of forsakenness,
naked and homeless.
How can I fold and suckle all its orphanhood?

Music, always music. Neighbour, are you the face
of that thief breaking in,
hollowing me out?
A tumbling violin
breathes its cries in me. I'm womb and mother.

Meditations

1 *After Niels Bohr*

Something in our nature enjoys twin truth.
An electron's double life: in turn a particle
And billow of guesses, waves of the probable.
Neither the one nor the other. World of both.

A thought in flows of the possible takes flesh.
Old Plato's lovely dream, undated and open;
The gain and shortfall of things as they happen.
Love's aims and journeys complement and mesh.

2 *After Alain Aspect*

Two quanta of light are shot contrariwise.
Then, pin one down travelling whatever line –
Already the other moves right-angled to its twin.
Separate togetherness. More a joy than surprise

As though the core knows what nothing has proved.
Unimaginable wholeness. A twitch in a filigree
Shimmers and ripples across a fragile city.
Of course, I still belong to anyone I've loved.

3 *After Werner Heisenberg*

Twin truths. And yet I can never gauge both.
Fix a particle and we've missed its impetus,
Fix its momentum and its place will elude us.
Every bid to fix catches us all in its truth.

Creation delights in this play of peekaboo.
I try to measure your nearness. You abscond.
Your gaze folds me into its infinite beyond.
Fugitive. Ungraspable. I can only love you.

The Bulldog O'Donnell

Chorus of tables and declensions. *Mensa, mensa.*
Latin or arithmetic. Both he'd made us sing
Aloud, his ruler slapping out a rhythm and pace.
Self-reliant and certain of gender and case.
'A sound mind in a sound body.' *Mens sana...*
Bulldog O'Donnell seemed so sure of everything.

Ah, the shattered self. How we'll fall to doubt.
Such tables turned, a temple tumbling down.
Our words. Our gender. Suspicion in commonplace.
Mistrust. Fragmentation. Irony's roundabout.
That long bony finger in the accusative case.
And who am I? All the whitened faces of a clown.

All my shed skins. But I hear him growing hoarse
With his questions: *What's the nominative in Latin?*
Who speaks? Who does what? Whose is the story?
Who's responsible for what? His own mandatory
Reply leading the choir: *The subject, of course!*
I ponder again the swish and metre of his baton.

My foibles, my moods, my myths. Even the sham.
For all that, I still weave a fragile city
Of trust. Blame me, friend. Praise me more.
What's best in me is what you love me for.
Our gazes intersect. And yes, here I am
So inconsistent, yet someone is counting on me.

Amo, amas, amat... He is pointing fingers
At himself, at me, at a neighbour. His chant
of boundaries: first, second and third person.
Conjugations of love. Was he really so certain?
That huge foot slamming the floor, a cincture's
Swayed scansion: *amamus, amatis, amant.*

FEAST

You must sit down, sayes Love, and taste my meat:
So I did sit and eat.

GEORGE HERBERT

Abundance
(for Marie)

To be there, childlike, when it happens.
Nothing I've ever earned or achieved.
Delight. Sudden quivers of abundance.

A whole glorious day with a friend.
Brunch. This honeyed bread. Talk.
All the time in the world to spend.

Those icy stings and a gladdened vein,
an autumn swim tingling my nape,
dousing pleasure on a sleepy brain.

Watching children on a bandstand floor;
some irrepressible urge to celebrate,
squealing, tramping, pleading for more.

November birches with leaves of apricot.
After a long walk in the frosty air,
to warm our palms around a coffee-pot.

Waves and moments of energy released.
I hoard them. A child with sweets and cakes
chortles at prospects of a midnight feast.

So much is that might never have been.

Pond

We'd been netting minnows in the pond all morning.
I knew he was palling with a boy from the avenue
I'd never liked. I still hear my jealous warning:
'If you play with him, then I won't play with you.'

Today a friend greeted me with a fleeting kiss,
Which seemed to glance traces of moments spun
To hours of lovemaking. Is it that I've known bliss?
That riddle of one in many, many in the one.

I remember how he'd smiled and didn't say a thing,
Just idly tossed a pebble to the middle of the pond.
Its plump and sucking fall expanded ring by ring.
A fiesta of hoops keeps swelling beyond and beyond.

Tight-wire

Strolling fields behind the tent I glance
Figures leaving glares of light.
Wild applause inside.
Elephants to dance;
Now the acrobats delight
Children, now the juggling clown.
Someone hands a faded dressing gown.
Steadied, out she'll stride

Over guy-wires, over littered mud and cans
Past an empty pony stall
Slipping in among
Hung-out clothes and vans.
There she'll seem too small and frail.
No one saw who stepped the wire.
Those who clap her clap their own desire.
Someone always young

Slinging ropes between two garden sheds
Full of reckless festive grace

Seems to dare to flout
Endless overheads –
Nothing underwrites but space.
Thrills of business just for fun
Touch the dreams of things we might have done.
Steadied, she'll step out.

Wireless

The word 'certain' and deep down I remember
a late-night newsreader's somnolent timbre
signing off just before the National Anthem.

A cabinet wireless square and solid as a world
around us, that row of knobs I'd once twirled
to eavesdrop on crackles and exotic noises

Riding the empty air. An innocence unravelled.
So much of what was certain a dominance veiled.
Suddenly it's a world multiple and bewildering

As foreign rumours and echoes we couldn't gag
when the tuning needle meandered over Europe:
Berlin, Stockholm, Paris, Hilversum, Prague.

Traces of static. An opulence breaking in.
I've grown to love the grit of interference.
Sizz and hubbub. So many cities of conversation.

Still a longing for the certain and overall.
To reach for timeless skies if only to fall
again into the deeper moments of what's ours.

Radiowaves vault to an overlayer and bounce.
A search for order in one man's resonance;
lives hueing and colouring the words we share.

Coherence hinted. A wager. Something guessed.
Echo of echo. Traces. Rumour of rumour.
This feast at which I'm both host and guest.

304

Michaelmas at Glendalough

Twin-lake valley scattered with remnants
Of praise and work and damp silence.
A path between the upper and lower lake
Greases with leaves. Is it the heartbreak
Of a season or the still ghosts of prayer
Hiding in birches? There's chill in the air,
Soon these leaves will fossilise in frost.
Something living stiffens and is lost.

Clusters of monks gathered in a first
Burgeoning, that strange lyrical outburst
Of separate worlds just newly spliced:
The lush blackbird, the eastern Christ.
I sense one watching from his beehive hut
As the upper lake gleams its sudden cross-cut
Of sunlight and epiphany and the lower lake
Clouds with all that's ordinary and opaque.

He stares. He'll bring his gleam of sun
To Europe after the Visigoth and Hun.
Will it all go so wrong? The dominance,
A loss of boundaries and shades of nuance.
Somehow everything's distant and mediated.
The sacred blurs. Too veiled. Too weighted.
He's staring at an ideal. Let his face
Turn back to the shadows of the commonplace.

The lower lake darkens towards October.
He gazes. The waters are deep and sober.
Freedom and dignity, a love of the profane;
Some Luther is hallowing the ordinary again.
The best when spoilt will soon be worse:
Roundhead and votary of sweet commerce,
Then soiler and technocrat, a male caged
By a reason too controlled and disengaged.

Old ghosts of desire stir the undergrowth;
Two worlds and we crave the best of both
On this greasy path between two cisterns.
Michaelmas at Glendalough as a century turns.
My feastday. The air fills with fragility,
The choices and wounds of double polity.
Now in the shadows, now in the sun;
Can angels of this heart and mind be one?

Leisure

What does it mean?
Suddenly, effortlessly, to touch the core.
Mostly in the glow of friends
but today just strolling the length of a city street.
Carnival moments.
The apple back on its tree
in a garden lost, a garden longed for.

I move among traders.
Stacks of aubergines, rows of tiger-lilies.
Rings of silver and cornelian.
A feast of action.
Crosslegged, an Indian plays
music on a saw-blade glittering in the sun.

In the sweat of thy face
shalt thou eat bread. First hearing
that story, I'd bled for Adam.
I bump into an acquaintance and begin to apologise.
'Taking a break,
Be hard at it tomorrow.'
Puritan me, so afraid of paradise.

Anaxagoras the sage
(a century before Plato) mulled it over
on a street like this in Athens.
First question: *Why are you here on earth?*
Answer: *To behold.*
No excuses called for.
Contemplation. Seeing. Fierce and intense.

This majesty. This fullness.
Does it all foreshadow another Eden?
The air is laden with yearning.
I can't say for what and I can't be silent either.
Rejoice. Rejoice.
To attest the gift of a day.
To saunter and gaze. To own the world.

Invitation

Anywhere and always just as you expect it least,
Welling or oozing from nowhere a desire to feast.

At Auschwitz Wolf hums Brahms' rhapsody by heart
As Eddy, thief turned juggler, rehearses his art.

Fling and abandon, gaieties colourful and porous.
The Mexican beggar's skirt, an Araner's *crios*.

Irresistible laughter, hiss and giggle of overflow.
That black engine-driver crooning his life's motto:

'Paint or tell a story, sing or shovel coal,
You gotta get a glory or the job lacks soul.'

Abundance of joy bubbling some underground jazz.
A voice whispers: Be with me tonight in paradise.

Celebration

Once our days were years. Now years are days.
A guest glances a clock on a kitchen shelf
As though he'd suddenly woken from a daze:
It's gone so fast I must have enjoyed myself.

The tiniest ticks in glacial ages of stones
Or even less on crueller scales of stars;
A man with dreams of past and future zones
Loses a self in aeons of clocks and calendars.

Lines with loops of days or months or years.
We don't know how to begin to think of time:
Memory, expectation, our shy hopes and fears –
Easier to word the taste of mango with lime.

Which Native American people used to say:
We never come to time, it comes to us?
Unwind the clock and let it come as it may,
Turn or spiral, a plot thickening and viscous.

But image on image seems to return to one:
A medium in which our doings move, a continuity
Inscribed and cumulative, all done or undone,
A chain of traces across a fragile city.

Delicate filigree. Tables of face-to-faceness,
Years of talk and laughter's shooting star.
The healing moment mango and lime caress.
To choose to say we're glad we've come so far.

Expectation

Waiting for you it's all those years ago,
Flutters of courtship smile in your approach.
Is it the gypsy earrings, the enamelled broach,
Native amber beads I'd brought from Chicago?

Doublespeak of dress that hides and flirts.
Little hoists of ceremony: tilts of a cap,
Hints of calves fattening over an ankle strap.
A giddiness of feasting gathers in dusky skirts.

Delight

Let the meal be simple. A big plate
of mussels, warm bread with garlic,
and enough mulled wine to celebrate

Being here. I open a hinged mussel
pincering a balloon of plump meat
from the blue angel wings of a shell.

A table's rising decibels of fun.
Such gossip. A story caps a story.
Banter. Then another pun on a pun.

Iced yoghurt snipes at my temples.
My tongue matches a strawberry's heart
with its rough skin of goose-pimples.

Conversations fragment. Tête-à-tête,
a confidence passes between two guests.
A munch of oatcake thickens my palate.

Juicy fumes of a mango on my breath.
(A poem with no end but delight.)
I knife to the oblong host of its pith.

Wine sinks its ease to the nerve-ends.
Here are my roots. I feast on faces.
Boundless laughter. A radiance of friends.

Courtesy

1

I bring my basketful to serve
Our table. Everything mine is yours.
Everything. Without reserve.

Poems to which I still revert.
Gauguin. Matisse. Renoir's pear-shaped women.
Music I've heard. Blessed Schubert.

Ecstasies I'll never understand –
Mandelstam's instants of splendour, the world
A plain apple in his hand.

Lost faces. Those whose heirs
I was. My print-out of their genes,
Seed and breed of forbears.

Whatever I've become – courtesy
Of lovers, friends or friends of friends.
All those traces in me.

The living and dead. My sum
Of being. A host open and woundable.
Here I am!

2

Tiny as a firefly under the night sky,
We try to imagine stars that travel
Two million light years to reach the eye.

Long ago on a stormy and starless night
Old people used keep a half-door opened,
Anyone passing could make for the light.

The Russian cosmonauts leaving after them
Bread and salt for the next to dock
At the station. Small symbols of welcome.

Who's that outsider waiting for you?
We try to imagine how destinies unravel
Across the years towards their rendezvous.

A space for wanderers, lone or dispossessed.
At this table we've laid one empty place,
That old courtesy for the missing guest.

3

Never again just this.
Once-off. Ongoing wistfulness.
Wine loosening through my thighs.
Closeness. Our sudden huddle of intimacy.
These hours we're citizens of paradise.

A nourishment of senses.
Such fierce delight tenses
Between affections and the moments
When, like a theatre after its applause,
This house will fall again to silence.

Let gaieties outweigh
Their own misgivings. Emigré
And native, my desire attends
The moment in and out of time
Which even when it ceases never ends.

I feed on such courtesy.
These guests keep countenancing me.
Mine always mine. This complicity
Of faces, companions, breadbreakers.
You and you and you. My fragile city.

Dance

1 *Weaving*

So tables aside! Any dance at all.
I'd loved our flight from the formal.
Our broken observance. Rock and Roll.
The Twist. Disco. Sweet and manic,
Our blare of rapture. Alone. Freelance.
But I yearn again for ritual, organic
Patterns, circlings, the whorled dance.

Sweated repetitiveness of reels that grew
To their ecstasy. A shrug. Yelped *yeoo*.
Quadrilles without the high buckled shoe,
Ribboned wigs, swallow-tailed elegance
Of Napoleon's court or Paris ballroom,
Figures needling an embroidery of dance,
Chaine-de-dames. Fan and perfume.

More a passionate sameness than grace.
Hospitality. Feelings of inclusiveness
As we lined up there. Face to face.
Expectant. Keats's lovers in the gaze
Of a moment but ready to step it out
Across the swollen belly of a vase.
Tableaux of memory wake in that shout:

Take the floor! The first batoned tone
Of a *céilí* band. *The Mason's Apron.*
Humours of Bandon. The Bridge of Athlone.
A swing. A turn. The skipping march.
Limerick's Walls. The Siege of Ennis.
Side-step and stoop under the arch.
Our linked arms. A scent of dizziness.

Openness. Again and again to realign.
Another face and the moves must begin
Anew. And we unfold into our design.
I want to dance for ever. A veil
Shakes between now-ness and infinity.
Touch of hands. Communal and frail.
Our courtesies weave a fragile city.

2 *Play*

Is music a love-making? To dance in rhythm,
our bodies sharing these humours and fancies.

Low-necks. Just glimmers of beautiful limbs.
The changing and same ballet of intimacies.

Yet all that talk of 'playing with fire'.
The puritans have put us through our paces.

Dante's lustful shades were doing time,
relearning for eternity swift embraces.

This arm around my waist. That shoulder
leaning on mine the freight of its histories.

Blouses. Men with cummerbunds. The gleam
and sizzle of dresses. To glorify what is.

No matter what this dance will be here.
Blessed be its weavings and its intricacies.

O fragile city of my trust and desire!
Our glancings. No longer any need to possess.

Tiny dalliances. Middle ground of playfulness.
This dance shuffling our warmth as we pass.

3 *Glimpse*

A few are sitting this one out: spectators,
Thinkers on the outside, catching a glance
Of how the dancers turn like Plato's stars.

Dance in a cosmos, cosmos in the light of dance.
An ancient image, I know, stuff of visionaries:
Harmony, music of spheres, the mystic's trance.

The whirl of it! Barefaced and fluid boundaries,
I'm watching through a window, sipping iced beer
In the night air. Ripe images. Old quandaries.

To dance between infinites of quark and star,
Lost in a labyrinth we ourselves have planned.
Detached and involved. Half-god, half-creature.

Glimpse from a stillness beyond rhythm's command.
An inner stillness in the shifting views of dancers.
To stand under heavens you can never understand.

4 *High*

Rhythm of now. Now the beat.
Forever. Forever.
Our *qui vive* of listening feet.
Sweetest seizure.

Such ecstasies as maddened Corybants:
A *bodhrán's* crescendo,
Frenzy of bones knuckling the dance,
High wire of let-go.

A reel with all its plans. Drumbeat,
Steps or turns,
Stubborn ritual. Some dizzy heat
Of spirit yearns.

Forever. Forever. How to remember
In each move and pose
Even the music's pitch and timbre
Crave repose?

Leaps in an infinite womb. I yield.
The dance's yes
Teeters on the rim of Achilles' shield.
Vertigo of gladness.

Our Double Time

(1998)

For those voices within, my love and thanks.

Plus la joie est extrême et plus elle est fuitive;
Mais j'en garde portant la memoire si vive,
Que mon plaisir perdu n'est pas de tout passé.

The more extreme the joy, the more fleeting;
Yet even so I keep its memory so intensely
That for me a vanished pleasure never fades.

PHILIPPE DESPORTES

Rien de rien,
Je ne regrette rien,
Car ma vie,
Car ma joie
Aujourd'hui
Ca commence avec toi.

No nothing at all,
I regret nothing,
As my life,
As my joy
Today
Begins with you.

CHARLES DUMONT AND MICHEL VAUCAIRE
Sung by Edith Piaf

WAKINGS

O sleep, O gentle sleep,
Nature's soft nurse, how have I frightened thee,
That thou no more wilt weigh my eyelids down
And steep my senses in forgetfulness?

WILLIAM SHAKESPEARE
King Henry IV

Dream

Floating, downhill, dreamlike
Through a mind's laissez-faire
A boy free-wheels on a bike
His legs oaring in the air
Outwards, downwards, a rodeo
Of flings, whooshes in a flow.
Pedalling again, he launches
Into space. No hands. See.
Tiny inclinations of haunches
Steering his whims of energy.

One knee-jerking ironhorse,
Racing the tail wind of a bus,
He bends over the handlebars.
Vertigo. Some mad Pegasus.
Fingers curled on the brake.
Faster. Faster. And I wake.
Fifty years? Is it really me
Cycling and cycling? It seems
I lurch into a half reverie
Trying to hold on to dreams.

Hurtling. Reckless. Delirious.
The hot funnel of a wind-break
As the oily exhaust of a bus
Hugs and sucks him in its wake.
Full tilt. Headlong. Knock-kneed.
This frantic tunnel of speed.

Faster. Furiously. Jackknife
Limbs pedalling a slipstream
Of trance. Is this my life?

Faster. Faster. In a dream.
And do I ripen? Such aches
Of regret. Even so a joy;
Whatever endlessly re-awakes
That boy inside a boy
With the same expectant face
As in a slow bicycle race –
Brakes squeezed, front wheel
To one side and motionless –
Concentrates on some ideal
Poised on rims of a stillness.

Thief

This bed is so ancient and so knowing,
A history of tosses bears up squarely
Throes of lovemaking, coming and going.

I can't even imagine nothing. A vacuum?
My tinyness seems infinitesimal and vast,
A oneness of gone, of living and to come.

Our entries and exits, passion's caprice,
Naked trajectories across a bed of being;
Everything still somehow all of a piece.

But I love bodies. Their saps and juice.
The swished delight of silk against skin.
Tipping of tongues. Flickers that seduce.

O thief in the night, coward and faint-heart,
I tremble at old Dante's dolorous notes:
Naked you came in…and naked you depart.

Interrogation

Sudden panic. Old sweats of fright:
This one by one of moving up the line,
Stealthy generations forsake the light.

Have I lived at all? Or too engrossed
In *tournaments of hunchbacks*, too taken
With dreams, will I when we dead awaken
Cry again what's next to Plato's ghost?

Even in my terror one word will borrow
Another. That hum and relief of lines.
Tomorrow, then, another poem. Tomorrow.

At one remove of words. Old stratagem.
But the heart of night remains unmoved.
The chill interrogations of three a.m.:
What have you given? Who have you loved?

One tiny night in eternities of August
Drawn on the rack and screws of doubt.
And will you trust? And will you trust?

Turning

I turn to a woman's embrace.
A child is engrossed in play
In another time and place,
She sleeps miles away.
Her dreams, clouds that scud
Over cliff-tops of childhood
Summers, she stoops on a beach
To angle and skim a stone
Those years beyond my reach.
I think we're playing alone.

Solo. And so utterly apart.
A body still tosses and frets;
Secret gardens of its heart
Fill with dusky regrets.
Bittersweet. Half and half.
Sorrowed exuberance of Piaf.
Rien. A flamboyant lullaby.
Non, je ne regrette rien.
Nothing. But yes. I cry
For all that might have been.

For dunes of memory where
Silences of unuttered love
Hang, kestrels in mid-air,
Hovering delicately above
What might but couldn't be.
Rien de rien. Mais si!
Evenings etched in delight.
My boyhood's Dodder when
We watched in dying light
A stark and lone heron.

Small and hollow hours.
Errors. Pleasures forgone
That still haunt. Remorse
For all the things undone.
Must the end be so alone
As evening's heron on a stone?
A chill ordeal. And yet
Slow bleedings to be wise.
Even in shadows of regret
Am I grateful for what is?

Whenever

Those stiff-necked years when I'd woken.
Leveller? Reaper? Angel or night-thief?
Lingering? In fullness? How or when?

A reflex of vague childhood anxieties.
My mother ill and always on the verge.
Osmosis of worry. An ingrained unease.

Icy memories of such terrors inside me.
One evening when some older altar-boys
Ganged up to lock me in the mortuary.

Those grown-ups persuading me to touch
A body. Better to remember and forget.
Oozes of fear in my hand as I approach.

Little by little I might dare to palm
The forehead. With the years my panics
Lessen. Has old nature begun to calm

Me down or is it my friends who allow
This ease? I unclench into their warmth.
It doesn't seem to matter when or how.

Imagine no tenderness. To stand alone
In emptiness. A closing-off and down.
Slow desiccation to a core of stone.

The blank of having no one to love.
However. Whenever. And I tell myself
These are things to be afraid of.

One

Great Leveller. Azrael. Lord Pluto.
La Faucheuse. Sweeping and grand.
Was Donne right? *Thou art not so*.

More a humble boatman. Old Charon
Ferrying us singly across a river;
Just going, as we came, one by one.

Yearning. Longing leaving its trace.
One agony. One grief. A staring gap.
Unique memory of one enfolded face.

Surrender

Soon I'll begin to forget how often before
Furies of the tiny uncaring hours of night
Drove to despair. Face to wall. Heart-sore.
Everything zero. Nothing can imagine light.

Endless and narrow caverns of satin dark.
But those hauled back from the edge talk of
Gentle slippage in a tunnel towards an arc
Of light. A sort of carefree hovering above.

Will dark hollow spaces for a day that loves
All unforeseeable? A richer logic of surprise,
Like Rainer Maria's handful of tumbling doves
Thrown out of the caves of night at sunrise?

To give in and up. So, just to yield, let go.
A time in love-making when you know that soon
You'll surrender, go sweetly with the flow
In mellow concentrated moments of a swoon.

A child is floating to sleep across a bedroom
Towards the night-lamp a mother once left lit;
A half-remembered leave-taking from another womb
Funnelling down to what's open and indefinite.

Nightmare

Was it an anger as I began to search
That morning I lost you on a street?
Could you just leave me in the lurch?

All I'd taken for granted rived apart.
Panics. Nightmares of loss. I reel.
To search. But where even to restart?

Imagine winding years where the lines
Of memory no longer lead to a present
Or a future. An ache sinks and resigns

Like a Piaf crying within. *Mon Dieu,*
For me to prove that I still care...
The time we... the days so few.

Thought and imagination out of phase,
I keep on saying things to an absence
As if my body mimes itself in a daze.

Look! You're there! Flash of affection;
A window you'd dallied to see, you say,
Joking, laughing in your resurrection.

Joy. My delight gliding in an embrace
Of warm connivance. *Mon Dieu, mon Dieu*
Just one day. Eternities of your face.

Everything. Everything I'm capable of.
O fallenness fallen short of fullness.
To know I'll never have loved enough.

Thread

At dawn I'm leafing a biography of Sigrid Undset.
A thread of her being travels portrait to portrait.

That childlike look caught glancing towards the lens.
Already her shy half-smile. Woundable and intense.

Or Mademoiselle in her hat, just a little perplexed.
It's as if each picture wants to foreshadow the next.

Then, the woman steady and sure in her womanhood
I gaze at, absorbing the warmth she seems to exude.

Different and the same. Something lovely and elusive
Constant in her face like a promise she has to give.

A woman who loves and is loved is always beautiful.
The lineaments ripened. Broad and mild and whole.

Journeys of *Kristin Lavransdatter* or *Olav Audunssøn*
To a last achievement. For this everything a preparation.

A frame left blank. That ambiguity of empty space
Where we must imagine final obediences of a face.

Twofold

Fit. Summered. Thoughtful. Balanced. Urbane.
Broken as a reed in bending humiliations of pain.

Has a world ever been so carefree, so debonair,
That morning you fetched me from Intensive Care?

Trees, touch of your hand, colours of your blouse,
Snatches of street-talk, hues of a pink-bricked house.

A first walk in the garden linking you my Eve;
Your body as it curved to pick up a fallen leaf.

Richer and richer and richer. My endless paradise.
But more than to seize the day, to hold it twice!

A moment doubly relishing its tang and flavour.
Once just to taste and then once more to savour.

Folded intensity of living in the light of mortality.
And yes! half of what we love is love's fragility.

Will this morning be that morning all over again?
Coward that I am, I still praise. Amen. Amen.

Looped awareness vibrates like a twofold rhyme.
Sweet density. And I want to live in double time.

Sweep

Years sneak up on me like other people's children.
Pinch yourself, Van Winkle! Where have you been?

What have you been doing? Whistling in the dark?
Scraping and scratching, anything to leave a mark?

That which is done is that which shall be done
And there is no new thing under the sun.

Vanity of vanities. A history's whim and vagary.
Most of Sophocles burnt in Alexandria's library.

Long rises and falls of empire and great cities.
Again the preacher's clamour: *vanity of vanities.*

Vertigo of an overview. Too far above and beyond.
Old temptations to take the high road and abscond.

In vast reaches and weaves of history my own knot.
Gentle and alert. Just that one ligature in the plot.

The nodes and ties and textures of time's sweep.
Choices made. A kiss given. Promises I keep.

Will this livelong day be long enough for love?

Somebody

I remember a friend's decline we grieved;
The way I'd dreaded the last leave-taking,
How that face gave more than it received.

Lingerings and draggings of a slow end.
I can fear the throes more than the going.
Who'll love me? Who'll be my friend?

But some woman somewhere is my daughter,
Her presence bending so carefully over me
Dabs and gentles my forehead with water.

That somebody is waiting to be my son,
That this face of mine calls out to him:
In my fall am I still lovable for someone?

Dread

Just imagine growing old and dour.
Unrecognised genius with his grudges.
Chips and gnawings. A private rage
Of half-envies that fester and sour.

Young transgressions are flings of bliss
Beside such nursed or bitter umbrages,
The brooded resentments of old age.
That, Donne knew, was the real abyss.

I ripen now daily beyond my prime.
A fiftieth year. The sap and juice
Slow, thicken and fix in concentration.
All the more I live in double time.

A precarious joy. The tear and let-rip,
Sweet compulsions, obsessive innovation,
As Madam Jazz improvises to seduce
One heart still glorying in its courtship.

More than anything I think I dread
The set jawbone of grim resignation.
Nothing to expect. Nothing to discover.
The sullen greyness of the living dead.

I go when I go. Let me go a lover.

Passivity

All those nights I woke in dread.
Francis Thompson found dead;
A poem he'd begun, a scribbled note

326

Shoved in the pocket of an overcoat.
Thoughts he thought he might forget.
First gropings for a line. And yet
It seems with hindsight by design
The perfect ending to his storyline.

Closure is foreclosure. Even so
Lives take aim despite the shadow
Of disjunctions or a sudden breach.
The arrow's curve may never reach
Its fullest arc and fall too soon,
Its aim and journey out of tune,
An end discordant with its story,
Narrative of nameless broken glory.

The chance and story integrate,
A plot transmuting chance to fate.
There's so much to be grateful for.
Broken youths of plagues or war,
Whole generations went *en masse*.
And I was blessed. I made a pass
At Madam Jazz and she said yes.
Our love-making just to acquiesce,

To glide and let the sleeve unravel,
Allowing it simply be. I travel
Like Proust: a touch, a scent, a sound,
Both past and present now refound,
Necklace of moments rich and twofold,
Silver and onyx, garnet and gold.
To leave the arrow trace its arc.
To trust the jazz of Madam's dark.

Flickers of foreplay before foreplay,
Notes and scraps of things to say,
And fifty years in a fragile city
Gather sweet nothings of passivity.
The tune and jazz become the plot.
O wise psalmist who knew how not
To try to overview or even understand:
Madam, *My times are in thy hand.*

Rehearsals

Those giddy piggyback rides we called 'broncos'.
Giggling charges, feigned bucking and neighing.
I plead in half-light 'O Father let's keep playing!'
'All right,' he said, 'Then just three more goes.'

Passion's careless caring for a man so carefree.
I travel the universe of Kristin Lavransdatter
As scene by scene her life worms into me,
Making mine whatever time had taught her.
Somehow a story's contours shape my own.
All her desire, her grudges, her joy, her conviction.
Year in, year out it almost seems I've grown
Through her, as if I've been apprentice to a fiction.
I watch with her, struggling, lingering heroine,
As she takes off the wedding ring she entrusts
To her friend and glimpses a finger's scarred skin
Where love had made its mark beyond its lusts.
So silence and a piercing light. I was there.
Rehearsal and preview for one grand première.

Antigone's sisterhood, Creon's rigid city.
And gods egging on that mix of choice and fate
As a chorus admonishes us in terror and pity:
'You've learned justice, although it comes too late.'
Antigone distraught embraces her bridal tomb,
Stern Creon, a man so stunted in his growth.
'Any greatness in a human life brings doom,
Rigid citizen and sister.' And am I both?
Heroine and hero. Part and counterpart.
My Antigone hankers after perfect dreams.
In Creon I cry: 'O crimes of my wicked heart!'
Antigone bereft. Antigone departed in her prime.
Like Lazarus, I return to live in double time.

Giddy up! Giddy up! I spur my bucking bronco,
Shoulder-high and giggling for all I'm worth.
Redoubled delight of only one more go.
My father lowering me gently back to earth.

Snow

Born before the snow began;
Flurries I keep imagining I can
See, those drifts of '47
Still shaping an image of heaven.
Every winter some migrant within
Always wants to renew, a pigeon
Homing northward; again I'll go
Back to the hush of a first snow.

Cross-country limbs soon ease
Hitting the metred stride of skis.
Muffs on wires, a skull on a spike,
Snow sculptures in the featherlike
Porous fluff of last night's fall.
Glints and winks of crystal recall
Children once bending in delight,
Gathering diamonds in the sunlight.

Shush! Shush! Shush! Shush!
Steady rhythmic stab and push.
Long-haul, *langlauf,* overland,
Sweated opiate in a pituitary gland,
Heel uplifts and the foot shove;
Somewhere a gleam hovers above
Body and limb; my spirit's glow
Floats and drifts in endless snow.

Here I loom just over the track.
Time is doubling on and back,
What was or will be taken up
Into this moment's flowing cup.
Old woman plucking her goose,
Eternity falls unbidden as spruce
Branches give up sudden intense
Sifts of snow. A dusted silence.

So, will it be like this to yield
Up the spirit? Over a snowfield,
Breath and élan, whatever is me
Unenveloped, a soaring energy,

Self expressed in another equation
Slowly retuning incarnation,
Insider outside, dazzled and finite
Riding this shaft of piercing light.

OUT OF EDEN

Denn wir sind nur die Schale und das Blatt.
Der großen Tod, den jeder in sich hat,
das ist die Frucht, die sich alles dreht.

But we're merely the skin and the leaf.
The grand death one has inside oneself
Is the fruit on which everything turns.

RAINER MARIA RILKE

Sunday Morning *Chez La Masseuse*

Muscles unkink, all my frettings a dough
Kneaded to ease. A mother of so long ago
Folds and presses the damp, podgy flour,
Leans and rolls and flattens. A whole hour
Sinks, child's play in flesh of remembrance.
My heart slows. Not sleep, more a trance.
She pulls and stretches every toe in turn;
Piecemeal a body learns how to unlearn.

One little piggy went to the market and one
Little piggy stayed at home and I've begun
To slip back past the angel's flaming sword.
Mother is tucking pastry, the apples cored
And sliced, she sprinkles flour over the table.
Cain hasn't yet stalked his brother Abel
And I had never scaled the orchard wall
To steal the apple. This is before the Fall.

A garden eastward in Eden before fig-leaf
Or apron, these the soothing hands of Eve
Rub camomile oils on my temples, caress
My brows, smooth me back to timelessness.
Palms clap and pat the blood up to the skin.
Swoon of well-being. What can I know of sin?
Here in the land of bdellium and onyx stone
I live forever in this sweet flesh and bone.

Towels pleated around me limb by limb
Like pastry doubled over the dish's rim,
She prods a knot in me she tries to undo,
A fork pricking a tart to let air through.
Shakes of powder, scented and featherweight
As a pinch of flour strewn on the oven plate.
The mind fidgets but let the body obey
A finger-tip swishing along my vertebrae.

Palms of oil ooze across my shoulder blade.
A warmth of water bottles wrapped and laid
Under a towel seeps up towards my midriff.
This animal plenitude as if, as if, as if
I'd never bitten the apple or didn't know.
Now is enough. Enough to be. To mellow.
So unashamed and naked, at home in my clay.
Paradise unearned. And still the seventh day.

Hale-Bopp

I watch your face; still an amazed and desolate
Eve on her first night outside of Eden's gate.

'A star with headlights,' you say, 'a comet that nears
Earth once in four thousand, four hundred years.'

One gritty snowball of hurtling dust and ice
Offers a sun its luminous two-tailed sacrifice.

Yet our warm bodies feel some need to soar.
A swooning infinite mind. The worm at the core.

Across the aeons our stars still wink and beckon.
Why did we bite the apple and learn to reckon?

Cherished ambitions, burning fame and fall.
And so fragile against the majesty of it all

Our tails of light. Do the frail bones of our story
Matter to a cosmos? Even our bruised glory

Dreams of meaning, our secret hero cravings
To count a little, to weigh in the scale of things.

Radiance of a look, a smile, a voice, a name,
Some print-out of infinity in this brittle frame

Flashes. A sudden caress. A squeezed hand.
Just our fondled moment held and spanned.

A trust caught in the orbit of one embrace.
Nothing so lovely, so lonely as a human face.

Spending

Intensities of one tiny fragile sojourn.
A comet's tail blazed, a face that shone.
All a being's throughput. We burn. We burn.

Those steely words still there to haunt;
Twenty years a-growing, twenty in bloom,
Twenty failing, twenty to hardly count.

A tape of genes plays out its master-plan.
Wear and ravages. Cells' subtle attunement.
The price of such adapting, our human span.

So what. So what. A son's prodigal return
To paradise. Just to spend a life being spent
By life, privilege of some Eden we re-earn.

Scarrings, those arteries that narrow and crust,
Unspoken sorrows that widen a heart's room,
Pinions and springs of a body begun to rust.

Even in broken goings, do we shape and adjust
Those lives we touched? A handing over and on.
Something enhanced, a world now left in trust.

Orchard

1

Once the gardener took us with him on his rounds
To show us fruit trees, the neat gravelled pathways,
Plums and greengages, walls with their wire stays,
That sunlit orchard which was always out of bounds.

'Let's box the fox,' the second-former had said,
'Give's a leg up.' We clambered a pink orchard wall,
Then tugged at branches to get those apples to fall.
'Nix! The gardener!' We pocketed a few and fled

Down the narrow laneway at the back of the chapel
Into the field with the big ditch where our gang
Had built a fort. Do I imagine I recall some tang
Of regret as I bite into that bitter unripe apple?

2

First go around, it seemed enough to succumb
To the telling, wonder how a plot would unfold,
A one-way journey towards whatever outcome.
But is a story richer the second time it's told,
And beginnings subtler seen in the light of an end?
A knowing ferments in us, a ripening enzyme,
A looped story where the start and finish blend,
Two-way traffic, a sort of doubling up of time.
In limits of vanishing life, a radiance of a whole,
As if our own plots thicken because we know
We're born to die and the worm is already turning
Deep in the core of those apples we once stole.
Are we what we are in what we long for, as though
Orchards lost shape the orchards of our yearning?

3

Once the gardener took us with him on his rounds
To show us fruit trees, the neat gravelled pathways,
Plums and greengages, walls with their wire stays,
That sunlit orchard which was always out of bounds.

And were there really those miles and miles between
Endless rows of apple trees or against the pink wall
Plums so richly purple or the greengages so green?
'So here, young fellow, you can eat this windfall!'

Now, what is it in that taste I think I still remember?
The gardener is opening a gate beside a conservatory
And everything stands still, suffused in a September
That casts some slanted light across my history.

Ageing

1

What's this new inwardness of our middle years
Poised between that hope and our remembrance?
For all the ambition, gnawings and strife of careers,
Beginnings of recollection, the backward glance?
For the young it isn't memory or the long recall:
Everything forwards, aims and plans and hope,
Our unbroken prime clambered an orchard wall,
Fresh and hungry for the full venture and scope.
So even the will to endure grows meditative,
Turning from the fire to slower gentler embers
As we recollect our once uncollected childhood,
A going with it, some ease of live and let live;
In the cumulative weight of what a heart remembers,
Things tipped in a scale of yearning and understood.

2

It wasn't the devil-may-care bit or even the folly
Of so much of what we did, but more the way
We just espoused a kind of cavalier melancholy:
And does it all mean nothing? One long decay.
But broken down, backed up against nothing,
Emptied, then came that shock of second sight.
That all might be well? How hard I had to cling
To a rumour, a desire, a single welling delight.
And now it's both. Almost as if I'm possessed
By a strange northern rhythm that sways the heart,

One of those long wistful folk-tunes from Sweden
When you imagine low-lit miles of spruce forest
Where darker joys absorb a wishful counterpart
And you know you've begun a slow return to Eden.

3

The apple bitten and that quick damp kiss,
Such moments tasted or moments overjoyed,
Happening after happening, this then this,
Moments follow moments and sink into a void.
All shift and turnover but somehow still traced
In remembrance or held in a long unbroken vow.
One kiss recalled, that recollected aftertaste,
Each memory and hope woven in a dying now.
Does a seed cast in the ground change creation?
Even as it passes every moment still banishes
Brokenness, sows a deeper yearning for duration.
Something won't just vanish with what vanishes,
As though a moment outpaces its own fleeing.
Yearning light shines through my broken being.

Knowing

Somehow freedom must always be a knowing.
In this knowing our yearning. A stick is bowing
Again and again that mazurka-like leitmotiv,
A Swedish folk-tune which turns its joy to grief
Then doubles back to resurrect a double joy.
Falling semitones that seemed at first to alloy
A line with doubt burnish some perfect desire,
As though knowing to what our hearts aspire,
Praise whatever muse called us into a being
Where in every coming we're already fleeing.
So agonisingly unique we are and yet to know
That brokers in this process we too must go
Quickly as the painted lady's fluttered days.
And yet so beautiful. Promises in a lover's gaze,
Giggling children, candle-light in a wine carafe,

The sumac's crimson leaves, a friend's laugh,
Rings on fingers, laburnums' clustered racemes,
How in recollected moments, the way in dreams
We play a play of belonging and not belonging
And know that knowing is just our naked longing
In face of all our frailty. An infinity of laughter
Hangs between the orchards of before and after,
Our endless yearning among things that sunder.
A majesty and awe, but even more the wonder
That something is where nothing might have been.
Even in our brokenness a beyond is breaking in.

What If?

1

After deep honey-like sleep I sometimes sense,
As I think I did as a child, everything is given;
I'm waking once more to worlds of munificence
Before barter, trade-offs, hard bargains driven.
Sun and shadow. Yet a chosen innocence prevails,
A kind of delight in open-handedness, a Maecenas
Garden of bestowal. Some lavish lop-sided scales.
Business is business but things go deeper in us.
Giving birth or heart or giving up the ghost.
All this expenditure at our core. I'm sure I've
Begun slowly to understand how the spendthrift
By some paradox keeps growing richer, almost
As though the more we give the more we thrive,
Our loss-leaders in delicate economies of gift.

2

Often no more than a glimpse. Just a side glance
At a passer-by and yet that sense of a life-span
Rerun in flashback. Is it an aura? A radiance?
This frail nobility in the gaze of one old man.
You know for sure you knew him once as a child
So fresh-skinned, eager, that first day he outran
His father. You remember how his father smiled,

A sort of flash forward to this passing ageing man.
Moments double and never again can you escape
A feeling that in a stranger's face a light is thrown
On all your hopes and memories, even things rued,
On some unique story your life is trying to shape
This journey to whatever end will be our own.
Small and bereft. Full and glorious in our finitude.

3

For some that fear of rivalries, of eye for eye,
Coheres us, and whatever goaded Cain to slay
We exorcise in scapegoat rituals, as if we rely
On victims to unite us and keep feuds at bay.
For others all the checks and controls; of course,
If it comes to the push, then, always the stronger.
Cohesion of threat, weights and balances of force.
Can it really be, I wonder, so simple any longer?
I know the layers of things unconscious or hidden,
How in our brokenness we travel from dust to dust.
And still. And still. Those times push came to shove
From nowhere that warm embrace, the hug of trust.
There's some bigger engine unbiddable and unbidden.
What if, I ask, what if the only rhyme is love?

Whatever Else

How it is, how long they reckon it may be.
When my time comes, tell me straight.
Please, no fudging or playing along with me.

Earthling that I am, forgive me if I shrink
In dread, rage, refuse or despair.
For all my talk, forgive my shying at the brink

Of this darkest leap of trust my life achieves.
To yield before the mind can know.
Imagine an apple tree that fruits before it leaves.

Remind me of images that in their shortfall gave
Some inkling of what remains beyond me:
How energies of a particle re-feature as a wave

Or how our music of being, though made in time,
Keeps on resolving beyond its silence,
Architecture of flux, both transient and sublime.

Tell me while there's still the time to mend
Breaches or even ask for pardon.
Whatever else please for my sake don't pretend.

Just tell me gently. Then, love me to the end.

But If

I imagined a gentle courtship: a widowed magistrate,
The younger hospital doctor with her quiet confidence.
The risked dignities of some first tentative date.

How the darings of intimacy would throw their bridge
Over so much before her. I wonder did she hesitate?
The accruals of companionship. Time's slow brokerage.

She couldn't have been that much older than his son?
Now this crucible. And when I admired her courage
She smiled as though to say: *But if you love someone...*

Those strange things begin to happen that perhaps
At first were just shrugged off. Hints of oblivion,
Oversights, non sequiturs, a blotting out, a lapse.

From the start she'd known the onset, how bereft
Of certain nervecells the mind begins its collapse,
Those transmissions fizzling out in a brain's weft.

Rocking. Ceaseless walking. A pitiful restlessness.
Outbursts. The day he suddenly accuses her of theft.
Now even unable to remember his own forgetfulness.

Can a heart still deny what the intellect must know?
The apple is bruised to the core. A piecemeal progress
To childishness. This long roundabout way to go.

Small relentless slides towards some twilight zone.
Her lover and friend. So then, the cruellest blow:
A mind roaming a youth she couldn't have known.

Odd flashes when she knows he senses her presence.
Moments when a heart outweighs Sisyphus' stone.
An unbroken love still hostage to this living absence.

Three Wishes

1

A good leaving. This moment I try to rehearse,
But will it come the way I've least expected?
Unfulfilled desires, dreams I needed to nurse
Left undone? Regrets? Energies misdirected?
For all the beauty of what's brittle and finite
I'm loathe to go. So heal what can be healed.
Beyond that, kindly don't spin out my fight.
However well meant, I think I'd want to yield.
That long corridor of light or is it the glare
Of those cherubims' daggers? I fear my agony.
Ease, then, whatever pain, gentle me toward
Eden's gate, just hold me as slowly I prepare
To let nature's blade have its way with me,
To fall softly on my angel's blazing sword.

2

All those rituals trying to ease a departure:
Opening windows, wakes, keenings, devout
Observance of old ways that seemed to reassure
The living, to appease a spirit travelling out.
The same crying need for patterns, some way
To cope with our bafflement, just the relief
Of routines, customs, things to do or say,
Fragile ceremonies shaping a space for grief.
But for me only the plainest rites of farewell.

Nothing elaborate. Maybe a meal you'll share,
Some recollecting, a little time for reassessing
How places will be reset around our table,
The half-dozen words of that Jewish prayer
I love: *May his memory be for a blessing.*

3

That some will depart early, others wait till late.
One by one by one. That someone will be first
Among contemporaries who wove each other's fate.
And someone lone and last. Is that the worst?
For all its doubling my time is still an arrow,
Something I know yet can't quite comprehend;
That my sacred friends too will leave and go,
That even a plot's richest moments will end.
Will there be those still able to tell the story,
A few to recall how my chapters were numbered,
Or how in the light of an end to begin to frame
Some overarching design, this life's trajectory,
Someone to shape out of the silence an afterword,
Or to say this was one narrative's perfected aim?

Ambition

A week or two after my stint in intensive care
An elderly woman across from me on the bus
Flashed a smile. But had she a knowing stare?
Her deep clear eyes still so warm and sensuous,

As she leant over to whisper and clasp my hand?
Only we, she said, who've had our share of trouble,
Who go to the edge and return, ever understand
How precious time is. Everything we do is double.

I imagined her as some young *cœur d'artichaut*,
Her generous spirit bestowing what gifts it can,
A once lavish Eve, all favours and overflow,
An artichoke heart with her leaf for every man.

And when I smiled back, I think I thought I knew
How precious it was. Golden beyond all measure.
But then my goals and ambitions, so much to do.
Where are garnet days you promised to treasure?

That elderly woman, I'm sure, is long since dead.
The pat of a hand, a glancing caress, and here I'm
Recalling her touch, and how she'd smiled and said,
You're too young, you'll forget our double time?

Her hand stroked my cheek lovingly as she passed.
What is or will be? Which is the sweetest one?
The paradox of a day that's both our first and last,
To live will be to have things we'll leave undone.

Trio

1 *Millennium*

Evening on an eleventh-floor balcony at Poitiers.
There at the horizon Charles Martel would win
Against the Saracens in 732. I seem to survey
All time since Eden and my head begins to spin.
Arab children are playing in a courtyard below
As I lean over to watch. What goes around comes
Around. The future reels, one endless vertigo
Of coming and going. Do we count in millenniums?
In an opposite block a neighbour is lighting a candle
On a table she has reverently laid. A giddy devil
Says cast yourself down from the temple. Somehow
The old steeplejack in me still manages to handle
This dizziness, as fixing my eyes at my own level,
I keep on gazing lovingly into this here and now.

2 *Recorder*

Some uniqueness of self I think I need to prove.
A trying too hard, some virtuoso inner strife,

The world kept at bay in musics of one remove,
A kind of holding on to Eden for dear life.
Strange how that holding becomes a letting go
And sounds of a woodwind plays low and tender,
A tenor saxophone, the slow penetrating oboe
Or a recorder most myself in a self-surrender?
And the utter fragility of every passing note,
Our world of grails, things mortal and makeshift.
O my Elsa never ask from where! A Lohengrin
I too have to return in that swan-drawn boat.
All said and done, is everything love's gift?
I clean, I tune and wait until I'm blown in.

3 *Nocturne*

Chopin keeps playing such longing in my heart.
The first climbing roses are nearly full-blown,
The huge yellow glory of the St John's wort
Shines another's memories, become your own.
And o so easily in this garden I could falter,
Suddenly so rife with recollection and desires,
Forget-me-nots you picked for the Virgin's altar,
Lupin pods played with, the orange-streaked iris.
May and June. Already a July is taking stock.
This is our double time and now riper August,
A nocturne in E flat minor is a season turning
Towards the lily and black-blooded hollyhock;
A slower regained paradise of unbroken trust,
A music grown richer in disciplines of yearning.

Dated the Fourth Day of April

Here signed, published and declared by the said
M.O'S in the presence of us who at his request...
I'd put it off and off. I suppose some dread,
A signing up for mortality years suppressed.

Worse still Esau, Adam's quarrelsome breed,
Mess of pottage or squabbled-over heirloom.
So here just fifty, at last I am doing the deed.
Pausing a moment in the solicitor's anteroom,

Through a window I see a secretary on a phone
Smiling and gesturing as if to say 'I understand';
Someone down the line hears mimes in her tone,
How she blushes or cribs her face with one hand.

Shades of inner conversations with the absent,
Those long-distance callers laying it on the line:
'If I were you...' O my voices forever present
I listen and ponder. Those mentors always mine.

Today there's some past subjunctive in the air.
Hereby revoking former wills and testamentary
Dispositions, this the last will... If I were there,
This is what I'd like to say. Can you hear me?

I give, devise and bequeath my residuary estate
To hold the same or proceeds of sale thereof...
A strange solemn language stumbles to celebrate
Listings of these final tangible signals of love.

Goods and chattels, whatever I'll leave behind,
To some friends with whom my heart is smitten.
In witness thereof I have hereunto signed
My name, the day and year first above written.

Triptych

1

Voices on telephones, screen messages keyed in,
Letters in cyberspace, belongings of mobility.
Each stranger's open face. For us then no Eden,
Just the dared and chosen fragilities of love's city.
Was it easier to leave worlds numinous and staid,

Neighbours who'd trace seed, breed and generation,
Plunged churn-dash or the narrow ridging spade,
Implements sweated on, fondled and passed on?
There's my mother regal in her morning bed:
Another Davin gone, may he rest in peace.
Births, deaths, marriages. That suburban wife
With Tipperary genes, arms fathoming to spread
And refold her newspaper along its resisting crease,
Facing squarely the whole broadsheet of her life.

2

Our neat divisions: birth, bestowal and decease.
I think of an old man telling a college researcher
How the fabric of existence was all of a piece,
Just one seamless garment of nature and nurture.
Was it a kind of frisson that first time I read
How those young girls in Madagascar sang
About labour pains as they buried their dead?
The opening of tomb-cave and the birth pang.
A flow renewing itself. The boisterous and rife
Wake games, the Bara burials that seem to flaunt
Our parlour rites, a dance's giggles and screams
Circling in a tense double time of rewound life;
Horseplay, bawdy refrains and sexual taunts;
Our being's folded cloth touching at extremes.

3

I wonder is it youth's brimming urge to divide
Their world from ours, as if the great leveller
Sealed us from them? Our side and the other side.
Have all the boundaries already started to blur?
The hallowed we learn from, tiny gestures inbred,
Doppelgänger of the mind, ghosts in the genes,
Our hero figures, those friends who went ahead,
Those fluttered spirits shuttling go-betweens.
Maybe the shades draw us slowly in their wake
Or deep down in me a flame has begun to waver
As little by little those spirits become our peers
And the darkly-seen-through glass less opaque.
Weights of memory shift gently in their favour.
Some need to name the gone grows with years.

NAMINGS

Tapestry

That they should simply vanish. Could that be?
A great divide. Cessation. An absolute cut-off.
Somehow they still encompass and transfigure me.

And so to ponder again rituals of our ancients.
Skull in the rafters. Urned bones. Or nearer us,
Pilgrims travelling barefoot to graves of saints.

Our shapers always with us. Hovering. Hands off.
Both here and hereafterwards. Shuttling spirits,
Invisible negotiations in hints and traces of love.

An embrace. A caress. Just the memory of a kiss.
Tiny dovetailed threads in tapestries of being.
An eternity or two to unravel an inch of this.

The moment of a single weft. The time of quasars.
Be with me now all beloved and bequeathed gone.
I must grow older among my saints and stars.

Glory to the fallen, all gone on,
And what loves refuse oblivion,
So loomed and knotted in a history,
Textures shuttled through in me.
My women loved, the fathers sought,
All movers, shakers of my thought.

A music heard, the good word said,
Wound in the tensions of a thread:
Complex now the pattern and design,
My friends who grew so slowly mine
And the more mine, even though you
Looped around and out of view.
The pull and ease of every thread,
Traffic between my living and my dead,
Behind in hidden warps of tapestry
The loved and gone are steadying me.
In all the daily weft and stain,
Ridge in my fabric, still the grain,
Though long woven over and undergone,
Glory to the fallen, all gone on.

So many lives gone on, woven into history.
Combed and subsumed. So many unnamed to whom
We owe the achieved or changed. Small refinements,
Picks of threads gathered into one tapestry
Of time. Minutiae. Infinite detail of obedience.
Painstaking millennia over a low-warp loom.

How we count in light-years for so little.
Of course, our high and mighty youth said no.
Black hole of despair. Meaningless whirlabout.
Let the gone be gone! Words too dry and brittle
Had begun to falter. Nib of ecstasy peters out.
A last breaking down. An emptying out of ego.

Only again to learn the inching tempo of creation.
No longer the darks or sudden hankered ecstasy,
Some steadier love makes all us weavers peers,
A surety in praise, sweated delight of vocation.
In just two hundred and twenty-five million years
Our sun revolves once around the centre of a galaxy.

Nothing and everything. Blind journeys to perfection.
Those Beauvais tapestries, their grain close and fine –
Up to forty threads an inch. Now humble and sharp,
This nib earns its slower ecstasies of reflection.
In mirrors lowered through a still unwoven warp,
The weaver's tilted glimpses of ripening design.

Promise

All bodies turn and turn about their axis:
Moons around planets, planets around a sun,
And suns around the centre of their galaxies.

In all this time and motion, again one face
Smiles and breaks the childish heart of a son.
Mother, why that smile whenever we'd embrace?

Promise? I ask, promise you'll only be mine?
You smile your smile: O there'll be many women,
All those stars to which you'll take a shine.

And is that child a young man, stoic and brave,
Who'll fling a white rose and watch its petals
Scattering like a dwarf star over your grave?

Or that young man this greying, trusting Thomas,
No hand in wounds, just glimpsing in every face
Traces of a woman smiling at that cry of promise?

Planets, moons, suns, galaxies, expanding space.
So small in hugeness, so huge my desire. Promise?
O promise a meaning in the promise of each face?

I smile your smile and know how you were right.
In your absence never before so present in me.

An exploded star still travels down its light.

Revenant

(i.m. David Greene)

They had gone forever into the great uncharted.
But the longer gone, the closer now they seem.
Shades and revenants. All my hallowed departed.

Deep, so deep again a single voice in me;
Sudden sweeping advices of his fatherhood,
Wide-browed, loud and bearded bonhomie.

Why were the fathers I'd choose so sonless?
Or in their sonlessness did they choose me?
Whatever. Enough to be grateful. To bless

A bulky presence that hovers and chortles again.
An endless urge to explain, to chart, to share.
His expansive tone when I talk to younger men;

Wonder if they can hear that boyish loneliness
In his heir, the quiet maimings of a childhood
Saying some no that keeps on becoming yes.

Yes and Yes. For all the wounds a celebrant.
But in our sonlessness always still your son.
We travel side by side, my lonesome revenant.

Rubato

(i.m. Caitlín Maude)

Here I am once more colloguing with her shadow.
Remember a nineteen-year-old callow, awe-struck?
Surges and *tremolos* of song, passionate bravado
That must soon consume her. My Piaf of Rosmuck.

A life drawn down on accounts always overdrawn.
Pageboy fringe and that singer's vulnerable gaze
Lamenting *Barbara Allen* or *The Rocks of Bawn*.
That I should be the one to survive those days?

Death has never danced so close to me before.
Youthful passion. A fling. Loneliness. A lust.
The blind led the blind in our need to explore.
That I should be the one to walk in her dust?

Rubato. Life wavered in intensities of a trill.
And it would be the first warm weekend in June
We'd lay her bones in the clay of a Dublin hill.
Rien de rien. O that defiant and giddy tune.

Non. No regrets. Yet still a desire to lament.
A blossom dropped so stealthily in full bloom.
A star flared and faded across the firmament.
A thread stretched and pegged, a warp in a loom.

Who'd guess which of us would outlive our youth?
Her songs still croon in my bones. A hum. A buzz.
Me the survivor. May I grow wiser for us both?
Everything that happens must happen as it does.

Etty Hillesum

Here goes. A two-year diary close-knit and small.
A match for most of life's problems
But deep down something like a tightly-wound ball

Of twine binds me relentlessly and at times I'm
No more or less than a frightened creature
Refusing to climb to the future one step at a time.

Amsterdam, November Tenth, Nineteen Forty-One:
Mortal fear in every fibre.
Complete collapse. Lack of confidence. Aversion.

Everything so heavy in me. I want to feel light.
I've taken from mankind and given nothing
Back. Sometimes I feel as though I'm a parasite.

A journal unselfing the self. Advices. A caveat.
Reprimands. Talkings to. 'Come on my girl!'
'Don't overdo it, Etty' or 'Never forget that!'

No swoons or wallowings. No earth-shaking thought.
Some sort of clarity through your work
For others. And that's what it's really about.

A heart big and anxious is beginning to unzip.
The turned down bed, the orchid spray.
Our desire must be like a slow and stately ship.

During these months something had matured in me,
All I'd to do was let it flourish.
Just to have grown enough to accept my destiny.

Every pretty blouse I put on a kind of celebration.
I feel so light and radiant and cheerful.
In suffering we share our loss with all creation.

No admittance to Jews. The air I breathe is mine.
That man cycling on Beethovenstraat,
His yellow star of David a crocus in the sunshine.
Such ripening strength. Gone the Bohemian waif.
I want to be there at every front.
I don't ever want to be what they'll call 'safe'.

Forty years later, indelibly that diary will stain
A mind's cloth. Slow-release epic
She'd dreamed of making, a postcard flung from a train

Window as moving out of transit it began its pull
To Auschwitz. We left the camp singing.
A poem whole in its interruption. So given. So full.

I can see the lopped-off tops from where I lie.
Ack-ack fire and filaments of light catch a tree
Bare and forked, glistening daggers at the sky.
A joy or a vanity that these two men can love me?
Tissues of voice whose chambers and depths beckoned,
Some human warmth took me over. And *homo sum*...
I pass from the arms of one to those of a second.
And what sort of person are you, Etty Hillesum?
Under the night sky all my tendernesses poured out,
Everything unspoken even to those whom you love.
Overflow of overflow. From all the caves of doubt
This heart thrown up like Rilke's tumbling dove.
Such cries of my body and spirit struggle to mesh.
Off-balance. Out of depth. Saint and star of flesh.

A kiss. A breath that passes through us both.
Delicious moment. Our lips pursed, then slack,
Sipping the quick dampened textures of a mouth.
That and no more, this ecstasy of holding-back.
A blitz of insight and all is suddenly clearer:
I mustn't yearn to spend a whole life with him.
But needing him less I think I'm even nearer?
Encounters and farewells; everything an interim.
More in small gestures than a wildness of night.
By phone sometimes we're closer than any embrace.
Things left unsaid. Woven nearness of distance.
In the timbres of his voice love's second sight.
How long can I live on the afterglow of a glance?
That he'd be taken from me? I fill with dread.
So ill and so, so terribly tired. My sweet,
Be ready to start again, pick up the thread.
Please, above all, don't take him from me yet.
Barely time to kiss a dry and withering mouth.
A husk. Two small rooms whose walls overheard
Our têtes-à-têtes for two woven years of growth.
My heart will always fly to you like a bird.
Much was beautiful, much was too hard to bear.
All the demons, passions, the goodness, the love.
Struggles and weakness, everything found in a man.
I carry your spirit in me. Nameless and everywhere
Those wings of yours must still unfold and move,
A dove at sunrise gauging heavens with its span.

And now I'm alone and here for everyone.
To bear all, growing stronger in the bearing.
Where I'm cut short, someone will carry on.

Joy. Memories of jasmine. My blistered feet.
Pogroms. Unspeakable horrors. All one whole.
To live long enough to fathom a little of it.

The dumpy woman with such greasy black hair
I imagine behind a washtub on Jodenbreestraat.
A hunchbacked Russian with that big-eyed stare.

All those worries about clothing, about food.
I want my life to turn into one great prayer.
So happen what may, it's bound to be good.

Is life glorious and magnificent? This desire
That we build some day a whole new world
A spring in my step as I walk by the barbed wire.

Are we given more to bear than we can shoulder?
And beyond that will we break? Some younger
Ones seemed shattered in spirit; those older

Take root in this wasteland soil. An eyesore.
A few lupins and seagulls. But my father smiles:
Jews in a desert? We've seen the landscape before.
Waxen faces. Registrations. Friskings. Process.
Roughly seventy people to a sealed goods wagon.
Bucket in middle; for the sick a paper mattress.

A fine-grained message as wagon No.12 careers
Towards Poland. Some farmer stoops to pick up
Her final postcard from those crammed years.

The web-spinning spider lets its thread unwind,
Then follows on. A life stretching beyond itself.
We were singing as we left the transit camp behind.

Heloïse

Once. A split second. A palm laid on my shoulder.
My own hand's flicked reaction as hers withdrew.
Memories of that touch still seem to enfold her.

Grazing of fingertips. That's all it was or is
Or ever would be. Pleasure both full and finite.
The sweet passing ghost of Abélard's Heloïse.

Her dove-eyed hunger. All his intellectual pride.
Honeymoons she'd turned his mind to flesh and then,
Amour courtois until their bones lie side by side.

Yearning seen through the lens of age after age.
History or legend. Moral. Romance and tragedy.
A story we keep on weaving into our own image.

The heart wants to hear what must be unsaid.
Even her letters may be sermons or voice-overs.
What queen did not envy my joys and my bed?

Flared lust. Abandon womaning into the vehemence
Of her cloister's rule. Still my desire to imagine
Listening eyes, her voice, that utter presence.

So much unspoken. A brush. Ointments of a glance.
A ghost once laid a hand gently on my shoulder.
Dream a love blessed and blessing in its absence.

Across quiet distances of passion finely tuned,
Poised abbess, caress again his monkish flesh.
A greying man is healing in his crying wound.

Trace

(i.m. George Ford)

Sometimes it's almost as if I'd seen his face.
Vignettes. Things said. That living residue
A veiled and hinted presence, a vague déjà vu
In his son's gestures. Voice-prints. A trace.

As though I'd seen that son, a twelve-year-old
Hugging a widow-mother floundering in distress;
Sensed his father finding in him a steadiness:
'Out of this loss all our lives will unfold.'

Forever a young man dreams of his children's
Future and doesn't care how days are numbered.
I always see that face still staring forward,
Steadfast and patient now even in its absence.

And so long gone before I'd ever met his son.
Already a great-grandchild stirs in the womb,
Turns and kicks, crying out for elbow room.
Galaxies of genes begin what must be re-begun.

His son will be my friend, a peer and brother.
Friend once meant kin. Such frontiers of love
Always open. Tones. Gestures. A rubbing-off.
Almost thirty years of ripening in each other.

Do hopes and memories keep weaving into one?
Those twists around a single warping thread.
It seems the past both passes and lies ahead.
This man I never met shapes me in his son.

Trinity College Chapel, Cambridge

Already four centuries since Herbert's birth.
One hand touching heav'n, with th'other earth.

I see him lighting candles in a chapel's dusk,
His demeanour somehow both gentle and brusque,

That ambitious aristocrat earning a humility.
I hold for two lives and both live in me.

Poems *such conflicts as no one can think.*
The draughty taper's star seems to wink,

Flickering this way, that way, back again,
As an eye between the glory of two women.

His doubting: *Have I no harvest but a thorn?*
Before my sighs did drie it, there was corn.

A universe self-completing in a single soul.
In just one weft the perfection of a whole.

Steady me, my Herbert. Lay your hands on me.
Thy skill and art, what music would it be?

My wobbling core. The heart such a maverick.
So tiny the flame tapered from wick to wick.

[Sunday 7 March 1993]

355

Rilke

To have made music among the dark and gone,
To share and eat *the poppies with the dead,*
Then you'll never lose that sweetest tone.

Me and Madam Jazz, you with your wild Orpheus;
Those landscapes where music, always the alien,
Expands our heart-space and still outgrows us.

Your hand fits mine. Too well I know that boy:
How angels of hurt send him again and again
To find those elusive fathers. Rodin. Tolstoy.

Anything we know learned from ripened women:
The warmth of Lou Andreas-Salomé's praise;
Magnifying silences, minds so open and human.

Little wonder then the fig tree is your symbol.
Hardly a blossom, straight to the fruiting phase.
Rainer Maria, singer of what's vast and whole:

And you stars, isn't it from you the lovers
Delight in the loved-one's face arises? Leave
Them bloom infinite caresses under the covers.

Why do you invoke the stars or the souls' birds?
They mustn't see the Rilken thread in the weave
Or what wounds hide behind the arras of our words.

Let your lovers play and glory in their laughter.
All in the kiss. All with the weave and grain;
How verses cast their shadows before and after.

Cold and passionate. Stone-givers. Broken reeds.
Tubes of stops and gaps. O Madam Jazz forgive
Us our off-notes, these words noisier than deeds.

Enough to laud the ring, the clasp, the jar.
Shapes, the light, colours. No need to explain.
Just as they are they become more than they are.

Transformation is everything. A brokenness obeys.
Bow down in the shadow-world of words and live
To say, to extol, to hymn, to sing, to praise.

Islander

A palm spread on the brow or tipping the hands
Would somehow help to both remember and forget,
Clay on clay, our old rituals of acceptance.

From the Jersey shore New York haloed a horizon
That night word came. It might have been Galway's
Shimmering skyline as the steamer left Inishmaan

Thirty years ago on his first visit to that city;
Reluctant pioneer, lover of the way things were,
Last unwilling convert to slates and electricity.

Oceans apart, my memory strives to fix its image.
'A man without help must depend on himself.'
He crouches and pokes his potato-sets in a ridge.

There was such delight, a sweated awkward dignity
Prides in his skills. And that half-smirk half-smile:
'So that's the way it's done. And now don't you see?'

For him no cities, his Promised Land an inheritance,
A stewardship between the gone and the yet unborn.
Always he seems to touch his earth with reverence.

All agog I'm standing there and once more a son
Learning to spread seaweed, how to mould the earth.
A man with a gift and where will he pass it on?

At eighty it's Dublin for radium. Still stubborn,
Alarmed at that lump, he defers a final pilgrimage.
'If I go now, sure I know that I'll never return.'

A thread of shoreline vanishes in the sleepless glow.
Lean radiance of dreams. Skid Row. Babbling towers.
Insomniac Camelot. Huge city of get-up-and-go.

I'm trying to imagine the podgy cold of his forehead.
He's kneeling to palm down a fistful of damp clay.
Quick stab of his dibble, the set darkens in its bed.

Patrimony

A down-turned palm, just the way he'd smiled,
That same gesture, even his tone and emphasis
As I stoop to hand a note to a friend's child:
Here, son, get yourself something with this.

Those years later, a student visiting him,
I saw a man breaking. Still, an extravagance I loved:
I'm James Hallinan, the parish priest of Wishaw
And you're a first cousin at *least* once removed.

Pour me a wee dram, I'm such a terrible sleeper.
Trails of stockpiles, noggin bottles I'd discover
In wardrobe nooks hidden from an older housekeeper,
Who fusses over her tearaway, a mothering lover.

Another dead bishop! He empties whiskey bottles
In the small hours. Terrors he'd tried to suppress
For years begin to leak as he weaves and shuttles
Between a shy bonhomie and blurts of loneliness.

We couldn't. We hadn't the time to fall in love.
Even those long warm summers at home from college
Always the harvest, the hay that we had to save.
Will you promise to help me out in my old age?

Police knocked us up to ask if I'm a relation.
A heart attack. The race against loneliness won.
Like an echo that sally from our last conversation:
Writing books? Sure, won't you give us a mention?

Here's to your open-handedness, my cousin priest,
As you stooped: Here get yourself something, son.
A whole smooth half-a-crown pressed into my fist.
Now allowing for inflation, I pass my fortune on.

Snag

Such flaws those Greek choruses knew.
Then do as I say and not as I do.

I am who I will be. An inch of history.
What if soiled hands smear the tapestry?

I have a dream. Or at least to try;
Saint Luther King, womaniser on the sly.

Must we too suffer and suffer into truth,
According to our measure cut our cloth?

Who knows the affliction of a falling star,
The slow slow healing wound of Abélard?

Remember the snags in my thread with pity.
So frail. And even as fragile as the city.

Double Edge

These long spare shadows in the grain,
The darker strands in my father's line,
Hairbreadths between sane and insane,
So inwoven in this temperament of mine.

You, my grandmother that I never knew,
(Father had told us that you were dead)
Did a country shame of madness hide you?
Poor Delia Garvan gone in the head.

Something had given. Maybe a foreboding
That a favourite son you'd kept so close
Would die 'out foreign'. A star imploding
In a night's despair. A lonely overdose.

That granddaughter too by her own hand.
Generations of nightmare, a fearful myth
You couldn't wake from or ever understand.
My marrow knows what you struggled with.

The gift and brunt of a giddiness inbred.
Double edges of your make-up. The madcap
Bobbin shuttles the cradle of its shed.
So tautly drawn, a warp can easily snap.

Your troubled spirit still hovers near me.
Every day of my life a wager and a choice.
All sweets and darks of such intensity.
I know the costs. I've chosen to rejoice.

Apprentice

Qui apprendait aux hommes à mourir leur apprendre à vivre.
He who taught men to die taught them to live.
MONTAIGNE

In my moment, host to all my saints and stars.
Host and apprentice. Everything numinous, charged.
Auras of friends recalled. A photograph on a shelf.
Everything at once itself and sacrament of itself.
Such long quiet accumulations of joint and skill:
A dormer sunny and double-glazed against the chill,
A dowelled chair, the silence of a mortised floor,
Persian gardens in a rug, hinged mystery of a door.
That *d* for door was once a Phoenician triangle,
Shape of a tent's flap Greeks in turn will call
Delta, a sign the Etruscans conveyed to Rome.
All those words, cognates that shift and resume.
So much hidden and beyond our conscious reach,
As a grammar extemporising in whirls of speech,
All ad lib. Improvisation. Vertigo of performance.
Newness without caprice: tiny, endless brilliance
Of variation, sameness of ceremony subtly broken,
Language acquired in a dizziness of what's spoken.

Learning. Always learning. And we re-edit our past,
Anxious as revisionist historians for a plot recast
To say this or that was our life's one watershed
Or maybe to say how every move we'd made just led
To where we are, as though we keep on yearning
For one thread to follow. The thread is learning.
In our newness, rhythms of reflection and return
Show us faces we wore before we're ever born.
We wager on a story both open and ghost-written,
Thousand times shy, a thousand more times bitten,
Weaving and bobbing among the warps and combings.
Traces of shades and revenants shape our becoming.
Herbert's green and fresh returns. Rilke's Orpheus
On saxophone playing his variations for Madam Jazz.
Mother forever smiling I beg again your promise.
Be with me now, my Hillesum, my Maude, my Heloïse;
Two *coeurs d'artichaut*, one surefooted as her vow.
All my loves and sonless fathers be with me now.
Host and apprentice to citizens of sweet by-and-by,
Slowly in my living I've begun to learn to die.

CROSSLIGHT

> Tonight the moon is blond.
> His sideways light bends inward to cheat
> the dark. That's why he's here to hand me
> the white shawl knitted beside some missing fire.
> When he sets it across my shoulders
> I'm lowered gently down
> and made to sleep again on earth.
>
> TESS GALLAGHER

PART I *Threshold*
(for R.L.)

Rowan

Early August and we're walking under a portico
Of rowans, weighing up the world. Then you begin

To tell me how a friend wastes and doesn't know
From day to day; how still she keeps a discipline:

Time in the garden watching how fuchsias grow
Daily to their glory and pods fatten on the lupin;

Hours listening to a late Beethoven adagio,
Latticed yearning for a peace she wants to win.

By night she laughs and cries. A constant flow
Of chatter in her sleep. He's now ghostly thin

And speaks of when she's gone. Must it be so?
The long struggle to joy of a quartet's violin

Wonders if she'll make it to when the sumacs show
Crimsons a summer's lushness has hidden within.

362

Naked

Naked from my mother's womb. Naked to return.
Nothing but starkness. Throes. A night's misery,
A body thrashing the dark. Why this? Why me?

Distillation. Exchange. Energy's shifting guises.
The salt still unseen before the vapour rises.
Our images fall short, too narrow and unearned.

A good woman crying out in the face of destiny.
A pitcher broken by the spring, a pillar overturned.
Even Job would die, *being old and full of days*.

In the morning light, her face harrowed and ashen.
Hours in a garden where a chalice will not pass.
Everything I know is nothing. Nothing but compassion.

Spiral

Spiral of dialogue, a quartet's yearning twist,
An outpouring and her mind wanders. She'll return
To a violin grieving over moments she has missed.

Even the most voluptuous sound is already gone
As she listens, that one sweet touch of a rim
Against the ground and the wheel is rolling on.

Still the touch, a wonderful kiss as we meet.
My friends, my friends, the sliding bow knows
How every tune is faring. We part as we greet.

Stabs and cries ascend A minor's stairs.
She wants to hear and hear her heart out.
Why must this cadenza catch us unawares?

And lest ye be like gods. To learn the fullness
Of finitude, a joy always in the light of an end.
This music she loves keeps preparing its stillness.

Angel

A stumbling over stones of ancient agonies.
The self-same questions as once in Job's cry.

Even the same answers. How it's beyond us.
A threshold. *Hast thou with him spread out the sky?*

Departures. Successions. A zillionth in a hugeness.
My words are frivolous. How can I try to reply?

Or because you've loved, you're trusting to surprise.
One final show of confidence in Madam Jazz.

Sacrifice. The old song of the bruised servant.
Then, when the angel comes, to want to say yes.

Stumbling over the stones of ancient agonies,
I begin this long apprenticeship of assent.

Virtuoso

As she listens to a quartet I seem to sense
A lifetime passing there before her eyes,
Just as they used to tell us years ago

How in the space of a fall you'd experience
That grand recapitulation or how in Paradise
Our sins could appear written on our brow.

The violin is breaking into a long reprise.
A descending theme. So big and intense.
Decades of apprenticeship travelling the bow.

The widened excitement of a brisk arpeggio.
A music spindling onwards to its flourish,
Both holding at bay and preparing silence.

That sudden blind play of a virtuoso.
No longer what's known but more how to know.
Sweet obediences of this once-off cadenza.

Intrinsic and jazzy and so unselfconscious
The fingers themselves begin to improvise.
Braille of flair and skill. Our letting go.

Something

Something that's both there and still not there.
Those random snapshots snatching at five decades:
A bride in a garden, schoolgirl with hair in braids,
Whatever she is, always half-hidden in her stare.

Dreams. Fears. Projections. All she'll discover
In being discovered, the way first desire, unsure
Of love, outgrows the passion of its own departure.
Is she staring now at some invisible lover?

For months now this tumour bloating unawares.
The years of growing selves and skins we slough,
So many rehearsals for one final shaking-off.
That something that's still her still stares

And stares as she watches a coal tit's sudden flight,
Relishing every detail. How lavender stems lurch
Under a bee's weight. First yellowings of a birch.
A midge swarm in the last shafts of sunlight.

Namesake

Travail of coming or going. Pangs of creation.
Her people lived here generation by generation.

A granddaughter just born is given again her name.
Light into dark into light. Claim and counterclaim.

Bara women of Madagascar lamented their birth-pains
Dancing and wailing around a neighbour's remains,

While elders rapped on an ancestor's tomb to say:
It's your grandchild born here, don't send it away.

Blunt and upfront. Everything now out in the open.
So weeks. A month or two. But hardly a season.

For both the counted days that unfold and enfold.
A crossing over. Namesakes greeting on a threshold.

No Stranger

No stranger the angel now and the moist
Parting kiss. Things loved not coveted.
Blossoms of moments tremble in relief
Against the sky. So much yet unsaid
Or unsayable. Silence at the core of grief.

Slowly and now. The slowest of nows.
Obsessive, detailed as courtship. Remember
Stares, the savoured glances and scents.
The plums will ripen, but that's September.
Days turned years turn back to moments

As though our finitude allows us love,
Paradox of a spirit that attaches, detaches,
So wholeheartedly among and never of;
Twin birds clinging to a single tree,
One eats the fruits, one fasts and watches.

Royal Red buddleias have grieved July's end.
Intensity. Unbearable vividness of the word.
The orange-and-lemon montbretia. Iris
Into iris. The gladioli's piercing sword.
Sweet, sweet fruits. Heartbreaking kiss.

Light

Perpetual light shine upon them, my mother prayed.
In memory, at least, everything sure and downright

As the fall of beads or the rhythms of words obeyed.
I search among the echoes for some image, an insight.

Complementary flesh and spirit? Energies displayed
Sometimes as particles, sometimes as waves of light?

A city of light? Then, what of these atoms that clayed
A spirit, this body of mine with its dark delight?

What about dancing, swims, Scotch with white lemonade,
Feasts, or lovemaking outdoors on an August night?

All-loving Madam Jazz I've second-guessed, betrayed
My trust. Let me take up my tune again, so finite

And full as all the undreamed-of echoed and relayed.
Fountain of life in thy light shall we see light.

Still

Still so still by the French windows to the garden
She watches and listens, alone, caught in crosslight,
The porch lamp picking up where the sunlight fades.

A woman already begun to slide away to the shades.
Surely a time for compassion not for philosophy.
See! she delights, the sumac has started to turn.

That it will be there when she's gone? Why yearn
For such crimson completeness? It seems an abundance
Keeps making us even more what we already are.

An apprenticeship over, a long preparation singular
And hers, a once-off in the whole journey of time.
False starts, returns, open-endedness. Now the assent.

At last a perfect obsession with the crimson moment.
An end and present fuller in the light of each other.
That face so animated, so glorious in the crosslight.

PART II *Variations*
(for R.L.)

Madam

In the beginning the jazz. An uncontainable theme
Spills out its tunes. Both whole and spendthrift

As though full grows fuller. O insatiable Madam
Of variations, self-fulfilling in your self-gift.

Immensity of a theme just for a while unwombed
In me. And small wonder our spoilt bodies bend

Under its weight. Variations unique and subsumed;
A music sustains us and brings us to our end.

Chaos in order, order at the heart of chaos.
Theme and overflow and all that sweeps between them.

Spilling of contingency shapes the ends of a theme.
Nourish me, my jazz. Play this tune to its close.

In Crosslight Now

In crosslight now all faces of my friends.
Every minute still so full, so precious,
A furious intensity of knowing it ends.

That everything happened just as it has,
A variation expanding the glory of a theme;
That I bear the mystery of my mistress jazz.

To fill with gratitude, even to soar.
That one swallow that shall not fall.
A caring less which means my caring more.

Each small gesture, every utterance,
The glances I hoard. Some love is mine,
And always mine. A peace. A radiance

I've wanted to word but can't. My part
My own variation shaping this history
Of a theme as though one narrow heart

Contains the fractured voices of humanity.
Rhythms chosen, riffs of light and dark.
Autumn seems so steeped in her eternity.

Clarinet

Another variation, sudden flare of munificence,
A clarinet exploring its notes and a sixth sense
Of rhythm reshaping a theme you thought you knew.

And the more you listen the more remote it seems.
Unknown, unknowable. Charge and allure of a theme's
Enigma fractioned in the funky plays of a clarinet.

Lean and mellow as that voice of Etty Hillesum
Ripening in whispers and rumours of a coming pogrom:
To the last moment life has beauty and meaning.

Her passion hums the reed. *You can no longer do*
But can only be and accept. Then, her adieu:
We must be ready to act as a balm for all wounds.

The night-lamp parents kept lit against your fears
Of letting go. That half-sleeplessness for years.
To know more the dark, to live more in the light.

Like a sigh that began so deep, deep down in you
The bittersweet clarinet scales on into the blue.
A silence somehow richer because a tune was heard.

That in the End

Here and now and maybe. To play is everything.
Interflow of mind and emotion caught in the doing.

Broken tempos of anguish seem to feed our joys;
Unexpected cadences, a tale of twelve-bar blues.

Moody solos. Unique. The stamp of one voice;
Then pure concert as an ensemble improvises,

Hearing in each other harmonies of cross-purpose,
As though being ourselves we're more capacious.

Music of paradox. Music of now and metamorphosis.
Nothing unearned. A trust unconscious and precise

That in the end, whatever I become or am or was,
I loved my friends, I praised my mistress jazz.

March On

Always this urge to begin and re-begin.
Armstrong's trumpet swings and skips
O when the saints go marching in.

As if rhythms keep needing to recompose
This determined joy of passionate blues,
His melody shatters the stricter tempos.

He can't imagine it and still he must,
A garden where beginnings and ends collide.
Every image is trying to widen our trust.

Valhalla's vivid and endless carouse.
Blacks downing burdens by the riverside.
Promises of a father's many-mansioned house.

For me just my friends. O jazz eternal
Give me their warmth, the talk, the glory
In faces of saints, boisterous and carnal.

O I want to be in that number, when...
His trumpet ransacking the melody's secret.
Satchmo of the horn, march on, march on.

Underwritten

Trusted and ample double bass. Rhythmic plump.
Pacemaker. Guardian *profundo* of bottom lines,
Dark-toned and ruminant in the stomp.

Paternal, ever-present rumble of a tempo given.
Upholder. Timekeeper. Counterpoint of a tune
So open-ended and pulse-driven.

Rhythm of abundance. Logic of music's overflow.
Above a clarinet hums its vertigo of desire.
Of course, I can never know.

And only to need to love it just as it is.
Underwritten in the murmured promise of a bass
To grow into such harmonies.

The freedom of it! Liberty of simply being,
Urge of at last to have looked an end in the eye,
As though even just seeing

The shape of finitude is still enough to glean
Something of that interplay of melody and rhythm.
My jazz moves in between.

Uncertain

Are tune and rhythm one in the fullness of the play?
Art Tatum is fingering *Someone to watch over me.*
My jazz, my jazz, will tomorrow be my dancing day?

Those years you begged just to let one moment stay,
That one slow moment trembling towards an ecstasy.
Are tune and rhythm one in the fullness of the play?

Keats' kiss-poised lover in my vase of brittle clay
Sings the melancholy of what might but couldn't be.
My jazz, my jazz, will tomorrow be my dancing day?

To know now you wouldn't wish it any other way.
A music bolder in the light of its own fragility.
Are tune and rhythm one in the fullness of the play?

The way it happened I must praise again and say:
What is, what comes, I kiss its sweet uncertainty.
My jazz, my jazz, will tomorrow be my dancing day?

I assent and still this flesh will cry and pray:
When the angel comes, let it not go hard with me.
Are tune and rhythm one in the fullness of the play?

My jazz, my jazz, will tomorrow be my dancing day?

Flightline

At the core of all the jazz's lavish promise:
Just to keep on playing, to improvise what is.

Saxman Keith Donald told me when the solo moves
It's loose and certain as the promise of loves.

'I'd know,' he said, 'the true line after one bar,
As if trusting one another we'll play what we are.'

Those riffs foregone, adornments you had to eschew,
The siren's sweetness that wails so deep in you,

Between moments endured and moments of the dream,
Singleness of purpose, utter obedience to a theme.

Nothing show-off. Lean flightlines. Grace to soar.
Shaping and shaped by a promise at the music's core.

Both

Cotton picking or dogging around Chicago slums,
Those *Basin Street Blues, Never No Lament,*
Get Happy, whirl and muddle or bewilderment,
And there in the banal the jazz still hums.

Swing! Brother, Swing! Shoe Shine Boy.
Out There. Back in Your Own Backyard.
Dancing in the Dark. Bye Bye Blackbird.
Big Butter and Egg Man. Stompin' at the Savoy.

Before-the-beat, around-the-beat, passion's tone,
Just on and on, swamping up those rhythms,
Afro, Creole or Latin, the Baptist hymns,
Even marches, she's making everything her own.

Someday Sweetheart. Bird of Paradise.
Nobody Knows. All God's Chillun Got Rhythm.
Garden of Souls. A Love Supreme.
Embraceable You. Smoke Gets in Your Eyes.

Ordinary down-to-earthness, so heaven-minded,
Both how it is and how we must refuse it.
The body breaks against the crying spirit.
This gaiety where all ends are open-ended.

Vertigo

To the end the jazz, pulse of surprise, off-chance,
Raveller and unraveller of tunes, wooer of margins,

Song of the servant, cotton-picker's rhythmic urge,
Whatever in evolution will always choose the verge.

Was Plato mad to dream up some infinite perfection,
Musics of fullness where the rhythm and tune are one?

Pure need of memory and of aim? A hunch? A guess?
Still this becoming, my finite rhapsody of process.

I grow older and it seems the silence that surrounds
Each tone is keener, the intensity between the sounds.

Love's moment so infinite and perfect in the flux.
Have I begun to understand something of that paradox?

A vibrato at the music's brim, my gift and privilege.
Lady Jazz, I'm your brinkman still dizzy at the edge.

VOICES

I thank you for your voices: thank you:
Your most sweet voices.

> WILLIAM SHAKESPEARE
> *Coriolanus*

Amour, tu as été mon maître,
Je t'ai servi sur tous les Dieux.
Ah si je pouvais deux fois naître,
Comme je te servirais mieux!

Love, you've been my master,
I've served you above all the Gods.
Ah, if I could be born twice,
How I'd serve you even better!

> CLEMONT MAROT

Overflow

The jazzmen say to improvise is both to hear
And answer at one time. Careless and austere,
How a knitted music revels in its discipline.
Friends and lovers, discrete polyphony within,
Where voices intersect, resonant and polyglot,
Do all our conversations tangle in one plot?
Skyscraper, tower of some monolith truth,
Did old Babel dream up the dreams of youth?
O city of my voices, fragile and uncontrolled,
Scattered oneness of what's woven and manifold
Braiding your melodies of part and counterpart,
Line and texture of those voices in one heart,
Voices of silver and onyx, of garnet and gold,
Wind and layer what complex stories we unfold,
Fabric of counterpoint, our shared fixed song,
Webbing this double fugue where I belong.

Nothing woos like voices. Those breaths haul
Ribs and midriff like a bucket handle. Of all
Kisses this wells deepest. Diaphragm-dance.
Air pumped to the head's cavities of resonance.
Windpipe. Soundbox purr. A throat's hum.
Tongue-shaped waves tap against an eardrum,
Shivers in two folds of mucus and membrane
Echo in erogenous chambers and zones of brain.
The lips' friction, a last consonant's hiss,
The pursed and gathered plosions of a kiss.
A breath now voices in me its trembling strings.
Every sound makes love. My body sings
And sways to a tune. Sap leaps and rejoices,
Juiced and warmed in this lavishness of voices.
All praise my lovers, and listen how I grow,
My voice welling in your voices' overflow.
Completing a completion, abundance overspilt;
As if I keep on filling what's already fulfilled.

O voices within shaping everything I do,
Even in my soliloquies I collogue with you.
Always, everywhere, ballet of voices in me.
The long climbed scale, the waifs of melody,
Our motet swapping tales, our this and that,
Small shared yearnings of a love's chitchat,
Sounds wooed and held in a rhythm's poise,
In an endless room of choreographed noise,
Motifs that echo their gentle counterclaim,
Phrases repeated, the same never the same.
Still our minuteness. Tiny figures in a theme
Subsumed in glories of some richer scheme,
A banquet of voices within steadying me
When night's angel croons her minor key.
Every leap, every turn our histories take
Will have been a music we lived to make.

Matins for You

Come again glistening from your morning shower
Half-coquettishly you'll throw
Your robe at me calling out 'Hello! Hello!'
I turn over stretching out to snatch
A bundle from the air and once more to watch
That parade across your bower.
Jaunty, brisk, allegro,
Preparing improvisations of yet another day,
As on our first morning twenty-seven years ago.

Sit on the bed-end and pull a stocking on,
Slip that frock over your head
Let it slither a little, ride your hips, then spread
Its folds and tumbles, flopping past those thighs
To swish against your ankles. I'm still all eyes.
The thrill and first frisson
At the half-known but unsaid,
At hints and contours embodied in a dance of dress
I'm ogling snugly from this your still warm bed.

Now you're hurrying, business-like and ready to go.
I wonder if I've ever glimpsed you
Or if all those years I even as much as knew
Behind those hints and suggestions I admire
What inmost aim or dream or heart's desire
Calls out 'Hello, Hello!'
Flirt and peekaboo
Of such unwitting closeness, our take-for-grantedness,
Complex web of intimacies where we slowly grew.

Sometimes wells of aloneness seem almost to imbue
Your silence with the long wistful rubato
Of a Chopin nocturne or is it a *sean-nós* tremolo?
'*Má bhíonn tú liom, bí liom, gach orlach de do chroí.*'
'If you're mine, be mine, each inch of your heart for me.'
That infinite longing in you
A girl racing to follow
The bus's headlamps to meet your father at Bunbeg.
He steps down from the platform. Hello! Hello!
You smile your father's inward Zen-like smile.

And yet its light shines outward
As when I watched you helping a child to word
The coy, swaggering pleasure of new shoes,
A muse the more a muse in being a muse.
That inward outward smile
Delights in delight conferred,
Fine-tuning those strains and riffs of wishes unspoken,
Desires another's heart doesn't yet know it has heard.

Now I see you, now I don't. The doubt
And loneness of what's always new,
Moments seized in double time, love's impromptu,
As when late last night you started telling me
How even as a girl you'd known your dream would be
Bringing others' dreams about.
This once I think I glimpsed you,
You my glistening, lonely, giving Mistress Zen.
Thank you. Thank you for so many dreams come true.

Secrets of Assisi

Behind the lavender, the buddleia and the roses,
Behind a darker screen of trees that closes
On the path, there before the boundary wall
Il Giardino Segreto where you imagine all
The forgotten têtes-à-têtes, the words apart,
Deals cut, some whispered heart to heart,
Lovers withdrawing, moments out of sight
And mind while in the busy open sunlight
Out in louder days our lives go on;
There in secret gardens voices of the gone
Speak their lines in overtones of history,
Harmonics of the past refiguring our story,
As though the narrative selves of long ago
Somehow in their wholeness seem to throw
A shape on ours. No, not even an elegy,
More a being that slowly enters me,
A different life, improvising and *ad hoc*,

Between double time and the demon clock,
Between surge of now and a non-stop line,
Flux and trust of another somehow mine.
On summer evenings when we eat *al fresco*,
I hear in a secret garden voices of Francesco.

At San Damiano once on the shaded bench,
Maybe you heard a quiver in my voice's reed
As I recited a troubadour's lovesong in French?
The closer we are, the more secrets we need.
Awoken by my heart's sudden flutter and leap,
My long uneasy nights sweated and turned,
Begging just the honeyed canticle of sleep.
Even in a carnival time of dreams I yearned.
Am I to blame for a love's unbidden foray?
Break me. Break me into more than I understood.
Tue so le laude la gloria e la honore
O Lord, most high, all-powerful and good!
Beautiful and radiant *cun grande splendore.*
In my darkest broken hour, yours the glory.

Think of wounded Abélard meeting Heloïse:
Sweet disciplines, the long haul of a soul,
Codes of one quick kiss, a hand squeeze,
Swift greetings at once fugitive and whole.
Secrets shared in a garden before we parted,
Hurrying again into the Umbrian nightfall;
So much guessed but always still unsaid,
Each with our own, a life, a service, a call.
To keep faith, to trust an invisible caress,
Long-standing, long-headed, long-range patience,
As unseen stars keep sending unseen rays.
O Chiara! Chiara! Chiara! clairvoyante, abbess!
Out of this broken yearning, a glow of absence,
A love thickening the more that love obeys.

Watch over us in our clay, brittle as we are.
Mi Signore, per sora luna e le stelle
Be praised, my Lord, through moon and star.
I hear children asking Chiara out to play.
The same laughter, a voice gentle and forthright,
As a young woman's strong will ripens in office,
In maternal tiptoeings across the chills of night

To spread extra rugs over some feebler novice.
Bower of advices, strange determined radiance,
When I wobble you're the one who is wise.
Daring, down to earth and still the sudden glance
Of an ardent girl behind the steadiest of eyes.
Who knows in secret gardens how a love may earn
Its keep or how in its boudoir a heart can yearn?

Beyond the lavender, the buddleia and the roses,
Behind a darker screen of trees that closes
Over bequeathed secrets we learn to repossess
In hints and traces, those words we must guess
Or thoughts which ricochet, the echoes and signs,
Riddles of what we read between the lines,
This tick-tack of things we still negotiate,
The silent interplay where we'll translate
Those unheard words that in a heart betoken
All of all which must remain unspoken.

High in the upper partials of our loyal past,
Those Umbrian voices ring true and steadfast
Across our common heritage of predicaments
As we travel in turn beyond a first innocence
To comb and choose what each needs to reveal,
To count veils and know the heart may conceal
As much as it discloses and yet not harden
Or grow suave. In green shadows of this garden
When lovers withdraw, in moments out of sight
And mind, beyond the busy open sunlight
Out in louder days where lives go on,
I broker faithful secrets between the gone.

Northway

The sun has burst over the island of Dursey.
I phone a friend from a kiosk on an ocean's rim:
Dursey, Dalkey, Lambay, a troché rhythm,
Digits years by heart, north-eastwards
Zeroing in, by island, by archipelago,
I home like a Viking. Islay, Orkney.
My suspense as I wait for two toned words:
Ja, hello!

Straight to the core of inner lakes and trees.
Heartland of corn, megalith graves, ornaments,
Lichened aspens, twigs, stones, sediments
Slowly and forever taking shape.
Sways of spruces hush against my ears,
Rock-a-bye of unfathomed intensities.
Ja, hello! says a voice. *I've lived in this landscape*
Two thousand years.

Down a line of centuries I'll hear her listening;
Gentle, anxious, keen, generous, intense,
All that giving and gift of utter presence.
Was it Chopin's Waltz Number 8?
An ailing mother filling her childhood with awe?
A wistful joy, as outside the snow was glistening
In spring light where spruces and lakes still wait
For another thaw.

Is the frost still deep under five months of snow?
Across dim and fretful winter afternoons
A child's heart skips to Chopin's anxious tunes.
That angst for time lost or squandered,
A body overwhelmed by its own intensity;
Where, where must the next note go?
A girl is falling asleep as the music wandered
In its minor key.

Somewhere in her dreams the blurts of a saxophone
Mere ville, mere hete enn mitt hjerte kan forstå
'Wilder and warmer than my heart can ever know.'
It's a long-lit Norwegian summer night

And there's a row-boat creaking across a lake
Towards some bluesy lure and moan,
To an island where a woman dances in fierce delight.
Then she'll wake.

And how it all pans out. Our choices or chances.
In Chopin's yearning waltz did that child hear
A choreography of lives tripping the inner ear,
A ballet where we'd so slowly grow?
That poise of her attentiveness, the passionate answer.
In her welcoming hug, Isadora Duncan dances
Wilder and warmer than my heart will ever know.
A listening dancer.

The wistful joy. Once again the major key,
As grateful for what is, a music gathers in
Sweet dissonance of all that might have been.
The sun bursts out over Dursey
And here I am phoning just to let her know.
A ringing tone as I wait anxiously
For the infinite moment when one voice will say:
Ja, hello!

Quartet

(Beethoven's String Quartet No.12, Opus 127)

1 *Allegro*

Swooping melodic fourths. And higher.
Ranging and looping. *Sempre dolce* of desire.

Even in this *allegro* I hear a wistful violin
Skipping scales of all that might have been

That spurt and strive towards a leading note,
So full of yearning. The tone that underwrote

Every ascent now seems to draw the bow
Homeward. And still this tension to and fro.

What is it breaks the heart when I hear that voice?
Si, je regrette that I had to make that choice

Between such longing and one golden promise.
My heart, I plead with you to praise what is.

2 *Molto Cantabile*

Slowly from a silence just one expanding tone
Enters some inward world of ripe Beethoven;
As if tears of marrow are shifting in the bone,
Acceptance and yearning carefully interwoven.
And then, out of a playful theme he'll fashion
Five variations. A benediction seems to underpin
A whole movement's dark and bridled passion,
Irrupting twice in dance, then again reined in.
Do the muses only mend the hearts they break?
To know how easily a voice can suddenly waver.
Hold the note. You hold it for the music's sake.
Clear and true. Precision of a demisemiquaver.
Unbearable joy. A gaiety grieving and intense
Of phrases looping upwards back to silence.

3 *Scherzo*

Pizzicato fanfare and an urgent cello:
Must we succumb? Must we succumb?
And one by one that faithful threesome
Of women. A viola darker and mellow
Takes up the motto: we will succumb!
Yes, say the violins, till kingdom come.

A fugal energy, riven and high-strung,
Fits and starts of turmoil and liaison,
Sudden long passages in unison.
As if speaking a different mother tongue,
Three women's voices are held in tension.
Is the polyglot cello a tenor holding on?

To risk chaos and still not to sunder.
A music on the edge, upbeat suspense,
Cross-rhythms both fractured and dense
And the cello's throb zigzagging under
Three women's voices. A jagged silence.
Swift and driven, a *fortissimo* cadence.

4 *Finale*

At the core of longing tears of sweated stone.
Is it just that voice? Or is there in every tune
Some endless desire, a wistful undertone?

Yet again, this hankering for everything to meld
All that might have been between the lines
Of voices counterpoised and voices paralleled.

A note struck early, a sound held on longer.
A phrase hungers for discord, some offbeat
Trust in resolution. Does my music grow stronger
In its own dissonance? A darker, deeper sweet?

A man both yearning and loving what's his.
So what is. What is. All glory to what is.

Oak

How can I describe my friend for you?
Gentle, strong, playful, innocent, wise?
Does that seem a paradox?
I want like a child to fetch my crayon box –
Red and yellow, green and blue –
And sketch a great, broad, hunching man,
Big brow, a smile and stars for eyes.
Or maybe I'll draw an oak with limbs that bend
Over a boy and say 'This will be my friend!'

That vast and deep-rooted system of an oak.
The sturdy entry of a twelve-year-old boy:
Today, my Daddy died.
He was the best daddy in the whole wide...
Almost as though at one stroke
Grief and pride of all in each
Hollows an anguished heart for plunges of joy.
Ein süßes Schrecken geht durch mein Gebein
'A sweet shudder travels this body of mine.'

Then I sit down beside a tall young man.
There we are, our backs against the furrowed bark,
Our early side-by-sideness.
A sweet travelling shudder? O yes! O yes!
A ramifying joy? We promise. We plan.
Our scheme of years cupped on a swaying stalk.
Things to do. How we'd make our mark.
The split-openness of an acorn, naked and new.
Our daring to say 'Love me as I love you.'

And plans unfold in ways we'd never planned.
Overtaken by surprise, caught again unawares,
As all the expected unravels.
Still and always a sweet shudder travels
The bones, our stretching to understand,
To desire according to the desire of another
As stage by stage we climb the decades' stairs.
Dreams, tasks, troubles, secrets we confide,
Double openness of growing side by side.

Who are we? Springs, falls, branchings out,
By turns Telemachus or Mentor, father and brother,
That loyal reassuring voice
At every change or fork of choice
Steadying my obsessions, recalling in nights of doubt:
Ein süßes Schrecken geht durch mein Gebein,
That first promise we keep for one another.
An acorn rooted and ovate leaves unfurled.
My friend. An oak for all the world.

Widening

A startled double-take at such an unexpected *hello!*
From nowhere our circle intersected,
I'm caught off guard by 'love's sudden show'.

Quando m'apparve l'amor subitamente...
My spirit's rhythm speeds with delight.
But the mind is busily signalling *lentemente.*

Slowly. Is it too late? This giddiness upends
And dazes me. A jagged tangent.
I have and hold the tighter circle of my friends.

Again I'm sitting in the crotch of childhood's sumac,
Our exclusive club. That voice at the edge
Says *What about me?* And again I'm taken aback

By that stare at the rim. A greeting face of intrusion.
Hello! it asks, *Can I play too?*
Here at the core, will I dare to trust this inclusion?

That over the unknown, all the unshared heritage,
Over so many missing years,
Amor subitamente throws its invisible bridge.

Yet more a return, like something meant to be.
The best robe, the fatted calf.
This feast is doubling its double time in me.

Overwhelmed. Almost as if there's no choice,
A circle gapes and opens its embrace.
Hail and welcome! My new and prodigal voice.

Handing On

1 *Prelude*

Reticent, maybe, when I first knew him
But light-legged, tall and slim,
A stride becoming more sure of itself.

Then one summer he'd confide in me
He'd determined it would be
Medicine. That change and long haul.

Squeamish, swoonish, twice out cold
And lugged away. Self-controlled
His resolute return to the theatre table.

Something so assured, quietly forthright;
The same boyish delight
In detail, wonder at the lore of everything.

Meditative hours at a Bach prelude.
Precise fingerings of gratitude
For what's both given and handed on.

Action! Sangfroid, lithe, efficient.
The severed finger of a patient
Fetched in a jar and sewn back.

Humble, decisive, kind yet swift,
Every trait and gift
That all my life I've fumblingly admired.

2 *Postlude*

I knew my friend as a boy the moment I saw his son:
A glance with its blend of tenderness and painstaking
Precision, every instant seemed a poem in the making.

Even in that voice his father's heart still breaking
And yearning to undo things so imperfectly done,
Longings of a father whose father didn't praise his son.

The awe of unfolding, everything a playful ceremony.
His endless attention to a new game, another toy,
These dozen years he'll devote so singly to that boy.

Loving explanations, a sort of teaching by joy.
I recalled a fishskin shoe he'd once shown me
Near his grandparents' fjord, an Icelandic pampootie,

But thinner, shinier, with its delicate mermaid beauty;
Or those tiny sticks fishermen used to prop their eyes,
Sleepworkers, gutting and salting sunrise to sunrise.

Then quote that favourite line of Tómas Guðmundsson:
Og enn ég hveð mér hljóðs til πakkar πeim
'So, once more I'm making a poem to thank them.'

That eager and shy boy, his by nature and name.
Another generation. A saga begun and rebegun.
I've never known a man so gentle with his son.

Tongues

Quando m'apparve Amor subitamente...
Love's sudden appearance to astounded Dante

Astounding again. Is each of my voices a mother
Nurturing me in the secret grammars of another?

Og enn ég hveð mér hljóðs til πakkar πeim
So, once more I'm making a poem to thank them

For hungry yearning words in breaths we draw.
Richness of what was becomes a murmur of awe

Mere ville, mere hete enn mitt hjerte kan forstå
Wilder and warmer than my heart can even know.

Unbidden utterings, strange blowings in my lungs,
These gurgled sounds, singing flames of tongues:

Má bhíonn tú liom bí liom, gach orlach de do chroí
If you're mine be mine each inch of your heart for me.

Macaronic nights I thrash, a wobbling Thomas,
Doubling new lines to keep one golden promise:

Ein süßes Schrecken geht durch mein Gebein.
A sweet shudder travels this body of mine,

As dark throws into dawn its tumbling dove,
Some unbearable joy fingers my spirit's glove.

Cadenza

The ranging sudden leaps. Lower. Higher.
Runs and roulades a *coloratura* of desire.

But in her timbre I hear the wistful violin
Climbing a scale of all that might have been

And pausing just a beat on a leading note
So full of yearning. The tone that underwrote

The whole ascent now seems to draw the bow
Homeward. And still this tension to and fro.

What is it breaks the heart when I hear her voice?
Si, je regrette that I had to make that choice

Between such longing and one golden promise.
My heart, I plead with you to praise what is.

St Stephen's Green

Only a stone's throw from here I was born.
As though pulled by navel gravity I return

To a first fountain, a gift from post-war Germany,
Three bronze women measuring out man's destiny.

Fateful spinners: What was, What is, Will be.
The three Norns Urður, Skuld and Verðandi.

Or a childhood's gentle women in German counterparts;
Roethke's Frau Baumann, Frau Schmidt, Frau Schwartze?

Yet I think I still know them by their cut and poise.
I imagine I hear their laughter bubbling in a voice

That wells underneath this fountain's fall and hiss.
I think I hang by their thread of golden promise.

That *all shall be well.* A gift I'm trying to accept.
To believe that promises given are promises kept.

Is and was and will be. A trust's open-plan
And will I then return to where I first began?

These three faces will watch and shine above me.
I know now who they are. I know they love me.

Our Double Time

1

A morning leaving hospital, suddenly the height,
The breadth, the depth. Autumn of my overhaul
When senses seemed to double. Rilke was right:
Some fruit in me keeps ripening for a mellow fall.
Scalpel and needle of growth. A wound's suture.
Etched wonder of what's both brittle and finite:
Two girls linking arms and so full of the future;
The unbearable joy of a sumac's crimson light.
Had I been too busy to notice all this before,
Too concerned to catch the obvious rhyme?
Everything vibrates. A voice. A scent. A colour.
Charged and marvellous. Everything in double time.
To have been to the edge, just to be allowed return
To moments of utter in-loveness, utter unconcern.

2

So I'd wanted it all. The whole noisy city.
Every unpetalled moment. And even as a boy
My mother's sick-bed, a piercing sword of pity.
O why this turning worm in my crimson joy?
A nagging unease, a thought I'd tried to shirk,
Some hazy dread. At last I think I'll dare
To face it squarely; even to trust its work.
Such release! To care more and not to care!
Twin intensity of knowing that now is now.
All time is borrowed, borrowed and double.
Two-sided, it both belongs and transcends.
Like Eunan's vision, mine is a carnal Tau:
The fun, the gossip, a town's hubble-bubble,
Criss-cross of voices, the laughter of my friends.

3

And yet nothing for granted. A face of a friend.
A glance, a touch, a word. *La joie de ma vie,*
Time doubled in the light of our open-end.
The day nor hour nor how the going will be.
Sudden cut and tumble? A flickering tragedy?
My heart knows brokenness and still rejoices.

But will these lines yet haunt a coward in me?
Whatever. Whenever. I trust I'll hear my voices.
Does Rilke's inner fruit now slowly mature,
Seeding and settling, a long working within?
So, in the meantime, friends, just to be sure,
Kiss me, caress me, stroke the outer skin.
Fondle this husk and pod, my spirit's cell,
Warm the gourd still ripening in its shell.

4

The stubborn will and then the loss of will.
Millennia of survival printed in nature's idiom
The way in making love we rein in until
A point of no return. Given over. Overcome.
As in the beginning yield again to the heave,
Years of volition keep the muscles in check
Till minutes before the foetus readies to leave,
A knee-jerk unclenching opens a womb's neck.
And the whole of my life preparing just for this.
D-day. H-hour. Zero moment. The splendour
Of piercing light. The distant face of Beatrice.
The passive voice will hum its last surrender.
Then, take me. Sweep me in that overflow.
Sweetness of holding back. Sweeter let-go.

5

Here is my life. These my friends and voices.
No fixed measures. Just moving with a word
As though I belong in counterpointed noises,
One of those fervent motets of William Byrd.
Across all the aeons, my one humming breath
Poised in this motet. Steady, even sublime.
To think this year will have been my fiftieth!
From now every single moment our double time.
Not that I've grown blasé or no longer care,
More a deeper listening to a music's densities.
No matter how or when, no matter where,
The feel of a line sung with consummate ease.
I love and am loved. All my tinyness rejoices
That I'll have been a voice among your voices.

The Gossamer Wall

POEMS IN WITNESS TO THE HOLOCAUST

(2002)

For those who died, for those who survived,
for those who told

A bite for me, a bite for you, an extra bite for Bella...
I felt her presence everywhere, in daylight, in rooms
I knew weren't empty... Watching with curiosity and
sympathy from her side of the gossamer wall.

ANNE MICHAELS, *Fugitive Pieces*

...the Devil is known to lure people into forgetting
precisely what is vital for them to remember....

ARTHUR MILLER, *The Crucible in History*

Cataclysm

In each human moment as in the time of stone
Such build-up before a lava fumes in the cone.

Cumulative time, a gradual hidden crescendo,
Those lids of the earth's crust shifting below.

Rifts in a magma chamber, a vicious blow-up;
Bombs and cinders spewed from an angry cup.

Sleep Vesuvius that once covered up Pompeii
With pumice-stone and ash. Sleep and allay

What fears we must both remember and forget.
Sleep Vesuvius. Within us all your molten threat.

And yet. Another beginning. Another landscape.
Can the sun still sweeten even the sourest grape?

Shared scars of forgiveness, our fragile hopes;
The fruits and vines tended on your lower slopes.

LANDSCAPES

Vemen vil er gor gevinen?
Vos zaynen mir a flig?
Loz er undz a skhus gefinen.
Oy, es zol shoyn zayn genug!

What's He trying to put over?
What are we, flies in the wind?
Is there nothing in our favour?
Enough! It's got to end.

Song of the Balta Pogrom (1882)
translated by David G. Roskies and Hillel Schwartz

Numbers

1

As though the digit shifts of centuries
Disconnect what is from what has been,
Some magic in numbers seems to lure us
And wants to wipe our old slate clean,

Somehow to forget that it may well be
That on the shaft of its middle decade
(And not its end) the twentieth century
Turns, or to think those ghosts are laid

And can no longer remind us how
It's best another generation remembers
Never to forget it could happen now.
No, not so much to rake the embers

But to recall how something not faced
Goes underground and then reappears
To haunt us. An image of Iscariot traced
Wandering across two thousand years,

His embezzled silver, his turncoat kiss.
Deutschland erwache, Juda verrecke!
Two millennia blurring Jew and Judas;
Even in the betrayer's name an echo.

Beware, beware a beast that slumbers.
And so, both to remember and celebrate
A year turning on the axis of our numbers.
A new millennium. An ancient slate.

2

A half a century on, last camp survivors
Will still wear a number on their forearm;
A tremblor rippling fifty miles beyond
Its epicentre, patterning a garden pond.
Telltale figures, eerie signatures of violence.

In an aftermath the fortunate huddle together;
At least a marriage each day at Bergen-Belsen.
Obstinacy of survival, slowly reassembled life.
Why was I one of those chosen to survive?
For children, grandchildren? A demand to tell?

Masks of resilience gradually become a self;
Work and getting on against all the odds.
Always the long-shadowed crux of that past:
Remember too much, the *Kapo* laughs last,
To forget breaks sacred promises to the gone.

Still the stamped forearms of first witnesses.
Indelible warnings: this might happen again.
Still a moment when testimony and story meet
Before the last attesting faces will retreat
To echo chambers of second-hand remembrance.

3

An intersection, at once cadence and overture,
Hinge and turning point, the moment when
The pasts we shape begin to shape our future.

Etty Hillesum recalled how her father had said
'Jews in a desert? We've seen the landscape before.'
Babylon, the Temple's fall, six million dead.

Give ear to my cry, don't hold your peace at my tears.
Is this the moment where testimony and story meet?
A passing guest, an alien like all my forebears.

Teach us, cries the psalmist, to number our days.
The exile, the scattering, now the ovens and marches.
Isaiah's world still stumbling onwards in praise.

Have I not told you from old you're my witnesses?
The desert through which we pass will bloom again.
I did not speak in secret in a land of darkness.

Remembrance

A word absorbed in an ease of childhood's garden
you think you've heard a million times over
suddenly will sink further in. A depth charge.

Or a piece you begin learning note by note,
slow practising by rote, a dreamlike repetition;
years go by before you re-awake to its music.

As though things can be too big for us close up
and need the slow-down of both time and distance;
a wider angle, the gradual *adagio* of truth.

So complex, so tangled, as if we have to wait
on some riff of imagination to refract detail,
some fiction to shape elusive meanings of fact.

Time to find the chronicles below the debris
of a cleansed ghetto, for piecemeal unearthings
to air their testimony against false witness.

Just quiet moves and shifts in geological tempo,
or the way climates show changes over decades
of slow landscape. A long redemption of time.

In a rest between notes a music's bridled silence,
or in our fictions those things still best unsaid,
a tacit crying out for the forgiveness of the dead.

Forebodings

Rumbles in bowels of myth. Again and again
Eruptions, sulphurous gases of blame.
An inwoven scapegoat down two millenniums.

When Pilate had washed his hands: *See you to it.*
Then answered all the people and said
'His blood be on us and all our children'.

Scatterings. Ghetto. Yellow badge. Pogroms.
Who was it poisoned wells to spread
Black Death among Christian folk? *And they spit*

Upon him and took the reed and smote him
On the head. So Europe at fever pitch.
Crusades. Over again the Goyim's fall guy.

Outsider inside. Love–hate's merry-go-round.
Blood-baker, healer, *Jude Süss.*
Even while the myth sleeps, a waiting victim.

Those angular planes overlapping and awry,
Tragic fault line within us,
Moody engines of prejudice underground.

Hankerings

Upheaval broods in the cauldron of an age.
Those thirty years of such faithful war –
Then Europe must struggle with her rage
For everything certain and hierarchical,
Three long centuries lusting after order.
Intolerance brews in her earth's mantle.

Rage for axioms, timeless abstractions:
Newton's laws, old Leibniz's universal;
Species, genus, our races and nations,
Europe hankers after all things steady.

A narrowing. A Renaissance in reversal.
A nervous urge to tame and already

We hunger for overviews, flawless stock,
Unblurred theories, the pure nightmare
Of ideal boundaries, *ein Land, ein Volk.*
Übermensch of dark-willed Nietzsche.
Outcastes, outsiders, freaks, beware
Our tick-tock reason's overreach.

What happened to Macbeth's carousing porter,
Montaigne's wry and carnival knowledge?
That marvelling at being just as we are,
Our lovely jumbled here-and-nowness,
Particular, once-off, centred at the edge,
This cussed and glorious human mess.

Lull

White noise and the chatter of foreshock
Along a fault; only the focus silent,
Some darker core of resentment.
Black shirts and polished boots,
Slogans of marchers with high-armed salutes.
Sultry Germany racked and knuckled under.
Tremblors wait in proud compressions of rock.

Versailles's humblings and rubbings-in;
Europe of boundaries settles bitter scores.
Too long a licking of sores
Rankles, a sour backlash
As after a first hard-won comeback the Crash
Of '29. So many half-hungry and idle.
Wounds fester under the earth's thin skin.

A wobbling trust. Dangerous subsoil.
At first too harsh, then a guilty placation.
Jutland, Somme, Verdun.
Thirty-five million.
And no, this could never happen again.

Seductive quiet. Sweet lulls of peace;
A seismic gap before a second turmoil.

Still yearnings for the glories of empires.
Dread of Bolsheviks. Upper crust and bourgeoisie
Longing for any certainty
Somehow appease and backslide.
Strut and vaunt of so much bruised pride.
All hail *Volk, Übermensch und Lebensraum!*
Let not light see my black and dark desires.

Spasm of precursors. Invisible shivers.
Lamentings heard i' th' air, strange screams of death.
In the sullen underneath
Slabs buckle in subduction
And prophesying with accents terrible of dire combustion.
Rock bends and strains towards its rupture.
A struck bell, the fabric of a planet quivers.

Reverberations

1

An old order to soldiers to lose their shape
As they march onto a bridge,
To break rhythm and march out of step

For fear concerted tempo might somehow match
Sways in the span and arch,
In case metered footfalls could catch

And amplify a beat to something vaster
Than just the sum of their paces;
A tapping into stone ripe for disaster.

2

After Napoleon the western ghetto
Vanishes. New epoch of citizenship,
Their loyalties now to flag and nation,
Rights, adaptations, *aggiornamento.*

But in vasts of White Russia, Poland,
Ukraine, Lithuania, Yiddish enclaves;
Always an outcast to Orthodox Slavs,
Catholic Poles, Lutheran *Volksdeutsch.*

Gulfs of language, religion and scorn.
Europe of nationhoods and borders,
Older jaundices, seething mistrusts;
The enclaved with nowhere now to turn.

Troop-carriers rumble over bridges:
Oder, Vista and Bug to a landscape
Already ashiver with deep grudges,
Bitter resonance of creaking divides.

Stress and strains of broken history
Prime a ruthless moment. A reverberation
Unleashes rage, a vicious licence
For minor Macbeths and *Übermenschen.*

In a sweep between Baltic and Black Sea
The Reich's own and echoed fury;
Chiming hatred, a boosted violence,
An ashen zone on Europe's hazard map.

   3

Wavers on a seismogram, a wider scribble,
Shifts and jostlings along a seam until
The moment mother earth bucks and quavers.

Violence spreads out on every side,
Frenzy of pulses radiates and woe betide
A jellied soil, any sympathetic ground

That dances to its rhythms. Shocks caught
And magnified. Even worse havoc wrought
Far from the epicentre. Consonance of terror.

Wilderness

How on the Day of Atonement Aaron came
In linen garments to choose by lots
For the Lord one of two goats,
And the other, sin-bearer for the Children of Israel,
He drove, a scapegoat into the wilderness.

Assimilated. Established. Even heroes of the Fatherland.
Liver of blaspheming Jew,
Gall of goat and slips of yew…
Once more the butt of every simmering prejudice
For th'ingredience of our cauldron.

Mischief bubbles. Strange conjunction of forces,
Hoarded pressures under duress,
Whatever slow or insidious process
Belches from its maw pent resentments
Through old hidden rifts and fissures.

In neighbouring shadows of politburos and commissars
The manufacturer, the entrepreneur
Still seem threatened and insecure;
Blond and blue-eyed redeemers of lost territory
Askance at swarthy interlopers.

Cornered every way. Marx the Jew boy,
Arch-Bolshevik, ogre and bane
Of commerce or just non-Aryan,
Sallow-skinned, jet-haired rogue insider,
Hinge and axis of German shame.

Or is it some scheming international Rothschild,
A plot of dangerous infidel,
Shylock way out of scale,
Sly, alien, worldwide tissue of collusion
Menacing a stooped and brittle *Volk*?

Whatever the angle, same kinetics of mistrust.
Sweet incense beaten small
And bring it inside the veil.
O Aaron so unsuspecting in your linens of atonement.
Target of all. Our consummate scapegoat.

Signatures

1

Freylekh, Bulgars, waltzes and Klezmorim
Playing with such a confused abandon
Dances at once rumbustious and sad that seem

To summon up centuries of teeming ghetto life,
Weddings, bar mitzvahs, circumcision feasts,
Hoisted out of the ordinary into some repetitive

Delight in sound – almost like those *céilí*
Bands melodeoning out their tunes
Battered and entrancing, a kind of cyclical gaiety

That goes on gathering its own quickened logic
Of unbroken desire. Or do they recall
Zigzag tensions and rhythms of Gypsy music?

And suddenly you hear the raucous joy of a trumpet,
A Black cotton-picker's reveille
Against the blues line of a wandering clarinet.

Then a Yiddish alto: 'There is my resting place'
Dorden ist mayn rue platz.
Each of these millions, someone's remembered face.

2

Surely all tragedies are both singular and one;
Those arcs of island over our human fault zone.

An uncouth and ruthless Georgian's litany of woe.
Ten million scorch-earth kulaks.
Purges and riddances. The Gulag archipelago.

Hatches battened on a reek of fevered steerage
Skibbereen to Grosse Île,
Ghosts of famine cross on their ragged voyage.

Some of their ships had once cargoed slaves,
Sugar drones and cotton-pickers,
The northern cities' Black slums and enclaves.

Middle passage of the dispossessed. Long transit
Of coffin-ships and camp trains,
Gangways and stations where their shades meet.

Hidden signatures of pain in a planet's hearth.
Quakes and eruptions linked in the underearth.

3

And yet there's no Richter scale of tragedy.
How to measure suffering? A calculus of pain?
Behind each agony a name, a voice, a face.

A quarter million Gypsies, the gays, the insane,
Soviet prisoners of war. The Slavs would be
Hewers and drawers under the master race.

But an unhinged and single-minded bid to erase
Every man, woman, child? Police and bureaucrat,
All will connive. There'll be no resting place.

Factories, trains and railroads now gearing up,
Machinery of oiled governance in a modern state;
Grindings and cogs of greasy calculation

And the one strain singled out for elimination.
This breed apart. A whole apparatus of hate
Bent on wiping a people from Europe's face.

Entrance

1

Convulsions in mother earth, the trembling rock;
Blind forces, a chronology of fault segments.

Ground swell of history, compulsions of an epoch;
Part of, tied into, caught up in grand events.

Marionettes? And yet decisions made, the ties,
The hitches, the twists which ravel us into a plot

Too intricate to comprehend. The eye tries
To follow its loops but strays in baffles of a knot.

Implications of grand doings and small choices.
Both bound up and binding. A complex ligature

Shaping this history that's also shaping us.
Could there be a Desolation without *der Führer*?

2

Enter the Austrian, history's fevered catalyst.
Vaulting ambition, which o'erleaps itself:
Shy, artistic and would-be watercolourist.

Volunteer artillery spotter, brave courier,
Three times wounded, twice an Iron Cross;
Now discharged corporal, disgruntled gurrier.

A somnambular voice invokes a latent anger,
His eyes singling out yours among the crowd.
Sleek-headed Chaplin. Mesmeric hate-monger.

Human, we want to explain away the villain.
Remember him only for the number of his victims.
Human? Is something already drawing us in?

3

And how to contain this unbearable evil?
Grails of theory, myths of explanation
Struggle to pin down one psychic upheaval

To make a make-up more easily understood.
Skeletons rattle in the ogre's cupboard,
A spirit tainted by a stain of Semite blood?

Grandmother Schicklgruber's seedy blackmail?
One-ball thesis? An apocryphal Jewess?
Strivings to bring a monster down to scale.

Part compassion, a *there-but-for-fortune*
Instinct stretches itself to analyse
Primrose paths, to understate the demon.

Part consolation, craving for simple clear-cut
Formulas, somehow to tame the untameable,
Undo inexplicable tangles of this blackest knot.

4

A bottomless puzzle. No matter how we rummage
So much eludes us,
So much remains hidden
In shimmies and connivances, a stage-managed image.

Clearance to Madagascar that will slide even further
On highs of a Russian invasion,
A gradual Final Solution?
Or from the start intent on some bureaucracy of murder?

Poisonous ideologue, deluded purger of Jewry,
Half-possessed messianic?
A cunning manipulator
Scheming determinedly in a cold-blooded fury?

Or both? At first a cynic's deceiving art,
The gestures, the counterfeit;
As the crowds feedback belief
A bestriding actor overcome by his own part.

Hungary, Poland, Czechoslovakia, the Ukraine,
Headiness of triumph, hubris,
Believing his own image.
Till Birnam forest come to Dunsinane.

Unwholesome radiance. A devious implacable will
Outpaces all explanation.
The black sun shines.
Quantum leap in some darker mystery of evil.

Signals

Electrical changes, rumours of foreshock,
Hints and tremolos sensed by animals
Tuning in to some seismic signals;
A dog yelps and chickens jitter.

Can no one hear the yearning oracle?

Heine's premonishing a century in advance,
A forlorn Cassandra
Warns the *Heimat* from exile in France.

A Munich newspaper's near-daily reports
Of fatal beatings
By gangs of thugs and party cohorts,

Break-ins, demimonde of counter extortion,
Dirt on rivals,
Nexus of blackmail and poison pen.

Editor Gerlich will be lifted by the Gestapo,
Steel-rimmed blood-spattered
Glasses returned to a soon-to-be widow.

An English civil servant writes to London:
The Jew is to be eliminated –
A cold intelligence is planning in Berlin

The fate of a kulak or a Turkish Armenian –
And the State has
No regard for the manner of his elimination.

Processions to Britain of opposition emissaries,
Coolly rebuffed,
Suspect double-crossers in Europe of boundaries.

Strange vibes and currents in rocks
Reptiles sense before earthquakes;
In hoar-frost the hibernating snakes
Stir from a warm underground lair.

Will no one see when the serpent rises?

Vignettes

1

'I was with A.H.', his secretary will remember,
'When he arrested Röhm and the SS chiefs.'
The last hours of June 1934
At Bad Wiessee. Night of the Long Knives.

Brownshirt leaders, outliving their usefulness,
Barracked overnight for morning executions.
'Back at the Chancery canteen,' she recalls,
'He'd joined me (both of us were vegetarians)

'But left for an hour, then called from the door:
So Fräulein Schröder, now I've had a bath,
I'm pure as a new-born babe once more.'
Relished moments. That knowing laugh.

2

Bathhouse there? A cleansing furnace?
Architects pore over detailed drafts.
Steps to chambers and then ramps.
Someone's busy working on an elevation.
The space where trains can pull in,
Perhaps a selection area just here?

And there'll be the minutiae: a pipeline,
Conduits, switches, the width of vents,
Probably a time and motion study
To check smooth running of machinery.
But for now, just a sense of proportion,
All focus still on the overall design.

Aesthetic of function. Delicate efficacy.
The tall pleasing line of a chimney,
A low contour of a kitchen and laundry.
Gate motto: ARBEIT MACHT FREI.
Work makes you free. Arch-joke
For connoisseurs. Malign surrealism.

3

Underground. Eastern Front command post.
Midnight tea and cakes. At two mein host
Grows expansive, holding forth until dawn.

Table talks. Monologues. *Der Führer* oracular
As a secretary shorthands each thought for posterity;
Art, philosophy, literature, the state of the war.

Tonight's guests Heydrich and Himmler. *Macbeth*
Does murder sleep. Trio of would-be virtuosi:
The watercolourist, violinist, architect of death.

Gradual bonds of complicity, a 'blood-cement'.
And no written orders, just a word to the wise
Making its way down to middle management.

Needless violence of the camps. Yes, gratuitous
And yet somehow even more a painstaking
Theatre of malice, *ars gratia artis.*

Extermination? 'Silly,' he says. 'A silly rumour,
We simply park our Jews in the Russian marshes.'
A nod and wink. *Der Führer* in high good humour.

From this instant, there's nothing serious in mortality.
All is but toys. A play of nudges for the gallery.
An ironic distance. Three great artists of evil.

Brink

Shelves of the earth shunt on different levels;
Forces of conflict
Climax in violence.
But this human tangle of evil almost unravels;
A turn of events,
One sudden twist,
A bitter history's last minute head-over-heels.

His vote now fallen, a waning star,
Der Führer holds a splintering party
With veiled threats of self-murder.

Hindenburg, tottering junker president,
About-faces. A backstairs deal turns
'That Austrian corporal' to 'dear young friend'

And haughty Papen thinks he'll rein in
The beast and can not see *Tarquin's
Ravishing strides towards his design.*

Tainted by the Night of Long Knives,
A first smear of the blood-cement,
Soon the arrogant Reichswehr connives.

A fractious left in one-eyed disorder
Squanders their last-chance majority,
Too busy settling some old score.

'A miracle', *der Führer* calls his success.
Thousands torch-light Wilhelm Straße.
The opposition slips away into darkness

As entering his office the new Chancellor
Confides to someone in his entourage:
'Nothing will dislodge me alive from here.'

How nearly it didn't happen. Fortune's somersault,
Blind worm of disaster,
A blundering drama,
Tragedy of this black knot somehow tied by default.
Sophocles watches.
The flaw. The downfall.
So little might have brought a juggernaut to a halt.

DESCENT

S'brent! briderlekh, s'brent!
Oy, undzer orem shtetl nebekh brent...!
Un ir shteyt un kukt azoy zikh
Mit farleygte hent...

Fire, brothers, fire!
Our poor town's on fire...!
While you stand there looking on
With folded hand...

MORDECCAI GEBIRTIG
translated by David G. Roskies

Northeim

Heimat

Thirty-one-year-old and tanned Wilhelm Spannaus
peers out of a rundown train window
on his return from seven years in South America.

1921, after a rising in the Rhineland
none of the glory of the Wilhelmine Reich
he'd left. Is the fatherland to be a Marxist shambles?

A brother had fought and perished in the world war.
Another in academe. Wilhelm will run
his father's bookshop, the first one ever in town.

Scion of old burghers and his father's gentlest son,
friendly with everyone, soon he'll be
intellectual drum and energy for his midland city.

411

Staunch Lutheran, acquaintance of poets and thinkers,
he'll fan the embers of recalled glory
to become the first of the Party members in the burgh.

There's a distrust of visionaries, and rumours abound
of thugs and power-lust, but people will say
Wilhelm Spannaus is involved, it must be in order.

To tidy things up. To revive a lustrous German soul.
Every pane is broken in the whole rumbling
train that snakes across the heartland into Northeim.

Northeim

In the fallout of defeat a city of ten thousand
nooked where the Leine and Ruhme meet,
this snug county seat plump in the heartland
rides the slump as a thousand other towns
where a seventh of Weimar Germany resides.

A cloister under Charlemagne, a Guelph city,
self-driven Hanseatics, then Lutherans
besieged and riven in the Thirty Years War.
Merchants surrender but the have-nots resist.
A broken power with its relics of old splendour,

Steep-roofed, small-paned jumble of houses
with timber designs; a medieval wall
defines a core of narrow cobbled streets.
Centuries of a comeback: a market and garrison
town become a pivotal midland junction.

Spur-lines, goods yards and a sugar refinery,
as commerce expands towards the Leine,
a retinue of railroad hands, tradesmen,
artisans, government clerks, teachers, newcomers
freighting Marx's credo to a rifting Northeim.

Beyond the wall a bourgeoisie northward
Toward the Ruhme, on a hill to the south
the wealthy nest as the lower ranks spill
west to the railroad hub; a cleft geography
soon mirrored in every beer club and choir.

Two hundred and fifty-three Northeimers dead
in Wilhelm's war. An inbred love
of marching is fed by fife and drum bands,
a complaisant town rife with slogans, banners,
and a military zest still not chastened by history.

Desires and ruptures no one will heed in time.
Self-betraying Northeim, a burgh still
smug in its divides until under pressure
of Nazi assault its wedged boundaries sunder
along an old fault line. A fissured city.

Kingpin

Ernst Girmann, the Party dynamo, an angry
Twenty-six-year-old son of a Northeim incomer;
Hardware merchant, cool, grey-eyed and hungry.

Like his *Führer*, an Iron Cross from World War One
Where a brother fell. But whatever died within,
Here's a man ruthless, consumed by ambition,

His dark blond hair split precisely mid-skull
And sleeked to the sides, thin lips and cleft chin,
A young ruddy face too knowing and vengeful.

An engine of upheaval. Every ruse and stratagem.
Short-fused and underhand; when drunk maudlin,
He despises Northeim, for years they ignore him.

An endless programme of unrest until the city's
Fissures gape and the group leader can begin
To weed his rivals out, to purge committees.

The Bürgermeister ousted, opponents collapse
As Girmann seizes power, local kingpin
In a regional gridiron of smaller Party satraps.

Once in control, a round of graft and patronage,
Resentments against an aloof elite, driven
By chips and grudges of *petit bourgeois* umbrage.

Vendettas. Anyone who'd crossed his path before.
The former city manager flees to save his skin.
A usurper's long memory for any unsettled score.

Failure to suppress the once supportive Lutherans
Galls him. He learns the tyrant's oldest chagrin:
To settle for the half-cheek of ritual obeisance.

As the Americans approach, his final orders are
To defend the city to the death. Unfrocked Girmann
Loads his *Schnapps*, decamps for the hills by car.

Three years interned and he'll settle in a town close
To Northeim. Later some stubborn tug of origin
Will return to its own an ageing and sullen recluse.

Fever Chart

Suddenly a fringe of zealots in from the cold.
The panache to hold a town at fever pitch.
Flags, a flash of black on white on red,
torchlight parades, blurted radio speeches,
children wearing swastikas, vertigo of elections,
rumours of the Gestapo, fracas, stormtroopers,
book burnings, cheering rallies, brass bands.

Suddenly a fringe of zealots move mid-stage.
Speakers planned to engage a middle class.
'Only one God in heaven we love, one fatherland,'
A Lutheran priest exhorts a crowd who applaud
rapturously. Girmann and cohorts tack and trim
to meet demands; self-tuned feedback of success,
a balance sheet of members, dues and votes.

Suddenly a fringe of zealots centre of attention.
Funded from the ground up, tactics hinge
on the leader's flair to sound the local mood;
once the coffers fill, the Gauleiter doesn't care.
To elude a backlash, Girmann soft-pedals Jews
but stokes every feud and panic in a riven city.
One clear-cut goal: the *realpolitik* of power.

Suddenly a fringe of zealots into the limelight.
Fuzzy talk of kin and forebears and blood
but there's an élan, a vehemence about the men,
a sense of purpose that seems to promise some
new ordinance, a millennium on earth. Farmers'
sons from Northeim County swell the marches
as old dreams well in the citizens' giddy hearts.

Suddenly a fringe of zealots in from the wings.
To keep things on the boil until the burghers
tire of all this turmoil and rancour and begin
to hanker again after the fist of certainty.
Anything for order. Riots dismissed as a phase,
the crowd cheer, sing the Horst Wessel Song.
A dizzying city skitters along the brink.

Butt

In fevers of stoked upheaval
How come the decent won't stand as one
Or somehow see behind the show and pageantry
Sleight-of hand, a jugglery of evil?
But none
So blind as those who will not see.

A left wing lose their way.
No bridges to the middle, their dreams
Of sweeping change a rhetoric out of touch;
Shadow marches, the *Internationale*,
And schemes
For a counter-coup, a phantom putsch.

415

Imagining themselves bereft
Of wealth and power, the Bourgeoisie
Hatch fears of a shake-up. A need to condemn
The *bête noire* of an upstart left
Won't see
The beast they feed will feed on them.

Communists gloat: at least
The spineless left is dealt a blow!
Guelphs still fight the ghosts of a lost cause,
Both fall prey to the hungry beast
And so
A town succumbs to tragic flaws,

Feckless squabbles, disunities.
A Blackshirt machine adjusts or shifts,
The thinner end and then the blunter edge,
A *coup d'état* by stealth, as a city's
Rifts
Widen to the bullying butt of a wedge.

Wilhelm

The Party digs in. A legerdemain of office.
Graft. Gravy train. Shuffles of embezzlement.

In Spannaus' bookshop mumbled dissent.
Was this the dream they meant to espouse?

Corruption could only undermine *das Volk*,
they grumble up the line to the Gauleiter

And no one listens. Girmann sews it up.
The black sun shines in blacker satellites.

Teacher friends hounded, Spannaus clings
to belief: *der Führer* would clean things up.

Wide-eyed trust. And many in town still say:
if Wilhelm is involved, it must be in order.

416

Power

1

A sudden caller to Schulenburg throws
a Swastika pin on his table: Put that on
or else! The aloof county prefect caves in.

An eye to preferment, civil servants join.
Spouse cajoles spouse, for our sake apply.
Rumbling momentum as a bandwagon rolls.

A tavern installs a radio to tout *der Führer*'s
speeches; Girmann's blunt brother puts out
signs on a shop-front: First Member in County.

A party of some hundred paid up the January
before. Now a scramble to become a member.
By December a fifth of Northeim's adults enlist.

Baskets of requests. The *Gruppenführer* sneers
at how after years fair-weather friends convert
and rubs his old opponents' noses in the dirt.

Some who oppose him enroll, want to give
the whole a leaven of decency, some dither
watching to see just how the wind blows.

The despised appeasers. Once in, no leaving.
Once compromised and in, the squeezers on,
A marked man while the black sun shone.

2

It spread by rumour
That one evening at a party in the town
Ruhmann the doctor after a drink or two
Had let his hair down
And did his take-off of *der Führer*.

Next morning his hostess
Reports his behaviour for fear it may redound
On her that the doctor had done his party-piece.
The word gets round
Better not to party just in case.

Better to stay
At home. Clubs they'd once joined
Have been rearranged or merged 'to aid cohesion'.
What's the point
When you watch every word you say?

Nothing too clear.
Talk of blacklists no one lays eyes on.
Everybody wonders who the moles are, everybody
Warns someone;
Shadow efficacy of hearsay and fear.

A few disappear,
Enemies cold-shouldered and driven out.
A news photo of a camp some hours away
That's whispered about,
Vague menaces in the atmosphere.

Enough just
For numb compliance. Terror seems to travel
And amplify like a myth as frail bonds of friendship
Begin to unravel.
Tacit threats. Meltdown of trust.

3

Now to warrant Girmann's iron hand
grand schemes to smarten Northeim
and prime a pump of Nazi upsurge.
A splurge of paint on medieval buildings.
Things on the move, a massive overhaul.
The wall around the town repaired,
an uncared-for chain of defence mounds
that surrounds the city landscaped to create
ornate parks or gardens, and the one-time
Northeim moat becomes instead a ring
of flattering lakes for swans. Everywhere
an air of purpose. A brand new
venue The Sacred Place (which stood
in a wood of tall oaks a henchman
of Girmann sold for a favourable sum),
a stadium which lures tourists to town.
Rundown areas cleared and re-planned,
demand for uniforms heartens business,

an address by Girmann to entrepreneurs
avers the end of the slump is in reach
if each of them employs more. Spend,
lend or borrow, above all consume.
Boomtown in the making. A house scheme
the regime they'd ousted tried they now
allow, though they stymied it before.
More public works. The Shirts know
how a show of action will for a while
beguile the burghers. Lulled for a time,
Northeim believes what Northeim desires.

Them

Girmann had threatened to expel some members
for hobnobbing with them. As the Reich began
to settle, a determined plan to freeze them out.

A haberdashery that a year before toasted two
hundred and thirty years. A grocery store.
A draper. A broker. Six score in ten thousand.

A newspaper names every store and office
to boycott. Few Northeimers dare to ignore
the SA man posted at the door of a premises.

A chance to capitalise on not to be missed.
A sign: GERMAN MERCHANT now vies with:
PURELY CHRISTIAN FAMILY ENTERPRISE.

No one credited the rhetoric before the Reich;
now from fear neighbours start to shun them.
Their slide to isolation has already begun.

A burgher urged by another to flee shrugged:
'*Verstehen Sie*, here I'm Müller the Banker,
anywhere else I'd only be Müller the Jew.'

A discreet push from a Veterans' Shooting Club
and Ballin the doctor crosses over the street
so as not to greet and taint his gentile friends.

A Shirt on his door, Ballin crumples. Numb
to the core, he keeps repeating: Was it for this
I spent four years to defend my fatherland?

Friends, colleagues, clients that shied away.
Slow isolation. Unprimrosed slide to a hell.
Blind-eyed Northeim doesn't want to know.

Stand-off

Northeim's *Geist* dumbed
Down to passivity. Numbed
And shrunken. What could you do?
Who would you trust or turn to?

As the Reich settles in
The once mirage of a genuine
Millennium fades. Disillusion.
Apathy. Denial. Accommodation.

A pretended daily compliance,
A sort of determined indifference
Where no one quite knew
Who was fooling who?

A need to keep the facade,
A zealous mutual charade:
The town dresses its window,
The Party approves the show.

An agreed unspoken stand-off.
Secretly many now scoff
At a dull regime; small
Comforts of inward withdrawal

That achieve nothing to halt
The iniquity. A spirit stalled,
A willed and grievous oblivion
While the black sun shone.

Huff-no-move of acquiescence.
Soft collusions of silence.

Battalion 101

Point-blank

Blueprint for a cleansed Europe. *Judenfrei.*
March '42 to February '43
at least three-quarters of all the butchery.

Timetablers, a retinue of paper Rommels
shunt millions until there's only a residue,
a last few rump ghettos and labour camps.

Feats of planning. Meticulous follow-through.
But who rounded them up in scattered villages,
sealed the trains or slew the lame and frail?

Everyday men. The plain and run-of-the mill
as Battalion 101 whose rank and file
would shy at first from point-blank slaughter.

Truckers, stevedores from Hamburg's docklands,
waiters, factory hands, clerks and small-time
salesmen; an average trawl of average citizens.

A mean of thirty-nine, too old for soldiers,
but drafted as *Ordnungspolizei* to clean up
Poland between the River Wisła and the Bug.

Men long grown before the black sun shone
from a city well-known for ease with outsiders.
Peer conformity, some bone-bred deference

Or any war's need to annul the victim's face?
Humdrum murder, dull and commonplace
as weeks lull them into a norm of violence.

Resettlements. Proceed as usual. Smoothly
again without incidents. Immunities of routine.
Ordinary men hardening in their daily carnage.

A Polish Village

1 *Débutants*

After the onslaught in Russia they know
a tour there left their men distraught,
but in June when a mainline to Sobibór
was under repair Globocnik had soon
started to prepare for more shootings.
Under his care in Poland there's still
almost two million to kill, and though
he'll use Treblinka and Bełżec to slow
now would lose momentum. Clearly
slaughter is troublesome for men, yet
just then a war dangles in the balance
and summer is a chance he can't miss.
For want of better, the firing squads
of débutant Battalion 101.

2 *Rumour*

A few had guarded the sealed wagons
of Jews and Gypsies eastward, knew
from what they piece together better
not to wait, and the escort commander
Gnade decided on the late train

and fled straight back to Hamburg.
A police battalion still unblooded.
July 12th when less one company
they mass, a few had begun to wonder
if this meant their cue for *Judenaktion*.
The one dissident platoon commander,
a Hamburg timber merchant, warns
his battalion commander's adjutant
he won't do it; as officer or merchant
he can't gun down bereft women
or infants. Unknown to his captain he left
to escort the 'work Jews' to Lublin.
A sergeant's caution to any who'd shirk:
he wants no cowards among his men.
Captain Wohlauf of First Company
Tips some off to next day's interesting
projects. Spare ammunition and whips
distributed. Everywhere there's rumour.

3 *Aside*

Roused early, some few are aware
what's ahead for them at Józefów
as trucks loaded with reserve bullets
jounce and swerve the dawning road
east to pounce on a sleeping village.
A weeping commander starts to speak
of a terrible task. A bleak assignment.
But after all orders are orders and
remember in Germany bombs fall
on both women and small children.
The Jews' American boycott harmed
the Fatherland. Armed partisans among
the three thousand eight hundred Jews
in Józefów just had to be kept in hand.
Fit men apart, the residue of women,
children and frail must now be shot
on the spot. Any who shied from the task,
should please immediately step aside.
One. Then a dozen more will seize
this last chance before the massacre.

4 *Lesson*

Company platoons surround the village.
Fugitives are shot. The others round
them up in the market. Anyone gives
trouble, gun them with infants or feeble
or any who hide. Able-bodied men
set aside for camps as 'work Jews'.
The rest shuttled from the market place
to a nearby forest and the firing squads.
A swift session in how best to kill.

The battalion doctor (a gifted piano
accordionist at soirées) in order to show
the ways you ensure an instant release
depicts the contour of a human head
and shoulders, shows a fixed bayonet
set on the backbone above the blades.
Freighted forty at a time to the woods,
victims climb down to be assigned
a policeman each, lined up and pressed
to sites in the forest Wohlauf chose
and made now to lie in rows, a bayonet
as prescribed above each shoulder blade.
The sound of a first fusillade. Work-Jews
Throw themselves on the ground and weep.

5 *Haste*

Wohlauf all day keeps on the go
choosing sites so the incoming batch
won't see corpses. Two squads despatch
truckloads in relays. A messy business.
A blundered aim and blood sprays
anywhere. Splinters of sundered skulls.
The flurried officers begin to despair.
Men from the market are brought in.
Everyone ought to shoot. Hurried
changes to the process: a two-man escort
to the sites for speed. A few who ask
are sent to a different task, but Wohlauf
refuses his men any other assignment:

'If you can't take it, then lie down
with all the Jews.' A cigarette break.
In the afternoon, alcohol for the squads
as more approach their platoon leader
to be excused from the gore. Some shun
the shootings, others after one ordeal
on a pretext will dodge or steal away.
Some just delay the action. The evening
of a long summer's day and a feverish
drive to finish; as darkness falls
none will survive. Reloaded trucks
head west into the night, leaving
a strewn and looted dead behind.

6 *Nightmare*

Back at the barracks horror sinks in.
Dismayed or angry they begin to drink.
Oblivion of the bitter and afraid. Again
Trapp will calm his men, tell them
others are accountable. Orders are orders.
Best not to dwell on it. But those not
in the forest will neither ask nor pry
and those who were will try to forget.
Suppressed despair. Józefów
a taboo by consensus and self-excuse.
Jews were doomed no matter what,
so one more shot counted for little.
Not everybody can yet execute infants,
but one could only shoot the youngest
as he just can't bear to leave an orphan.
Some men declare they'd go mad
if they ever had to do the like again.
One wakes the night after Józefów
riddling a barracks roof with bullets.

Papa Trapp

Iron Crossed veteran of World War One,
at fifty-three a career policeman risen
through the ranks with his *esprit de corps*
but short on the blinder zeal of two captains
Wohlauf and Hoffmann who can't now conceal
young, arrogant contempt for their commander.
Yet Papa Trapp is popular among his men.

God, why did I have to be given these orders?
That day at Józefów he'd cry for the bloodshed;
aloof and riven he'd paced his headquarters
but not the forest. Things commanded not faced.
In despair he'd shed tears and confided to one
of his men *If ever this Jewish affair is avenged
on earth, then have mercy on us Germans.*

As the police reboarded trucks at Józefów
a ten-year-old girl bleeding from the head
appeared, he took her in his arms and said
You shall remain alive. Horror-struck
he'll console troops, overlook the truancy
of men who stole away or stepped aside.
Patron of all who flinch. A major who wept.

Come September a sergeant slain by ambush
and Lublin demands a minimum two hundred
punishment shootings to subdue locals. Trapp
still balks at Poles but with a mayor's consent
he'll kill just down-and-outs; instead the Jews
from a nearby ghetto can overfill his quota.
And Papa Trapp has no more tears to shed.

Measures

Apart from the merchant who first stepped aside
Or a dozen more who took a stand,
The trouble is the new recruits are horrified
By slaughter at first hand.
Squalor and gore are a burden,
Such distress could well unhinge their men.

True, a mind gets used to almost anything.
But a conscript tailor on a second relay,
Given a German mother and daughter for gunning
Sought release from the fray,
Returned to the market place.
The trouble is these killings face to face.

A merchant encountered among the men
In the market a Hamburg Jew;
Another's first job a war veteran from Bremen
Who'd begged in vain for rescue.
Morale will only improve
If the dirty work is kept at one remove.

Yet once posted to Lublin District everything
Seems at least more bearable.
Treblinka's death engine is in full swing.
A blind eye turned to hell,
Trapp's *Ordnungspolizei*
Elude the horrors of seeing how victims die.

Still violent round-ups. *Schnell! Schnell!*
Poke and herd. The murdered slow
Or fragile, the sweated driven pell-mell
Of parched human cargo
Nailed in a cattle wagon,
A freight of Jewry penned and shunted on.

Ukrainian, Latvian, Lithuanian, underfed
War prisoners, the dreaded *Hiwis,*
Move in if there's any more bloodshed.
Measures taken to ease
The burden. A system refined.
A butchery out of sight and out of mind.

Lieutenant Gnade

A few courageous dissidents,
some who tend to skulk but take no stance,
the bulk of ordinary men who toe a line
of slow inurement;
in others a beast awakens.

Hartwig Gnade, Lieutenant
Mercy, who only eight months ago went
by late train back from Minsk so not to know
his cargo's fate,
now turns cruel and violent.

As they dig their hole he'd choose
twenty greybeards to undress, and to amuse
himself compels them to crawl before their grave,
yells at his officers
to club these naked Jews.

Wobbling and enraged he'll sit
on a mound above the trench firing on it;
as teeming bodies shove into this tumulus
he's screaming drunken
abuse from the edge of the pit.

And in the colder late autumn
he'll institute his strip-search for every victim
to loot valuables. Returned their underwear,
they leave en route
for Treblinka shamed and numb.

Surges of a deep and molten
fury vie with *Hiwis* for cruelty; sudden
vicious shifts of humour terrify even
his men. An anger
amok. Vesuvius within.

Hoffmann

Another bred in a youth movement,
a touchy and headstrong twenty-year-old
ten years in the SS, then captain of a company,
a careerist who loves to parade his full insignia,
his white gloves, and whose men dub him
'Hitler's cub scout'.

At Józefów when the timber merchant
withdrew and one of Captain Hoffmann's men
was among the few who dared to follow suit
he openly abused his recruit for breaking ranks,
but Trapp excused the man and reined
his captain in.

Until October Company Three
Still eluded the worst. (At Józefów
they hadn't seen the shootings at first hand.)
Now a command to clear a northern ghetto
and Hoffmann's turn to read the orders
to proceed as usual.

But the captain has stomach pain and dysentery.
Often it's best to refrain from motion so instead
from his bed he fusses over small details.
His men soon notice he tends to fall
ill on the eve, bedridden
before the action.

With Hoffmann on sick leave Trapp
asks Berlin to relieve the captain of his command.
Moved to the front he'll win an Iron Cross, belie
his former comrades' snide remarks and heal
his bruised pride. The spirit willing,
had the flesh refused?

Wohlauf

Vice-Commander Wohlauf, chief of the battalion's
First Company, an officer with belief in himself
And a lust for success that often came to grief.
Schooled in the regime, the SS by twenty-three,
recalled from duty in Norway for lack of restraint
and here at twenty-nine he's back in favour
as Trapp nurses his career, but his men still see
a pretentious man, their showy 'Little Rommel.'.

This is a captain of romance. Due to marry
in June, out of the blue his battalion is sent
to Poland but Trapp will relent and he weds
but returns to command a company at Józefów.
Soon Wohlauf has his new spouse visit him.
A wartime honeymoon. His greatcoat draped
over his bride, she'll climb aboard his truck
alongside her captain on an August round-up.
The head of his convoy Wohlauf issues orders.
Hiwis already sotted are shooting so wildly
even his police take cover and everywhere
corpses as Jews make their way in thousands
to the marketplace one hot late summer's day.
Those who faint are shot. Frau Wohlauf,
already four months gone, takes off her coat,
stands in her dress at the market looking on.

To a man his First Company now take offence
that a woman sees their violence. A trace of shame
as a horrified Trapp must face his officer down.
After the Serokomla massacre he and his bride
pass some days in Hamburg. The honeymooner
returns but stays only weeks as ill with jaundice
he seeks recall. His one brother has been killed
and his father just dead, as an only living son
his request is granted. Exit Captain Wohlauf.

Culmination

After massacres and cleared ghettos
a hunt for any fugitive disappeared
to live underground, daily outings
to hound absconders hid in forests
now tracked by faeces found in snow,
or giveaway chimney pipes attract
stalkers to the prey. Farmers' stolen
crops betray their hungry presence.
A hunter drops a grenade in a bunker,
any survivors sprayed with gunfire.
A dozen or two at a time, entire
families perish as volunteers pursue
the chase. No duress just a tenacious
tracking down. Once again the face
to face of Józefów as Battalion
101 clock up another thousand.

Seniors withdrawn, others moved on
in the turnover and still the battalion
blooded at Józefów participates
in the Harvest Fest as inmates
of Lublin labour camps march
to zigzag graves. Speakers blare
music to mute and counterpart
gunshot, and lined along the route
Reserve Battalion 101
sentinel a cortège to extinction,
the Germans' biggest single *Aktion*;
in three November days alone
forty-two thousand Jews slain –
half the battalion's whole campaign.
Such ordinary men now lend a hand
to kill some eighty-three thousand.

FIGURES

Shtiler, shtiler, lomir shvaygn,
Kvorim vaksn do.
S'hobn zey farflantst di sonim;
Grinen zey tsum blo.

Still, still let us be still.
Graves grow here.
Planted by the enemy,
they blossom to the sky.

SHMERKE KACZERGINSKI
translated by David G. Roskies and Hillel Schwartz

Summons

Meditate that this came about. Imagine.
Pyjama ghosts tramp the shadow of a chimney.
Shorn and nameless. Desolation's mad machine
With endless counts and selections. *Try to see!*
For each who survived, every numbered
Arm that tries to hold the wedding guest,
A thousand urgent stories forever unheard;
In each testimony a thousand more suppressed.
A Polish horizon glows with stifled cries:
Who'll wake us from this infinite nightmare?
Out of the cone of Vesuvius their lives rise
To sky-write gaunt silences in the frozen air.
A summons to *try to look, to try to see.*
A muted dead demand their debt of memory.

Arrivals

Clamourings for water, even a handful of snow.
By day the glimpsed places, in the dozed night
Groans or bickering until their wagons slow
And crash open in a station's eerie floodlight.
Uncanny ordinariness. 'No Baggage', they're told.
A dozen SS men with a stony indifferent air
Move among the arrivals questioning 'How old?'
'Healthy or ill?' and pointing either here or there.
Men won't abandon wives. 'Together afterward,'
They're reassured. Some mothers unreconciled
To leaving small children are soon transferred:
'Good,' they say, 'Good, just stay with the child.'
A finger is pointing. Caprices of fate allotted.
Frozen silence of lives unseamed and parted.

Figures

After days and countries of a roughshod ride
Dishevelled children edgy and overstressed:
A boy scolded won't stick to his mother's side,
A miss who hugs her doll against her chest.
Boarding-school girls clamber from the train
In hats with blue ribbons trailing in the air,
Pleated skirts and socks straightened again,
Five by five, holding hands and unaware.
A fifteen-year-old will recall how she loses
A mother who opts to leave her on her own,
A neighbour's child so forlorn that she chooses
The other side. A waif shouldn't vanish alone.
Figures forever sealed in a molten Pompeii,
Marrow spread as bone-dust in Polish clay.

There

Non-stop. A sweated shift of *Sonderkommando*
Remove remaining traces of a previous batch
And hurriedly prepare the set for another show,
Another intake into this theatre of despatch.
A clothes-peg carefully numbered still forestalls
A final panic. Such a well-rehearsed scene
With signs hung on the changing room walls
To extol in several languages merits of hygiene.
A squalid journey and now the need to scour
Arrivals. *Remember your number*...unctuous
Reassuring speeches as spruce SS impresarios
Cozen and seal their victims into a shower.
Just affable ushers. No time wasted. No fuss.
In every heart one moment when it knows?

Here

After disinfection, broken oversized shoes,
Berets, blue stripes and the shaven head,
A large yellow Star of David for the Jews,
For criminals green triangles, politicos red.
Elaborate madhouse of rules and signs of caste.
Beatings. Starvation. A *Kapo*'s whim and sway
Unravel reason. Here no future or no past.
Maybe the sap and cunning for another day.
A ladle of watery soup traded on the sly,
A broom filched, a shoe-patch, rations of bread.
Each for himself. Father steals from son.
Parched but denied an icicle Levi asks why?
There's no why here. Shorn and striped biped,
A tattooed number who'd once been someone.

Qui vive

Always on their wits. Day by day to postpone
The inevitable in a brutal catch-as-catch-can;
As months draw skin tighter over a cheekbone,
Steinlauf washes to remember he's still a man.
When to queue to arrive as the soup is thickest,
To sleep on a pillow of belongings, not to leave
Bowl or shoe untended. Survival of the quickest.
Ruses and dodges of endurance. Endless *qui vive*.
The submerged or exhausted slow beyond caring.
A week, at most a month. Then the *laissez-faire*
Of the overcome and a last ghostly indifference
To hunger, squalor, beatings or fear. Just staring
Listless and vacant goners. *Muselmänner.*
A light in their eye already shines their silence.

Threads

Three a.m. rollcall of skeleton labour.
Chin up, chest out until the *Kapo*'s gone;
Hands tucked under armpits of a neighbour
Huddling the glazed will to carry on.
Phantom bodies move outside their mind
As cold claws and ices deep in the marrow.
On the double! Various teams, assigned
A ditch to dig, sand and stones to barrow.
Weeks totted from when they first arrive,
Argued over, checked so someone could say
For certain, if any of them manage to survive,
So and so died on such and such a day.
Just somebody to pass another's story on;
Tiny threads of time loop beyond oblivion.

Night

Night after night they sink in muds of dream:
There among their own in warm midsummer
They tell their story to friends who always seem
Distant, somehow unable to hear a homecomer.
Attuned to the sound, old hands wake but hold
Back and so are sure they'll arrive in between
Bucketfuls, never are sent half-clad in the cold
To empty warm urine into a frozen latrine.
They drift again towards a sleep that gnaws
And lures the mind with phantom food until
Many lick their lips or work their jaws;
Dreams both tempt and cheat the hungry will.
Short fitful hours when a Tantalus replays
In feverish stereo broken nightmares of days.

Ensemble

In summer by camp gates an ensemble's concerts:
As squads of inmates are filing past in fives,
On stools in their pleated navy-blue skirts
And lavender scarves they play for their lives.
Chosen by an exam, many who'd been *virtuose*
Now grind a music complicit and empty-eyed;
A band conductor from a famous Vienna café
Parodies for all she's worth her life outside.
Brisk marches to keep everything on the go.
In strict tempo marionettes in rags they slept in
Jerk their stiffened joints and swollen feet.
Then *The Blue Danube* or even *The Merry Widow*
For a commandant who loves waltzes. A violin
Is singing against the grain its hollow upbeat.

Ravens

They untangle, lug, stack and kindle the dead.
Chosen on the platform for brawn, broken in
Hell for leather, men clubbed and goaded
As still among the bodies they recognise kin.
Shirkers are shot. Others harden to endure
As stokers of hell, well-fed privileged caste
High on their pickings. A three-month tour
Of duty before they in their turn are gassed.
Sonderkommando, Levi's 'crematorium ravens'
Fallen beyond his compassion's greyest zone;
Soiled by fellow blood, vultures and cravens,
Cain sucking his marrow from Abel's bone.
Pity these ravens for what driven ravens do;
Bitter complicity that Jew should oven Jew.

Elite

Stars of the show they strut their daily stage:
Roll-call, undressing-room drama, the rite
And frisson of power, rivalry, bursts of rage,
Gratification of swaggering in this limelight.
'Caps off!' The slowest to remove their caps
Are plucked out in rows of five to undergo
A routine of physical jerks until they collapse,
And battered then to death by a block *Kapo*.
An elite trained by public shamings to comply
Now turn humiliation into ritual bloodshed.
Snappy and insouciant the SS cast an eye
Over the count to check the newly dead.
Thrilled by quivers of fear in lives they own,
They crunch paths gravelled with human bone.

Lily

Lab women and men in SS gardens consort.
Lily is engaged to a Pole in an undercover
Courtship. Her striped dress tight and short,
Lily is twenty and styles herself for her lover.
Never face on, their whispered rendezvous,
Cigarettes from a ration, cucumbers he thieves,
Small forbidden gifts and their billets-doux
Hidden for pick-up under a pumpkin's leaves.
Her fiancé sent to another commando, his friend
Fetches a note and is nabbed. A coded complot
In sweet nothings? Prepared to take the rap,
He's beaten but refuses to tell until in the end
The Pole owns up to save him. All three are shot.
We are, she'd written, *like plants so full of sap...*

Chinks

Here Jew, politico and gypsy, misfit and thief,
This underworld where push comes to shove
In a squad's *esprit de corps*, moments of relief,
First rough fellowship edging towards love.
Under the chimneys shows of gratuitous aid,
Things forgone, a gesture for a friend's sake:
Lulu offers a tea ration to a parched comrade,
At rollcall fainting neighbours slapped awake.
Wolf hums his repertoire while Levi advises
Bandi, innocent Hungarian, to steal to survive;
In the black of night Lorenzo the mason rises
To filch soup which keeps his protégés alive.
For some, for a while, bitter and sweet parallel
As rifts of light blink through the walls of hell.

Alone

Sprawled barracks, shacks, a conglomerate
Of *Kapos,* commandos, a shifting grey zone,
Clutches of friends, dices of time and fate
And each satellite camp a globe of its own.
Bunked head to feet in a jam-packed hut.
Polish. Hungarian. Greek. Every new arrival
Reshuffles the cards. Flux and through-put.
Bonds of language, a connivance of survival.
Each somewhere someone's remembered face.
At Buna, Monowitz, Auschwitz and Birkenau,
For most an unheard passing leaves no trace
But eking their starved wits a few somehow
Endure to witness through one memory's lens.
The silent alone fathom the depth of silence.

REFUSALS

Unter dayne vayse shtern
Shtrek tsu mir dayn vayse hant,
Mayne verter zaynen trern,
Viln ruen in dayn hant.

Beneath the whiteness of your stars,
Stretch out toward me your white hand;
All my words are turned to tears –
They long to rest within your hand.

ABRAHAM SUTZKEVER
translated by Leonard Wolf

Spoors

Murmurs

Under black sunlight the will to endure;
A victim dares to overturn her soup bowl,
Warsaw's ghetto defended sewer by sewer,
Reckless White Rose of the siblings Scholl.

What to do if Germans evacuate Amsterdam?
Frank gossips to her diary in an annex room.
In Bürgerbräukeller Elser primes his bomb;
Wolski the gardener is hiding Ringelblum.

At Birkenau, Salmonovitch shins a flag mast.
'Nearly a hundred,' he replies when they ask
His age. Six hundred boys beaten and gassed.
A crematorium log buried in a thermos flask.

Crackles of resistance. Cussed moves to stall
The beast. Cards flung from trains, spoors
Of memory, whispers behind a gossamer wall.
Static of refusal. A grit of risk and gestures.

440

Blumenfrucht

Sosnowiec, June of '42 and Germans
in hospitals threw infant Jews from a window
to trucks below. The rest leave for Auschwitz.
Five youths somehow sought to thieve arms
from a German's quarters. Blumenfrucht caught,
he wants to shoot but an officer's dog sinks
teeth in his hand. Resolute as they set alight
wooden chips stuck underneath his fingernails;
even a two-day session on an iron net fails
to break him and when he screamed he said:
I will not speak, I am dead no matter what.
A mother brought to cajole him. Still he refuses.
Captors esteem such self-control but something
in his mettle unnerves the regime. By right a Jew
is swung in daylight, a warning to *Untermenschen.*
Blumenfrucht hanged before his morning broke.

To Life!

On the lookout, ready for any fate,
Dabrowa Tarnowska's prayer-shawled
Rabbi Isaac would wait
With followers. Found and hauled

From their hide-out underground,
They're herded to a Jewish graveyard.
Someone unseen by their guard
Passes a vodka bottle around

And facing each waiting assassin
They drink their toast *lechayim!*
As linking hands they begin
To dance. At once mowed

Down. A preventable episode.
Enraged the squad cuts
Their bellies and tramples on them
To spill their mutinous guts.

Praise him with the timbrel and dance.

Hallowing

1

At Kelme, the ditch dug, Daniel
Rabbi asks a commandant's leave
To speak for a while to his people.
'All right, speak, but make it brief.'

Unhurried in the face of the commandant:
The sanctification of the name, trace
And travail of a shadow-desiring servant,
No longer to act, simply to embrace.

Time to end – an officer butts in.
Willingly, lovingly to accept our fate.
The ditch graves gape and wait.
I have finished. You may begin.

2

Ringelblum beaten for nights on end
Refuses to name any gentile friend,
Asks: Can death be so hard to bear?
To deny their gloating over his despair.
A Warsaw bunker someone had betrayed
And all thirty-eight caught in the raid.
A switch of cell? Prisoners contrive
His rescue. Slim chance to stay alive.
And are his children doomed all the same?
So it's the way of Hallow-His-Name.
Kiddush Ha-Shem. Humble acceptance.
For many just the sign of their silence.

Recording

And will anyone ever know?
In Vilna they wanted, in case,
Someone outside the ghetto.
I'm the victim. I'm the witness –
A camp slogan. Defiance
Of record. Charged remembrance.

Birkenau's chronicler Lewental
Buries his thermos in the ash
Of crematorium III, journal
for a final revolt, a cache
Of testimony, resistance of word,
Troves of memory interred.

Four hundred pages of diary
In the minuscule hand of Etty
Hillesum, a crammed story
Of sudden ripening that forty
Years away will resurface.
Spoor of a life. A trace.

Survival

1

As smoke from burning wood the will
To survive leaves a ghosted heart;
Parents and sons of Olga Lengyel
Chambered, her husband once sighted
Through the wire, she tilts to the brink
Till drafted by camp resistance. A part
To play: intelligence link by link
Along a human chain the underground
Flits contraband, a parcelled explosive
Hazardous as the angle of a *Kapo*'s head.
At least to die for something beyond.
We lived to resist. We resisted to live.

2

Pell-mell nights in a parched cattle car,
Parted from loved ones into a bizarre
Seesaw of eerie calm and rampage
Of the *Kapos'* random virtuoso rage;
Broken by ghettoed months, too numb
With disbelief to adapt they succumb.
A few by grit or hazard can adjust.
Ruses of refusal. A shared crust.
Carmen's bartered pail for Delbo's
Drought. More than his soup, Lorenzo's
Resistance. A gesture of human rapport.
Levi's something still worth living for.

Just

Leopold the thief feeds his protégés,
tends their needs in his *pied-à-terre*,
a Lvov sewer. Laundry. Prayer books.
A year to liberty and ten survive.

Freelance, Albert the local masseur
bicycling Jersey to rub his clientele;
his fee in kind duck eggs and bread
secreted to his fosterlings underground.

After *Kristallnacht* Priest Lichtenberg
protested against transports to the East,
prayed for Jews and internees. Arrested
for his prayers, he dies en route to Dachau.

Austrian Anton Schmidt, the sergeant,
sought to flit Jews by army truck
to Białystok – still thought safe.
But caught, he too forfeits the light.

A Gruszka Zaporska unnamed tended
Six in his cowshed. Raided he's gunned
As he fled for his life. Gendarmes return
To wipe out wife, daughter and son.

To save just one is to save the world.
On bitter ground the wind-blown seed;
Lone random flowerings of courage.

Haunted

Dazed in a sudden comeback from oblivion
Displaced huddle into a surge of rebirth,
Children named after their ashen gone,
Firethorns lavishing berries on stony earth.
Swaying in a brittle future so many cling
To one another, pooling their orphan genes,
Their broken youth lived out in offspring,
Angels of their parents' interrupted teens.
Vulnerable vessels, survivor urge to protect.
Fragmentary disclosures. Eavesdrops. A tattoo.
We must be ready after what happened to us.
Children tabbed by anxiety. Always checked.
Stains of what happened seep slowly through.
Aroma of mistrust, distant fall-out of Vesuvius.

Deep in the memory gene a black sun.
History is over, be happy like anyone.
Would they help, give bread? Delbo
Asks every face. No assumed tomorrow.
Defiant normality. Success of reborn day
Almost holds nightmare moments at bay
As they make their lives. The busy scarred.
And yet to know not to drop your guard,
Never to count on another human being.
You're alone. Something always missing.
Undertones of grief lurk below a crust
Of everyday. Half-smile of broken trust.
Behind a flimsy partition ghost parents call,
Siblings eavesdrop behind a gossamer wall.
A doubleness only revenants understand.
Wounded alone know the wounded land.

Even the numbed and busy daylight cracks
A survivor's mask. A subconscious goblin
Triggers surreal *déjà vu*, flashbacks,
Replays, clusters of torments breaking in.
The dentist's drill smells of burning bone,
In a car behind a bus the choking fumes,
A crane's gibbet dangles inmates to atone
Escapes, a cinema queue for shower rooms.
Delicate balance between the dark and light:
Ordinary work-filled days with nervous rifts
Weigh against the nightmare's haunted realm;
Grown older, days again brim with hindsight,
A psyche lopsiding as its fragile poise shifts
And burdens of memory threaten to overwhelm.

Voices in the bowels of the ark cry out:
Hear us too! Cracked voices of drought
As from cattle cars hosanna faces stare.
Primo Levi now steps so softly into air.
Points thrown, a barbed unerring train,
A rifted trust never quite trusted again;
A keeper brother unkeeps Jean Améry,
Still red embers burning into memory.
Es mus azoy zayn. Who witnesses a witness?
Celan's burden of so much ash to bless,
Insomniac being, silent in the Undivided
He marks: *Sometimes his genius goes dead
And sinks into the bitter well of his heart.*
One by one by one our witnesses depart,
Softly the shaft, the orphan's satin despair
Over the parapet, down the well of a stair.

Against the odds unearthed diaries, fragments.
In milk cans and tin boxes Ringelblum's blow-
By-blow journals, sudden cache of documents
Dug up out of the ruins of the Warsaw ghetto.
Planting a tree some Polish children chance
On thermos-flasked notes of Salmen Lewental,
The Greek Jew's slow-release resistance,
Birkenau *Sonderkommando*'s time capsule.
All fugitive chronicles sealed into airtight
Jars interred with rubble and sunk below
Rebuilt houses, lives still waiting on the light.

Write and record. That a world may yet know.
Dubnov's orders, *shtetlekh* and ghettos wiped
From the earth's face: *Schreibt un farschreibt.*

Cry the shibboleth in an alien land.
Trucks of half-skeletons, the demand
Of the rabbi's son, desolate Elihu:
Show your power. This is against you!
Nothing happens. No lightning rod.
Sonnenshein shouts *There's no god.*
Six million brothers Cain can kill.
Black sunshine. Ratchetings of evil
As chill winds blow across a bowl
Of stars. A world rattles on its pole.
Broken vessels of a god in hiding,
Agony's grinding down, a sliding
Back to sacred nothingness that hovers.
Beckonings, maybe. No more. A lover's
Invitation rumouring through the dark.
Rustles of absence in a silent ark.

Le Chambon

Hinge

Whipped by one of those skinflint winds
that blows in across such exposed tableland,
a thin dark-eyed woman shawled in snow

Picks her way to *rue de la Grande Fontaine*,
that led beyond its curve to a staid presbytery;
In Le Chambon, they said, someone might help.

Remote sanctuary, ice-skinned city of refuge,
tombstone grey, wind-bitter Huguenot village,
stubborn asylum on the granite Plateau du Velay

447

where Chazot the preacher once burnt at the stake
and Nantes's promise breached, a thousand or so
more Protestants had sought refuge and settled here.

Rocky ground, steady and fertile in its remembrance
of the centuries' outbursts, nest of unarmed resistance
sentried to the south and west by spent volcanoes.

Over the German border into northern France,
and now her final chance she has fled southward;
in Le Chambon, they said, someone might help.

Wind and snow whirl off the Lignon River.
A half-numb tap. Swinging on a hinge of memory
The door opens. '*Naturellement*, come in, come in.'

Divergence

Holidaymakers gone, the twin granite villages
Le Chambon-sur-Lignon and Le Mazet winter in.
Three months of yellow summer, nine of grey.

Curt streetscapes and stoic cut-stone homes,
bleak outskirt of somnolent farms and forest
where dissident Huguenots once hid their pulpit.

Two craggy villages paired in a single story,
four centuries of shared and broken ground,
the same prepared soil before this ordeal.

A deep resistance sways on its stealthy roots,
urgent offshoots of risk, a subterranean hum,
in a humus of quiet trust, Le Chambon burgeoned.

Everything aware and ajar. The secret room,
webs of messages and kitchen *savoir-faire*,
Teams of guides to dare the mountains by night.

Somehow bitterer winds now blow in Le Mazet
to chill the marrow. No apron of sensuous grain.
No scatterer. No sower. No Spring. No *grande fontaine*.

Against the stranger's need, Le Mazet's shut door.
A ground so harrowed though no seed is sown.
My neighbour is only my own. A narrowed love.

Pastor Trocmé

'Death, death, death,' his sigh on arrival,
'I'm entrusted with helping a tiny village die.'
Through the ashen stone walls of a presbytery
deep slanted windows ration their sunlight
on a Basque-style tablecloth. Yellow, red, black;
colours warm and volatile enliven a room.

Driven, turbulent Trocmé. A boy of fourteen
he'd seen a jawless German after the Somme.
An etched image. Or was it Kindler, born-again
telegrapher, refusing to bear arms at the front?
A flicker of sun-caught yellow in a cloth's design;
what must be done to save this village's soul?

Here the hungry depths of Huguenot memory.
Jews? But we only know one human kind.
Throwback of whispers among old outsiders
as Trocmé trudges in snow to far-flung farms.
Kitchen to kitchen. A tremolo of counteraction,
a calm obstinacy spreads its undertow of trust.

Still that temperament. Yellow, red and black
as doubts that will often plague his mind by night.
A few hundred or even thousands sheltered?
Too small a thing to do? And was it cowardice
to shun all force? Bitter chaffings of despair,
a blood-red desire to gun the Führer down.

No time for idle compassion. A violent man
bridled by love, Trocmé has begun to sow
in the long-readied soil of grey Le Chambon
his stubborn mustard seed of quiet resistance.
A stranger's face caressed. A door ajar.
City of refuge, lest innocent blood be shed.

Impresario

Great summer clumps and bushes of wild broom
yellow and warm a desolate hinterland before
it greys back to a wasteland nine-month winter.

Even then the bony withered fingers of *le genêt*
warm again, yielding their acrid perfumes
to thaw the chill stony rooms of Le Chambon.

The pastor's wife is tending her kitchen stove
snapping and bending the broom's wizened branches,
She hears a numb tapping on the presbytery door.

It's the hunger she notices in the snow-haloed face,
a half-glance preparing to retrace her steps
through the entrance porch. 'Of course, come in!'

'Come in!' She bustles a stranger toward heat to hear
her news, fusses her to eat at their long wooden
table, her sodden shoes shoved in the oven to dry.

In a blizzard she crosses a square to the Town Hall.
'But no,' says the mayor, 'just run her out of here!
'Will you save one woman and destroy us all?'

No arguments. Madame Trocmé exits to snow,
reluctant impresario of an underground trust.
The first of hundreds lying low, secreted

in safe houses and farms near the pine forest,
over mountains out of harm's way to Switzerland.
A city of refuge. A hamlet for waif and stray.

But where else could they go? A Chambonais' shrug
Plays down the dangers. We had to take them in.
I couldn't close a door against a stranger's face.

Contagion

Out from the hub of Le Chambon's counterstand,
Slow spread and rub-off of their bedrock love.

In childbirth, Magda had nearly bled to her end.
As Trocmé watched by her bed in his dark heart

he knew he'd relished survival; even as she sank
his mind raced with plans, how he'd begin anew.

But shouldn't he yearn for two to meld into one?
A broken mystic so shocked at his self-concern.

Later she mends and he confesses his own dismay
at how his spirit could stray in a future without her.

'Oh never mind' – her bifocal nature that understood
those gradients of love and let-go always undefined.

Her earth-nearness countervails his earnest strain,
holding a tense balance in the scales of a passion.

His ardour still never sure where to draw the line;
perpetual apprentice in the yaw and pitch of things.

Two intense temperaments contrary and at one.
The nave of their resistance fanning outwards.

Risk

Besieged centuries of dissent and lying low
These still waters lodged in a spent crater,
a mountain people silent, cunning, secretive.

Something stirred. Swirls in a brackish pond
as word spreads of a summer round-up in Paris;
rumours of Jews massacred in the far east.

Stonily refusing to betray any broken stranger
Le Chambon's grey dissenter presbytery becomes
a hub and clearing house, an eddying centre.

In the temple they ask *Which now of these three,
thinkest thou, was neighbour to him that fell
among the thieves?* Somehow an interrogative mood

ripples and widens out across the community.
And about thirteen leaders, *les responsables,*
discuss and relay the same implacable question:

Who is my neighbour? The Gestapo tightens its grip
but a daring begins to outweigh every new risk;
the Chambonais already grown surer of their answer.

More and more fugitive children are housed.
Madame Eyraud's *pension* forever open door,
her fourteen or so boarders mothered and homed.

Then a pacifist school of makeshift classrooms,
An ease of welcome and deft rule-bending
blending both refugee teachers and pupils in.

On the periphery houses with back doors that open
onto woods where the hidden flee when the farm
dogs bark their alarm as a round-up approaches.

Sober Chambonais spontaneity that needs to move
less from above than outwards. An *esprit de corps*
quickens in the margins. Some centrifugal love.

Swift and decisive responses, no over-command,
almost as though they thrive on risks just taken;
this village alive in the jazz of its chosen danger.

Nameless

Maybe it comes from the garrison city of Le Puy.
A hasty call from a nervous employee
who somehow contrives to forestall Gestapo round-ups.
Those lives in his hands as he lifts a phone;
unknown amateur mole, his heart in his mouth.

The same warning from the same nameless voice.
Beware! Beware! Tomorrow morning!
No one knew from where the call had come.
But whoever it was was always right,
just one night's notice given to raise the alarm.

All houses in Le Chambon and nearby combed.
Routine call for identity papers,
Machine-guns poised, doors hurriedly unlocked,
walls knocked for a hollow sound,
cupboards, attics, cellars but no Jew found.

Throughout the day invisible messengers flit
beyond the village, make their way
to warn the outposts of a coming daybreak raid.
Uprooted from another makeshift lair,
evacuees prepare to vanish into the forest.

At the core some anonymous urge to disobey.
His quick staccato communiqué issued
before the click on a swiftly recradled receiver:
Attention! Attention! Demain matin!
A furtive courage crackling down the line.

Trouble

Trocmé and two right-hand men are incarcerated.
First distrust, then respect for these Huguenot
Inmates, a camaraderie of spirit almost as though
Another Le Chambon grew as they met and debated.

453

Fragile city of trust, an innocent countermine
Far too dangerous to handle. The camp supremo
Ordains their release. And just before they go
An oath of allegiance two of them refuse to sign.

Back in the huts fellow internees are horror-struck:
Refuse to sign? A scrap of paper in a dossier?
You must be a skunk with skunks! Even Trocmé
That stubborn night would doubt the line they took.

'Pack your bags – we want no trouble in the compound,'
They're told next morning. Orders come from on high.
And no need to sign. They return to say goodbye.
Holding hands closest comrades gather around,

Sing *au revoir* to the tune of 'Auld Lang Syne'.
The Huguenots survive. *Only* au revoir *my brothers*.
Freighted to Polish camps or Silesia the others
End in the chambers or the maw of a salt-mine.

Misgivings

Years after Magda Trocmé will recall
and still regret that first bitter deceit,
counterfeit cards made for a Monsieur Lévy.

Without a faked identity the man would die.
And yet to lie? A slide to the demimonde?
Once beyond Eden some candour forever lost.

These faked forms, papers forged or falsified,
Things denied, fudge and ruses of concealment,
Each silent half-truth went against the grain.

More a time for action than for contemplation
or an old temptation to keep our hands clean;
would we've been purer if we'd shut our door?

A shed innocence. Impure metal of humankind.
'Never mind,' she shrugs, 'What else could we do?
Who could they turn to if the Chambonais balked?'

Le Forestier

1

'A lonely, young, sad and beautiful man.'
This was how years afterwards the Chambonais
Recall him, brown-haired Dr Roger Le Forestier
Who settled in Le Chambon before the war began.

Villagers warm to boyish irresistible innocence,
Sober Chambonais drawn in by his spontaneity,
A strange, colourful figure who lives so vividly
His life seems much more real than his absence.

He falls for Danielle with all the swarm and whirl
Of a nature utterly guileless and open-hearted.
'A woman as handsome as himself,' they said,
'How he couldn't stop being in love with the girl!'

From the outbreak eccentric surgeon to the Maquis,
Patching up injured guerrillas until he'll refuse
The partisans his red-crossed ambulance for use
As a troop-carrier. Shunned, he blunders to Le Puy

To prove himself, trying to have two Maquisards
Released, but underground passengers have played
Into Gestapo hands, Sancho Panza betrayed
By a gun they'd hid on the sly in the boot of his car.

He pleads his beliefs: *lest innocent blood be shed*
Chambonais had hidden Jews. His youthful candour
Moves Schmehling, Le Puy's garrison commander;
To free him if he goes to tend German wounded.

A chance to flee but his gratitude refuses to shirk.
Already Schmehling's acquittal has been subverted
By messages to Lyon the Gestapo have sent ahead,
They nab him as he sets off to Germany to work.

Later Danielle tracing her husband Le Forestier
Learns of a hundred and twenty murdered near Lyon,
Rummages sacks of their belongings. In the final one,
A button with the name of his tailor in Montpéllier.

2

A score years on the Trocmés visiting Munich
sought out Schmehling (now a retired schoolmaster
living in a bomb-damaged house), enquired of him
why those last grim months while they scoured
villages nearby and knew Le Chambon was a den
of resistance, why then did they desist from closing in?
'I believed,' he replied, 'Le Forestier had told the truth,
nothing in our violence could kill Chambonais dissent,
and I worked to delay the Tartar Legion's round-up.'
So why, the Trocmés press, was Le Forestier murdered?
'That Gestapo bastards should gull me! At night
I wake and that beautiful, beautiful woman is there
with her two small children begging me for their sake
to spare her husband. I see them as they take leave
of that man, her confidence in me that he would return.
What must she think of me?'
                        1944,
August 20th, some days before the liberation
of Paris, a Gestapo squad ablaze with a night's
drinking had herded from Le Forestier's jail scores
of prisoners out to an abandoned farmstead where
they were gunned, stacked, doused, set alight,
their clothes packed into sacks. Neighbours had heard
the screams of those the bullets had failed to kill.

'What must she think of me?' His eyes now fill
with tears. In a low voice André Trocmé replies:
'She has not as yet been able to forgive you.'
Voilà tout! The Trocmés leave him to his grief.

PRISONERS OF HOPE

הֲיֵשׁ בִּלְתְּךָ גּוֹאֵל, וּבִלְתִּי – אֲסִיר־תִּקְוָה ?

Is there any redeemer like you?
Or any prisoner of hope like me?

JUDAH HALEVI
translated by Nicholas de Lange

Round-up

Whoever it was took this photograph

Zeroes on a boy's eyes that want to grow
Bigger and bigger the more you gaze,
Deeper and deeper in the sideways
Sunlight asking us how we can know

The words to put in the mouth of another?

Dust-veil

1

*Three millenniums and minds still rake over
Hekla's third post-glacial outbreak, uncover
ash interred under a thousand beds of ice
tephra that spreads to Uist and Shetland.
Had this dust-veil produced such changes,
not just immediate havoc but shifts of climate
ramifying right across a northern hemisphere?*

*Those years Ireland's oaks had narrowest rings,
Norway's snowline fell and the Caspian rose;
even the Alpine winter now grows harsher,*

457

the Danube overflows to flood the Hungarian plain.
Does the great Mycenaean reign end by drought,
famine rout the Hittites from the Anatolian plateau,
Hekla's outburst unsettling over half our globe?

2

Still in autumn harvest feast of Sukkoth.
A fugitive garden hutch, a fragile booth,

Lonely tabernacle, wilderness *pied-à-terre,*
Wandering other always at home elsewhere.

Is there any redeemer like you? Poet Halevi
Asked, *Or any prisoner of hope like me?*

Roaming three millenniums: Mesopotamia, Egypt
By the Nile, Babylon, Nineveh, the same script

Of exile and bondage and wilderness sojourns
Crying towards Jerusalem. Caravan of returns.

The battered wife of a God she can't forsake,
Even an enemy's bruisings a lover's keepsake.

My love encamps where'er you pitch your tent...
And chastens the body your sweet blows have bent.

3

Liberator on the move, knife on the throat.
Thousands of lives herded westwards;
laggards, stragglers riddled and ditched.

We were not allowed to turn our heads
but we knew what the shooting meant.
Sometimes five hundred shot per day.

At Blechhammer marched into huts
to sleep, then torched. Burn or run
the gauntlet of sweeping gunfire.

On a cliff-top road beside Palmnicken
gunners mowed them five abreast
dead or alive into the freezing Baltic.

Rhyme nor reason. Knife on the throat
as a black sun sinks. The Reich
pared to its bare skeleton of hate.

4

After Liberation Socha the thief is struck
Down on a Lvov street by a passing truck;
Poles cross themselves as his juices ooze
In a gutter. *God's reward for aiding Jews.*
London's streets dance as war ceases;
In Poland still a rondo of hate's caprices.
Bełżec, Sobibór, Treblinka, Chełmno,
More than all the Auschwitz archipelago;
Treblinka, Chełmno, Bełżec, Sobibór:
Of two million, a hundred and nine endure.
Testifying in Lublin one of Bełżec's two
Killed as he homes from court. Bastard Jew!
Five Auschwitz, Mauthausen and Buchenwald
Survivors the Polish Home Army halt
In a car near Nowy Targ stripped and slain.
An angry shadow falls on the face of Cain.
At Kielce eight-year-old Henryk Blaszczyk's
Pretended on July 4th of '46
That Jews had seized him for special rites.
A medieval rumour fanned now re-ignites
And forty-two are shot, axed or stoned.
More than half the survivors flee Poland.

5

Hierarchies of doubt among the blessed few.
Another man's wounds? Who slept with a *Kapo*
To cheat the hungry kiln or made it through
Dancing moonlight naked to pleasure Gestapo?
Hoarded brunt and guilt of unspoken years.
Business as before. Over and over nightmare
Of ghostly homecomings where no one hears.
To endure to tell the world but do they care?
Heels are taller and hem-lines lower again.
A glittering eye can't stay the wedding guest
Who shirks the bony hand of too much pain;
A world that lusts for life soon loses interest.
For years tattoos of memory travel incognito.
They didn't understand, they didn't want to know.

6

Slowly a cone has bled its anger,
red lava cools off and browns.
In Northeim Girmann's ousted enemy
comes back to run the City Hall.
A policeman in Battalion 101
peached by his ex-woman and sent
to Poland names a sergeant, lieutenant
and major under whose command
he'd shed blood of Jews and Poles.
The policeman and Trapp are executed.
Gnade fell in action but most fled
like Lieutenants Hoffmann and Wohlauf
to Hamburg as career policemen until
in '67 an assiduous investigator
will accuse them. An eight-year sentence
(four for Hoffmann on appeal) but the State
withdraws. The conviction rate too low.
Who understands or wants to know?

7

Ancient Mesopotamian spring fest
Woven by the scattered or oppressed
Into a sombre history of complots
To erase a people without trace.
Feast of Lots.

Mordecai, outsider who wouldn't bow
And refused to kowtow
To Haman, jumped up Amalekite
That plotted to destroy the Persian Jews
Out of spite.

Mordecai and niece Esther outsmart
Haman the palace upstart...
At Minsk in '42 at least
Five thousand from the ghetto killed
To mark their feast;

Thirty miles west of Lódz the Gestapo's
Readied gallows
And Jews made play hangmen
To their own ten sons to avenge
Haman's ten.

For the festive bread of deliverance
A stone of remembrance
With noosed ghosts in bas-relief;
Ashen calendar of bitter eruptions,
Almanac of grief.

8

No gain or purpose. Just gratuitous hate.
Never before? And yet we can't be sure?
Cinders raked over in the earth's grate
Peoples buried in ash that left no spoor?
Thousands of Aztec victims paraded yearly
In Tenochtitlán, taunted up the stairways
To the killing stones high above the city;
American natives wiped by *Conquistadores*.
Even among narrow-eyed cruelties a shudder.

Time and motion as two masked figures unclasp
A canister dropped in a sunken bunker's eyehole.
Shift and breach of the known, an under-judder
As a volcano spits warnings through a fumarole.
Fallouts of tephra still blow beyond our grasp.

9

'Ten days it rained ashes and the rains were grey',
a chronicler writes with dismay: bitter weather,
dry fogs, dimmed suns, blights and failed harvests,
signs from heaven as the Shang dynasty runs down.

A Chinese eyewitness to Hekla's Far East fallout?
A spewing fireball spreads a dust-veil of desolation,
pall of travail, those broken and scattered peoples.
Destruction turns all their presence into absence

unless some testimony breaks their infinite silence.
In remembrance resides the secret of our redemption.
Out of this eruption, can we prepare another climate?

Sign

Lonely Yahweh breathes in
And out ten vertebrae of a human;
Another inhaling of love
But blown too hard to glove

Their bones and seven vessels
Explode into night, cells
Of a divine soul we bring
Back by deeds and prayering.

Talmudic riddles and lucid
Yiddish...joyously I stride
In Warsaw, Vilna or Lvov.
Other. Among and not of.

Unhomed. Smitten with eternities.
Thou shalt separate three cities...
Lest innocent blood be shed.
The milk and meat divided.

The wood, the fire and the lamb.
And I am tired as I am
A Jew, wading through blood.
I no longer have the hardihood...

Glatstein at fifty-odd
Quarrels with a wounded God.
We, your radiant vessel,
Palpable sign of your miracle.

Is this what haters hate?
The chosen choosing to separate.
Kedushah. Apart and vagabond.
Singled out. Bearers of beyond.

Paradise

The sea is the sea. A chimney's just a chimney.
Bride kissed through a veil of wounded piety.

I love the birth of light, the pure fantastic
Of the naked and the real. Without bombastic.

Shalom, to be safe, to be healed and whole.
A wood of candles now the Wailing Wall.

Down a corridor of history the booted pogrom
Still echoes a broken rhyme with crematorium.

Black milk, black snow, black sun, black bloom.
Paradise pushes its way out of my tiny room.

Maybe a half eternity of God's restless time,
How often to trust to heal such broken rhyme

In Abraham's breast? *And all my yesterdays*
I sense among blossoms of blood-flecked lilac sprays.

Babel

A city, a tower whose top may reach to heaven.
Has would-be Babel fallen all over again?

So sure we'd been of plot and *mise-en-scène*,
A tick-tock dénouement, slow but certain.

Visions of control, primrose track to hell;
Stoked ovens, gaunt shadows of Babel.

Broken forever old spinning-jenny's thread,
Our long and trusted dream of progress dead.

Bitumen for mortar, they said, *brick for stone*.
Paths of Auschwitz paved with ash and bone.

Still trembling in our galaxy's outer spaces
The crying silence of six million faces.

Stretching

So is all history one secret narrative of power
Broken in the brick and rubble of Babel's tower?

Hard-bitten Atlas, our hands thrown in the air,
Are we too disillusioned now to bother to care?

Our stories become labyrinths of irony that turn
On irony. Fiddlers fiddling while a world may burn.

He breaks me down on every side and I am gone.
O you who stalked the barren road to Babylon

Or walked the desert as second Jerusalem fell
And Titus of Vesuvius shattered Herod's temple,

Show us again some end to shape our storyline.
A feast of rich food and well-aged wine...

Isaiah's imagination stretches somehow to cope;
In Jeremiah's darkest scroll a jazz of hope

That stirs even in the deepest cries of silence:
Then shall the young women rejoice in the dance.

Glimpses

After a tough day selecting who'd live or die,
For light relief Mengele had the camp cellist
Anita Lasker play him Schumann's *Träumerei*.

But in concerts under Mahler's niece's baton
Hints of perfection outside a chimney's shadow.
Behind all hopelessness a kind of life went on.

Depths of survival. Klezmer or jazz or *céilí*,
A story squeezes at the edge clamours of music;
Out of darkest histories, profoundest gaiety.

A feast of rich food and well-aged wine.
Visions beyond loosening back into a world
Too deep and copious for black suns to shine.

Imagined surprises, surprises beyond our ken.
Dream and reality feeding circuitries of hope;
A promise to remember, a promise of never again.

Waking

Can how we remember shape what we become?
A criss-cross of testimonies in every medium.

Delbo says do not look in the eyes of the cellist,
A cellist recalls her music as a means to resist.

Walking ghosts in staccato clips of a newsreel;
Six million one face in the melancholy of a still.

Lucky Szymborska, *a hook, a beam, a brake*;
Celan's waking to *black milk of daybreak*.

Humble siftings, a patient tentative process;
Angles and tangents of vision, layered witness.

No closure. No Babel's towering overview;
With each fugitive testimony to begin anew.

Memory a frequent waking out of forgetfulness;
Dissonant cries of silence refuse to quiesce.

Imagine

More than ever seductions of Babel's tower.
New ways of control,
Accrued information, the software of power.

The overlords and barons of print and screen,
Oligarchies of news
Shaping our images. Everything overseen

By Argus whose hundred eyes never sleep:
Snooped bites of memory,
The bug and zoom to eavesdrop and peep.

A traffic camera that can zero in at will,
Constant vigil in the heavens,
Whereabouts triangled, tabbed by a mobile.

The benign are keeping a watch over us.
Imagine another black sun,
An all-knowing stony insomniac Argus?

As never before we promise never again.

Never

That any poem after Auschwitz is obscene?
Covenants of silence so broken between us
Can we still promise or trust what we mean?

Even in the dark of earth, seeds will swell.
All the interweavings and fullness of being,
Nothing less may insure against our hell.

A black sun only shines out of a vacuum.
Cold narrowings and idols of blood and soil.
And all the more now, we can't sing dumb!

A conversation so rich it knows it never arrives
Or forecloses; in a buzz and cross-ruff of polity
The restless subversive ragtime of what thrives.

Endless dialogues. The criss-cross of flourishings.
Again and over again our complex yes.
A raucous glory and the whole jazz of things.

The sudden riffs of surprise beyond our ken;
Out of control, a music's brimming let-go.
We feast to keep our promise of never again.

Repair

Never, never again. Pleading remembrance
Whispers through the gossamer wall:
Promise us at least this. An insisting silence.
We begin to repair, to overhaul

Soft habits of the psyche, trying to find
Fault lines, trembling earth-shelves,
The will overreaching limits of mind
Grounding worlds in private selves.

Wounds always ajar. In its aftershock
Our earth still trembles and strains.
Tentative moves. Even to probe a rock
Stratum, to map the fault planes?

White noise and quivers. Shifts of geology.
What might be salvaged? Hesitance
Of first mendings. Delicate *perhaps* or *maybe*
Tracing detours of repaired advance.

Faces

Neat millions of pairs of abandoned shoes
Creased with mute presence of those whose

Faces both stare and vanish. Which ghetto?
Warsaw, Vilna, Łódz, Riga, Kovno.

Eight hundred dark-eyed girls from Salonica
Bony and sag-breasted singing the *Hatikvah*

Tread the barefoot floor to a shower room.
Friedländer, Berenstein, Menasche, Blum.

Each someone's fondled face. A named few.
Did they hold hands the moment they knew?

I'll change their shame to praise and renown in all
The earth... Always each face and shoeless footfall

A breathing memory behind the gossamer wall.

Soon

Soon now their testimony and history coalesce.
Last survivors fade and witnesses to witnesses

Broker their first-hand words. Distilled memory.
Slowly, we begin to reshape our shaping story.

A card from a train in Warsaw's suburb Praha:
We're going nobody knows where. Be well, Laja.

That someone would tell. Now our second-hand
Perspective, a narrative struggling to understand.

Victims, perpetrators, bystanders who'd known
Still cast questioning shadows across our own.

Some barbarous. Mostly inaction or indifference.
Hear, O Israel still weeps their revenant silence.

Abraham pleaded for the sake of the ten just.
Our promise to mend the earth? A healing trust?

Reprise

To remember to break the middle *matzah*
To lean to the left and taste again *maror*,

To pour salt-water on eggs at the Passover,
Share around the untouched cup of Elijah.

Risks. Fugues of detours. Spirals of reprise.
A feast of rich food and well-aged wine.

A light too broad for any black sun to shine.
Scope of conversations, brilliance of what is;

To love the range and fullness yet to recall.
Your golden hair, Margarete, your ashen hair...

Next year in Jerusalem! Parting toast and prayer.
And still they breathe behind a gossamer wall.

ACKNOWLEDGEMENTS

The Gossamer Wall is a distillation over several years of various aspects of the Shoah and it is hoped that it will encourage readers back to the primary sources, in particular to the first-hand accounts of witnesses in which the poems are grounded, but also to historical or scholarly studies and the imaginative literature which undergird them.

Among the numerous testimonies of survivors are Primo Levi's *If This Is A Man, The Truce, The Drowned and The Saved* and *Moments Of Reprieve*; Charlotte Delbo's *Auschwitz and After*, Elie Wiesel's *All Rivers Run to the Sea*, Etty Hillesum's *An Interrupted Life*, Anne Frank's *The Diary of a Young Girl*, Jacques Lusseyran's *And there was light* and Anita Lasker-Wallfisch's *Inherit the Truth*.

Some of the historical works which the poems draw on are Sir Martin Gilbert's *The Holocaust*, William Sheridan Allen's *The Nazi Seizure of Power*, Christopher R. Browning's *Ordinary Men* and Philip Hallie's *Lest Innocent Blood Be Shed*, along with many other studies such as Ron Rosenbaum's *Explaining Hitler*, Christopher R. Browning's *The Path to Genocide*, J.P. Stern's *Hitler*, Joachim Fest's *Plotting Hitler's Death*, and Aaron Hass's *The Aftermath*.

Other books which the poems point to are Richard L. Rubenstein and John K. Roth's *Approaches to Auschwitz*, Inga Clendinnen's *Reading the Holocaust*, Edith Wyschogrod's *An Ethics of Remembering; Contending with Hitler*, edited by David Clay Large, and *In and Out of the Ghetto*, edited by R. Po-Chia Hsia and Hartmut Lehmann.

The imaginative literature dealing with the theme includes Anne Michaels' *Fugitive Pieces* (from which the title is taken), Elie Wiesel's *Night*, David G. Roskies's *The Literature of Destruction* (which provided several epigraphs), *A Treasury of Yiddish Poetry*, edited by Irving Howe and Eliezer Greenberg, and John Felstiner's *Paul Celan* and *Selected Poems and Prose of Paul Celan*.

I'm grateful to Dr Elizabeth Maxwell for inviting me to read from these poems as part of the international conference *Remembering for the Future: The Holocaust in an Age of Genocide* at Oxford where I had crucial conversations with survivors, scholars and those who teach and hand on the history of the Shoah to another generation.

I'm deeply appreciative of the advice and support of my friend Professor Peter Ochs, as well as Dr Margie Tolstoy, Dr Nicholas De Lange, Professor Gila Ramras-Rauch, Dr Wendy Whitworth, Dr Guy Beiner, Angela Gaw and Dr Margaret Gowan. I'm also grateful to David Arnold, Paulette Goldstein, Batsheva Dagan and Oren Baruch Stier for their interest. I'm especially thankful to friends Vigdis and

Erik Bjørhovde, Marie Rooney, Dermod Dwyer, Helen O'Sullivan, Robert Kruger, Hallgrímur Magnússon, Ken O'Brien, Valerie Hannigan, Audrey and Walter Pfeil, Daniel and Perrin Hardy, Deborah and David Ford (for his constant encouragement and counsel) and, above all, to Bríd.

Acknowledgements are also due to the editors of the following publications in which some of these poems first appeared: *The Harp, The Patterson Review, Remembering for the Future: The Holocaust in an Age of Genocide*, ed. John K. Roth and Elizabeth Maxwell (Palgrave, 2001) and *Third Way*.

Love Life

(2005)

For Bríd

Three dozen years. Morning, noon, night.
Love life. Our being bathèd in the light.

CRIMSON THREAD

> Your lips are like a crimson thread
> and your mouth is lovely...
>
> *Song of Solomon*

Homing

1

Longbow years of longing
Bends an arc's wooden U.
Tenser stretch, fiercer shoot.

An arrow rigs a violent route
Gathering into a shaft of yew
Dreamed eye of a golden ring.

Cupidinous. Desire overdue.
A goose cock-feather quivering.
No hard-to-get. No pursuit.

Come what may. *Coûte que coûte.*
I finger a silk-whipped string.
My life takes aim for you.

2

O Eros ravish and enlarge us.
Just to gaze, to listen, to mingle.
Sweet fusion. Carnal relish.
Break me again with outlandish
Desire my prowling Mademoiselle.
The arrow of our time discharges.

3

A shaft so full of amorous remembering,
Déjà vu of yearning's consummate fit
As I stoop to fondle a hollow in your nape.

As if such hunger coiled up in a man
Wakes some reminiscence we relearn,
I kiss in your flesh your spirit's kiss

Like Hermes' son fallen for Salmacis.
Our nature divides only to return.
I've known you since the world began.

A woman's desire now bends to shape
The long elucidation of my spirit.
An arrow homes into its golden ring.

Long Song

Fragrance of your oils.
L'amour fou. Such sweet folly.
Your haunting presence
Distilled traces of perfume.
Resonances of voice
Dwell in my nervous body.
My skin wants to glow,
All of my being glistens.
Divine shining through.
Your lips like a crimson thread,
Your mouth is lovely...
You're all beautiful, my love.
Honeyed obsession
Of unreasonable love.
Pleased, being pleased,
I caress this amplitude,
Eternal roundness.
Voluptuous golden ring.
Sap and juices sing
Eden's long song in the veins.
Spirit into flesh.
The flesh into the spirit.
A garden fountain,
A well of living water,
Flowing streams from Lebanon.

For Real

A first gazing at you unawares.
Wonder by wonder my body savours

The conch-like detail of an ear,
An amethyst ring on your finger.

Could I ever have enough of you?
Juiced cantaloupe, ripe honeydew,

Slack desire so I desire you more.
Laugh as no one laughed before.

Vivid more vivid, real more real.
I stare towards heavens you reveal.

Yellower yellow. Bluer blue.
Can you see me as I see you?

Sweeter than being loved to love.
Sweetest our beings' hand in glove.

Milk and honey, spice and wine.
I'm your lover. You are mine.

Candle

I think I've fallen in love again with Eve
Who coded your genes so perfectly for me
And sent them replicating down an aeon.

With every needed break or loss or siege
Chromosomes mutate to bring you in the nick
Of time to be this beloved face and name.

Amazed once more I hardly dare to believe
I fall heir to whatever you choose in me;
Fluke and mould of planned unplanned liaison.

Shulammite, Laura, Beatrice, Bríd.
In double-corded spirals of a candle's wick
After such ages helixes of yearning flame.

Healing

Think that I might never have happened on you,
Mate and match;
For all the work of genes so many *ifs*.

Supposing in the bebop and noise of youth,
In turns and riffs,
In fumbled serendipities of time and place

I'd faltered or somehow failed to recognise
My counter-face
Or Eros hadn't led across the Rubicon?

Imagine we weren't ripe for one another –
Me blundering on,
Strung up, burning the candle at both ends –

Or if I hadn't suffered breakage under way?
The broken mends.
Burnt not shy. Wounded enough to heal.

Complementarity

Golden halo of early lust,
Arrow that trembles and aches
In a looped bow of suspense

And still delights in anticipation,
Part an aiming and part
A relished moment loth

To let go the silk string.
So, the Rubicon.
Yield and quiver of returning

Until we two are each and both
Wave and fired dart,
A misty integration.

Soft combat. Honeyed violence.
My female being awakes
Dewy-eyed with trust.

Sun

A fireball I cannot hold a candle to –
Light-years more giving, ample and rife
With desire, magnolia chalice of body

I touch petal by petal and undo.
Like an overcoat a wife must last for life
My poor sober father had cautioned me.

Paced madness. Patient furnace of sun.
Shape me, kiln me, cast me, love me,
Mate, mistress, queen, courtesan in one.

Our naked nothing. Wing-giving delirium.
All caution to winds and kings of Jericho,
In Rahab's window tie a crimson thread.

Jag of bliss. Drowsed and overcome
My life for yours. Ravish me! I grow,
I sweat, I ripen in your pleasured bed.

Rhyme

No courtly sighs. No amorous unattainable.
Come to me a woman in flesh and bone

And wander slyly past the mind's sentinel
As my hand strays along an erogenous zone.

Unpetal a whole purple chalice of magnolia.
And let it be all the crimson spill and stain.

Amor, senno, valor, pietate e doglia –
Love, wisdom, courage, pity and pain.

At Avignon Francesco Petrarca hums his Laura.
The way you moved? An invitation in your sway,

Gentle persuasion in the swish of a body's girth?
A spirit's glance. A mood. A fragrance. An aura.

That was that. I sleep into my life's *canzoniere*
And wake to see the tracks of angels in the earth.

Exposé

O mind and king of thinking
Unbend limbs, come out to play.
Abdicate a little while, uncrown

A head with pleasures sinking
In, our dénouement and disarray.
A mellowing out, a meltdown

As mute beguilements of attire,
Soft options of *yes*'s and *no*'s,
Incentives of an inner trousseau,

Lingerie of gathering desire
Scatter every slither of clothes.
Fetish trail. Pell-mell libido.

Throats murmur expectancy,
Endearments gone beyond word,
Sweet nothings, double Dutch.

Babble and purr of fancy
Uncage a reason's hummingbird.
Pamper my *Geist*'s temple, touch

Sacral nooks and alleys
Of lovemaking's stop-go calculus.
Nerve-blitz and spirit-bond.

An unzip of passion dallies
In misty chaos glazing over us.
Glisten. Doze in the dew pond.

Approach

First touchings almost by the by,
A back glanced, a patted thigh,

Feathery recall secreting in a gland,
A thrill I hold in the palm of my hand.

Gentle wooing's amusements or whims,
Every pleasure now haunts my limbs.

Wild Héloïse recollects in the choir
Relish and burn of her veiled desire:

The amorous delights we had tried.
Abbess of the Paraclete once gratified,

Set on remembering. Earthy. Unresigned.
Movements of my body betray my mind.

Novice, I hug the outward and extern.
How slowly maleness begins to learn

Just to bask in whatever it is is you.
And still I travel the body's avenue

To uncover a being. I stroke and grope
Your spirit's curves and envelope.

Concertina

1

I know Herrick's secrets.
Another naïve man
I too begin to flirt

Taken by folds of skirt
Which like a Japanese fan
Flicker accordion pleats,

Sways of silk redundancy
Whose melody's fall
Of light and dark caprices

Concertina creases
To play my nerves and call
A rousing tune I fancy.

2

The first relaxed chords
Before a tune gathers speed,
The *rallentando*
Of our toysome unswaddlings,
Switch and swop of roles,
Homo ludens make-believe
Master or mistress,
Geisha of dentelle and thong
Or Amazon queen,

Gentle games of the chamber,
Licence of delight,
Time-beguiling and time out,
Our playful anything goes.

3

Festina lente. The love-maker's paradox.
Haste made slowly, pleasures of vigilance
As *accelerando* rhythms in a squeeze-box
Now gather towards the zenith of the dance.
And we clamour for an Eden we still grieve
To let this moment eternally melodeon on;
Adam in his garden cries out to his Eve:
O do not abandon me in my abandon!
A melody peaks, evens out and mellows,
Soft cadenzas beckon childhood's sandman
And dream the pliant frame of a ballerina
Forever dancing to a tune's pleated bellows
Trembling into the narrows of a reed-organ.
Paradise squeezed in folds of a concertina.

Match

Testosterone or gene, whatever obsession
Craves the chase and catch,
A stalker picks up the trail and siege anew.

And why do I never get enough of you?
Quest and scent match,
Hunter pleasured in glories of repossession.

In you desire seems to need to improvise,
To shift, to grow, to dare,
Beatrice anxious more to focus than to tame.

To pare, to trim and oil a steadier flame,
To cup a wobbling flare,
Shape-thrower and temptress who was wise.

Voluptuous both. Passion's infinite devotion.
Sudden crimson blaze
And all my male-drawn lines again are blurred.

Right from the start, deeper more inward.
Slow burn of always.
Love that holds the sun and stars in motion.

Name-dropping

Do friends notice when often by design
I somehow steer the conversation around

So casually to seem to drop your name,
The once-tapped *r* and long *ee* sound,

Charge of a consonant and vowel spliced,
Slipping you in like a hidden billet-doux

As though apart I need to stake my claim
On this lovely incantation of your *Geist?*

How even in your absence I conjure you.
I've called you by name. You are mine.

Filling In

Beyond a springboard of concupiscence
All the morning-after tête-à-têtes

Unfold and fill the years of fancy-free;
Optative mood, co-optive present tense

Of past friends we both promise to share,
Stories that we now want to turn to faces.

Early tentative encounters, our début,
Friend by friend, coming out as a pair.

The shock to find so many *you*s in you
And still refind the *you* who chooses me.

Slow transfer and knitting in of kismet.
We move among others who move in us.

Yearning

Though not here Madam
Your body still haunts me
With its scented rockaby.

You go and silence falls
Flake by numbing flake
Across a forlorn room.

Alone and too entire,
Self-contained entropy,
A too perfect balance

Craves again a *jouissance*
To break and shatter me.
I wobble in my desire.

A night's noiseless boom
Of absence and how I wake
As my fumbling hand recalls

Glance and shapes of a thigh.
What yearnings for eternity
Burn in my dreamy palm?

Wobble

Deep down am I already sure of you?
At first green moments, even jealous

Huff and puff of childish self-defence;
Boy sores, gaps and rifts of confidence.

Does a world of eyes see what I too see?
Iago drops a scented handkerchief in me

A night you climb my stairs on tiptoes
To tell how a flame returned to propose.

The dull Moor in me imagines Cassio.
Soft you. A word or two before you go.

Promise me our years of trust and ease.
What wound did ever heal but by degrees?

Wound

So and so our wound and mingled yarn,
Lovers' daylight knockabout:
'Who, tell me, said that I said that?'

'Yes, but you're the one who started it!'
Infinite retrospect unfurled
As each other word borrows another tiff.

Was it me snapping at you began the row,
Calling your concern a nag,
All my blustering a hidden self-reproach?

No good the 'Let's call it quits' approach.
I hoist surrender's flag,
My climbing down the only let up now.

Hands in the air. A white handkerchief.
With you I take on the world.
A flaw, maybe, in love I cannot fight.

Eros Venusson smiles at such a spat.
Our making up a making out.
A fabric stitched and toughened in its darn.

Making Up

A male mix of inroad and protection
As I play my part and counterpart,
A pioneer and wooing troubadour

And Madam is my slowing sorcerer
Both holding back and drawing on
As waves of pleasure ebb and flow.

In our marrow drunken angels waft.
See how my soul breathes and glitters,
How I invade and spill my joy in you.

A cry and shiver as *entre nous*
A pebble of desire hops and skitters,
Shimmering in the sea's dark shaft.

Rise and flood, the slack and low
In the moon-pull, the earth-melodeon,
What infinite arousal are we made for?

Ancient *tristesse. La petite mort.*
So must we die? Must we part?
Native of Eden, I ache for resurrection.

Globe

It's just the way I girth the chart:
Above and below, ping-ponging
Anxious to hold the line and probe

My reason's measured tit for tat,
A cooler tapered zeroing in,
Narrowing girdles of equidistance.

Not that I love you less as such,
It's just my east–west attitude
Forever parallel and concentric.

A Capricorn, my sweated tropic –
Whatever my line of latitude –
Always concurrent, unable to touch.

Your longitude a steadier stance
Latticing me through thick or thin,
Logic or instinct, this and that.

In your constant loops of our globe
Warm meridians of noon's longing
Diverge to fondle poles apart.

Play

You, my all in one, my one in all,
It's still summer, will you come out to play?
Let's make love inside the orchard wall.

Coy, bold, knowing, insolent, outré
Madam, goddess, nymph, vamp, flirt;
Play each woman you know how to play.

Strip me back to my core, tease, subvert,
Dig out, scour, clean, make me ready,
Flushing and purging any wound or hurt.

Unhead this wary head, unsentry me.
The ears of Cherubim begin to tingle,
I come to my garden of myrrh and honey.

O vigilant gate-keeper wink one single
Moment, sheathe again your fiery sword.
Once angels we return. We fuse. We mingle.

Let's make love again before the Fall.

Moments

That we can hurt each other deepest and still
To know it always had to be you and me.
Sometimes then the upturned coin of bliss.

A sudden barb, an answer a shade too curt,
Love's dagger has probed a delicate zone,
Double-edged knife that cuts both ways.

Again we whisper our unbidden covenant:
I am my beloved's and my beloved is mine.
And how dewed membranes glint and shine!

One breath, one pulse, one skin, one delirium,
Rhythm and dazzle of a body's oil and shine.
All fancy and fun, all on song and consonant.

So willingly those rare moments out of phase
When an intimate rapier stabs too near the bone,
A dissonant night numb in a womb of hurt.

Some do it with a sword, others with a kiss.
Only in our unbroken promises are we free.
You are mine. Do with me what you will.

Covenant

The first moves we played by touch and feel,
Mutual come-on of glow and counterglow,
Share and share alike, our seesaw deal,
Some subtle paralleling of a *quid pro quo*.
Or so it seemed. But how we turn spendthrift,
As already we've begun our foolish potlatch,
Spiralling upward in endless covenants of gift.
And so hopeless it becomes to try and match.
Je t'aime à la folie and make no bones
About my bargain. Nothing asked or sought,
Quits before we start – neither getter nor giver –
We travel on beyond the tables and the stones.
No barter. No pay-back. Gratis. For naught.
I desire you. Just love me now and forever.

COVENANTS

Then happy I, that love and am beloved
Where I may not remove, nor be removed.

WILLIAM SHAKESPEARE

Launch

1 *Knot*

Right over left and left over right.
Or the other way around. Symmetrical plot
Of two mutual loops drawn tight,
The squared-off weftage of a reef knot.

Double and single, a riddle of ligature.
Functional beauty sacred and profane;
A history of knots, a rope architecture,
Easy to loosen but tighter under strain.

Plied strength in our tying up of ends,
An emblem, one tiny glorious detail,
A sign becoming what a sign intends.
We tauten the love-knot, hoist the sail.

2 *Splice*

Braid by braid to unravel
Our weave as stripped
We intersperse
For better, for worse
Our strands; a whipped
And knitted re-ravel

No longer a knot with its come
And go but more
To have and hold
Our splice's twofold
Purchase, a rapport
Tougher than its sum.

I take whoever you are
Or come to be
Till one of us perish
To love, to cherish.
Steer by my burgee.
I hitch to your star.

3 Hitch

A moon hoops earth and earth the sun,
Planet hitched to planet, swung like a stone

Hoisted into the taut whirlwind of a sling.
A month's wax and wane, neap and spring,

The tides of things, our orbits loop and pitch.
What is this trust which underwrites a voyage?

Our world-weight and giddy let-fly, a tense
Counterpoise of gravity and centrifugence,

Outward gyres held by their contrary force,
Some push and pull that covenants a universe.

4 Plunge

A balanced helm, a beautiful sail trim.
But over again surge and sweet of deviation;
A moment's perfect bearing another interim,
Our ark of covenant still steered by variation.
Under a bowl of sky watch and weather-eye
Alert to luff and camber, telltale breath;
Close-hauling, compromise of full and by
And how *the wind bloweth as it listeth.*

That perfect bearing already a moment ago.
Are lovers trimmers? O my Ulysses
Sail on, sail on! Our fleeting *status quo*,
Perfection neared in a series of near misses.
Globed in a bowl of oil, a gimballed compass
Bobs and pivots to hold its northern promise.

Voyage

1 *Reckoning*

After the offing, below an arc of skyline
A passage dips behind a glimpsed horizon,
A mirage that beckons and recedes to where
We think we travel, felt somehow our future
Lay, the position line, our plotted course
That didn't count sudden squalls or detours
We now dead-reckon, things so sure on land
As charts and tidal curves once gone beyond
A harbour arms now so unknown and giddy
And we're in our element and still all at sea.
Pinching hard we narrow down an airflow
To thud the waves to leeward El Dorado;
Ease the sheets a touch then bear away
But re-gathering speed luff up to stay
As near on course as can be as we begin
To fathom a long haul's mode and routine;
Steady notchings on a sheet winch's ratchet
Beyond our first beam reaches of delight.

2 *Log*

Who'll take the tiller? Whose hour? Whose turn?
Rites and habits of each;
Day by day by day a ballast of pattern.

The lovely bulb of a spinnaker blooms on a run;
Then on a beat our stubborn
Keel counter-drives and harrows us on.

And how many different tacks? Our two lives
Even still at one;
A hull's streamline moments as it connives

With cloth and tide and bearing, glorious reach
Of a vessel that never arrives,
Years logged in schedules of vigil and watch.

3 *Echo-sounder*

A life's canonical rhythm,
Monk-like tempo of days;
Muscle, sinew, limb
Learn mundane strategies,

Passages crossed, re-crossed,
Courses steered by degrees
As a pianist's fingered trust
Sleeps across the keys

Or wrist movements retain
Ordered strokes of Chinese
Characters, a graven routine
Which both ties and frees.

Hoists and binds that gird
Days of rites and liturgies,
Halyard and curtain cord
Clothes lines, hanked stays.

Echos in a mind's chamber
As a boat heels and sways
Stirs a cradle we remember
To lull a freshening breeze.

A wind-moment's once-off
And ready-about novices
We wear our habits of love.
Even keel of our ease.

Below

The companion way
Down into our boat's hollow.
A whelk's honed spiral.

Cooped and warm below;
Lockers, a galley and bunks.
Children playing house.

This cabin all our homes:
Parnell Street to Booterstown.
A tortoise desire.

Shells we didn't build,
Houses just loaned to live in,
Hermit crabs squatting.

At last Trimleston.
Our pebble-dashed habitat.
Clams exude their shell.

Trimleston

1

Premises hereinafter described and intended
A plot of ground at Trimleston, Booterstown,
Parish of Taney, part Barony of Rathdown
Shown on the map therein outlined in red.
The way we'd only taken just minutes to decide
And yet how it's years before our lives are sewn
Into the fabric of these walls' brick and stone,
Our plot and promise shaped slowly from inside.
Immediately we'd loved the house's light and feel.
Demised unto the said William Henry Watson,
To Cecil William Buggy, to Eileen Dundon...
Our turn to set our hands and affix our seal
In the presence of all who named these rooms home;
Our dreams their memories woven on one loom.

2

But is this house chameleon?
Different modes and shapes
As pictures drawn by a child,
Moods coloured in crayon.

Hail on the window and again
Snug and huddling schoolboy
I nestle in a garden dugout
My secret fort and den.

And when the wind blows
My garret is a tree-house
Slung and roofed in an elm,
Hideaway of reverie that knows

Lone watches before the mast,
The lookout's agony,
Cries of sirens in the marrow.
Rootless me. And you rootfast,

Embedded, indigenous, earthbound,
Deepen canals of nutrients,
Limbs' mirror image
Anchoring underground

My crow's nest and hermitage.
Rock-a-bye treetop dreamer –
And when the bough breaks?
I feed once more on your rootage.

3

The Whit-weekend we came were we aware
The loom would shuttle here our middle years?
Lovemaking, meals, guests, moments of despair,
For all our secrets here these walls have ears.
To perform and observe covenants contained within
Which expression where context admits or requires
Shall include what is and what might have been,
The yin and yang of even our silent desires.
By diverse main assurances and acts in law,
Events and ultimately by indenture of assignment...

Haunts of others' memories bought and sold.
Throughout May we'd talked of plans and paint,
Children with crayons, bricks and straw,
Dream and mortar of promise. Delicate roothold.

Dwelling

1

Our passion's juices coil piecemeal in;
Delights of flesh, oil and ooze of core,
Being hugged in an inner porous skin,
Small beginnings of less becoming more.
Gentle leakings, a gradual *savoir-faire*,
Drip by drip a mantle secretes its lime
As calcium hardens to seal an outer layer
And molluscs secrete their own good time.
A clam distils its house as needs may be;
Always complete and still scales accrue,
Whatever calcareous dreams years filter
From inside out, a slow process of beauty,
Contours and angles of life seeping through;
Our geometry of warmth, shell and shelter.

2

Season by season
Slopes of light that home
Our daily rondo

To caress a horizon,
To fondle how our bedroom
Curtains with Navaho

Designs emblazon
Slants of wall with autumn,
So it's as though

It stands to reason
Brick and mortar enwomb
Our being and know

The stairway's treason
Of creaks and humdrum
Whinges, the tiptoe

Of Rilke's frozen
Music in the shell we assume,
Ebb and flow

Of suns that crimson
The sea-urchin's dome
In our gable window.

3

Patterns just understood, thoughts unsaid,
House habits, order and rule of our cloister;
Squatter's rights to chairs or sides of a bed,
In rooms of dailyness, the world our oyster.
Do steady minds make everything their own?
In a bivalve's hollow even the tiniest grain
Layered over can work a precious stone,
Love's somnambulance and legerdemain.
The up-and-over door a castle drawbridge,
Our converted attic crow's nest and garret,
Under the drain cover outside the garage
The Count of Monte Cristo's oubliette.
In the clammy ear of a mollusc oceans swell;
Grit that sands and pearls our chosen shell.

Guests

1

Our dugout, lair, our haunt, fort and den.
Snuggle and crouch of a schoolboy hideaway;
First delight of privacies but soon again
A deeper urge to invite others into play.
As a Chinese sign with a treadle hindering a gate,
A single word for both barrier and concern –
The nestling exclusion of our tête-à-tête,

Withdrawal and marking off the better to return.
Cloister and burrow, whispering inner sanctum,
Our bolthole and refuge, our own place apart,
Hugger-mugger of warmth through thick and thin
With doors that close only to disclose a welcome.
Space for munificence. Open hand. Open heart.
Steadiness of seclusion becoming a beckoning in.

2

A thought-through menu.
Their last visit what was it?
Enough white and red?
A day preparing *la cuisine*.
Dressed up and ready,
House-proud excitement of hosts,
Blue napkins folded
And tall glasses anxious.
To bring extra chairs,
To fix our table placings,
We check kitchen timings,
Guessing the first to arrive.

Boisterous humour,
Conversations tuning up,
An evening's wine
And food weave their dynamic.
Gossip, jokes, flirtings,
Things partners didn't dare say,

Hidden sides revealed
In festive mediation,
Our household gods smile.
Attentive hosts topping up.
We preside over
The din and mischief of fun.

Reluctant break-up,
Riotous drawn out farewells
And soon again hugs,
Final noisy gate goodbyes
As hall-door waving
We turn to tumbling silence
Of low-burnt candles,

Cheese, last half-empty bottles
And scattered napkins,
All the débris of a feast,
A huddle of gaiety
Absorbed into the fabric,
A warmth hoarded within our walls.

3

Our lean-to conservatory in falling light,
The cactus bowl already in out of the bite

Of autumn, our words gentled to and fro.
Both of us host and guest as we tiptoe

Into our dance of love. Quivers of attention
And we unveil our seven veils one by one.

Between breathes a darkening space that listens
As the spine-proud flesh of cactus glistens

In the prolonged summer of a sun porch shared.
Opulence of knowing someone else has cared.

4

On our walls paintings we chose and saved for,
Hung carefully so every space seems imbued
With another abiding presence, a silent insider
Whose hues and shapes tinge our daily mood.
Spines on a shelf, a long coloured melodeon,
The rank and file of permanent house-guests;
While intimates and shades we most rely on
Slouch at ease between our bedside bookrests.
Blurred lines between what's in and outside;
No matter how steady, a home always porous,
A loose-fitting and breathing coated skin
Thrown over a dugout where we loved to hide,
A child's wigwam, tarpaulin pulled to enclose
The warm round yes-ness of sojourns within.

Study

1

Here in our attic room
I bend lovingly over my only heirloom,
My mother's polished bureau,

Drawing Japanese characters
For the word *study*. Over and over I rehearse
Twenty-one strokes,

A half-stroke for each century
Back to the Yellow River 2000 B.C.
On bones and tortoise shells.

Strive and *strong* combine
To mean study. For *study* the first sign
A squatting figure, a woman's

Genitals and legs spread wide
Suggests birth struggle alongside
Tensed biceps for effort.

My strength a drawn bow,
I crouch in over my mother's bureau.
Love's hard labour.

2

Slow summers I recall
Reading for an autumn exam:
Lovely months of process.
No need for grind or cram,
Relishing each small
Detail, every finesse,
Crescendo of long haul.

Pulse and surge of insight,
Some falling into place,
Skull-thrill of illumination,
Glimpses *in medias res*,
Moments taking flight,

A child born again
In the *aha!* of delight.

Days when ideas churn
And settle, connections made,
A synapse tenses and eases,
Things grasped in delayed
Reaction, a dawning pattern
Distends my mind and pleases;
I think I'm happiest when I learn.

3

High in my dormer I see you hunching below
To nurture a patch slowly made your own,
Host to cuttings or shoots and happy although
The garden you work is always a loan of a loan.
Travail of signs borrowed from hand to hand,
As I lean on my mother's bureau to write *study*;
In a daily welcome of struggling to understand
An orient of brushed strokes incarnate in me.
Your father in you stoops to hoe and weed,
Fondles a shrub to know it grows and thrives,
A guest tended and given pride of place
As down by the Yellow River I strive to read
My tortoise shells and the seeds of invited lives
Now breed in us worlds we bend to embrace.

Watch

1

Transit of dreams, rite of passage
As a pencil traces ground tracks,
Skims and plots
A course, harbours of refuge,
Charts, almanacs,
Pilot books, our rate of knots.

First intimacy, the in-your-face
Of loneliness dares now accept
A middle distance,
Delicate growing space
Of watches kept
Across beam and draft of silence.

Mute nearness, sweet abyss,
High and low waters of mood,
Time and tide;
Love weathers to what is,
An ease and latitude,
Parallels that needn't meet.

To know enough to know hiddenness,
Sunken hulks, an unmarked ridge
Or reef or shelf.
To have and never possess;
Each a hermitage,
Cave of heart, cache of self.

Chartered years of bell-shaped lead-lines,
Riptides, overfalls, height and shallow.
So much unfathomed.
A sandbank drifts and realigns.
Echo by echo,
Shoal by shoal an ocean plumbed.

2

A fresh turn of phrase
The flurry and throb
Of words tuned for a first time.

Often with strangers
A surprise role shift,
A different demeanour.

Some detail untold:
'I must have mentioned that?'
Sudden sidelong playful air.

Staunch in narrow straits,
Steady in squalls like
A craft closer to the wind.

503

Explorer's pleasure
In unworn waters
Another channel charted.

Still sides never shown,
Faces unseen before
Glanced through our darkened glass.

3

Each shape and lineament of day by day,
Positions to plot or check in nightly dialogue,
Line of sounding along our double headway,
Intimacies of thoughts we share and log.
To follow every knot, warm and closeup
And yet to hold the near and far in balance
As if we slacken a little to allow for scope,
Lull and driftage, love's adaptive distance.
Dreamy horizons outline another reality
As finer details cross the mind's screen;
Turn and turn about and still to watch
Moments shifting focus as needs may be,
Zero in, drawing back or in between;
Chart scale and voyage we make and match.

About

1

Habits and habitat
Everyday this and that
Of nod and half-response
Or crossed communiqué
But what had you started to say?
As if a broken utterance

Like the chatter of the gone
Somehow travels on
Infinite megahertz
Lurks forever in the ether
Of some promised weather
Or in the hum between the words

The boat's radio
Suddenly blurts below
The deck. Channel 16
Hisses and waits to snatch
Alerts or warn; our watch,
Ship to shore and go-between.

In a tack's heady
Moment do they steady
Us as we go about,
Voices of the past
Shadows that forecast
to underwrite a word spelt out

In waves of high frequency?
O muse of the ordinary,
Medium and alter ego,
Reverberate in names
Our salvage claims
Lima, Oscar, Victor, Echo.

2

Foot, head, tack,
clew, luff and leech –
Bob McCune seadog
names me parts of a sail.
I thought of Japanese *sensei*
'a life before', 'a teacher'

and stowing the sail
each term sung in me,
a gleam and engine of sound
precise and weatherworn
as meticulously back and forth
we folded into the cloth

sailors of Mesopotamia,
Egyptian mariners,
boatmen of the Middle Sea,
Barbary coastal pirates
or nosing the Indian Ocean
Arabians on their dhow.

Moves of hands that listen
to so many lives before,
long benevolence of the gone
as down in their debt we tap;
leaf-trace and rootstock,
tutoring guests and ghosts.

3

Under the swung boom
Unordinary delirium
Of Joshua Slocum

As out of a morning east
Sudden glimpses of coast.
My father's ghost

Knuckles a barometer
On the bulkhead. *Higher*,
He mumbles, *the better.*

Better high than doldrum
Mood, but better the sum
Of both in the room

Of living. Bunks, galley,
Bilge and heads, greasy
Ballast of the ordinary.

A dovetailed whole.
Deck, hold, hull.
Glory to it all.

4

The unkinked dead uncoil in our routine,
Even in a sea-change their codes and ritual,
Mundane orders, the shipshape of discipline,
Past masters closest in the sweet habitual.
Ready about! Our square-rigger's cry;
Turns prepared, moments weighed up well:
A trough just as our bow luffs through the eye
Of the wind to nose into rhythms of swell.
And *jib ready!* Shouted back as though

These older rites can both alert and calm
The body before the mind even understands
The gone keep showing us the ropes. *Lee-oh!*
As tacking a tiller switched from palm to palm,
Our sea-craft still steered by revenant hands.

Dedication

1

Who in his tenderest years
Finds some new lovely thing
His life is high and he flies
On the wings of his manhood:
Better than riches his thoughts...

Five lines from Pindar's Pythian
My friend had inked neatly
On the title page of our wedding
Gift: *The Icelandic Horse.*
The thump on earth and ice

Echoes for a thousand years:
Forehead to muzzle, shoulder
To loins and ear to hoof
They quivered under our touch.
In the first blue of summer.

The sand trembles and shivers
In the thud of a burden beast,
An out of season thistle
Flower droops in the wind,
A breath of autumn descends

As the clatter of hooves dies
Away in a hollow distance
The sky fades in the rivers,
And fresh young voices
Sing again old songs.

2

Towards the end we'd both been exhausted.
Yet buoyed up by noise, *les joies de la vie*
Of an evening we'd enjoyed as well as hosted,
But still loth to lose the last of the company.
And should we clear up at such a late hour?
Two young couples aproned at the sink dismiss
Our feeble gainsayings. Diminished horsepower.
No, no, we're taking over all of this!
Under orders and banished from our kitchen
By might and main, by hammer and tongs,
But happier than Lear I've willingly resigned
My realm to my two nieces and their men.
And fresh voices will sing again old songs;
Waves of energy are surging up behind.

3

Two nieces and their knights.
So it's live and let live
As we slip Pegasus' golden
Bridle and say tonight's
All take and no give.

Who in his tenderest years
Finds some new lovely thing,
His hope is high and he flies...
No end in sight. No frontiers.
So young and easy on the wing.

Light years away incalculable
Echo, a moment's spin-off,
Seeping trust diffused
Through membranes recall
Slow osmosis of love.

Ten to Seven

1

At ten to seven still I want to wake;
A boy for five years and ours for life –
A habit ingrained I was never able to break.

Everything decreed by whistle, hour and bell,
Drill and dressing down in order's name;
Of course, for years what could we do but rebel?

And decades later bit by bit to learn
To stamp my time, shape the template of a day.
Blustered journey out. Delicate return.

Day by day rhythm of sweet discipline,
Silent moments kept between two tasks
Reflect and prepare before we re-begin.

From a study window, contented anchorite
After hours and slow patterns of thought
I watch the tumbled dim of evening light.

A boy five years and ours for life the Jesuit
Motto promised. Gladly I bend to the rule.
A monk in me has grown to fit his habit.

2

Paradox of a steady passion,
Trappist lover's feast and ration;

Clearheaded joy, sober kick,
Trembling music's arithmetic;

A clove hitch that holds when taut,
Perfect rhymes that shape a thought,

Flow and sand of filter bed,
Tip and tig of heart and head;

Wings lift-off, a braking fin,
Words run wild my pulse reins in.

3

Another dawn watch begun at ten to seven
As light breaks into the wind's anarchy;
A steady head but no haven heaven,
Hopkins forever out in the swing of the sea.
To know the ropes, always to think ahead,
Again same shipshape rule and routine;
Everything coiled, made off, cleated,
Sails flaked or stowed, a readied unforeseen.
Over and over a day's lone discipline
As my white horses whelm and overcome,
Waters brimmed and harrowed in a wind's fetch,
Crests ridden, the troughs weathered within,
The green swell seldom in the haven's dumb;
In every squall a heart's range and stretch.

House

1 *Storeys*

Hub and core
Of our daily round
A bottom floor;
Kitchen, lounge, porch
Suit us down to the ground.

But sorting realities of day
Climb one flight
To shadow play
In sleep and dream
Second-storied night.

Then, win or lose
My attic tenancy.
Floored by the muse,
A hard landing.
Top-flight of fancy.

2 *Corners*

Softly and aside
Forgotten by the vacuum
Forgiven by the broom
In dusty half-lit angles of a room
Our daydreams ride

Their cock-horse
Ring-fingered, fancy-free
To bell-toed Banbury,
Footloose music of reverie
Running its sweet course.

O Wizard of Oz,
Memory's wand,
Tip our too fond
Balance, somehow slip beyond,
Conjure what never was.

Make-believe. Our delirium.
Dreamer and sojourner,
Little Jack Horner
Sit in your delighted corner
Pulling out your plum.

A world in the head.
But deeper, wider,
The muse insider
Unreels from Miss Muffet's spider
An endless silken thread.

3 *Echoes*

An underground desire to bloom
Sows
And grows
The damask rose
Of hopes that now as memory recompose.

Harmonics of abode, geography of echoes
Embrace
A trace
Of daily footpace,
Fall and print on years of staircase.

Our covenants loamed in time and space
Become
The shalom
Of every room
We walk. Mellow somnabulance of home.

4 *Shades*

How still all holders of our house abide
In an ether where secret decibels relay
Things mumbled under breath or cried
At night in a dream's *esprit d'escalier.*
Half-sentences of an interrupted story
Our lives and space seem almost to subsume;
Creaky resonance of each imagined memory
In the infinite daydream of a lived-in room.
How shadows caught in silence overhear
Voices of those who come to take our place
For this late supper *à deux* by candlelight
When swapped news allows a day cohere
In broken bread of evening's face to face.
Across a room our ghosts now smile goodnight.

SEASONING

Passing, passing
The blossom gives way to the fruit...
The grape on the vine
Is wine in the making...

RUMI: *Mathnavi* 1, 2930
interpreted by Raficq Abdulla

Settlement

1

Day and day. Board and bed.
Hardly even a thought unsaid,
As frets shared, dreams joined,
Slow changes, shifts of mind,
Delights that ripen, things rued,
Stretch and spread a heartwood.

Night and night, as joists cool
And sigh, time again to settle.
Mortise and tenon. Bedfellows,
Knees tucked to knee-hollows,
Belly to butt until we swap,
Tandem-turning in our sleep.

Year and year, still alongside.
Invisible seams. Apart and allied.
Different sap, different firs,
But collateral snug-set timbers
Tried and weathered in every mood,
Living, creaking, breathing wood.

Seasoned as cedars of Lebanon,
Sanded lumber beds down,
Dips and buckles of white deal
Floorboards worn to reveal
Planed, knotted parallels of love.
Honeymoon of tongue and groove.

513

2

How our new flush boards had scented a room,
Its fresh-skinned deal
Sap-shiny, plumb,

Veined with arrow-headed and oval curlicues,
Ingrained tramlines
And brown tattoos

Of random birthmark knots and flooring brads
A foot apart
Like silver ear-studs.

How gently under varnish daylight sallows
Pale-faced timber
As its fibre mellows,

Honeys slowly down to a melon hue
And the grain darkens;
Out of true

A house in its wisdom settles and a whole floor
Trusts to the slope
And lean of tenure.

3

So flush a deck, so similar in our grain,
Lines between us sometimes almost blurred;
The moments when joints gape under strain,
A give and buoyancy promises undergird.
Here and there against the grain a scar,
Cut and relayed boards marked by slits,
Seams of private grief and *aide-mémoire*
To map another world of hidden conduits.
Ease and sprain, delicate dovetails of stress,
Sudden honeymoons when the juices move,
A long wear and tear of side by side,
Whatever seasons in a rub and shine of process.
Shifts. Mellowings. Years of push and shove.
Come with me from Lebanon now, my bride.

IOU

1

Two brass pans hung from a scale-beam
On a balance of years –
One with childhood hurt, one with a dream.

Once a cocky young man with somersault
Moods and humours,
Huffs and counter-time, a jibbing colt.

The iconoclast bravado of damaged memory
Shadow boxed
A father's shadow in all the powers that be.

Deeply a body remembers and seems to nestle
Kinks and clinches,
Reflexes of old injuries in sinew and muscle.

Knots and hang-ups. So many demons to redeem
Or hold at bay.
But a boy in me still carried an infinite dream.

Two brass pans hung from a scale-beam.
O love me long enough to counter-weigh.

2

Fumbled bids to thank you
Fall on different ears
According to your moment's ebb or flow.

Sometimes a dismissive overview:
'No matter what with the years
Somehow you'd have had to mellow';

Others nothing (I hope) you rue
Just a sigh that appears
To tot things up: 'I don't know

'How I managed what we went through!'
In swings and mood careers
A relentless singing vertigo.

515

So again a scribbled IOU.
I sought him in streets and squares...
I held him and would not let him go.

3

Faithful voyager as push comes to shove
There you are again to bail me out,

Thimbling dry an ocean out of love.
Or for years it must have seemed like that

As the restless boat of my nature changed tack,
Shifted so suddenly onto a different course,

Me almost overboard, you dragging me back.
Full and by, zigzag beats and detours,

Or learning to slacken sheets and bear away,
When to ride it out or go with the flow.

Rack and pinion, the long haul of everyday,
Course made good, years of common cargo,

All that weathers us in what we weather.
Still my mistress mariner. And still together.

Tending

1

Of all images always this one:
You're sprinkling plants begun to jade
In the brittle hothouse passion

Of an attic study. More shade,
Keep away from direct sun.
A nourishing wet crusade.

Rain-fosterer, bringer of water,
Smiling and bending to touch a blade,
More and more your father,

Just the way you'd called and said
'Look! How happy those leaves are!'
Sap and stem delighted,

A foliage moistening it's *cri de cœur*.
Even a moment's loneness placated
In a glad yearning nurture.

Aqua vitae of stalk and vein,
Sweet beads that lush a verdure
Of damp pliancy and sheen.

My heart so dry and narrow to wife,
A world not big enough to contain
All you want to give.

2

Two-timer, I confess
Gleams of woken desire that shone
All those years ago,
Flashes of dreams long forgone
And long beyond redress.

Once more I second-guess
The flirt I dance attendance on.
A jealous muse's gigolo,
Still I tend a double liaison
Under sweet duress.

Anything to assuage a mistress,
Whatever glimpses I melodeon
Into words to slow
Time down, a sound compulsion,
Things I needed to bless

Or a craving to repossess
A moment, a scratch against oblivion,
Fear of letting up or go,
Crippled wool-gathering Casaubon
Feathering a loneliness?

3

A time more for pruning than for grief.
With what toughness you reserve for rescue

You stoop to pluck any dried-up leaf,
Then stake a tired stem with a bamboo.

Always with hurt or flaw your closest rapport,
A desire to heal beyond all commonsense.

Was it the outsider in me you'd fallen for,
Love's call to tend a wound of absence?

Sometimes in a spring birch's first sway
Even yet an old dream's leaves will waken.

No easy closure here. But what to say?
Choices now the wake of choices taken,

I take the gift of whatever gift I bring
To juice endless taproots of your longing.

Three Minutes

1

It was one of those three-minute machines.
Passport size. The black curtain drawn
Aside, we huddled together for dear life
on a wobbly, twirlable stool and waited
forever trying to hold onto our smile
till the explosive bulb fixed us in its blitz.

It must have stuck in at the back of a drawer.
Anyhow, the other day we dropped on the floor,
your hair loosely pinned up behind
and there I am in a yellow summer shirt,
your arm around me, squeezing into the booth;
yoked and both facing into the light.

2

Riddle me a riddle of how we season.
We change as our world changes;
Conspiracy of time, a growing treason

Of never ever the same twice.
The minute we kiss and touch
A slippage, an elusive paradise.

Hidden in a mind's skittish inscape
Our half-desires and fictions,
We juggle even dreams we shape.

Biographies we delicately rearrange,
Selves we slough off,
Constancy of constant change.

Flesh sapped five years ago,
A hide already shed,
I sweet a body I barely know.

3

Zigzag and detour. All our wafts and drifts.
Broadening in ways we've vaguely understood.

Targets a minute alters as our viewpoint shifts;
Things we do we never thought we would.

Light, shape and size a varying assemblage
Our lens can either narrow or magnify.

Yet somewhere in the brain we hold an image
As if there's more to seeing than meets the eye.

Remember π a stylish dolmen in a row
Of easy figures? The terms 'constant', 'variable?'

Diameter and circumference a constant ratio
In any circle however big or small.

Our growth ring widens its looping parallel.
Breadth and compass. Love's proportioned circle.

Weathering

1

Winds back and freshen
As mare's tails, wispy and thin,
Puff and huddle and darken.
Although the signs were ominous –
A depression moving steadily in –
How easily a gale creeps up on us!

Too fretful about a squall
To see the moment, too deep in detail
To notice the overall
As clouds had gathered and huffed.
You could teach the devil himself to sail
If only he could look aloft.

All seemed plain sailing.
Then, suddenly, as though from nowhere
A moody gust. Yet seeing
How I'm just as thin-skinned,
Why didn't I sense the cooler air,
Prepare to slacken and spill the wind?

2

Mostly a tiff that seemed about nothing
Or anyhow something that had nothing to do
With what we'd begun to argue about,
Although from the start I knew
I'd have to winkle out
A hurt you'd been for weeks mutely nursing.

I think we'd fall into a pattern.
It's you who'd held our lives steady,
So how could I ride out a billow
Of sudden humours? Already
My psyche hits Skid Row
As we seesaw and gainsay out of turn.

A heated logic's riddle-me-ree.
But I'd fail to find the middle ground
And play Hamlet at the end of his tether
Until you'd come around
To pull us both together,
End up blaming yourself for blaming me.

3

In the eye of a storm still to find perspective,
To slide a lens from zoom to a wider view

And set a moment's detail against our life.
In holding off, my love, I'm holding you.

The years it takes to learn a double vision!
I'm standing back a fraction for your sake

Trying at once to pan and zero in on
How everything and nothing is at stake.

Bifocal ardour. A space to allow me to keep
On trusting even if you seem to stand aloof,

A close-up that still retains its wider sweep
And holds my need for warmth at one remove.

Imperfect metal tempered to a new resilience;
My presence somehow nearer for its distance.

Stains

1

Honeyed in our aftermath we lie
Hand in hand to stare at where
A drink I spilt above had left
It's watermark tracing out
Across our boudoir ceiling exotic
Archipelagos of browning lands,
Mini-continents with sandy shores

Thrown up on a plaster fault line
That seems to map a travelled world
Voyages charted in oceans of white.

I drift in and out of sleep
Content in a hazy borderland
Between the real and understood
An interregnum in the mind when
Our time together begins to flicker
And gather in one moment before
It again disperses around a sepia
Atlas of half-memories that shift
And float along a landmass shelf
Dreaming onwards side by side.

So many regions unexplored,
Exotic islands of pleasure foregone,
Realms left forever unseen,
Atlantis of the might have been,
Or even an ordinary country passed
By, some *terra firma* where
We might have settled but knew
We had to keep a course and steer
Our ship by each other's star
Or be a lotus-eater left behind.

2

The ways things would spill and fall,
Blotches and seepage of how it is,
Chances of lives that overlap.

With someone else who knows who
We'd have become: another map,
Unlike patterns, a different stain.

If I hadn't let myself be chosen
Who do you think would have lain
Here now catnapping in your bed?

I puzzle over what never was
Gazing at the watermarks overhead.
Your mission to bring an outsider in.

Anchor of loners, tender of wounded.
I wonder who else you might have been,
Of all your odd men out which

You'd have wifed? The sergeant dreamer,
The gambler who'd later strike it rich?
Good night then Madam Millionaire!

3

Each choice has left another choice behind
Among all the *we*'s we might have been.

At every turn our design redefined.
Indelible ink of being. Our stains are in.

A living batik of knotted dips and prints
Where gain is also loss and every tie,

Anything chosen at once loosens and tightens,
A steeped folding soaking in its dye.

Whatever now our map, our seeped traces,
The stains of other selves are long outdated,

Our story absorbed into the other's face's
Lines and creases, both of us implicated

In all the twists and hues impressed so far.
Tell me your love. I'll tell you who you are.

Tandem

1

Perhaps just one of my so many vagaries,
A whirlwind idea I'd talked you into
And off we pushed uphill against the breeze

Riding hell for leather our sheeny new
Black heavy metal roadsters. I think
We both pedalled a phantom bicycle for two,

Each of us secretly striving to keep in sync
With the other's alternating second wind.
Down in Kilkenny there's marble black as ink.

Afraid to let one another down we'd grinned
And borne our knee-jerk reaction to the strain –
We should have said, even been more disciplined.

But to choose the foothill of a Wicklow mountain
The long way around, such sweated circuities
When we could have travelled a duller Kildare plain?

Our manic headlong pedal-driven intensities.
One hand steers, the other urging our knees,
We climb the greasy dream of marble cities.

2

So few days before we'd got together.
Headfirst we struck out
Hot in our leather
Learning as we went
A mutual comether.

And only weeks before we'd both sign on
For wherever it would lead,
Fragile liaison
Of whispers and covenants,
Our tender marathon.

Even from the start I'm sure you'd found
The going tough. An obstinate streak
The contrary high ground,
Slews and swings,
The long way around.

If only I'd understood the highway code
But we rode against the wind;
We might have toed
The line, instead we went
The mountain road.

A rough ride far over and above
Anything you'd reckoned on;

524

Push come to shove,
Holding a delicate balance
Ad-libbingly you love.

3

Down in Kilkenny it is reported...
Our boneshakers parked in a yard below
We're fetched up on a lodging house bed
Hearts pumping and drumming *fortissimo*,

Too exhausted to even think of making hay
I've wandered off into an infant sleep,
Begun again to breathe the flush and sway
Of wind as poised we tackle another steep

Mountain road apace and I wonder whether
Bodies have a will of their own or if we relax
Into a double rhythm pedalling together,
Each of us picking up where the other slacks.

A trade balance subtler than *quid pro quo*,
Intricate lovemaking of motion in tandem.
I yield control and let the steering go.
Please don't wake me out of this dream.

No-man's-land

1

Still my boyhood's Aran trance.
At bedtime when I lit a sconce
Already I'd begun a long fall,
An actor who came to be his role.
Perhaps to understand is to become
Whatever it is we yearn to fathom.

No distance. At any rate not for me
The chill removes of anthropology
Or pieced shards of a scholar's vase.

I can only say whatever it was
I'd known I had to learn by love.
From inside out. Hand in glove.

O woken Belshazzar of Babylon,
Over against the candlestick and on
A whitewashed wall a hand has written:
Be glad you weren't so hard-bitten
Or so old so young to notice where
A shadow's fingers wrote despair.

To drink Belshazzar's empty cup?
So hard to say the game is up,
My heritage on me a speckled bird.
Though I can no longer risk my word,
A hopeless hoping swings between
What is and still what might have been.

2

Before we'd met you'd long decoded
The scribble on the whitewashed wall
It would take me years to read.

Did a young man's fever renew
Your yielded hopes or was it
All that's big and lavish in you

Going with the flow of how I was,
Eternal woman falling again
For a driven male, a man with a cause?

The same abundance that understood
When sobered Belshazzar had seen
The ghostwritten scrawl and could

No longer jeopardise his muse.
Once watching as you lit a candle
I ask why you came to choose

To love me. Laughing you tell me
How much it weighted that I had been
A citizen of your childhood country.

3

And yes, yes, things will fade, things change.
A millennium or two tiny in a bigger scheme.

The star-gazing grave builders of Newgrange,
Movers and shakers all dwindle in a daydream.

Did they too once read the shadow's scrawl,
Know the strange forlornness of no-man's-land?

Even when we decipher the letters on the wall
I suppose we changelings never understand.

To love what is and not what might have been
I serve my craft. But yet we keep our word.

Year by year I've lived my boyhood trance.
A sonority, turns and vibes of phrase, my live-in

Lover's unbroken code of bed and board.
What lonely ghosts sleepwalk our dalliance.

Ceremony

1

I want to remember Friday evenings
We dressed up just to go nowhere
and carefully laid a table for us both,
pretended we were each other's guest
and host as we lit a scented candle,
wooers tending the smallest need
we talked as though we rarely met
allowing ceremony undo the hex
of everydayness, of half-said things,
what we should have heard but missed
as if round and routine both bind
and cast a spell we need to break.
We date, we dally, paying court
to broach the sabbath of ourselves.

2

Slow repetition of sober days,
An actor's lines over and over
Till every twitch of the tongue obeys.

Sluggish mornings a struggle to cope.
Tumbling, tumbling acrobat
Behind the smiling dancer on the rope.

Scaled hours against the flow
A pianist's years of finger drills
Before the encore and the low bow.

Hell, highwater. Thick and thin.
Gain and build-up of steady pace,
A refusal to give up or in.

Slack *accelerando* of covenant,
Strange freedoms of discipline
Pirouette in the glory of an instant.

Acupoint of joy. Harnessed catharsis.
Everything new and possible again
An old actor's glow. All for this.

3

Bird flight at sundown.
Afterwards the aftershine.
Infinite moment.

Selves

1

Right from curtain-up a jangle of rapport.
Though maybe even in our first delirium,

Waiting in the wings, selves we'd fallen for
Trusted the shuffle of what we'd yet become.

Improvisation, a plot still in the making.
Utterly involved and still detached enough

To love; double-eyed actors always taking
Our cue from the other, maybe we'd pull it off?

Long steady dialogue of gain and surrender,
Theatre in the round, coarse grain of living

Where both can be a borrower and a lender,
Ourselves as much in taking as in giving.

Mix of endless mongrel *you*'s and *me*'s.
Cast and ragbag of our hybrid psyches.

2

Who's this woman I know I've never known?
After thirty years surely through and through

But now out of nowhere a fresh come-on,
Awe and tease of some other stranger you

Who probably didn't exist those years ago
But more than likely ripened as you grew

To play this leading lady I desire to know.
Enter then this queen of hearts on cue

To say if you still recognise the figure I cut?
Prince Hamlet lulled by his tragic flaw

Who somewhere along the line lost the plot
Or a consort whose dream you dreamt you saw?

We both usurp the selves we thought we'd be.
Am I the surprise for you that you're for me?

3

Now a lover and now an *éminence grise*,
The quick changes, the moods we display,

Parts we swap or learn to switch with ease,
Gamut of a self's *dramatis personae*.

Fever and fright. Each lead and cameo,
Long years through our paces and routines

With me your opposite star and antihero,
Triumph or flop, all the shifting scenes.

Then suddenly to surge and lose control.
My *femme fatale* again I ogle and squire.

Forever new our throwaway lines of play
As we slip in ripe delight from role to role

To strut our hidden stage of old desire.
Love my glory. Love my feet of clay.

Darkroom

All recreation alone
Off a landing halfway up
A dormitory stairs
Our hightech co-op,
Red-light chamber of pleasures,
Twilight zone.

Patrick McGlade S.J.'s
Photography club,
Den of potassium odours,
Brown bottled lab
Of fixers, enlarger, rollers,
Tin plates to glaze

A slow foggy image
That under my forceps
Begins at last to unblur
As something develops
In a dish I seem to stir
Until you emerge

Some two score years
Off in a haze
Of all that's yet to shape
Logics of fuzz,
Chaos dreams that leap
Their grey frontiers

To redefine a story
While we wait
In the darkroom of a moment
Shade and light
For some future determined
To become a memory

That may have been a dream
On which we focused,
A single rapid exposure
We have to trust
But never can be sure,
A sort of dim

But deeper recollection,
Vague and filtered
We bit by bit adapt
And funnel inward,
A dusky shot snapped
On a lens of perfection

Now fixing in a murk
Of stock solution
Gradual matters of fact
On a bromide silver emulsion,
A Rembrandt effect
Ripening in the dark.

Parkinson's

1

Stealthily. One day that quiver in your ring
Finger. Or my impatience at your squiggling

Such illegible notes. Just your astonishment
Noticing the absence of an old lineament.

Once speedy genes, high-geared and fleet;
At twelve the school's swiftest athlete.

The oils of movement slower to lubricate.
Stiffness, a tremor, that off-balance gait.

A specialist confirms Parkinson's disease.
Failing dopamine. The brain's vagaries.

Then moments of denial. Again so strong
And confident: Those doctors got it wrong.

Your fright is pleading with me to agree.
I bat for time: Maybe, we'll have to see.

What can I do? These arms enfold you.
No matter what, I have and hold you.

And so you must travel painful spendthrift
Windings of acceptance. Giving turns gift.

Together. But is there a closer closeness?
Yet another shift in love's long process.

2

Flustered now by stress,
A need for time,
Days planned, a gentler pace;
Any breeze shivers in your limbs,
My aspen mistress.

Hardy, deep-rooted, light-loving
You learn to endure.
Pioneer tree in fallow or clearing.
A random sigh flutters in your leaves:
O God, I'm tired of shaking.

3

Often I wake early to taps on my pillow.
Last evening's tablet at the end of its tether
Your forefinger begins its morning *tremolo*
As if counting in sleep hours lain together.
I think at first you'd pitied an over-eagerness,
My jittery hand that spilled half your coffee;
A headstrong giant-killer wobbly and nervous
That slowly over time you'd steadied in me.
Blurs and transfers between fellow travellers.
I couldn't but see your half flirtatious sidelong
Glance at me that both asks and reassures:
Even if I shake I think my spirit is young?
Our years side by side tongued and grooved.
A face is beautiful once a face is loved.

Driving

Often a shade quicker to react
You alert your duller half.
Yet another misfortune staved off.

But sometimes not. I'm all thrown
By a flash countermand
To what I've already reckoned on.

What I ask you do you take me for?
Ah, you wonder how to tell.
And then just supposing I hadn't?

Damned if you do, damned if you don't.
Cleft stick of devotion.
This note on a windscreen to say I'm grateful.

Mistress

Even at the door I hear your school voice,
And am awkward as I slip into your sanctum

A timid copy-bearer approaching with a sum
You'll tot and tick off, doling out your praise.

I sneak a voyeur's glance before you know
I'm standing there at sides of you I rarely see,

Heisenberg cheating a principle of uncertainty
I'm peeping now at this mistress *ex officio*.

Steady performer, gently in charge of it all
'Up you come to the table and show me your sum!'

But I've been spotted. A rumour across a room:
Look teacher! Teacher, look it's Micheal!

Flagrante delicto I glimpse your metamorphosis.
A flash smile turns to reassure my gaucheness.

FULL AND BY

In sailing 'full and by' the aim is to make the best possible progress to windward, the best balance between high pointing and fast footing.

Boatwords (Denny Desoutter)

Savoir donner cette sérénité au bateau, voilà tout l'art du bon marin...ce n'est que de proche en proche que l'on améliore la marche du bateau...

The art of great sailors is no more, and no less than this: to bring harmony to their vessels...you approach perfection through a series of approximations...

JEAN-LOUIS GOLDSCHMID
translated by Peter Davison

Gaze

Ordinary out of the ordinary
Moments
I eye again
Lineaments
That now contain
Traces of a fumbled history,
Love *a fortiori*
Scribbling in faces
Each other's story

And remembered infatuated
Glances,
First eyeings up,
Dalliances
Loop the loop
Of all the years we're mated

And derring-do
Drop in freefall
As I fell for you.

But a deeper wonder.
Greedy
I craved your all,
Needy,
Any withdrawal
Or doubt and I'd flounder,
Hamlet who'd brood,
And chafe or pout
A blackmail mood.

Some old damage inbred,
Decades spent
Determined to bless
A temperament,
An all-or-nothingness
So long wing-wounded
Or confused or both
At once. Slow
Blundered growth

With so many hurts unshown
Or unshared
Grieves lonely
Unrepaired,
If and *only*
Of how we might have flown
A different way
Forgive us now
Such feet of clay.

Yet what soars between us!
You and me
Flickering delight
In infinity,
Daily flight
In the sun. Madcap Icarus
Whatever I do
Whatever I've done
I home in you

Who has endlessly believed
In what we might
Or what we still
Become. Inflight
Invisible
Repair. Once a thieved
Sly, sideways
Lover's stare.
Now this gaze.

Caprice

1

Vibes that want to jar or risk the duo,
Passing notes too harsh, out of sync,

Mismatched phrasings, uneven tempo,
Clashes as melody hovers on the brink.

O the ease of steady lines! One to one.
Unnerved at every interrupted cadence

It took me years to trust to resolution.
Richness of each mended dissonance.

Caprice and ruses of wild lovemaking,
Flirted anticipations, playful tension,

Rising sounds retarded enough to hone
An urge, keep accelerating and braking

Pleasure. A quaver held in suspension.
Offbeat discords prime a sweeter tone.

2

Delicious liberty of notes to rove
Extempore
Con amore

As in between the lines we wove
Inaudible noise
Of a middle voice
Underwrites our undersong,
Cantus firmus
Holding us
In melodic progression, headstrong
Silent tenor,
Our rapport.

3

A trace in us, an echo of some tonality,
Whatever loves us before we ever loved,

What loneness ours even as we roved
Out, still signs its key in you and me.

Three decades everything shared and joint.
Flesh of my flesh, bone alongside bone;

More and more together and still alone,
Lines ripening in unison and counterpoint

We hold a pitch and measure as best we can.
The more our rock and rhythm correspond

The longer we long, the further on beyond,
Desire homing towards where desire began

As though from its beginning a tune returns;
Glory of our music how our music yearns.

Duration

1

Open stage, no hiding wings,
Mood swings, every scenario,
Dreams, hurts, coups, failings,

Space to let each other grow,
Our repertoire of knockabout,
Kitchen sink and passion play,
To know our parts inside out,
To choose rehearsed naïveté
Of moments taken one by one.
Often mothered in my wound,
Sometimes do I daughter you?
Subtle timings, shifts of cue,
Day by day played in the round,
Ad lib an ease of layered duration.

2

Cost analysis of gaffes and failures
As we number over older blunders
Balancing out and taking stock.

Designs, things hearts set on,
Blighted causes, a false dawn,
But how even hindsight wonders,

How we so often got it wrong?
Sometimes you'd known all along,
Both loving and doubting you yielded.

Recalled cringe of once phases,
Youth's labyrinth and vast mazes
And no short cuts across time's arc.

Let-downs, what didn't go to plan,
Gnaws and rubbing, even chagrin
Tie the slow ravellings of duration.

Again the ultimate sophistication:
To say like Ibsen's Terje Vigen
Best all happened the way it did.

Strange discipline of false scents,
Mistakes we count on now as portents.
Remembered shinings, forgotten dark.

3

But is now an error in some future date?
Pace again battlements Hamlet O'Siadhail

Or say *confusion is not an ignoble state*
(Imperfectly I rhyme with Brian Friel).

Chameleon days, divine dissatisfaction,
Changing scenes, lines I know I forgot,

The constant edits, rewrites or redirection,
And yet to believe we haven't lost the plot

But keep on relearning and switching role
As if to follow a plot but not the plotting

As if forgivingly we go improvising on
A performance art still beyond control,

Duration's every knotting and unknotting
Gentling us towards whatever dénouement.

À Deux

February night and a monastic gong of moon
high over Booterstown,
dangling weigh-beams of day steadying

we sit together each of us hunched in our novel
that's slowly unfolding
itself in a busy curious equilibrium of silence

as I side-glance a story flitting across your face
like noiseless hallowed
hours of living and find myself wanting to say

remember years your younger brothers stayed
to stew before exams
we joked about 'the cloister', spoke of 'our rule'

but don't and instead allow the eye-blink to hang
dreams in separate pans
that whatever their weight perfectly counter-weigh

while we tunnel inward along such different plots,
solitude *à deux*
down our steep divergent burrows of desire.

Is this shalom holding up a world for healing?
At each end of a couch,
Our two dancing balances brought to rest.

Anniversary

In the darted morning light of early autumn
Our first encounter's
Shivered hum,
A tuning fork
Trembling long unimaginable futures.

Jokes, myths, slow gathered connotations,
Wavelengths,
Metal oscillations
Under touch,
The tones we don't hear, we feel.

Every word becomes a knuckled gong,
A round deep
Monophthong
Humming *profondo*
Rung down into bones of time.

Kitchen Portrait

Above all I think it's steadfastness.
Even transplanted to Booterstown,
clay-wrapped Donegal roots

tapped downwards in limier soil,
smiling containedly as your father
you're bending over to slice a parsnip

not on a chopping board in full moons
but laid from palm to middle finger,
thumbed down for the quick knife

that carves lengthways, scooping out
long tapered wedges which fall
in a rhythm at once soothing and sure.

Mind-grounded. Heart-earthed.
All things seem to be at one.
A gentle paring back to the core.

*　*　*

This is Jimmy Nancy's daughter.
An inner unyielding ring,
A resilient core

Remembers District Inspector Martin
Struck dead in Gweedore.
Goaded and angry

Outside the church a throng rushed;
At sixteen Nancy an Dochartaigh,
Did your father's mother

Fling her shawl over foolhardy
Martin to blind and smother
Him for the bludgeon?

Craggy determined Northern breed.
A hardline circle drawn
Around the marrow.

542

* * *

You work a swift careful knife.
Kind, forethoughtful,
At ease and yet

No one oversteps
The mark. Your first option
The quiet life

But not for granted. Although
The dice of genes has thrown
Its gentle throw,

In the blade's steel glint
Nancy an Dochartaigh still
A flickered shadow,

Hovering foundation myth
Of where to draw the line,
To stand your ground.

Stern and generous seed.
Layers of independent rind.
Tender pith.

Pardon

Wise to keep things weighed up and prepare
In case a worm should turn within a rose
And catch us unaware.
God knows
Enough the after-clap when petals fall.

Mistress Bradstreet's homage back to front:
If ever man was content in a wife
Or woman who bore the brunt
So rife
With desire for a long underground haul.

Ample sap and green I'd darkly spent
Resisting the unalterable. Were you surgeon
To genetic discontent?
I burgeon,
Flex a little in the sun. Forgive me all.

Odyssey

For me a *déjà vu* in everything I'd learn,
More repossession than need or lack,

Strange glovelike feel of second sojourn,
Each outset a kind of coming back.

For you an urge to throw another shape.
How often you'd wondered what fad next?

Change follows change, a mutable inscape
That had you half-amused, half-perplexed

At how I seem to don another personality.
Post-Japan it's tofu, rice and chopsticks.

Und so suddenly I recover a German in me.
Sometimes homing must have taken weeks

As absorbed in conversations where I'd been,
Unconsciously drawing out an afterglow

I thrived a little longer in my different skin,
Still sweet on worlds I couldn't yet let go.

After France nights listening to *chansons.*
Ma plus belle histoire d'amour c'est vous.

Rife. Desirous. Restless. Driven. Chameleon.
In all shape-shifting I return to you.

Birthday Note

In an opal sky dawn winds stir.
Inching a morning higher
Over the hipped roofs of Trimleston
Through our double-glaze
The sun poured February 28th.

Would you like it all over again?
O yes! Wave the wand!
If you knew a little of what you know,
If we had it both ways,
You'd go back if only you could.

And me? Happier now than then,
Even as the years abscond,
Deep in a plot we're keeping on the go
I love its twists and ricochets,
Part sunk in, part understood.

The tumbling light begins to blur.
Our sun a drunken high-flier
Falls. As you go to switch a lamp on
In your hips longing sways.
The whole room holds its breath.

Breakfast

A chance in a million, a blue moon meeting
Where both felt completely understood
As if we'd known each other at least an aeon

Except this conversation just kept going,
So much to tell, so much to dream of
Here we sit talking two generations on

Fondling hot mugs and buttering *croissants*
At a table with a carnation in a carafe
And last night's half-drunk bottle of Chianti.

Eros has turned a promise into memory.
In wine the morning sunrays flood
Mellow, fermented colours of a history.

Hostess

In friendships I made the pace
Interfacing
Sometimes for us both; your way instead
A discerning, stable

Concentration of insight,
Jeweller's loupe,
A magnifying glass picking out
Minutiae of care.

Whatever my need to share,
Little doubt
In other friends the prism I hold up
Refracts your light,

Hostess queen of table,
Wide-hearted
Tenderer to guest or stranger, embracing
All I embrace.

At Sea

Jets whine overhead.
Who will be lonely for whom?
One silver gull cries.

Yoked we throw our light.
That one will be first to go.
A twin star untwinned.

Question

On our shed's south wall it's spring.
Clianthus puniceus has opened out
clusters of crimson parrots' bills,
drooped bunches of lobsters' claws.
In a neighbour's garden cotoneaster
fires with berries a chill sunlight.
Our two silver birches have shot
their buds to fuzz a colder outline,
in their limbs a Swedish refrain:
Det är ju godt att vi är två
It's so good that we are two.

These lines now since student days
a minor-keyed harvest folksong
vad jag fäller, du raker in –
what I cut down, you rake in,
And now three dozen years beyond
as we play out our third score
it's pining tune haunts the more,
winds down darker in our time
an austere three-time rhythm
Det är så tråkigt att ensamt gå –
So backbreaking to walk alone.

Would this be the hardest season?
Unshared days between our birches'
burgeon and when the soft lime
mouse ears so noiselessly unfold
And early March wind sways
a tandem leaning as their branch tips
almost touch. In the falling tones
of a melody again the low warm
swish of a scythe. *Bak i skuggan
Går en ängel och räfser in –*
In the shadow an angel gathers in.

If

Maybe
Together. If one must go
First? In imagined schism
Our tentative enquiry:
If you were

Alone
Would you fall again in love?
A slow chiselling realism
In your reply: enough
To shape one stone.

But me...
I don't know how to know.
Trusting hues of your prism,
If I was so lucky,
I think I'd dare.

Passage

So our boat ploughs on,
The bows still scudding with ease,
Old homing salmon.

Off course. No pinching.
A sail full and by the breeze.
One butterfly wing.

The tune yearning plays,
A song humming in the wire,
Wind sung in our stays.

Voyage we still dream.
Long perspective of desire.
Port's fugitive gleam.

Against

Every qualm or doubt
Thrashed out,
Talked over,
Non-stop Hamlet,
Sleep-tosser, night-walker,
Set

Against a fern's silence,
Calmly intense,
Contemplative,
A frond-still
Kind of live and let live,
Gentle

Unfolding in good time;
Steady sap-climb,
Leaf-stir
And shining through.
Shalom-finder. Heart-ponderer.
You.

Day

Our days forever.
Forever now one more day
New under the sun.

Double-blossomed lives.
Full and by. Then, to die well.
Gently petals fall.

Our love spooling out
Sun-up-ness and sun-down-ness.
Wisdom's crimson thread.

Cameo x 3

1

Warm but matter of fact.
Mover and dreamer. All your inbred
But's and *and*'s.

Rite-breaker and reverer,
Woman of action for all your worth
But visionary,

Both a doer and hearer.
Martha cumbered, down-to-earth.
Attentive Mary.

Twin strands.
Funambulist on a crimson thread.
Love's balancing act.

2

Daily affirmer.
Years at school conducting a class,
Whispers, laughter, murmur;
Your ruler a baton's hoisted upbeat.

Grown-ups you meet
By chance, sudden glances of delight
At seeing you in the street.
Recall a half-forgotten bond.

First face beyond
The home and cradle. Halfway house.
Life's brokeress. A fond
Voice calling towards the world.

3

In a mirror you hung on the wardrobe
Through our open bedroom door
A lampshade's white paper globe
Moons before
First light floods our gable-window.

I reflect how I'd thought years ago
You'd paint and already dreamt up
Some Van Gogh blue and yellow,
Large buttercup
Suns burning an Arles noon.

Instead a calmer composition of moon
Framed by banister against a crimson
Window-pane. *Clair de lune*
At Booterstown.
Our life together your still-life.

Crimson Thread

My love, my love along the slopes of Gilead,
This is our Eden before the bitter apricot.
How unimaginable now our story if we had
Never met, never shaped each other's plot.
Fracture and hurt of a once bruised youth,
Sores healed by wine and oil and spice.
Kiss of life. Shulammite's mouth-to-mouth.
My wounds bound up in second paradise.
Over and over. Season by season by season,
I'm older than my mother's crimson moment.
Our slow grown plot of risks and pardon
As father cries how things would be different,
If things were again. O heart's secret treason!
My sister, my bride...I come to your garden.

Again from under
Scarlet cords of winter fruit
A sumac burgeons.

We roved out all in our youth and prime.
Both real and unreal it seems somehow
Like reading a novel for the second time
To recall our unfolding in the light of now.
So much that fell almost as if by accident,
Twists and corners we couldn't see or gauge,

The plot gradually entangled as we went
That will have been our story page by page.
Two so close. Two so utterly different.
Clash and blur become a rich repair,
Secrets held to love more open-eyed,
Lives sweet against a crimson moment.
Chalk or cheese of what we are or share.
Lived-in paradox of decades side by side.

Deep deeper yellow
Prepares a crimson moment.
A sumac's leaf falls.

Dew, spice, honey, wine and milk,
Bone of my bone, flesh of my flesh
Wear again for me the damson silk
I take as given and still begin afresh.
Awake o north wind, come south wind....
Never enough just to have rubbed along.
Promise of promises nothing can rescind.
All or nothing. All is Solomon's Song.
I come to my garden, my sister, my bride.
Eat friend, drink and be drunk with love
And every moment I think I'm satisfied
Wakes me to desires I'm dreaming of.
In Solomon's blue curtain a cord of covenant,
A crimson thread until the crimson moment.

Globe

(2007)

For David, friend of friends

Our dance within the isotope
Ties and tears of history's robe;
Born in a land, I wake in a globe.

SHADOW MARKS

>...while memory holds a seat
>in this distracted globe.

>WILLIAM SHAKESPEARE

Given

Duke Ellington's It don't mean a thing
(If it ain't got that swing) juggles a gene
From within a phrase. Newness takes wing.

Our human being one second in three years;
As an atom to the planet our earth in space,
A single offbeat in all that jazz of spheres.

Still somehow the player's nerve to chance it,
Even to love a humbler in-betweenness
Of non-stop becoming, to flourish in transit.

O world as it is and not as it might have been,
Our riven map of this cussed here and now
Where webs and clusters of movers again begin

To allow the to and fro of things to arrange
And rearrange while another bridge passage
Prepares tomorrow's loops and modes of change.

For all our line's fragilities still dream-driven
As shifting landscapes shape and are reshaped.
Our one precious second. Our globe as given.

Shift

All generations face up to this
Slippage of what's familiar, slidings,
Differences of use and tone,
Subtle plays of emphasis,
Things
That steal up on us and push us on.

The way a word's meaning shifts
And though some resist or gripe
Most don't notice any move
As one strong verb shifts
Type
To settle down in another groove

Which bit by bit starts a pattern
That just may or may not take
But even if it does that too
Will of course in its turn
Break,
Making way for something new

So we slowly accumulate a past
In stirring of grammar's overspill
Which seems to allow us both
A sense of what's steadfast
And still
To feel the sway and pull of growth

Unless some sudden unforeseen
Upheaval or leap brings so swift
A change our whole context
Alters, a switch of scene,
A rift
Between one era and the next.

Under our noses this giddy pace.
Backfooted, an old paradigm
Unravels and all's at stake
As we melodeon space
And time.
Globe unmapped, globe we make.

Mobile

Once our globe of heartache, a long ago
Of emigrant wake and no return, but now

Across all busy skies the prodded phone.
Nihau! thumbs a sojourner in China Town.

Each node of belonging homed by satellite
Travels the dark fibres of a breakfast update

To touch digital nerves of daily memory.
'O you're my life that began...' *Enta omri* –

An Arab's Hamburg cab plays Umm Kulthum.
On worldwide webs our charted genome,

Eons of software copied from pod to pod,
A narrative mapped in one meandering code.

Lenses of time and space now telescope
And the long reels of a plot are speeding up

As lineaments of so many histories cross
A blurred zigzag between a "them" and "us".

Our line of country shifts and reconfigures.
We are the world. The face of the earth is ours.

Sputnik

Was it make-believe of childhood
That made the garden chosen seem
A time when our lives stayed still

Before the half-remembered thrill
At how a Russian sputnik hurtled
Ring-a-ring-a-rosie around an earth.

557

We didn't know they put a girth
On a patchwork fractious planet.
Tischa, Tischa, walls fall down.

A world that was a collective noun
Snapped from there outside itself,
A whirling clod once photographed

For good a delicate spinning craft,
Pocketful of posies we relearn
To tend, this fragile raft in space.

Everywhere becomes everyplace.
No man is an island Donne knew
Before the instant image wheel

Relayed the tube's mute appeal.
Hungry or broken, the wallfallen
Commands seen in Abel's face.

Tsunami

津
波

1

An unheard inner molten command
And the earth's maw begins to retch
Cracking the floor of the Indian Ocean.

Tsu: water and a brush in hand
To sign a sweep of sea, a stretch
Of deep for safe crossing, a haven.

Nami: liquid and a flaying hand
To symbolise a wave, as if to sketch
An ocean peeling off its skin.

Together a billowing towards land,
A tidal wave gathering its fetch
To deliver a long roll of misfortune.

2

Their flight visceral
And inborn as before it begins
An original
People still read the signs.

Nature's bonds
Broken by stilted inn
Or shrimp ponds
No mangroves hold the line.

Safer at sea:
In shallows the swells heighten,
Irony
Of a harbour now danger's haven.

Earthlings our toss
And turn frail in the sweep
Of a cosmos,
Humble riders on a moody spaceship,

A trembling globe.
Some hundred and eighty thousand.
Like Job
We cry out what is our end?

3

That all would have died sometime.
Any death as much a riddle as thousands.
So many together, unripe, in their prime?

Whole kindred with no one to claim
Their hurried dead or still to remember
A vanished face or a cried name.

Never to be called 'old man' *Bapak!*
Days into days stretch into weeks
And tides sweep over the crack

As an orphan blows her toy trumpet
Sumatra's grievers show signs of return
Setting out fruits at a morning market.

Durian, papaya, lime and mangostan.
Our earth is spinning across its seasons.
Fishermen cling to the skin of an ocean.

Underground

Scoops once cabled along an ocean's bed
Bounce their waves in space as each report
Lets us for a while turn brothers' keepers.

But news is news and another item dead.
A sense of stretching, always falling short;
Prisoners of each instant, global peepers.

Turnover. Overload. Through-put. Burn-out.
Simultaneous broadcast, performance of now,
Take it or leave it, our all-consuming present.

Choices. Options. Preferences. All about
Freedom to zap and channel-hop, to allow
Us our daily shop around in any event.

Cameramen fly on to break another story
Across a dimming or warming atmosphere,
A jet-stream of bulletins for fear we'd wake

To stale headlines. Our yesterday is history.
Through windows of planes beginning to near
A runway reporters stare down as though to take

A reading of another landscape's hints and signs
On patches of an archaeologist's aerial photo
Spreading under their vapour trailing air-bus

Shadow marks the rape's yellow outlines
Over sites of older settlements bedded below.
Underground shine of bones foreshadow us.

Touch-down

In all our moods and changes some groundplot,
Some sense of what was to give us bearings,
A recorder tuning in to where we were;
Even in such doubting days when we're aware
How grand flight plans so often clip the wings
Of underlings to justify the have and have-not.

Cold comfort in the cosy no-man's-land
Of huffing theorists busy trying to climb
Out of history, seeing everywhere deceits,
The half-aware cheatings of previous elites
Or reaching back to chide another time
Where long ago is a city built on sand

Of disillusion at ideas so fallen from grace
Once they knew explained the line and sweep
Of certain progress, stage by stage ascent
Of man and so their fingers burnt they're bent
On undermining everything, determined to keep
Cutting off our nose to spite our face.

Hail! all smothered voices from the past,
Orphan written out, forgotten dissenter
And every saga left too long untold,
Come in now waif and nomad from the cold!
The margins edge out a blurring centre,
Let the broken come into their own at last.

Still in curves and echoes of polyphony gone
Before us, a tune that's both old and fresh
Among the ties and leaps of complex histories
Allows the resonance and unforeseen of stories'
Shifts and vamped progressions that seem to mesh
Plots wound deep in us and winding on

Into the blue of other flights and offbeat
Loop the loops to retrieve out of the lurch
Of fashion things we thought we'd outgrown,
Out of date jingles on a mobile telephone
Where we just scroll quickly down to search
Our main menu's options and thumb *delete*.

Deafness of now in each newsflash and cast
As if too present we only hear the status
Quo of notes, missing out the arch of sound
Soaring its riffs above some older ground
Base phrase where our ghosts still nod at us.
This touching down in the lift-off of our past.

Scenario

In a rim's touch and turn
Our moment's wheel of now
Already become what was.

All that's to come still jazz,
An unknown latent in know-how;
Our past a future we learn.

Perspective

1 *Middle Distance*

We learn the touch-and-go of being
Between, figures in a half-distance,
Neither a loom too close to view
Or a shape so vague as not to matter,
Rather brokers in the thick of things,
Movers in a loose focus of betwixtness,
We walk a canvas's middle ground.

2 *Wide Angle*

So deep our mind's desire for seeing
Grander sweeps, a craving to glance
An overall or in detachment to eschew

Events that seem no more than a spatter
Of foam on the tides history brings
To swirl our lives along regardless,
Broadbrush of aeons in the round,

Great vistas and trends decreeing
Our civilisations' first appearance –
Booms and slumps, how they grew,
Why they flourish, then shatter,
Rise and fall determined by curvings
Of coast or river, Nile or Euphrates
The land-locked or the outward bound.

Does what at first may seem a freeing
Turn us all to slaves of circumstance?
Our long slow story lines accrue
Clusters of growth in the teeming clatter
And confusion of so many happenings,
Thousands of encounters in our daily mess,
In the bigger picture's blurred surround.

3 *Close-up*

And some scale downward, fleeing
The muddle in labyrinths of remembrance,
In scents and musks of Proust's clew
Winding inward a psyche's chatter
With warts and all foreshortenings,
Chosen myopia of endless consciousness,
An insomniac's inner merry-go-round;

Recalls of detail that though guaranteeing
Darker oubliettes of self still unbalance
What we think and what we do.
A worn-in narrative is both flatter
And richer for our shared humdrummings
Where inner and outer worlds caress,
The commonplaces that still astound.

4 *Symmetry*

Even our own heartbeat is keying
Us to the middle of a cosmic dance;
Our pulse a geometric average of two
Limits: from the Big Bang's scatter
It's fifteen billion years, the swing
Of atoms a femto-world. O Antaeus,
Keep your airy feet on the ground.

Footprint

Sometimes ground vanishes under our feet
As tidal waves of change sweep in so fast
Over sand too shifting now for any retreat.

But neither fogeys nor spirit-rappers of a past,
All thumbs, slowly we text our mobile tidings
Copping on to Gr8 & c u @ 3.

The only rule of thumb to learn new things
As our middle voice tips towards passivity
Allowing another generation show us how

To program memories and delete what's old
Or out-of-date as making way we bow
With grace to let another crowd take hold.

Even in the thrill and confusion of letting go,
Strange continuities in this thumb tick-tack
A sign from school or invoices (*so and so*

Many @ such and such) makes a comeback.
Yet also some unease lurks in the marrow
That those who follow us may thumb their nose

At footprints we'd walked in, once numinous
Traces rubbed out by history's ebbs and flows
In the sifting sand-glass of our remembrance.

Under their thumbs one global city they build;
Their turn to find loops and detours of advance,
Keeping promises we're leaving unfulfilled.

Thread Mark

Who'll promise to remember us?
An angel of change has brushed its wing
against the frail contours of our lives.

A lighter generation now takes off.
Open-ended travellers. Will they become
globetrotters, strays and passers-by,

our turn a past they won't recall
as their own? Already a future forebears
once imagined now long outdated.

O angel of history, must we forget
those hard-earned vestiges in our clay,
sweat of heritage, arrears we owe?

The dues paid, the debt assumed,
our thread mark of owing between
those who were and those who follow.

Yes, to love the flow, to embrace
the shifting globe and yet the risk
of traces lost in giddiness of change.

In these fragmented times we wonder
will those who fit the prints we leave
remember feet that walked before them?

Slope

So frail the ways that we remember,
Episodes we fudge or blur,
The unconscious ember
We keep on raking over

And just ordinary hit and miss
Of human recall, hazed
In some failed synapsis,
A sign in our psyche's wax erased

Or even the way our status quo
Chooses a founding memory
It was always so,
How we were and how we'll be.

One narrative, an ancient nation,
Flag and parade and anthem,
Tyrannies of commemoration
Of us always different from them.

In our stumblings, even in our flaws
And gaps what else have we
But spoors in the mind, our gauze
Of story grown in a womb of memory,

Testimonies of what happened then
Probed and sifted through,
Unfolded and told again,
Our slope of past climbed anew

To fight against the grinding dust
Of forgetfulness and snatch
The absent back? We trust
Now traces of our gone to catch

Between rungs of time's vertigo
Memories of things done
And hallow the dead we owe.
For all our frailty, a risk we run.

Sifting

In all these leap years of change
How easily from heights of now
We view what was as obsolete
Forgetting how
So many things loop and repeat
As gain and loss rearrange,

How in this upping of our pace
What's knitted over centuries
Could unravel half-unnoticed.
Behind our ease
A velvet glove and greedy fist,
Soft tyranny of the market-place,

Bytes of facts and hardnosed
Figures, our problems best
Scanned by instruments. Screening
Out the rest,
We quickly lose a thread of memory,
The poetry in us so readily prosed.

Given a globe of sudden upheaval,
We thrill at change but fear chaos.
In dizzy worlds that begin
To criss-cross
And fuse, we can only trust in
Loops and circuits of retrieval

As trade winds shift and sweep
Over older boundaries
And faithful to our past's debt
We sift memories
For what to recall, what to forget
To steady us now before we leap.

Tension

Any variation a leap in the dark:
Forgetting too little or not remembering enough
We'd stray too long off the beat.

For fear that we might lose the spark
Of what's always more we dare or bluff
Nervy completeness of the incomplete,

Sweet tensions of not yet and memory
Between anticipation and fond repeat,
Interplay of riff and debt.

All our jazzing still an extempore
Of players who know freedom's bittersweet
In every newness they beget.

Brokerage

How begot, how nourished? Reply, reply.
Bred both in the heart and head
and nurtured in the middle ground
of our belongings,

friends, lovers, fellow-players,
darings of trust, clusters of conversation,
bedrock and seedbed, chosen garden
of our becoming.

Born and died on such a date
before we knew or cut short,
a fact of dust in public records
unless some

delight in our coming, meaning-makers
who, growing into shared memory,
mourn crimson moments of our end.
City within city,

Groundings of our kept promises
feeding whatever newness we attain,
brokering bonds and ties between
each and all.

Blend

Beyond each heartland over millennia
exodus, migration, scattering,
eternal Jew, Chinese sojourner
or wherever green is worn.

Remember how many thrived in Babylon,
exile and rover making good
or darker musics of belonging
blues, calypso, reggae.

As both before Europe's lines and maps
and in gaps and interstices then,
even more so now that all
our frontiers shift and leak.

Every homeland falls short of our desire.
...*che retro la memoria non piò ire* –
memory can't backtrack –
Dante dreams onward.

Uprootedness, estrangement, our starting again.
As in the beginning and maybe always
blends of memory, story, myth
cross oceans of longing.

Traces

1

An ocean only ever the sum of its drops,
All that we can, even though we know
That of course another generation chops
And changes, going wherever currents go.
But what traces will any of us now leave?
A comber's tiny eddy that froths and scums
As much as any of our lifetimes will achieve,
A fret in restless floods of what becomes.
No telling the way each sea-change behaves;
A ripple somewhere in the flux and motion,
In the rips and overfalls of loss and gain
Our pebble skims the water, a wave train
Overwhelmed by the flow, swept to an ocean
On ebbtides of stories that once made waves.

2

Still there are a few marked out for greatness.
Remember debates: *history maketh the man*
Or the other way around, so some innateness
Chooses doers and heroes catch as catch can.
Surely both a meaning someone wagers on,
A lifelong preparation but also no doubt
The way it happens, this or that liaison,
The fall and ravel of how it all plays out,
Every complex motive we sift and sieve,
The strands given, lines we splice or tie,
Node-workers, knot-tiers, hitch-makers,
Slowly we become our own movers and shakers
As plot and characters merge in reasons why,
Our histories still the tangle of lives we live.

3

Some looping in the least expected strand
Too early out may find they've tied a knot
For a world still not ripe to understand
And seem to stand outside the bigger plot.
The lucky may even get their timing right,
Knotting a moment's perfect knot and yet

Others, years ignored, may walk the light
Long enough to see their mend in the net.
Las Casas upsetting everyone's apple-cart
Or Galileo staring out beyond our ken,
Mendel's pea garden's state of the art
Like Meister Bach lost and found again.
A hitch too soon, on time or in hindsight,
The fingered loop or twist its own delight.

4

Over and over again a hasty dream that strives
To short-cut every shaky setback or hiccough,
All the ordinary fumblings of our frail lives,
Desires to broom the world from the ground up.
When too hurried visions have failed or faltered,
The pendulum swung again by those who frown
On any change, the opting out of nothing altered,
Everything imagined as it was handed down.
Bottom up or top down the same particulars,
Shifting minutiae of a slow working through;
In every doing something still left to be done,
Daily revision of broken histories rebegun.
Our knots must hold as easily as they undo;
And still we bless the memory of our stars.

5

For most nothing momentous or too high-flown,
Just some trace laid down, our mark made
In the give and take of lives, a loan of a loan
Passed on as mention of our names will fade.
It's mainly fallen angels with our clayed feet
And yet moments in stories no one has told,
Split seconds of our double time, a pleat
In a cloth of histories that takes so long to unfold.
A promise kept, something done for someone
As rumours of decency gone to ground for years
Re-emerge, the way suddenly in a niece's son
A gene that ducked and weaved then reappears;
Gestures of love on streets of a fragile city,
Memory inscribed in action, a scratch on eternity.

KNOT-TYING

The knotte, that why every tale is toold...

GEOFFREY CHAUCER

Fame

(for Johann Mendel, Bruder Gregor, botanist;
born 22 July 1822, died 6 January 1884)

Bend low in your garden, *Bruder Gregor*,
count and wait, count hybrids you resow
for eight years, thirty thousand plants
you choose to mate by axils, stems, seeds,
shapes and hues, the dwarf and tall you cross.
Watch how a pair of characters refuse to mix
but keeping one, will spare a hidden other
to flare anew across a later generation,
a lost grandparent again breeds through.
Kiss the ground, Gregor, fondle seeds
wrinkled or round, green and yellow pods,
calculate by night the odds for seven traits
to mutate another shuffled year of peas.
Bend, Brother, seize the wonder you unearth,
these throw-backs that neither blend nor thin;
Darwin knew he should but couldn't see,
switches and engines of our mongrelhood.
Now tell great and good how genes play
a mulish hide and seek. Misunderstood
friar snared in a foolish blindman's-buff,
go tell to your heart's desire your sidelined
wonder but is it we who are blindfold, don't
see how we chase and never can catch on?
Despatch reports to Herr Professors *Hinz*
und Kunz. That tiresome friar who somewhere
in his counting garden hunts strange equations
to answer questions that haven't yet been asked.

572

No basked in glory, Brother. A feverish talk
or two no one notices, a recessive hidden
in a Brno society's journal shelving dust.
So now become Abbot Gregor and wrangle
out your days in a tax row to die
unknown begetter of genes, a wax-winged
Icarus who'd never flown. Young Johann
Mendel, farmer's son, can we call you Hansel
and tell a boy dreaming in a kitchen garden
before a falling tree will maim his father,
before a nervous student flunks exams,
turns Augustinian *Bruder Gregor* by default
or Herr Professor Nägeli can ignore his find,
tell you how a generation after Jánaček's
organ music at your cortège and clearing decks
confrères burn your papers three unknowing
heirs in different parts laboriously repeat
something of the same experiments only undust
your name from library shelves? Mendel's Law.
Fame, Brother Gregor, a fragile gene
Another forty years beyond your garden.

Après Vous Monsieur!

*(for Emmanuel Levinas, philosopher;
born 12 January 1906, died Christmas Day 1995)*

A father's arms stretch out across a century
to touch five years from either end,
embrace weighted with presentment and memory
fathoming how to mend.
No 'because', just infinite command,
a face hiding more than it will show
calls you hostage and brother's keeper,
keeper even of your keeping me.
Child of Kovno,
Eighty years riding out the trends,
offstage whisper, sideshow
to Sartre, de Beauvoir, Derrida and friends,
unrelenting shadow.

Scene shift and it seems as though
lines, byplays, subplots all combined
to cue a late entrance as a slow
voice of asides and rumours wends
into the mind.
Silent weeper of dead barely named,
parents and brothers still behind
each word, each claim counter-claimed,
mined, then undermined,
fearing we might comprehend
a face we daren't even think we know.
One thing said and unsaid over again,
riff and midrash on the same unashamed
and urgent *ditto*:
I'm here, I'm here for you, *hineni!*
No I and Thou or *quid pro quo,*
Seo anseo mé, me voici!
Less equal than below
après vous, monsieur, we bow
between a world at Heidegger's clay feet
and long hidden Talmud years
under doyen M. Chouchani
merciless exegete,
between the realms of Abraham and Ulysses,
between a tent-dweller's incomplete
dream who always turns his gaze
to promised lands and the feat
of a homing voyager who may forget
his cunning journey, between the double helix
of heritage, good gene and true,
between Rabbi and Plato always
Jews and Greeks.
Eighty and his rumour flares and spreads apace.
Autrui, the other's face that seeks
me out, a presence already a trace
of what's concealed but speaks:
I am the one thou shalt not kill!
Traveller, traveller, where have you been?
Après vous Monsieur, Madame!
An outsider turns his insistent face.
Stranger, come in.

Lodestar

(for Patrick Kavanagh, poet;
born 21/22 October 1904, died 30 November 1967)

A star rides watery hills of evening gloom:
'Someday they'll say,' he'd insist,
'you dug this ground with me' – Lennon
his friend will recall. Then answer
yes, outside the whitethorn hedges of Ballyrush
and Gortin after the narrow tyrant's climb
no dreamer realises.

Some misfit gene long before the womb,
an awkward customer at best,
in school-books finds the leaven
for whatever codon or mystic enhancer
feeds the lone psyche's shock and rush
in clumps of nettles and glistening slime
love immortalises.

Never to allow the fame of rustic heirloom,
a Monaghan colourist;
that digger, Tarry Lennon,
you remember, no local romancer,
what's true for Drumnagrella is true for Bangladesh,
for this alone the stairs of broken rhyme.
No compromises

but to face a world of failure and yet resume
as above the tired *Weltgeist*
laughter-smothered courage again
begins to praise, cussed freelancer
tilting at grinding mills of angst and anguish;
another day a prophetic enzyme
still improvises

and Kitty Stobling's new outrageous bridegroom,
a wooer too possessed
to scoff at all the tedious men,
to tend to every dog and chancer
who couldn't see in any December whin bush
a wise king. So what the pantomime
of unwon prizes,

let the final Baggot Street sonnets bloom
when after much trouble blest
by canal water, born again
Zenlover whose post-cancer
no caring jag now surrenders afresh,
Meister Eckhart green and sublime.
O God of surprises!

Kafka's mad, Picasso's sad in despair's confining room,
a kamikaze careerist
batters out the sanity of men.
Eden-haunted angel-glancer,
What word in this cantankerous gene made flesh?
Behind, before, beyond its time
A star still rises.

Cue

*(for William Shakespeare, playwright and poet;
born 23 (?) April 1564, died 23 April 1616)*

What cheer, great and most elusive ghost?
All hail good master, so long engraved in us,
we both speak your mind and do not know
what story shaped an extravagant unerring spirit,
a tyger's heart wrapt in a player's hide
who tells everything and nothing, mummer
entering and exiting, leaving empty space
to conjure what happened, make the even truth
a pleasure flow. Child of April 23rd
coming and going, in and out on cue,
all parts and ages done by fifty-two.
Vague footprints still in bonds and registers
William Shagspere and *Anne Hathwey* of Stratford,
furnace-sighing lover shotgunned at eighteen:
Susanna; Hamnet, Judith sonne and daughter.
Lost years seeking the bubble reputation,
a name on lists of Bishopgate's petty debtors,
Johannes factotum learning the adrenalin trade
until poor grudger Robert Greene complains
'Trust them not there is an upstart Crow...'

At thirty Hamnet mourned before his teens.
Sudden mentions by poet Drayton and Southwell
and rivals are stealing copies both fair and foul,
now theatre shareholder with friends at court,
wise investor with eyes severe and beard
of frugal cut signing his deals and loans.
A score years, a million dazzling words,
half-dozen lived out a squire at Stratford
and all entailed to Susanna's male heirs,
just a second-best bed as an afterthought
for Anne his wife. Strange will indeed
outriddling Hamlet in riddles left behind.
No one and everyone as each role stares
into the eye and prospect of his soul.
An acorn's ambitious recipe of genes
well sunned and rained unfolds an oak,
nature and nurture scheme with such a will
to soak and breathe all our foibled lives,
a Hamlet echoing every voice around him
who picks bare bones of Plutarch, rakes
over chronicles to fire a brain with plots
he bloods and fleshes, shrewd mood-shifter
luring and juicing a rowdy London yard,
streetwise, no one's fool and yet the fool
in quips and banter glinting his vision's fabric.
There needs no ghost come from his grave
to tell how marrow sweats in every line
as prince, general, lord, queen and thane,
glutton, coward, lecher, soldier, braggart,
every foul-mouthed and calumnious knave,
tramp our patchwork show across the planks.
A long time ago the world began, hey ho!
hey nonny, nonny, o mistress mine!
In how warm a heart do our hearts bask?
Sponge, mimic, scavenger, hustler, clown,
but does the sonneteer occasionally unmask,
allow an actor's visor clatter down?
W.H. onlie begetter's riddle-me-ree
obsession with outwitting time's wrong
thou runnest after that which flees from thee,
so fickle a dark lady and yet to long.
Is passion shaped in pale-blooded veins,
past master in the cold comfort of an art

that dresses hurts while still the self remains
the hidden sum and cipher of every part?
This virtuoso heart that never can unclasp;
All otherness, it slips again beyond our grasp
as each gleaming mood swings on another.
'In youth when I did love,' a grave-digger sings,
Hamlet broods on a thrown-up skull;
Macbeth rinses trembling hangman's hands,
a drunken porter moans his brewer's droop.
Such timing well-graced actor to arrive
and enter at this creaking hinge of history
to strut a glittering stage as Europe wakes
out of a sleepy middle age to retrace
profaner youth, such flair to tread
the boards in this giant-world of feverish states,
hotbed of new voyages, emissaries and spies;
so barefaced and fancy-free at one
fell swoop to shape and hammer language,
daring all that Bacon's Latin couldn't dare.
Things dance attendance on fortune's knave,
a talent bursting through as a moment readies,
flawless match of chromosome and chance,
set, props, backdrop, every detail
of a plot conspires to cue the lead in
as Burbage lugged his father's lumber to frame
The Globe. As luck would have it the finest
London troupe and a will to hold the mirror up
to what we do, not what we should do,
to tell the story and let it tell itself
with shock and shadow-ironies that peep
between the lines from play to play to hint
at how a knowing voice and unseen eye
that qualms and scruples through soliloquies
still house the sonnets' dreaming realist,
applying fears to hope and hope to fears
as from now to how we ripe and ripe.
But did we hear the hint or imagine it?
Greatest mirror, most hidden holder up.

Admiral of Arks

(for Jean Vanier, founder of L'Arche;
born 10 September 1924)

Evacuated from Bordeaux at eleven Vanier
Saw an overloaded captain
Watching a tug of refugees driven away

Whose cries traverse his years and multiply
Among the marred and broken
And fix him with Lazarus's begging eye.

At thirteen as he opts to leave Québec on his own
For Dartmouth's British Naval College,
His army father trusting as though he'd known.

A butterfly collared cadet, chevron winged,
All day moving at the double,
No room for teenagery, tough and Kiplinged;

5 A.M. barefoot scrubbing decks at sea,
Turns below or on the bridge;
Three of his classmates all admirals to be.

A sailor inside sails against the stream.
If you can trust yourself
When all men doubt you. A different dream

As life pulls and loops strands to plot
Surreptitious ins and outs
And tie, as if by chance, the perfect knot.

A concrete asylum where eighty retarded inmates
Tramp their tethered days in circles
Charges his psyche with horror and fascinates.

Whose presence had his friend Père Thomas seen
Crying *I am who I am*
In some noisy muddled sequence of a gene?

To trust the grooves and habitats of love.
Soup, apples from village neighbours.
Raphael and Philippe. One tap and one stove.

Slobber of dailyness. Tasks begun and rebegun.
Small humdrum of the wounded,
Seizures, tears, rushes of anger or affection.

More listening than wanting to do things for,
Fecundity of nothing accomplished,
Ordinary unhurried to and fro of rapport.

No mask or echelons, a kind of upside-downness,
Osmosis of bare and broken
Takers and givers in a single fragile caress.

A flood of middle 1960s volunteers.
Americas, India, Africa, Jerusalem,
Flotilla of arks across some forty years.

By guess and by God, fellowships of need
Ravel decades of care and laughter,
Hurt or seeking minds slowly unmutinied.

Each new community he heartens to adjust,
Admiral of arks, servant-leader,
A father's voice still saying, of course, I trust.

Villagers overlooked, zealous finger-pointings,
Let live of breakage and passage,
And lose, and start again at your beginnings

As after two years' illness his return to hidden
Gradual rhythms of healing that heals,
A stiller brother's keeper who loves unbidden

Guests that might never be if it were known
Chromosome messages had so mistaken.
A refused slab becomes the corner-stone

Lain against the market's coarser grain.
Day by day a giving in
To banalities of love. Over and over again

To announce a vision, even to wear renown
And to fall short anew with every
Ups-a-daisied child let forever down,

A tug still fails all who'll never board.
Yet the joy in Abigail's cry:
To wash the feet of servants of my lord.

The Burning Bush

(for Sigrid Undset, Norwegian novelist;
born 20 May 1882, died 10 June 1949;
awarded Nobel Prize in 1928 for her historical novels
Kristin Lavransdatter *and* Olav Audunssøn*)*

1

A young thing basked on a sunlit slope
in warm Danish earth of infanthood
and clung to Papa, archaeologist back
at last for good, and already at two
could list names of Stone Age axes.
Once Papa in a heady moment
allowed his own Sigrid hold
Schliemann's terracotta horse,
a toy a proud child had handled
thousands of miles and years away
in Asia Minor's nine-layered Troy,
that slipped her fickle hands and broke.
Returned to Norway old wine of sagas,
Greek myths and Rome trickle down.
Keeper of finds he'd let her hold
torques and pendants from antique days,
while Mamma, free-minded Dane whet
a daughter's talents with Andersen's tales.
Home now shifted from flat to flat.
Her Papa ails and eleven or almost
Sigrid sat and read aloud
as engrossed he strove to close a work.
By forty he's dead. Barely sixteen
she chose to drop out of her co-ed.

Facts, they'd said, but often no more
than a prop, theory, a kind of try-out,
side-tracks in history's longer light –
her father's Trojan horse of doubt.
Right or wrong, enough is enough,
and Sigrid high horses into the world.

2

Dear Dea, I've sometimes even begun.
Nothing comes right. Burnt on the spot.
I must make art but haven't lived enough.
I think I'm possessed. But if it works or not,
Nothing grips me like this scribbling stuff.
Letters to a Swedish pen-friend, each one
Both dialogue and self-appraisal. *I too*
Want some day to fall in love but my ideal
Is maybe not so high as yours, I only
Want to love and be loved as earthlings do.
Constant passion for what's worldly and real.
Ten years as secretary, a woman lonely
In double life: by day her post; by night
Chaucer, Shakespeare, Byron, Keats, learning
Greek and Latin, Drachmann, Heine, beloved
Sagas. *Dear Dea, I've got only my yearning!*
Mamma worries that she's so late to bed.
The damned office all day, at least I might
Be let do whatever I want at night-time.
A decade breadwinner for mother and younger
Sisters she spent among the office Misses
Who whisper in one-room flats their hunger
For white-horsed knights with infinite kisses,
Dream their dangerous dreams in broken rhyme.
Once we'd authority. Freedom's a colder stone.
Dea, if only we women could be as women are...
Neither to vie or play the cards a man deals.
But has this prophet already seen so far?
Don't marry, Dea, unless head over heels
And sooner hell with him than heaven alone.
Ten years to fumble and open into her voice.
Still the whirl of stubborn genes and hardwire,
Her father's long-sighted perspective squirms
At Hamsun's Pan or Ibsen's selves of choice.
Art's a clamour between our nature and desire,

A crying gap between our angels and worms.
Her first refusal. 'And don't ever bother again
With historical novels. A modern one maybe
You'd never know,' condescends editor Nansen.
Bruised ego she both nurses and disciplines.
So the chic griefs of hapless Marta Oulie:
I've been unfaithful to my husband, she begins.

3

A break and book and a bursary abroad.
At last to Rome where something thawed.
In letters talk of new white blouses,
A black straw hat with roses, carouses
In cheap wine bars until sunrise
And her painter Svarstad, a streetwise
Loner, driven and against the stream,
Shining knight who'd walked her dream.
Happiness is a shooting star, a blitz
To always remember and wish on its
First caresses, still dizzy and new.
I kiss the earth for I never knew
A human could even be this happy
Or if I did it wouldn't ever happen to me.
Rome, Paris, London, Copenhagen.
A kimono. The loveliest I've ever been.
Home, another book and breakthrough.
Married in Antwerp, London for a few
Months, their first-born son in Rome,
And back to Norway to set up home.
A burning bush of temperament needs
To be everything. Mother of feeds
And changes, hostess and author
By night as she worries for a stepdaughter
And son as her husband's ex can't cope.
Painter Svarstad has begun to slope
Off to his atelier and overnight there.
One evening she let down her hair
And wore her olive-green from Rome,
But when Svarstad didn't make it home
From a frock that wowed Rome's carousers
She sews for her son a coat and trousers.

Separated in the country with children and pets,
visits from the step-family she frets about;
her second daughter never quite right,
another son, as still by night cigarettes
and caffeine to breathe new lives
Kristin Lavransdatter and Olav Audunssøn,
her passions worn and woven in.
Now more than ever twin strings of genes,
weighted sagas and Danish ballads,
a daughter's double strands laid down
beside a parted helix of two times.
How in a tangle of isms and fragmentation
to find an angle of vision where
love knows no rules and breaks them all,
not in a freefall of lone egos
but a knot in a greater story that throws
its light both back and forward to catch
the infinite in flight? Time wears on,
beliefs drift and we think otherwise.
Our human hearts can't shift. O lonely
office girls turn back to before
Enlightenment and yearn for a knight in arms,
give Kristin her head to fall
for a tearaway prince she'd meant to wean
from whim or foolery and shape the one
true cavalier he never was or could be.
Let her ripen strong and humble
to glimpse how from the outset in ecstasy or anger
his ring had bitten in and scarred
her finger or the way a love had underwritten
each fumbled choice, great or small,
undoing all the half-remembered bitter ends.
Light be light, dark dark,
a palette stark and realer set against
fin de siècle anything goes,
chiaroscuro of our consuming doze.
A prophet winding back to stare
forward and finding by retreat and detour
as soil-proud once transgressor
Olav Audunssøn strove to his end to uncoil
inner snakes of clay and blood,
worlds where light and dark interplay

5

A lone figure walks over Brooklyn Bridge.
Her daughter dead, a son shot
Skirmishing Germans in Norway.
Long banned by Nazis, they'd got
Her across to Sweden by sleigh.
Wartime in New York of essays and reportage
And a prophet comes back home wasted,
Her days doubled in nights,
Her life-sum in the red,
A seer with her Trojan hindsight
Whose long perspective watched so far ahead.
Would our sundered dreams of liberty end in tears,
Our broken fellowship
Pondered on a market scales?
Has civilisation begun to slip
As a fabric wears and fails
And a house of progress falls about our ears?
Oracle burdened with too great a convert's zeal,
A third order nun,
A Kristin stumbling to forgive
Those who'd shot her son,
To be, to burn, to live.
Dea, some day to fall in love but my ideal...
Kristin and Olav echo in us and amplify.
Older wine of hindsight,
And yet the bread is new.
Alone into the light,
Burn-out and burning through.
A flaming bush cries *Here am I.*

I've Crossed Famous Rivers

(Ndiwelimilambo enamagama)

*(for Nelson Mandela, former President of South Africa,
born 18 July 1918)*

A slow dripped stone worn by indignities.
No epiphany, revelation, moment of truth
just the long rotten row of African Only.

Die wit man moet altyd baas wes.
The pale man must always be boss.
Die kaffer op sy plek. Nigger in his place.

Rolihlahla, Mandiba, Dalibhunga, Mandela.
Tree-shaker, clan-man, chief à la Bhunga;
Russet, white-bellied, stripe-thighed impala

anteloping Africa. *I've crossed famous rivers.*
Less sprinter than long-distance runner coping
boundary by boundary hoping to let both

the bred Thembu kingmaker and royal mentor
first hit his stride as he shed skin by skin,
clan, tribe and stock but also to become

his names for all his people. Tree-shaker,
pathfinder, painstaker, a cross-country
pacemaker moving dangerously out ahead.

Even as a boy to win but never to humiliate.
Discipline inscribed in years and genes of grit,
a stubborn smile that seems to begin in an eye

of a student once expelled for making a stand,
a tearaway eluding a planned tribal match,
a gardener of Robben Island sharing among

prisoners and warders his overspill of fruits,
Antigone crying at Creon's unlistening will.
For 28 years never to stand still

Even on the same spot wearing out a shoe
to keep on and on running no matter what.
Talk, plot, debate, argument, growth.

Decades of gestation. A small village boy
he'd whiten his hair with ash in imitation
of his beloved father. Now parent to a nation.

Nkosi sikelel iAfrika. God bless Africa.
Laps of honour in a stadium of success.
Forgiveness. To win but never to humiliate.

Under a frost of grey a wise smile creases.
Yes, to father a country, but to have lost
my children's laughter? *I've crossed famous rivers.*

A Fractured Gleam

(for Mohandas Gandhi;
born 2 October 1869, assassinated 30 January 1948)

1

Detailed, fussy advice to family and ashram:
Avoid spices, cocoa, both tea and coffee;

Figs, raisins, grapes, an orange or a plum,
Home-bread, the clothes to wear, celibacy;

As for ornaments, beware dirt in nose or ears.
I's dotted, *t*'s crossed. A lawyer's ifs and buts.

South Africa a tune-up for 21 years.
'The saint has left our shores,' sighs Smuts,

'I sincerely hope forever.' Yet a personality,
A voice, a humour that captivates. Shy youth

That left become freedom icon in his dhoti,
Mahatma of lifelong experiments in truth.

587

2

Wire glasses, sandals, bone and loincloth
now tipping seven stone of inner strife,
Great Soul of India grown even thinner

than the outcasted unknown London student,
clone English gentleman in a silk top hat
and his own silver-mounted walking stick.

Violin, French, dancing. Practising alone
from Bell's *Standard Elocutionist* he'd intone
one of William Pitt's high-flown speeches.

It seems as though such shame once sown
must bloom full-blown and wither before
what's overgrown can push for the light.

3

In Gandhi's eyes a glint that won't let go,
His wily frame of energy.
So many conflicts in so small a torso.

Frightened boy harassing his child bride,
Minutiae loving dreamer,
A sensuous underlip curbed and denied,

Peacemaker, ascetic gatherer of fame,
Determined hunger-striker
Suffering to atone or gain by stealth his aim?

A drawn line falls short of Euclid's line;
In the so and so of living,
Pure soul and cunning clay combine.

Hopeless visionary and master politico,
Both guru and bargainer,
Aware how far to push his quid pro quo

Or so unerringly to choose a perfect token,
Salt and spinning wheel,
Fasts, vows, lockouts or laws broken.

Three times he's called in to broker power,
This maverick of self-rule.
I plough my furrow, I wait my hour.

4

To the hub's eye every spoke is an avenue.
Glamourless persuasion in villages and lanes;
Hindu and Muslim for ages muddled through
Long before an empire's sneaking trains.

One fall and we fall together. All is knit,
As a seed to its tree so our means and ends.
Why banish a tiger to keep a tiger's spirit?
States with bombs are feared even by friends.

Bitter shadow of defeat. A voice is fading.
Remember the salt march to the shore at Dandi?
But round and round a violent souring ring
As a Hindu mob clamours 'Death to Gandhi'.

How can I believe that I alone am right?
The Raj is withdrawing, the stakes are down.
Fragile bird of hope, barely still in flight
Winging out into dark. A seer or clown?

Between two hawks to die a dove for both.
No enemy or failure. One frail humanity.
Toothless foolish sage in his loincloth.
Garland him. Feed the lamps with ghee.

5

Gandhi the figurehead useful then as now.
A nation's father or *rishi* crying in vain
Would it have happened as it happened anyhow?
Source, head-streams, feeders, branches, creeks,
On flows the Ganges south across its plain
As water finds the grooves that water seeks.

Hungry the tiger, hungrier still the zealots.
Splits and wars and bomb-poised neighbours.
Though not the tiger, still the tiger's spots.
On flows the river and swings as a river swings,

The more involved, the more the way blurs;
Vision bogged down in the alluvium of things.

Has a globe begun to fear the tiger within?
An icecap melting down, our holed ozone.
The hours in prison he'd set aside to spin
And purify just one soul for the sake of all.
To stand against the world though you stand alone.
Mahatma's ghost still teaching green and small

And the views of Jain friend Raychandbhai:
No need to pit extreme against extreme,
The jewel can shine a face for every eye.
To love truth in one glint of a stone,
The live and let live in a fractured gleam.
Lonely Cassandra come into your own.

Whistle-blower

*(for Bartolomé de Las Casas, historian, Dominican missionary
and defender of native rights in the Americas;
born Seville 1474, died Madrid 17 July 1566)*

1

Young *clérigo* and conquistador on his first escapade
To take Cuba,
Shocked at seeing five hundred of *Los Indos* slayed,

But granted land and natives for some years he combines
His heart and gain;
On the make he sends his Indians to work the mines.

Was it a sermon on the feast of Pentecost 1514?
*To take away
A neighbour's living is to murder.* What does it mean?

Like one who kills a son before his father's eyes
Las Casas ponders –
A person who from the gains of the poor offers sacrifice.

A case for native rights once heard from a Dominican
Sinks in
To shake his being and undermine the businessman.

Abandon his Indians? Who'd be kinder than he'd been?
El clérigo hurries
To Governor Velaquez to relinquish his charges and begin

His unheard of mission. The king must halt this disaster;
He boards for Spain.
His peons drudge to their end under another master.

2

Ninety-two years of health and in overdrive;
Some dozen Atlantic crossings and still to outlive

Ferdinand the Catholic, Handsome Philip, Charles V,
And even to seem in the end to die at the zenith

Of his growth. Several lives in the breath of one:
Voyager, trader, radical, priest, historian.

A merchant's son with his Salamanca degrees,
By twenty-four he'd sailed with Columbus to the Indies,

So mission after mission between dominions and capital
Reformer determined to serve even in his shortfall.

For over three decades he travels to challenge king,
Cardinal or chancellor who just as they're enacting

Change will die. Endless buck-passing juntas
That kill with kindness or are rigged by Bishop Burgos.

Campaigner destined to fail even in his success
As every ban on slaves he cajoles Madrid to pass

The conquerors somehow override and undermine.
Shuttle apostle both catching and missing the boat.

3

Eight years of mid-life withdrawal
To a Dominican close, he has to refrain
From preaching. Days of study to renew
'The state of his soul'. Outside the wall
Cortés is conquering New Spain,
Alvarado Guatemala, Pizarro Peru.

A hate figure settlers now rejoice
To see ensconced and out of the way,
A trouble-making son of a gun.
In worlds of turmoil a lone voice,
Doubts cracking in his vessel of clay:
Perhaps he wasn't the chosen one?

Necessary methods must sometime hurt.
Better such modern means for reaching
Infidel so long as he comes to believe.
(Apostles had miracles up their sleeve.)
Conquest so much quicker than preaching;
Fill them with terror or else they revert.

To peach on his own? Nothing lower!
To win their slaves they'd marched
Months across uncharted terrain,
Toiled and bled. A small gain
For weeks frozen, starved, parched.
Boat-rocker. Whistle-blower.

Civilisations, plants, animals, lands,
Realms of discovery whirl by,
Unknown gold or precious stone.
To save a people and redeem his own?
Strands he'd so wanted to tie
Keep on slipping out of his hands.

African slaves play on his mind,
Mistakes made, his failed colony
Journeys to force Pizarro to cease
Terror called him, or had he pined
For action? In Guatemala his plea
To take the feared Tuzutlan by peace.

4

       Old mocking cliché:
'Try it', they said, 'Try with words only
       And sacred exhortation'.
       Clérigo and brethren
Are learning Quiché.

       A people who'd once known
Cities, temples, pyramids, palaces,
       Stars and warriors' fame
       Written by hieroglyph,
Sculpted in stone.

       Refusing the party line
Again Las Casas insists on trust,
       Tiny inflections of tact,
       Slow grammar of respect
To conjugate and decline

       Madness of hundreds massacred
As easy grindstones for Spanish swords,
       Bad faith of slavery,
       Trinkets, wine, bribes
And their broken word

       As conquistadors leave
Yet another cruel hierograph
       Inscribing the earth with greed.
       Ask the Mayan dead
Do stones grieve?

       Over four and a half
Centuries and poet Ak'abal
       From Totonicapán
       Writes what might have been
Las Casas' epigraph.

       Guatemala laments:
Ri ab'aj man e mem
       Taj xa kakik'ol ri kich' awem
       Not that the stones are dumb,
They hold their silence.

Unbroken

*(for Máirtín Ó Cadhain, Irish novelist and short story writer;
born 1906, died 18 October 1970)*

Fiery Cois Fhairrge teacher from a rugged line
Of storytellers,
Dismissed for his politics from his school post,
Interned in the Curragh at thirty-three,
Teaching other metal hut dwellers
Irish and spreading his wings: Ó Cadhain
Of Tintown Academy.

Tolstoy, Dostoyevsky, Gogol, Chekhov, Gorky,
Europe's extremes
Flirting in his busy head:
I'm learning Russian for all I'm worth.
His letters hungry for word of friends
And gossip, short stories begun, schemes
For novels, a stubborn humour, quirky
And down-to-earth.

Book after book pored over and underlined.
But how to undo
History? Our island as it ought
To have been. A dark road indeed.
A windswept tree bends to renew
And graft centuries of Europe's thought;
A vision of two worlds combined,
Few may heed.

Two long-parted strands tied in a node
Of frail dream
As the wind whines in stone
Walls and tells again in a gritty,
Nasal voice stories to redeem
An unbroken line who fingers to bone
Worked their life and tramped the road
To Bright City.

Burden of being both outside and within:
To count the cost
Because you've walked beyond,
To know the loss because you grew
Inside and feel so double-crossed
By your own who still can't respond
To your dream. Has the weave begun to thin
Unable to renew?

All the scattered energy beating the air,
Epistles or protests
Or scolding follies of the blind.
Can no one see? Will nothing halt
This unravelling? A tongue invests
Two thousand years to haunt the mind;
So rich a cloth so soon threadbare,
Fraying by default.

'Have you heard,' he glows, *ag déanamh na gcosa*
'A newborn foal *trying to find its feet?*'
His urge to include everything he'd heard,
Burrowing deeper to embrace a whole
Planet. Dried cowpats used for peat
In Aran that Tolstoy knew from Russia;
A globe inferred.

Under a cocky Rabelaisian carapace,
Tilt and wag
And his craggy snorting laugh
The bones of some story in the making
As he recalls lives that seem to nag
For words he plucks from history's riff-raff.
Behind a stern and pouting face
A heart is breaking.

WOUNDED MEMORY

Της λύπης είναι τέμενος η γη.
Αγνώστου πόνου δάκρυ στάξει η αυγή·
αι ορφαναί εσπέραι αι χλωμαί πενθούσι·
και ψάλλει θλιβερά η εκλεκτή ψυχή.

Earth is a sanctuary of sorrow.
Dawn drops a tear of unknown pain;
the wan orphan evenings mourn
and the select soul intones sadly.

CAVAFY
translated by Rae Dalven

Bushmen

1

Thousands of years they wander lands lush
With wild game and berries,
Nomads in Africa's southern veldt and bush,

Chattering bands of hunters and gatherers at ease
With how a cosmos behaves.
Short, apricot-skinned, eyes like the Chinese,

Come-day-go-day Bushman paints or engraves
An unbroken story in red
Ochre figures across the walls of the caves;

From Drakensberg north to the Zambezi the bled
Eland and hunter obsessed
And tall in ecstasy reaches for his Great Godhead.

Alone before the Bantu squeezed them north-west
To the Kalahari, before
Paintings of galleons and Dutch farmers expressed

Forebodings, still they dance a stalking metaphor,
The Masawara and San
Big in their trance as dreaming upwards they adore.

2

Around the fire they tend
Women clap up a chant and rhythm,
On a verge of trance
Dancers dance on,
Flux
Of buttocks
And ankle-rattlers prattle and hum

As the seated spirit's *n/um*,
Great God's sap rising to the boil
With yelps of *qai! qai!*
'Pain,' they cry out,
Rush
And push
Helter-skelter to the edge while

Stars and Bushmen reconcile
Their oneness in this dance they weave
And lay their hands to heal.
The sacred eland eaten,
Praise
The prey's
Own surrender to lend its life.

The surrounding dark is rife
With bawdy shrieks as a medicine man
Out on a limb stalls
And falters in his shivering
Dance,
His trance
Too deep willy-nilly he's lain

Beside the fire to regain
His mind. A kinship mends its dissonance
In this frenzy of togetherness;
Things done undone, every
Drift
Or rift
Healing in a hell-for-leatherness of dance.

3

Centuries of cross-purpose, claim and counter-claim:
They fence and graze where ancestors hunted game;
Poison arrowed Pygmies we never managed to tame.

Around the edges of farms, armies, factory or mine,
Diseased or lost or absorbed by default or design,
The tattered remnants of natives brought into line.

4

A dream that dreamed the Masawara's
Stars peters out. Some strays endure
Underlings in a Kalahari game enclosure.
What's gone a dumb show,
Mourn what was to become in all that was.

A broken twig, how grass stems were bent,
The call of a bird, even the shape of a spoor
Itself, the sacred eland's delicate signature
Touching the benign earth,
Whispered signs or hand messages sent

Along millennia. And then a line drawn
In the sand, the life-thread someone loaned
For a while and passed on. Nothing owned.
Firewood fetched by a wayside
Camp pitched at sunset, broken at dawn.

Dance for our healing, dance for falling rain
As greedy boreholes dry up the water table.
O Cain, o Cain, you murder brother Abel!
The Bushmen's shadows thin,
Poison arrows of shame have hit the vein.

Hyenas howl, the eye of the lioness glints,
Upright fall and stars shoot down the sky.
Hair on our heads are clouds when we die.
Praise names of our God lost,
Wind makes dust to take away our footprints.

Blizzard

(dedicated to Roman Vishniac and Eva Hoffman)

1

Teaming, quarrelsome, noisy world of *shtetl*
and ghetto, raucous melancholy of klezmer,
once scattered across Europe's eastern plains;

the Russian-born American Roman Vishniac
hurried to snap a last exposure to the light,
his lens shuttering lovingly each gesture of life:

shopkeepers, housewives, girls hungry to live,
milkman, printer, cattle-trader, stamp-collector,
Talmudic scholar in his fur hat and muffler,

cobbler, watchmaker, barber, second-hand dealer,
women gossiping with buckets at a vendor's door,
an elder stroking his beard in the *Beth Midrash*,

the salesman carrying his bags to the rail station,
a man, saw in one hand, his *tallith* in the other,
as dark figures in caftans bend into the snow,

Rabbi, cantor, tailor, peddler and beggar,
young men gathering to dream of Palestine,
a rapt Hasid walks along a swarming street,

where a merchant haggles over the price of a hen,
someone is inviting the local fool for dinner,
children are queuing up outside the *mikva*,

and *cheder* boys swat under the eye of a *melamed*,
a *yeshiva* student brushes his coat for the Sabbath
And a father fits his son with a cap for the blizzard.

2

Since Babylon in wandered Europe,
A nestling presence among not of,
Hunkering down and chequering in.

Cossacks, Turks, Swedes, Prussians.
Remember one side will win –
Watch well the way the winds blow!

Mystic, carnal dangerous other
But some *pogromchik* is lying low.
No hatred but we always knew

Side by side until the crunch.
Sorer still that Jew betrays Jew.
We shared sweet fellowship in God's

House. Two thousand years among
The *Goyim*. Together and at odds.
Bitter sigh between two sighs.

3

Shtetlekh seething with long quarrels of change,
Zionists, *Balabatim*, Marxists or Hasidim,

Tug and pull of custom and sudden challenge.
Some dreamers of *golden medina* cross to grim

Lower East Side sweat
shops beyond the Hudson.
O don't look for me where streams are playing,

O sukh mikh nit vu fontanen shpritsn
You will not find me there. Others are staying

To argue the toss of progress with endless fever
Of *Yashiva* students searching every midrash

For whatever meaning might still hide, whatever
Might yet have become before the hour of ash,

Before the looted sanctuary, the broken ark,
The silent klezmer. In a dumb fallen prayer

Their stubble glares like buckwheat after dark.
Don't look for me. You will not find me there.

4

A Pole in Bransk stumbles on grave-slabs with Hebrew
Nazis used to pave a lane and flags some hid,
Unheeded whetstones in barns or sheds he'll now bring
To where the Jewish graveyard was. Curiosity
becomes in time a sombre gesture of remembrance.

A ruddy sheepskinned leather-booted farmer's witty
'They'd cheapen for Christmas' sort of shrewd boy the Yid
Remark of one who'd once carted to graves a slew
Of dead. 'If that's what they want, you can't say a thing'
Even a sigh and sense of let-up, a jovial good riddance.

'Noisy as a *cheder*,' they still half-consciously repeat.
A scatter of Jewish words remain – the gone within,
A trace of woven *us* and *them*. The *Goy* and Jew.
'Richer but they too had their poor ones, *oy*, they did.
But one becomes used to people. I feel their absence.'

They are only truly dead who've been forgotten.
'Yes,' agrees another, 'I grew up on this street,
As I walk here I recall exactly who lived where:
Shapiros, Gottliebs, Goldwasser, Tykocki and in
The next house that man, what was his name, the one

Who did business with my Papa?' Once thick and thin
Of side-by-sideness slowly fades. The Gemora knew
To kill a human is to kill a whole world, to cheat
Them of all their children's children unbegotten.
A questioning prayer in the long anguish of a *shofar*.
Master of the Universe, why? O what have you done?

Palestine

1

On walls of Gaza City's government building
Someone wrote Vegetius's Roman words:
Let him who desires peace prepare for war.

General stickler and armchair conqueror
Whose fourth-century treatise undergirds
Every ruler's feet of rubble, gilding

Electric shocks and grillings used to keep
Mistrust at bay with supergrass or mole,
Intelligence and of course security for all.

Barak or Mukhabarat. And will we fall
And fall into Vegetius's blackest hole?
Walls that never talk must sometimes weep.

2

A handcuff drawn around an Arab substate
Glow-eyed martyrs dodge to freight a bomb.

Black and white of slowly simmered hate,
Another busload blown to kingdom come.

That Jews again should board a bus to die?
But now missiles fired to take a suspect out.

Each cold revenge of eye for eye for eye
And so this grieving turn and turn about.

The *saheed* wafted straight to paradise,
Sweet juices drunk to fête the newly sainted

But cameras watch the tell-tale swollen eyes
Of mothers wailing over their lonely dead.

This endless blindfold ring of anger vent.
Abraham's children pitch their mourning tent.

3

Abraham, Ivreham, Isdud, Ashdod,
Names that name a double vision,
Yibne and Yavne, Lydda and Lod.

Two millennia remembering Israel:
And she called the child Ichabod –
The glory of Israel gone, a frail

Look back at freighted golden days
Like some fondled childhood detail
Of vanished ghettos, yearning gaze.

Broken neighbours, prey to zealots,
Routed villagers, history's strays
Squat in camps or shacks, have-nots

In fruitless alleyways where men
In djellabas talk of figs and apricots,
Dream of villages, dream of then...

Foolish blood of right or wronging
Things gone that never come again.
Is every memory another longing?

Two rootholds grope the shifting sand
With all the tears of sweet belonging.
Two memories in vowels of one land.

Shalom and Salaam unreconciled.
Solomon takes his sword in hand.
Cry out wise mothers of the child.

4

Two separated domains cut off and brought to their knees.
Backgammon clacks as youths throw stones on the street.
Another permit that comes too late to visit dying kin,
A student thwarted, a pass withdrawn and ends won't meet;
At check-points trucks of fresh cut flowers wilt in delays,
Some minor Vegetius busy nipping hope in the bud,
Squeezed by settlers, gridirons of asphalt highways
Until their promised land becomes this no-win zone
Where victims fall in love with raging victimhood.
Day by day a gift of bread has turned to stone.
How, then tell me, can we make peace with Israelis?
Now another border closure to seal their anger in.

Is that Arab beside you preparing to pull the pin?
If our side loses of course the other will score.
Grind of *qui vive*, relentless doubt, suppressed fear.
Another suicide bomber shadows across a door.
Pizzeria, hotel, party disco, market, bus

And again today someone's lover's body sack.
We give them everything and look how they betray us.
Too long burdened victimhood, a haunted Jew
Too laden still and too intent on hitting back
To learn the stronger's generous move, derring-do
To stop the dizzy spiral, a giant too keen to win,
Samson bringing pillars down around his ears.

Layer on layer of yellow sandstone myth and years,
Hill of Zion, Mount of Olives, Dome on the Rock,
City of yearning and broken bread, city of *Salaam*.
Somewhere once you dreamed a peace beyond the flock,
Shalom of ripe commingling and let-live mosaic
Of all the thriving clamour of eastern streets and smells,
Coffee, *falafel*, *halva*, deals with upfront money,
Al Quds sunning itself in noise of give and take.
Old city of *muezzins'* calls, chants and swinging bells
The savour of your soil delights my mouth like honey.
Your Western Wall so full of slotted prayers and tears.
O fragile city! Jerusalem. Our earthly Jerusalem.

5

And so another road to Jerusalem loops both back and beyond.
Whose are still the voices where the past and future correspond?

Poet Aharon Shabtai like Amos dresser of the sycamore tree
Cries out *my lips mutter: Palestine! Do not die on me!*

A creature born of our people's love will burst forth into the blue.
Listen, his heart is beating through mine – I'm a Palestinian Jew.

Whirlwind, earthquake, then, fire. But even in the end you find
The stiller smaller voice. At last Elijah is learning to unwind.

O Abraham, could you not bear the fire-worshipper a single night?
As mystic Rumi's *cavernous shadows need the light to play*

And light alone can lead you to the light, so too, so too
Each soul will know what it has done and what it has failed to do.

The evening dove's olive leaf and the chatter under the palm.
Abraham, Ishmael, Isaac, Jacob and the tribes. Shalom! Salaam!

Doggone Blues

1

Home, village, tribe. Uprooted
Centuries of men and women
Chained, shipped, sold, branded.

First dim recall of Guinea.
No name or date. Master's
Jim, Esther, Ned or Jenny.

The lucky ones maybe roost
As cooks or house-slaves,
Few learn trades or crafts; most

From the day a child lifts a hoe
To work the fields until they
Drop between shafts of a plough.

Some drivers humane, some mean
And any spirit shown
Whipped until they're broken in.

We bake de bread, dey gib us de cruss
Wails the juba beater,
We sif de meal, dey gib us huss.

Nobody whose trouble nobody knows.
Crooned endurance in song
A story waiting to erupt in Blues.

2

So many "head of slaves" to tend the crop this year.
To buy a breeder and maybe bide until she mates.

The young man rides up, beckons the watching overseer
And says send me Juno or Missylene or Chlory
And then rides on into the trees, dismounts and waits

Or a young housemaid taken and soon set in pillory,
A wife's jealous cuffs and whippings sting the bone.

Quadroon, octoroon, their careful measures of mulatto.
Of course, give a coon an inch and he'll take a mile.
When you ain't got nobody you can call your own.

They'll take over the place. Yes, sir, we know Sambo!
And guilt stalks. Old shadowy nigger in the wood-pile.

3

Civil war. Then the Day of Jubilo
And slaves who still didn't know
Quite why? Tears on either side:
Owner and bondsman. Tongue-tied
Uncertain Blacks crowd a gateway,
A mind to leave, a mind to stay.
An' when your stomach's full o' slack
Some come begging to be taken back,
Others go stumbling on to die
On highways. *Brother, don't you cry!*
Saw-mills cotton-gins, lumber-camps,
Levee-banks, floods, glades, swamps.
Ought's an ought. Figger's a figger.
All for de white man, none for de nigger,
Sharecroppers rub your sleepy eyes,
Another slavery in another guise.
Started at the bottom, I stayed right there,
Don't seem like I gonna get nowhere.
Sourgraped South still juggles laws,
Klan lynchings or grandfather clause,
A Black finger as a pickled memento.
Who'd like a daughter to marry a Negro?
A ruse by any name to do them down.
Going to leave this Jim Crow town...
North, where they think money grows on trees
Don't give a doggone if ma black soul freeze.
Pittsburgh, Cleveland, St Louis, Chicago
No heaven on earth, Lord, wherever I go.
Nobody's nobody, a margin survivor,
Mule-skinner, rambler, steel-driver,
Convict, logger, pimp or whore,
Outsider, railroader, stevedore,
Boomer, number-runner, bootlegger.
First of 'twenty and odd negers'
Black Anthony Johnson steps down

From 'a man of warre' at Jamestown
The year of grace 1619.
All these years where have you been
Dogtrot cabin to shanty and slum?
Was it Fulani? But they left you dumb.
Flat-talk, dog-Latin, gumbo or jive,
An endless lust just to stay alive,
Migrant, loafer, roustabout.
All odds on a whiting out.
A chattel bought, a chattel sold,
Nobody's nobody's story told
In mumble, holler, scat or groan
Go tell 'em ivories how to groan.

4

Let everybody know the trouble I know.
A summer march to Washington King led:
We shall overcome August banners stream.

Before they overcome they shall undergo
Glower or backlash grudge of privilege shed.
Court by court a hard-etched self-esteem.

The sniper's rage is somewhere lying low.
But how to heal the white to love instead?
The preacher man calls out *I have a dream.*

For angry young an Uncle Tom too slow.
O black is beautiful! The Panther is dead
Or somewhere gone to ground in academe.

So the stalemate breadline snare of ghetto,
Gangs and drugs, lives hung by a thread,
Bias bound and hemmed invisible seam

Of half-forgotten scar and hickory blow.
The master's shadow falls years ahead:
Every lash and backlash a burden to redeem.

Turn about and wheel about, jump Jim Crow.
Satchmo, go bugle up the marching dead.
A ghost preacher cries *I still have a dream.*

Remember

1

Remember a long Armenian summer without dawn,
April 1915 to September 22.
Death cried for ravens and ravens darkened Van.

Young Turks tap on doors and Madame Hagopian
Hurries to hide her son in a mulberry tree
As ten thousand bodies float in Lake Geoljik.

Tricked and gathered. An *Ausrottungspolitik* –
Policy of elimination – a German diplomat reports
(Who'll later die for Hitler's bungled coup).

Behind the Great War's veil the soldiers slew
Or drowned thousands a day. Litany of slaughter:
Van, Trebizond, Bitlis, Sivas, Kharput.

For some a stoked-up envy, a chance to loot;
For many old cooped and brooded neighbour hate,
Abdul the Damned's contempt again overt.

Women and children over mountain desert,
Stripped naked, preyed upon and abused.
As vultures hover above the roadside dead.

Crawling, maimed, starved, begging for bread,
But south to a Mesopotamia most never reach,
A trail of rifle-butted shrieks and wailings.

Asia Minor black with ravens' wings
A million and a half Armenian dead before
The mulberry sheds the leaves of seven seasons.

2

A people's homeland for over three millennia.
Then word leaks out of slaughter in Armenia.

Their German allies hear but will see no evil.
A muted protest. Let nothing cause upheaval.

Waves of sympathy. Compassionate well-to-do
Funnelling millions of kindness dollars through.

'The broad interest of humanity', says poet Pound.
Woodrow Wilson pads the softer middle ground.

A cruel and merciless fate. Our words' slippage.
Editorials. Press reports and months of coverage.

The carrions rage across the blotted sky.
And in the bitter end the world stands by.

3

Under the soot-winged ravens
a torch. Brave Mary Louise
Graffam, missioner from Maine,
only alien to refuse to leave
Armenians from Sivas on their
deportation southward march
toward the Euphrates valley,
witness to how Turk and Kurd
(men already lured and dead)
robbed, beat, raped, kidnapped.
Everyone who lagged behind
killed... I saw hundreds of them.
Some died of thirst; others
went crazy. Like the rest,
I was all in rags. On the run
one end of the camp to the other.
Forbidden by the local mutessarif
to pass on beyond the Euphrates
she watches her pupils file across.
Back in Sivas to tend orphans,
underground aid, food smuggled
to mountain caves, trials for treason.
Thousands saved or alleviated;
above all an unflinching witness:
we kept carbolic acid on window
sills to keep the odour of dead
from coming in. There were
hosts of dogs feeding on bodies.
The sky was black with birds.

4

A drape of ravens flap their bitter wings.
Sleight-of-hand order, double directive,
Ceremonial secret oaths, sniggered codings:
'Departed convoy', 'provide with bread and olive'.
Deceit of trenches, diggers despatched on the spot.
Infants choked by steam, mad doctors, nightmare
Deportations (males or stragglers to be shot)
Long wasteland caravan, cortège to nowhere.
And who remembers the Armenian genocide?
Quadrupled blueprint, Hitler's upscaled *Vorbild*.
Of eighty-two Terpandjians, eighty died:
Grandfather, father, mother, brothers killed.
Megerditch, Garabet, Touma, Shukri, Paul;
A name for each three hundred thousand to recall.

Fallout

(after John Hersey's Hiroshima)

1

Island by island, Guam, Okinawa. To stun
Them to surrender sooner. To cast the die.

Cross-legged Dr Fujii read his *shinbun*
As widow Nakamura stood watching by

Her window a neighbour who'd now begun
Tearing down his house so he'd comply

With new defence fire-lanes and everyone
Wondered when and what? Three planes fly

Over before the all-clear sounds. None
Who'd survive that morning knew just why

A step this way or that had meant they'd won
What others lost. Imagine one step awry?

Enola Gay unloads. Below the August sun
Broad Island's hundred thousand woke to die.

A pilot logs: *My God, what have we done?*
Wounds of light enrage the hush of sky.

2

On pavements they retch, wait death and die.
Quiet ungrudged passing. All for the country.
Emperor, ten thousand years! Vive Majesty!
Tennō-Heika. Banzai! Banzai! Banzai!
Sudden fires rage out of the queasy murk.
All day still-living wander to Asano Park.

Maples, laurel, pines still green and upright
By rock-pool gardens. In the shades caress
Widow Nakamura's sick brood sleepless
With excitement. Her son sees with delight
A gas storage tank torching the night air.

Faces erased by flash burns are calling out
Mizu! Water! As Tanimotosan fumbling
His basin of water over corpses, stumbling
Apologies to the dead, relieves their drought.
Mizu! Mizu! One man takes and drinks,
Raises himself slightly, bows and thanks.

Then bloated drops of rain trounce the soil.
Out of a blazing city's convection swirls
Of angry uprooted trees; a funnel hurls
Débris winding high in the air a coil
Of iron roofs and doors. Eerie whirlwind.
Takakurasan shields his feebler friend.

Dr Sasaki, of thirty the sole unharmed
Among medics, dazed begins to roam
A broken hospital dabbing Mercurochrome;
Overcome by injured hordes that swarmed
To him, he wiped, daubed, bound and tended.
A hundred thousand either doomed or dead.

City of woe, scorched back to its bones.
Four square miles of red-brownish scar,
Crumpled bicycles, shells of tram or car,
Mica traces fuse in granite gravestones.
The lingering slough off their clammy skin;
The silent nurse a silent wounded gene.

3

Widow Nakamura's ten years'
penury as no one
wants the maimed leftovers.

Schoolgirls out to clear fire-lanes
disfigured rejects
sent to New York for touching up.

Tanimoto's daughter Koko
a jilted fiancée
deemed too smitten by fallout.

Beta particles, gamma rays,
lurking scars,
purple spots of leukaemia,

Broken wall of foetus cells'
strange aberrations,
stunted or skull-shrunk in womb.

Hibakusha. Outcast. Bomb-touched.
Victims' victims.
Sentence handed down in chromosome.

4

As only days after it fell the hidden
Roots of organs roused began to climb
Above the ground before their time

Lush over ashes and wreckage unbidden
Sickle-senna, morning glories and bluets,
Purslane, clotbur, goosefoot, Spanish bayonets

Wound the charred trees or anxious weed
Tangled gutters, roofs and fallen stones
To bloom wildly among the city's bones,

A million and a half so quickly now succeed –
After forty years one in ten survivors –
In this phoenix town of sybarites and strivers,

Of geisha houses, coffee shops and brothels,
Leaf-lined avenues chock-a-block with cars,
Born again in baseball and neon lighted bars.

Green pine trees, cranes and turtles...
Widow Nakamura sings once more in May
At flower festivals for the Emperor's birthday

As Toshio, her son, who never can forget
The fire, before dawn commutes once again
By train to golf with his useful businessmen,

And an older Dr Sasaki harbours the regret
That he couldn't label all the unearthed dead.
What nameless souls still hover unattended?

Eclipse

1

A myth of no losers, no few,
No inner other or need to warrant
Rights of tongue or belief.
Who has ever heard of Ainu?

Land of rising sun. Hokkaidō,
Honshū, Shikokū, Kyushū.
One seamless folk,
Archipelago of Yamato.

Hokkaidō? North Coast Road,
Renamed and annexed Ezo
Island of Ainu stock
Whose ways slowly erode.

Pioneers, missions, uneven trade.
Kindred of matriliny, node
And lattice of mores undone,
Their native gods renege

Who once steered the Kurile chain,
Sakhalin, Honshū. Origin vague,
But homeland for two millennia
Before the Meiji legerdemain

Surnamed and labelled them *dojin*
'Natives', surveyed the whole terrain
Changing place names to their own.
A blotting out. A sucking in.

2

By nineteen hundred two thirds extinct. The moral,
Smiles a law-maker over his smiling table,

By irresistible force of nature, a superior wins,
Our nation's duty to cure misfortunes of indigenes.

Prudent givers and takers, fishers and hunters
At pains to dispatch the souls of slaughtered bears

To heal the earth's sweet gifting wound.
Everything borrowed. Nothing ever owned.

The sphere of living, the sphere of gone or unborn
A seamless globe where dead in dreams return.

Their Ekishi leaders chosen to be open-handed,
Lavish keepers of nature, begin to trade

Their prey for sugar, clothes or sake and lacquers
To assuage their gods who turn unhearing ears.

Unwillingly they turn to farm bad land and fail.
Kindly, simple-minded, stupid, slothful. A nail

That's sticking up will be hammered down.
Nothing borrowed. Everything must be owned.

A light denied. A planet moves in between.
Two crossing globes of meaning. One unseen.

3

Nineteen eighties and an Ainu
Fell for a girl in Tanikawa.
When parents balked they knew
She had to elope. Petty bourgeois

Shame declares a daughter dead.
In Nibutani school a master
Complains the Ainu smell. Rounded
Eyes, a beard that grows faster.

School dropouts. Mostly jobless.
Some in summer revive rites
For tourists, show wares and dress.
Some just incognito urbanites.

More Japanese than Japanese.
In willed absorption a double
Loss: neither those nor these.
Gods forsaken still untouchable.

4

In eclipse peoples saw a body dying,
A darkened planet overcome,
A lamp obscured, a globe shadowed.

Old need for an upper hand. What glowed
Snuffed under another's thumb.
Outshone star. A by-thing.

Ishikaribetsu, o greatly meandering
River, once sacred to the Ainu
Describe your arc south and westward

To tell a forgotten name, a lost word.
No standing still. Grieve a residue
Swept along by history's slandering

Winners, mourn at every turn strewn
Kinships, lines waning or scored
Through. The map-wiped Ainu.

Solar goddess Amaterasu
Has raised her grass-mower sword.
A risen sun deletes the moon.

Outposts

1

Capricious Queen Bess insisting that she'd learn
To greet her foreign guests in kind
Had ordered her own primer of the Irish tongue

And cast a special font to spread among
The people books to teach reforms
For fear they'd choose Spain's Popish sway.

Vous êtres le gentilhomme de bonne qualité?
Quality. Calen o custure me!
Henry V's Pistol mocks French with gibberish.

Or was Shakespeare aware that this was Irish:
Cailín ó Chois tSiúire mé –
'I'm a girl from River Suir side', a melody

Borrowed for 'A sonet of a louer for a lady
And sung at the end of eurie line'
The original *Calen o castureme!*

But Edward Spencer's scorning throwaway
The bards which are to them as poets
Sows his seed of doubt that blooms as shame.

2

Nothing else but to make way by the blood of army
To enlarge their territories of power and tyranny;
That is an unlawful war, a cruel and bloody

Work...that the cause of the Irish native in
Seeking their just freedoms... Leveller Walwyn
Appeals before the Cromwell wars begin

In earnest...*is the very same as our cause here.*
Eoghan Rua of Tyrone back from Spain in the year
1642, a strategist they fear,

European *extraordinaire* and after Benburb
All but Dublin at his feet, when Roundheads curb
His power by terror. *To hell or Connacht* a proverb.

Driven from their proper, natural, native rights.
Cassandra-like Walwyn has the future in his sights
But no one cares. No one steers by his lights.

3

Thinned and broken by famine,
a scramble to shed the past;
teacher and parent connive:
for any Irish word a score
on a stick hung from the neck,
a slap for every notch.

To seem to move with the times.
Children reared to leave
and Mother Church's myth
how clearly it's God's will
that they'd embrace English
to bring the faith abroad.

A new state's doers soon
blind-eye a weary dream.
Report on report. Schemes
keep the show on the road.
A handful of honest souls
swim against the tide.

Still silly season letters
preserving a native tongue
or outbursts of self-loathing
they talk through their erse.
Cell doubling of self-doubt.
A tally stick in the mind.

Meanwhile school playground
by playground a balance shifts.
Household by single household.
Against seas of erosion
A few limpets of hope.
A cling of scattered outposts.

4

A TV documentary on Irish in Tyrone
With archived voices from the Sperrins,
Outlying vestiges. Lingering aberrance
Here and there on a hill's spur.
Raised by a grandmother, alone
Seán Ó Cairealláin in a stony redoubt;
Páidí Láidir left with a sister,
Loners and odd ones out.

Soundbites direct from Caisleán Glas:
Dreas 'a bout', 'a turn', 'some',
With its middle vowel a pet idiom.
A final eavesdrop. Fading noise
Of a dialect sinks in the dross
And waste of things as Sperrins' limestone
Caps hold their glacial poise
Over Tír Eoghain. Land of Eoghan.

An interviewed professor's explanation
How such communities erode:
Protestant minister, the main road,
A lame teacher who'd forced English,
The Board of Education,
A priest's *stop your gibberish*
And talk your proper language!

A young woman learner talking
In her parents' tavern
With a mountain man who'd return
To his shieling with a week's supplies.
Gaelic Leaguers bring
Their song and dance and medals won.
An afterglow they want to lionise
Until one by one by one....

Language's frail brinkmanship
Before it falls. Something age-old
Slips, lets go its last foothold.
Closing footage. The mood alters
A fraction as a cheerful clip
Of a bird-like voice lifts a song
A bar or two before she falters
Into English. *I forget...*

Crying out

1

Griefs written in wounded memories' song
Wind across our centuries saying no
To any easiness of why the world is wrong,

Irreversible lines of ordeals once borne
In sudden flattened notes, a long slow
Uncoiling strain of losses we need to mourn.

O don't look for me where streams are playing –
In sweatshops' *klezmer* a *shtetl*'s long ago.
No soft-pedalling such musics of belonging,

This knowing in the marrow how crops can fail –
Fair hills of Erin, *Bánchnoic Éireann óighe –*
Some coffin-ship is busy setting its sail.

There behind the jazz a soul is keening –
No heaven on earth, Lord, nowhere I go –
Holding open all our agonies of meaning.

2

The long mute pleas of the dead
For us to remember things
So beyond our ken we barely control

Our deepest urge to shun in dread
Their clammy-handed nobblings,
To flee the ghostly buttonhole

Of those whose testimony shocks
Too much for us to hear.
Of patterns we're destined to rehearse

Unless a patient listening unblocks
Such clogged up fear
Of our histories' ancient mariners,

Voyages we need to face and word,
Stories of dreams stillborn,
Tragedies that never found a voice,

Cries of agony yet to be heard.
So much we must mourn
Until our broken bones rejoice.

3

A history of our world unravels into histories,
The crying out of our once forgotten stories,

The mended reed of voices we've refound
Proclaiming all that was trampled underground.

But out of our darkest silences now instead
We risk becoming everything we dread:

The fractured clamour of each remembering victim
As deaf to the world as the world was once to them.

Given too many memories our psyche smothers.
Will our victimhood learn to keep this word for others?

4

Habits of mind reassure,
a sleepwalking that gradually turns its face
against the angel of change,

a slow silting up,
encrustations of recall, our deadwood,
long cortège of tradition

as the stare of stone icons,
remindings of misfortune inscribed in place
or mute testimonies of vestige.

How can we shift our gaze
to leave what has been, the *déjà vu*, the before,
and dare to spring the trap?

Memory, mother of muses,
wake us, shake us up out of this haunted
past that will not pass.

5

As we choose a friend
In the end
We blend or select memories to mend
Whatever engine moves
Our spirits on,

But don't efface
The place
Or trace of any lost or wounded face
Stained with its loves and lives
From our horizon.

Still we recall
The fall
Of all behind the gossamer wall.
Or when the thimbled bells of foxgloves
Summon the gone

We won't forget
Our debt.
And yet
To allow a spring night let
Slip our sleepless doves
Into the dawn.

ANGEL OF CHANGE

Who has not found the Heaven – below –
Will fail of it above –
For Angels rent the House next ours,
Wherever we remove –

EMILY DICKINSON

Overview

Giddy world of shuffle and hotchpotch
Criss-cross planet of easy mix and match.

Keyboards tap a galaxy of satellites
And monies shift in nervous kilobytes

Across a grand bazaar of cyberspace.
Migrants roam our busy market-place.

Noise and anguish of an age. Free-range.
Freewheeling. Nothing endures but change.

Given a globe where borders leak and flow
A violin pleads beside a sitar and koto

As nightly starving Sudanese now stare
Out of the tube. And no hiding unaware

Or folding out again an old cocoon.
No turning back. We've reached the moon.

Adam, atom-splitter, rider in space.
Is this our earth's frail and wispy face?

Hovering

We've seen how wisps of cloud scud
The face of the earth
Over such furrows of soil and blood,
Wrinkled maps of shifts and moves,
The lineaments of nationhood.

Gone the musket dream and bayonet,
Now our fusion
Weaponry, our Damocles threat
Of power-plants' silent leaks
Undoing the bones of a planet.

Clearly the pain of a torn cocoon,
Rip of unclosing
Hearts in manhood's burning noon
Who would follow in their footsteps
At the rising of the moon

On into the blue and risky unknown?
Flourish or perish
As we bend to caress the windblown
Face of mother earth weeping
Under her broken ozone.

Clearly a grief, an urge to keep
Faith even
With our own fond mistakes. A deep
Gambling unease, a last teetering
Chaos before our leap.

Mesh

Thrill of teetering as lines blur and merge
In medias res
Of this our mortal life and still our urge

To withdraw. Yet to refuse to second-guess.
Our step into space
Another free-fall in sweet confusions of process.

Campaigns, cross-border information flows
Keeping pace
Across an atlas, nodes and clusters of NGOs,

Eco-watchers or whistle-blowers who relay
The word in case....
An Ainu website, *médecins sans frontières,*

Circles of Buddhist monks, ghostly chat-rooms
Or face to face,
Amnesty, networks of dwellers in shacks or slums.

Boundless world of hidden loops and re-loops,
A noiseless trace
Of complex feedback and feedforward hoops.

Is something in the making, something new?
Another place
Over and under our boundaries, a reaching through

And linking up both in and beyond regimes,
Fuzzy embrace
Of overlapping maps, our mesh of dreams.

Mending

Something on the go. Something new?
But once our cities' mix and brew –
Alexandria, a nurse of every race.

Once west to east a silken route
Of questing swaps and barter, astute
Venetian Polo crossed to China.

A wrong bearing, any misreading
Unmaps a whole adventure leading
Us astray by slips and blunders.

A fractious Europe, greedy Minotaur
Wandering through thirty years of war,
Side-tracked in cul-de-sacs and alleys.

Then byways of flag and proletariat,
Goose step of ism and autocrat,
Grimmest hundred years of carnage.

Searching a silken clew to the maze,
We retrace steps to mend our ways.
Something old is harking onwards.

Seepage

Hybrids of old, all our songs and histories ooze:
London reggae, Yiddish tangos, pale-faced blues,

Chaîne de dames danced at *céilís, los gauchos judíos.*
Drift and flux of all that's open-ended and porous.

The words we loan that seem to wander and renew;
Proverbs, faiths, motifs, borrowings, seepings through.

Years of rubbing along or just letting things slide,
Ease of decades of trade, our muddling side by side.

Poland's memory of Khazars, Toledo's open mind,
The Koran's *ya ayyuha 'n naasu*, o mankind!

Right but maybe wrong, wrong but maybe right;
In huddles of cities, our days lived in each other's light.

Slow rite of osmosis, aborptions half understood.
Surges and ebbs. Our long sievings of mongrelhood.

Accelerando

Gone the leisure of change. No long, slow
Percolations, trade-offs of loan or swap;
A new upping of pace, daily *accelerando*
Of chance and switches, our choices' flip-flop.
No moss gathering, *Swaraj*, Ourselves Alone.
Together to shuttle a planet's shrunken girth,
Border-crosser, globetrotter, rolling stone,
All *grenzgänger* now we dwarf our earth.
Constant shadowing in, scumble of old divides,
Topsy-turvy world of shifting borderland,
So much of what we thought so certain slides,
To move the earth where's our somewhere to stand?
Glasnost of nanosecond and graven silicon;
Pole to pole our driven sifting cyclotron.

Giant

One-eyed market giant
Driven by haggle and deal
Straddling a whole sphere,

Plateau or atoll,
Desert or jungle basin,
Our earth's four corners.

High-speed, space-shrinking,
One sprawling, planet-girdling
Game of here-there-ness.

Foods or goods or tools,
All chains of commodities,
Our tastes and desires.

Mergers or movements
Of labour, takeover bids,
All the tricks of trade.

Hungry pliant giant,
Bringer of all invention,
Heeder of what works.

Lattice of silk routes.
Worldwide pitch. Grand casino.
Globe of all play all.

Seeing

Once a market's noisy playground,
split difference, spit and luck-penny,
higgle-haggle gossip of a souk,

horses and carts of traders gathered
in the staring light of a *shtetl*'s square
busy unpacking stalls and wares.

But lives eked in favelas and barrios
or bidonvilles as all the while
a giant rumbles across the earth.

Containers, wide-winged jet-craft,
juggernauts swallow all before them.
The strong stronger, the weak weaker.

Rock stars, nomad managers, tycoons;
under four hundred billionaires
belting half our planet's wealth.

Somewhere in slums or refuge camps,
in ramshackle sweat shops or shanty
with fists of stone and clenched teeth

a Gilgamesh grown angry in his youth
seals his heart to fell the cedar
and slay the all-preying ogre.

How now to yoke the avid beast,
a tamed Humbaba broken in
to see what one-eyed giants can't see?

Humbaba

Moody Humbaba, bull and bear,
One-eyed giant of *laissez-faire*,
In open rings no fake control
Up and up the greasy pole,
Make or break, boom or bust,
Winners all or bite the dust.

Life unknown, unseen face,
If a cut's better another place,
Stony eyes on the bottom line
To keep the shareholders benign;
Word from on high and incognito
Take up the silken tent and go.

So on. A circus can't second-guess.
Humbaba whispers success, success.
Full of options doubting Thomas,
Till death or we break our promise;
Where it shifts, where it flows.
Hazy despair of anything goes.

Vague unease. A rogue state,
A lone zealot big with fate,
Some ideologue or malcontent,
A button pressed, anthrax sent,
Half-lulled awareness of a messed
Habitat, our greed-fouled nest?

What unfaced face under the sun
Calls to account what we've undone?
Bargain-driver, giver and taker,
Homo sapiens, meaning maker,
Shaper or shaped, player or plaything,
Are we still masters of our ring?

Loop

Less a ring than another looping back,
Relearning to cross again an older track.

In nooks of harvest fields the forgotten sheaf,
Each seventh year's share-out and debt relief

Bent on offsetting our market's quid pro quo:
A tithe to Levite, sojourner, fatherless, widow

Binding alms beyond whims of goodwill.
Mohammed's urged levy for needy and ill,

For those hearts it's necessary to conciliate;
Ballast and even out, a counter-weight

To those bitter daily shadows of bony hunger.
Someone's birthright is only to die younger?

An overflow shared, our balance re-tipped.
Can we forget the starving years of Egypt?

Update

Given a globe of flash and breaking news
Where swarms of flies on a starving face
Crawl a screen of glass
Between comfort and hunger, refuse

To fade when zapped but leave a creeping trace
Within a psyche's magic lantern,
An after-image of concern,
Given a globe has watched the wasting face

We can no longer say we didn't know.
Gone the slow despatch, our alibi
For hindsight, each plea
Immediate and doubled in its nag and echo

Haunts the ear of every brother's keeper.
Bulletin by bulletin, update by update,
Famine's balance sheet.
Bitter wind-sower, whirlwind reaper

Still so world-foolish and pennywise,
Children's children know we know.
Tomorrow, tomorrow, tomorrow.
Abel's child now starves before our eyes.

Butterfly

Yes now and again to feel so overpowered.
Could anything we ever do matter a whit?
Would-be dreams, seeds that never flowered,
A world just as it is and there you have it!
Yet a fresh belonging, thrill of connectedness,
In the maze and jumble of whatever's new
As if a globe so imperfect in its glorious mess
Catches in spins and webs everything we do.

Beyond fluke or the end of fate's weary tether
Sweet chaos transcends and breaks old spells
As somewhere under the folds of summer sky
A flapped red admiral shifts a planet's weather.
Again everything matters to everything else;
Vision gathers in the span of one butterfly.

Ad Lib

A hazier vision both more and other,
neither state nor superstate, a melding in,
a ravel of pacts and stitched affiliations,

jagged ad lib of patchworks and deals,
sixes and sevens of bonds and ties,
plans caught up in random drift,

bits of schemes as we go along,
spliced, recombinant, spilling over,
shimmies of mimicry, on the spot design,

stop–start modes or toggle switches,
loose weavings, filigrees of consensus
thickening into webs of give and take.

No longer the view from nowhere,
citizens of a planet and still parishioners
we must belong now here, now there,

both a sizing up and a sizing down.
Given a globe of satellite footprints
one half knows how the other lives,

given a globe now to improvise
we hold each other again to account,
players all in our jazz of things.

Shuffle

Our clumsy fellowship of jazz,
Fast and loose of lines revised,
Tunes bedded in our roll and swing.

The jet-setters' razzamatazz,
Messengers of a past now idolised
And each demanding all or nothing.

High-flying soprano saxophone
So heady as it tries to soar
Homelessly above our thick and thin;

A solo trumpets what's our own
Dreaming soundproof rooms before
The blare and clamour, before the din.

O down to earth all players now,
The bob and riff and open-plan.
No opting out. The line evolves,

Even our hearing shaping how
It loops and turns as best it can.
In double listening a clash resolves,

Richer in remembered dissonance.
Argument over argument, by pros
And cons and shuffled compromise,

The counterpoint, the taken chance,
As discord by discord we recompose
And for the music's sake extemporise

Bluesy scales of how we cope.
Neither returning or losing the way,
All vision in rhythms of how it is.

Each-in-otherness, ad hocery of hope
Keeping all our difference in play,
Quarrelsome sessions of beloved noise.

Behind

White noise of all forsaken still insists
Across a high-strung rainbow of snare drums
On weaving in among the horn and sax

Pitchless sounds astray in cul-de-sacs,
Alleys of broken pasts, consortiums
Of static grief that summon still our shades

To thicken every phrase before it fades
Into indistinctness where soloists
Blur again amid the jazz reminding us

Of each travail and tragedy left behind us
And how out of bones of slaves music wrests
A syncopated note of gaiety that hones

The stories of affliction no one owns,
When brass jams and blows its moody idioms,
Weeping over the stillborn milk of history.

Clusters

Always our histories loop and so renew.
Schools, combos, zones of thought, a few
Tight clutches of friends, bands of dissidence,
Brainstorms, cross-breeding argument, dense
Huddles of players face to face that change
A rhythm's logic, curve our psychic range
To sift and fuse and rearrange progressions
That shape the mood of an age, jam sessions
Over time and the teacher-to-pupil baton:
Socrates, Plato, Aristotle on and on
Or chez Café Guernois Degas, Manet,
Cézanne and Pissarro busy arguing their way
Around their darker masters. Switched modes,
Nests and seedbeds, genealogies of nodes

As Satchmo Armstrong once played with King
Oliver and Jelly Roll. In musics of doing.
Yesterday's not today or now tomorrow's way
Which of course is never simply to say
That though there's no one way there's no
Yardstick and yesterday we sometimes know
Was better or not as good, just as tomorrow
May hoop either way to cobble joy or sorrow
In honky-tonks of being where rhythms swap,
cakewalk, ragtime, jazz, swing or bebop.
Dizzy's and Parker's chopped staccatos stunned
Munroe's Uptown House at 52nd,
A variation become as weighty as a theme,
Fractured melody hovers above a seam
Of chord sequences in a six-bar repeat
As accents land now on, now off the beat
In promises of process and substance blended.
Paradox of solo and ensemble in one splendid
Line that knows the moment of ordered freedom
When the brass blows down and yields to drum.
What a man does with his life when it's finally his;
Everywhere is local now exactly where it is.
Beyond a deadlock of perfection in notes that jar
We make each broken other whatever we are.
Polyphony of phrase, each open-hearted probe,
Clusters of goodwill in swap-shops of a globe;
Where music aims the music holds within.
The jazz is as the jazz has never been.

Tremolo

All that has been still an undertone,
Frets of memory half-heard deep
Below a hybrid croon of saxophone

Or when King Oliver's horn's darker
Notes warn a plantation child
He'd die an obscure poolroom marker.

A Bushman taps a hunting bow,
One end humming between the lips,
Drone of sound mesmeric and hollow.

At wedding gigs East Europe's blues
In moods of a harmonic minor scale
Blare a wistful *klezmer* rumpus.

Fingers strum a blown *mukkuri*
As swung against an Ainu's hips
A song of peace plucks a *tonkori*.

Once Turk or Khan, Rome or Greece,
Empires now where suns never fall,
A dominant bringing a dominant peace.

But one space of chosen nodes,
Mediant world of both/and plays
In flexitime, in different modes?

Given riffs and breaks of our own,
Given a globe of boundless jazz,
Yet still a remembered undertone,

A quivering earthy line of soul
Crying in all diminished chords.
Our globe still trembles on its pole.

Over the Kwai

Trembling, in tears, over and over
I'm very, very sorry. Nagasesan
a tiny man in an elegant straw hat,
loose kimono–like jacket and trousers
bowed in the heat as the sun clambered
a sky up over the morning Kwai.

Lomax, you will tell us, his once
victim remembered, *Lomax you will
be killed shortly whatever happens,*
a mechanical voice doing its duty
in its choppy menacing segments,
loathsome endless singsong questions.

An officer picked up a big stick.
After Nagasesan had interpreted
every query, a slow deliberate
blow delivered from head height
to his chest, belly and broken arms.
Lomax, you tell us, then it will stop.

The full gush of a nearby hosepipe
turned onto his nostrils and mouth,
a torrent into his lungs and stomach
choking and welling up within;
the voice of Nagasesan heard again
above his head and into his ear.

*Fifty years, a long time for me,
for suffering. I never forgot you,
I remember your face, even your eyes...*
Nagasesan's long rapids of remembrance
gathering up all unfinished histories
to span the Kwai and ask forgiveness.

Yurusu, to allow, accept, absolve,
a giving away hidden in pardon,
or *maitheamh* our own 'making good'
a victim's fifty lurking years
of lone recall and dreamt revenge.
Lomax, you'll tell us as you let go

the prey of so many broken pasts
walk to greet their once hunter
over a sweated bridge of a memory,
rapprochement of all our ghosts
cross timeless flows of atonement.
We can't forget. We do forgive.

Skeins

Never to forget the towering dreams
Of heaven-hankers before their time,
Brick for stone, for mortar slime

So many offered for madcap schemes.
Over and again some other fable
Of perfection: *Let us make us a name.*

Another skyscraper and still the same.
Fall and fall all spires of Babel
To lovely confusions of our gabble

Scattered abroad on the face of the earth
As slowly we relearn each other's worth,
Difference and sameness incommensurable.

In all our babble birds of a feather –
Aithníonn ciaróg ciaróg eile,
Beetle knows beetle – *Qui se ressemble*

S'assemble – all over flock together,
Skeins of hope, *gleich und gleich...*
Like to like, kind calls fellow –

Rui wa tomo o yobu in Tokyo.
Around our globe a netted Reich,
Of random trust, cross-ties of civility,

Farflung jumbles of non-violent voices
Argue our intertwining choices
To weave one planet's fragile city.

Strategy

Global city of nowhere and everywhere,
Comity of good will,
Delicate growth that thrives
On thriving and yet always so bound

Up with states and their staked-out
Limits, a brokerage between
Determined hit-and-runners
Who still think their bombs can pound

An earth to submission and the too naïve
So easily taken for a ride
By every thug and trafficker,
All the more hard-bitten on the rebound.

Our brittle city of Trojan horses,
Hijacked battering rams,
Poison on the market shelf,
Gas canisters in the underground

Or the underminers within the psyche,
Unmasked unmaskers of power's
Bleak and stalking beast,
Suspicious minds that never unwound.

Give us a policy? At least a strategy?
The slow hatchings of peace,
Our stumbled unfinishedness
Dealing with everything just as it's found,

A trust in openness, the barer daring
Of players out on a limb;
No iron curtain here,
Fragile theatre of worlds in the round.

Bridges

Around our Babel-fallen world
embedded in grammars of landscape,
jumble and palaver of simultaneity

as though on one Rabelaisian earth
in myriad difference grains of sameness,
Seeds of everything in everything else,

the way white light contains all waves
and a sound wakes its every partial
or from one cell any limb unfolds.

Still our heartlands and inner sources,
quiet meanderings of each particular.
Yet given a globe of such opulence

will one-tongued markets ever hear
how watchwords in so many lores
admonish against too muddied waters?

Over our years a Dante is warning:
l'aqua cheta rovina i ponti –
Stagnant water demolishes bridges.

Deepest river, least its noise
in worlds kept by core keepers
where stiller waters still run deep.

Session

Deep, deep
The legends and contours of every line,
Tune womb
Of our stories of who begat whom,
And as phrases part or combine.

So fine
A line between what's open and shut.
Proud horns
Above a shivering reed that mourns
What never made the cut.

Power's glut
Of power knows always what's true.
Somewhere
Against the grain, again the flair
Among a jazz's daring few

Some new
Delight in playing face to face
Grace notes
For a line that steadies as it floats,
Without a theory or a base,

Shared space
Holding what we hold and not to fear
Those bars
Where our history clashes or jars
And in lines unsymmetrical to the ear

Still hear
Deep reasonings of a different lore.
No map
Of any middle ground or overlap
Yet listening as never before –

No more –
Just hunched jazzmen so engrossed
In each
Other's chance outleap and reach
Of friendship at its utmost.

No host
And no one owns the chorus or break.
Guests all
At Madam Jazz's beck and call.
For nothing but the music's sake.

Only End

Music of a given globe,
Off-chance jazz forever bringing
More being into being
Out of history's tangled knots and loops
Spirituals and flophouse bands
In hymns and charismatic whoops,
In night-clubs' vibe and strobe,
Nothing buts now *everything ands.*

Our heads are ancient Greeks
Who think just because they think
A body's out of sync
With thought but maybe we relearn the way
Our mind can pulse to intransigent
Musics of once broken to play
Beyond perfect techniques
The livelong midrash of a moment.

Given a globe of profusion,
We players are no legislators
More like mediators,
Who extemporising seem to up the ante
To find the nit and grit that has
A universal image for a Dante,
An aim without conclusion
To play mein host to Madam Jazz

Playing without end.
Growling, wailing, singing Madam,
In anguish and joys we jam
As Davis's almost vibratoless horn
Wraps around *Embraceable You*
Somehow original and still reborn
Swooping back to mend,
Resolving just to clash anew.

All time to understand
Infinite blues of what ifs,
Breaks and tragic riffs

As traditions wander into other spaces
Zigzagging and boundary crossing
In clustered face-to-faces
Commonplace and grand,
Sweet nuisances of our being

On song and off-beam,
Hanging loose, hanging tough,
Offbeat, off the cuff,
Made, broken and remade in love,
Lived-in boneshaking pizzazz
Of interwoven polyphony above
An understated theme.
The only end of jazz is jazz.

Tongues

(2010)

For Eileen Hallinan, Hallgrímur Magnússon, Chie Nakamura
and all who nurtured me in tongues.

FOREWORD

Isn't language an extraordinary thing? And to think that everyone has a language! It's such a take-for-granted part of all our daily lives and everything we do. It's the most distinctive human gift. Not only do we all learn and know a language but a large majority of people as mothers and fathers know the joy of being language teachers, the delight of passing on their own mother tongue.

What is also amazing is how average four-year-olds, without ever being specifically taught complex rules, can not only speak grammatically but can come up with sentences they have never heard before. It seems that we have an innate facility to acquire language. There is good linguistic and even genetic evidence, that we're hardwired to work language.

Yet we never finish and never completely know even our own language. We go on learning all our lives. If we enter a trade or profession we learn the jargon. Someone uses a phrase you never heard before and you pick it up. Think of all the new words my generation absorbed in the technological revolution we're living through as we entered a new world of 'booting up', 'dropdown menus', 'taskbars' and 'spam filters'. If you take up a new sport there are 'genoas' or 'birdies'. Part of children's fascination with Tolkien's *Lord of the Rings* is the variety of languages he invents for the Middle-Earth. Any new cult or subculture we enter will teach us a whole new vocabulary whether it's the criminal underworld of 'fencing' or the 'consciousness raising' of a political subgroup. We're endless language learners.

And words are so strange. Each seems to have an aura of its own. Whole institutions split over a word. The Roman Catholic Church and the Eastern Orthodox Church parted from about 1054 over the addition of *filioque* (and the Son) to the Nicene Creed. People kill one another over words. Think of the use of 'ethnic cleansing' in Eastern Europe or how in the Rwandan genocide the Hutu branded the Tutsi as 'cockroaches'.

There are whole fields and networks of meaning. Over time meanings slide and change. When I was a boy 'adult' only meant 'grown-up'. Then it was used to convey 'suitable for adults'. Now it also means 'pornographic' as in an 'adult movie'. We're half-conscious of the transition. The shifts of sense and usage accumulate over hundreds even thousands of years within one language.

Then again languages are related. Even a quick glance at the word for 'mother' in, say, Spanish and Italian *madre*, Catalan *mare*, French *mère* and Portuguese *mãe* would lead you think that there was something in common. On balance if we compare these various words for 'mother', we might work out what they have in common and build up a picture of what word they might all be derived from. In fact, we know that historically all of them were originally Latin and so they all come from Latin *mater*. But there again if we take a wider angle and look at the word for 'mother' in, for example, Latin *mater*, English *mother*, Irish *máthair*, Greek *mētēr* and *mātár-* in the language of ancient India, by using the same comparative method, we might work out what word they should all have come from. Given the variations we'd reckon on a word like *mātér* as its origin. Here we don't know the history but we have to believe that in all probability this language existed. This hypothetical common ancestral language must have spread across most parts of Europe and in certain parts of India.

Scholars making use of the comparative method and what they call 'internal reconstruction', that is working out the original form within a group of closely related languages, have figured out with an extraordinary degree of precision not only the words but also the grammar of this hypothetical language, which they call 'Proto-Indo-European'. On top of this, we can get some picture of the culture, the society and environment, the economy and technology, even the religion and poetics of those who spoke this language. There is a lot of controversy as to exactly when and where this language was spoken. It's largely agreed that it probably had split into differing dialects by the third millennium BC.

While in an example like 'mother' it is relatively easy to see the relationship, this is not always so. The nexus of rules describing the developments and connections are so well worked through that words which, on the surface seem most unlikely to be related are revealed to have a common origin. For instance, at first there seems little connection between English 'queen', the Irish word *bean* meaning woman (which has entered English as the first element in 'banshee') and the Greek word *gunē*, 'woman' (which we see in the first part of of 'gynecology').

Of course there are many other large families of languages besides the Indo-European. There are Sino-Tibetan, Semitic, Ural-Altaic families and so on. Some have tried to find common origins for a number of these families, but this is highly speculative.

Why am I explaining all this? I just want to give a sense of the scope of the shifts and linkages. In meditating on words, I want to allow these relationships shine through and illuminate the intricate marvel of language.

As a poet I'm utterly intrigued by the rampant imagination of human beings. I think of Wallace Stevens's famous 'Thirteen Ways of Looking at a Blackbird'. Languages have infinite ways of looking at one thing. In English there is the 'presentation' of a prize. It has all the resonances of present or gift and has its origin in the Latin for something which 'is before' someone. That seems to a speaker of English straightforward enough. But then in French it's a 'delivery' or 'handing over' (*remise*), in German it's 'hiring out' or 'loaning' (*Verleihung*), in Icelandic 'a parting with or handing over' (*afhenda*) and so on. Again to an English speaker it's clear that you can wear hats, shirts, trousers, gloves or glasses, while in Japanese there is a different verb used for all of these. Or to take the example of an idiom in English, it rains 'cats and dogs' but in French it's 'strings' (*de cordes*), in Irish 'a cobbler's knives' (*sceanna gréasaí*) and in Welsh 'old women and sticks' (*hen wragedd a ffyn*). There's just four ways of looking at rain. But of course it's endless.

The great linguist Edward Sapir once said 'every language itself is a collective art of expression... An artist may utilise the aesthetic resources of his speech. He may be thankful if the given palette of colours is rich, if the springboard is light. But he deserves no special credit for felicities which are the language's own.' For a while in the first half of the 20th century, Sapir and another linguist Benjamin Whorf propounded the view that the language a person speaks affects the way that he or she thinks, meaning that the structure of the language itself affects cognition. The standard example was the number of words (later shown to be somewhat exaggerated) Eskimos have for snow. This view, though no doubt it has some validity, is too deterministic. Life is more porous and clearly we can acquire other languages.

This brings me to that unbelievable joy of learning a new language. There is a special delight in discovering how things can be said differently. The feeling of becoming a child again and being the butt of everybody else's knowledge. Yet being an adult you're able to be guided by a tradition of grammar and rules. You're trying to get your tongue and head to chime. There is a rollercoaster of feelings of elation and despair, of progress and shortfall. Sometimes there's a sense of *déjà entendu* as if some latent part of your personality is waking. And you're not just learning words but also a history, a geography, an entire culture. Then a whole new world of friendships is growing.

I mentioned the word grammar. This is in some ways an astounding phenomenon. We have here the basic patterns on which we can turn endless variations. It's a way of keeping the 'ecology' of the personal innovation and the possibility of community in play. It's the genetic code that allows for infinite mutations. Or to put it another way, it's the tune on which we can riff to our heart's content.

For many children of my generation the word conjures up hours of parsing and analysis and learning declensions and conjugations off by heart. I began Latin at primary school where we learned our verbs off by heart as we learned our tables. *Amo, amas, amat.* But looking back on the wealth of terms we used – 'the ablative absolute', 'the prolative infinitive', 'the sequences of tenses' and 'final clauses' – I'm amazed at how as children we just drank in these mysterious expressions. I wasn't surprised when I discovered years later that the word 'glamour' was originally 'grammar'. It was apparently a Scottish variant of the word 'grammar', which because it was associated with learning came to mean 'magic'. And so the meanings 'charm', 'allure', 'excitement', though often with a connotation of the ephemeral. But little did I as a schoolboy think... I want now to return, to make these terms my own, to enjoy the strange enchantment: *'verbs of hoping, promising, threatening, swearing are usually followed by the future infinitive...'*

Some years ago when my books started to appear in Japanese translation, with the help of my translator and friend, Professor Shigeo Shimizu, I started to try to tackle Japanese. I became fascinated by those fantastic 'characters' or signs. You know the way you've so often seen what seems just a blur of eastern squiggles on a restaurant or shop front but you couldn't for the life of you distinguish one from the other, not to mention remembering them or imagine how they could convey meaning. It began to dawn on me that we use such signs here in Europe too. We all know how a stylised figure of a man or woman signs which toilet we head for. Or how a knife and fork sign in a list of hotels tells us there is a restaurant. Again a stylised figure in a wheelchair indicates facilities for the disabled. But what may at first appear to us as squiggles is a whole system of such signs that has evolved over something like four millennia and which can be read by about a sixth of the world's population. But what grabs me is that these 'characters' can express all abstract thought. One thing is to draw some picture of a concrete object but how do you illustrate concepts like 'worry', 'meaning', 'experience'?

These signs or characters derive from ones which originated between 2000 and 1500 BC in the Yellow River region of China. The earliest were inscribed on bones and tortoise shells. Starting as simple they grew abstract, complex and highly stylised. They were brought to Japan by Chinese and Korean migrants about the third or fourth century AD. In Japanese, these signs can be read as Chinese loan-words or as native Japanese words. For example 言 can be read as *gen* if taken as a Chinese borrowed word or as *koto* if read as the native Japanese word.

Normally the Japanese are only conscious of the origin of the most transparent characters. Otherwise they are largely unaware, just as English speakers don't know the roots of most words they use daily. I'm by no means the first western poet to meditate on these signs. Probably the most famous example in English is Ezra Pound's *Cantos*. He had been introduced to them through Ernest Fenollosa's work. Fenollosa spent long periods in Japan and contributed greatly to Japanese culture. At one point he travelled through America with a magic lantern lecturing on these signs. The *Cantos* were written between about 1915 and 1956. But there is also the earlier French-language tradition with figures such as the Belgian Henri Michaux and later, such works as Paul Claudel's *Connaissance de l'Est* (1900) and Victor Segalen's *Stèles* (1912). And yet we've gone beyond any simple 'Orientalia' and in a culture bombarded by visual images, these signs remain rich enough to sustain endless meditations.

We live in a new oral and visual culture. Alongside the image comes the soundbite. In any language, proverbs are a source of metaphor and wisdom. When someone says 'there is no smoke without fire', nobody looks around to find a fire. It's like the third line of a haiku and we know at once this isn't to be taken literally. It sums up the long hard-earned experience of a community and saves it reinventing the wheel over and over again.

I find the variation in metaphors from language to language quite astonishing. Sometimes images must have spread from country to country. Other times the same image arose from a similar way of life, even though there probably was no contact. I love the nugget-like intensity of the proverbs; it's almost as if there was an economy of truth which is like gnomic Edda verse.

Then too there's always been a secondary, often facetious and formulaic layer of 'Wellerism' about in many languages. A Norwegian example is: Make haste slowly, said the farmer as he ate his porridge with an awl. I believe cynical proverbs were popular in Soviet

Russia. Perhaps there is some connection between the level of public trust and the frequency of these undercuttings of traditional wisdom. And they go on showing up in new circumstance or to turn an old fashioned sentiment upside down. Popular in Norway among women, for instance: 'when God created the human being, she began with a rough draft' or 'men will be men, strong and childish'.

Of course, the suspicion of language itself has been at the heart of many intellectual quandaries. Interwoven with Marxist, feminist and postcolonial critiques, language itself has been doubted. Jacques Derrida and Michel Foucault played with the Saussurean view of the sign as an arbitrary convention. Roland Barthes argued that the sign had to be seen as a sign in order not to underpin illusions of reality. Paul de Man went a stage further insisting that language is always weaving between the literal and the metaphorical which in the end renders it unreadable. And so on...

This line of suspicion largely derives from Ferdinand de Saussure's view of language as a complete system of signs. On the other hand the French philosopher Paul Ricœur has opened up again the whole question of the relation of the sign to reality and imagination. Clearly there is no one-to-one linkage but rather a complex interaction. Language is vital for history's narrative or for a judge's decision or for great works of fiction. According to Ricoeur 'through the capacity of language to create and recreate, we discover reality itself in the process of being re-created...language in the making creates reality in the making'. Our sense of who we are is mediated through language.

In the end I know all the dangers and suspicion and yet I must trust. Only by keeping the whole scope and richness of words and signs in play, by feasting on the fullness of language can we hope to allow this our unique human gift to flourish.

My friend the painter Mick O'Dea once told me how he has all his life been enthralled by paint, by the feeling of taking clay and the oils of the earth and daubing them on a canvas. As a poet I know nothing quite like the thrill of taking these organised sounds and signs we make and shaping them in sequences of rhythm and meaning. I want to hold up the wonder of tongues and say: How about this?

WONDER

Men hugse det bør vi:
Eit ord er eit under.

Yet remember we ought:
A word is a wonder.

TOR JONSSON

A Basin in a Kyōto Temple Garden

1

Built just before Byzantium fell
In Ryōanji's stone and moss garden
The *tsukubai* or 'crouching basin',

A vice-Shōgun's gift with its ladle
Waiting for a monk who'll bow and bale
A scoop of water to cleanse his soul

And ponder the Zen of these four signs:
Above a 5, a bird to the right,
Below a foot, leftside an arrow.

2

吾 唯 足 知
Ware tada taru o shiru
I only know contentment

Can humankind bear
Very much reality?
All that might have been.
Burnt Norton's five commands
Echo down this garden.

Go, go, go said Eliot's bird,
Quick, find them, find them.
Lost footprints of shaven monks
Time's arrow forgets
In basins of squared silence,
But scoop now deeper
This whole greater than its parts:
The pool too a sign,
With 5, bird, foot and arrow.
Clockwise these symbols read
I only know contentment.

3

Contentment? What am I doing here
At Eurasia's opposite end
A pilgrim on another island?
Iyashii 'lowly' their adjective,
The contented both rich and humble,
A bottomless well of contentment
Cupped up in a small bamboo ladle.
A Zenic moment. A lavishment.
But dippers stir a storm in ripples,
And there in the shimmering water
Once more I face my Madam Desire.

4

For the umpteenth time
To shed an easy-peasy
Native tongue, become
A player in other plays.
I reincarnate
A child soaking every word.
A strange *déjà vu*
Awakes an oriental self.
Born again, remothered me.

5

No Byzantium I sail to.
Glittering light, a cloud that passes
Caught in waters of reality,
Contentment always in the doing.
Five symbols and one to share with four

To keep both the whole and parts in play.
Did I ever choose to see that face?
O lifelong cupidinous arrow,
Footfall memory of what might have been,
O bird of desire still haunting me.

Rebirths

Thrill of such rebirths,
Pangs of growing to
Other take-for-grantedness

Until I forget
Any time before,
As though this was always me.

A favourite song,
Aroma of foods,
Jokes about neighbour countries.

Webs of reference,
When to thank or bow,
The meaning of a friend's name.

Babel's giddy world:
Once masks, now faces,
New ways I see and am seen.

Have I stepped outside
An innocent ring,
My garden never the same?

Still no turning back.
All houses now tents
A nomadic mind has pitched:

Finnegans Waker,
The only reader,
The perfect insomniac.

No complete sharer.
Polyglot loneness.
Rich creole of memories.

Unless

1

Unless you behave
As little children
These kingdoms too shut their gates.
After the first rush,
Kiss of new vowels,
Strange sound used and understood,
Again your childhood
Hangs on others' words.
Rollercoaster of regrowth:
That Japanese man
Blunderingly called
A widower to his face;
Misunderstandings
All my humbling *faux pas*,
Yokes of initiation,
Words over your head,
A whispered put-down,
Butt of everyone's knowing.
Feelings of despair
As progress plateaus –
What's the point in bothering?
Temptations to yield.
Never fully there.
Still a sense of belonging.
A world glimpsed I can't give up.

2

Unless venturing
A shy child within
No one dares to mother me.
An adult guard down,
Weakness my defence,

First move in a love affair.
New friends' protégé,
A grateful pupil,
Nurtured beyond my nature
I'm finding my tongue.

And begin to shape
Yet another persona.
Slowly I absorb,
Psyche tuning in
Like a diplomat returned
From too long abroad,
Stretching to adopt
Other angles of vision.
Lifelong induction –
Still an apprentice
I resound parent voices.
Echoing their gift,
In their light I learn
First to creep and then to walk,
Hold my own among the tribe.

Overlap

A hidden image lurks behind each word,
Some secret cargo stored below my mind,
A resonance, a coloured first-time heard,
Recalled frisson never quite defined.
And still each word remains a public tool,
Enough shared sense to manage all we mean,
Unconscious mix of anarchy and rule,
A subtle compromise, a go-between.
Associations half tied down, half free,
A zone at once both on and off the map,
All history and story interwound
In straddled borderlands of 'us' and 'me'
Where memories and kinship overlap –
Our inner echo room, our common ground.

Undertones

1

Please don't say the word 'highly-strung'.
My childhood wakes again in me.
What did whispering adults mean?

Whatever they were murmuring
Part for me, part behind my back,
Was it my fault, something I said?

Amati? Stradivarius?
The pegs tautening creakingly
Over my bridge and fingerboard.

Virtuoso temperament
Quavering from scroll to tailpiece,
Stick and rosined bow of passion.

Adult now, so not to my face,
But when I shed an old image,
Another dreaded adjective.

The moment I think I'm placid
Or reining in my eagerness:
Ah, but you're so very intense!

Violins pick up the rhythm
Pizzicatoing across the years
A sense of half-understood shame.

2

Well, well. What talk of violins?
'A person or an animal
Nervous and easily upset',
'Sensitive, excitable child' –
Lexicons keep our common core
But don't you hear background hum,
A charge behind the metaphor?

Perhaps it was once archery,
A D-shaped narrow-limbed longbow's
Arrow tense from nock to head,
Fletched and ready but still too taut
Before its moment of release,
A short linen fibre drawn taut,
So overstrung, so overwrought.

No, no! For me the violin.
A stick ricochets and bounces
Across the upper gut-strings pegged
Shamelessly tight. And let it be.
I can't care less. Rosin the bow.
My life played out against a pulse.
High tension of concert pitch.

Worlds

1

How many words have Eskimos for snow?
Do we only see what we already know?

For some no need to split their greens and blues.
We learn to break our rainbow into hues.

Our language our conspiracies of thought,
A web of metaphors that we were taught.

That futures lie ahead just in the mind,
For Ayamara the unseen lay behind.

Enigma interplay of thought and word
The lines of shape and shaper always blurred.

2

Die. They die and die.
Hundreds on our globe,
Waning to a last speaker.

All five continents,
Ainu to Zazao,
A to Z of dwindlings.

Lost in children's play.
Mothers who don't dare.
Languages move up the line.

Tongues fall to silence
Their worlds unravelling
Broken threads of might have been.

3

Once an Araner's lost blank stare.
In Dublin the ward nurses declare

Him deaf. He can't understand.
Once only he'd been on mainland.

Message clear (intended or not):
A world unsafe for a monoglot.

So fast our futures slip behind.
His image refuses to quit my mind.

Again the Ainu face in Kyōto,
The gaze of a Canadian Eskimo.

All standing still our slow downfall.
This flux and change I can't forestall.

Turnstile

'Adult and a chiseller,' father said
And I made myself as small as I could
When he pushed me ahead through the turnstile
Pleased with himself that he'd saved a tanner.

'I did, faith,' I imagine him claiming
Or 'Don't you bother about that, brother!'
Layers of language somehow glide from me
Like those years of quid and bob and copper.

Each generation's gradual slippage,
Ephemeral poetry of slang,
Idioms, patterns, soft shifts of meaning –
The day Middle English slipped to modern.

What is it in me that can't quite manage
That confident intransitive: *Enjoy!*
Or saying *cool* or how at last *I'd gotten*
To try out another *medication*?

No, this is life. I take it as it is.
Even such strange returns of older forms.
It's just I know my age. I bow my head
As the turnstile's bar clicks against my chest.

Grooves

1

Millennia hide behind each utterance
A silted mind below a shimmering pool,
Each tongue's conspiracy a matrix of nuance
In unremembered change and shifts of rule.
Such worlds of connotations left unsaid,
Our slang and jargon plots inside a plot;
So many depths, so many circles spread,
Within our own are we a polyglot?
Our voice a sound dispersed in time and tense,
Unconscious breath in any act of speech
Sending through its hum and plosion daughter
Dispatches, subtle overtones of sense,
Unfolding rings, circuitries of outreach,
Our every word a pebble dropped in water.

2

Smack and kiss of lips that spread around,
Feel of tongue shaping flows of air
Knowing how to streamline any sound,
Curl and arch of oral savoir-faire.
Sheer delight before the paradigm,
Buzz of groove and tooth with z between,
Jabberwocky thrill of nonsense rhyme,
Taste of words before the thing they mean.
Vowels ooze around my chortling tongue
Finding whatever curve they need to voice
Liquid music's humming jubjub bird;
Vocal chords a violin highly-strung
Freighting through my mouth a dancing voice,
Endless joy of one incarnate word.

3

My life of rubbings-off and overlays –
The way we gather from those we chance to meet
From day to day some word or maybe phrase
I've heard and half-unknowingly repeat.
However much an island, however clannish,
Our language too an archaeology –

For us the Latin, Vikings and Spanish –
It's Dutch or Portuguese through Nagasaki.
No archipelago to own outright,
We touch on hidden continental shelves;
No insulation, nothing's watertight,
We are such shifting laminated selves.
In any dream whatever rules we flout,
Each word a gene in stories we print out.

4

What unknown was first to coin a word,
Single imaginations breaking through,
Strings of sounds that no one before had heard
Someone dared to find and make it new.
Hoarded combinations still untried,
Meanings so rich and manifold,
Keeping within the metaphors they hide
Endless elbowroom inside the mould.
Prod and pull of untold slide and change
Editing a culture's omnibus,
Long communal art, experience wrought
Over years of drift and need to rearrange,
Generations shaping and reshaping us,
Ages carving out our grooves of thought.

5

Of course the easy groove of how I came.
Perhaps my cast of mind, a temperament
That opened up between the self and same
So I delight in all that's different.
Such once-offness, unique modes of speech
And yet the analogues I can't ignore
In spite of meanings overlaps and breach,
For all our unlike names one human core?
If only how we learn to analyse,
As children grasping grammars unaware,
Or even ways as adults we zigzagwise
Could find with time the door to anywhere.
Whatever universals allow us move;
My transit lives still slide from groove to groove.

Kyōto by Night

Night on endless night a Kyōto hotel
narrows its room around my sleeplessness
playing back a lifetime in my skull.

I'd read the door and all the bathroom signs,
proud of my *kanji*, found how the window worked,
whiled an hour with a local radio broadcast.

Tonight at wits' end the resident masseuse
plump and skilled tackles me part by part:
Fukurahagi she names my tensed up calves.

One of eight from Kyūshū, grandparent now,
each evening a half an hour by motorbike
for four sessions with her hotel clientele.

Her husband when he's drunk still beats her –
pon pon! she illustrates with her clenched fists –
bon no kubo, she presses the nape of my neck.

Twice a year back to her childhood island:
Lantern Festival or visits to her parents' grave.
'Too busy here,' she tells my impatient head.

Soon she'll home for a beer or two and bed.
Her story fills a sterile room with warmth.
I'm grateful and glad I came so far to listen.

Her thumbs print my brainstems with ease;
the press of *anma* elbowing into my mind,
I tumble towards an ecstasy of sleep.

Satō-san? Nakamura-san? Suzuki-san?
Have I forgotten to ask my kneader's name?
My anonymous grandmother is biking into the night.

WORD

How long a time lies in one little word!

WILLIAM SHAKESPEARE: *Richard II*

Lullaby

Stains are in, stains are in,
The instant our songs begin

To rock-a-bye my darling baby
Dreaming up worlds of maybe.

Then *byssa, byssa barnet*
Beddie byes my snowy Arne,

Quieter now and slumber-bound,
Rest in lulls of milky sound.

Ninna nanna, ninna nanna,
La mia bambina italiana.

Aja papaya, aja papaja
Doze so *meine kleine Freya.*

Hushabye and *nen-nen-yo*
The moon is high in Tokyo.

Bí bí og blaka Viking Anna,
Seoithín, seoithín, seó a leanbh,

All is well I wouldn't lie,
Trust again this bye and bye.

Valleys deep and dark unruly,
Dafydd Bach, *si hei lwli.*

663

Kuus, kuus, kalike,
My Tallinn child, night won't stay.

Sandman fallen, lullaby sung,
Sleep my love in a mother tongue.

Mother

Whenever I think of snow I think of her.
Barely a dozen days after she bore me
It began. Forty-seven and over a smother

Of soggy turf she folds a relentless nappy.
Summer the wettest in decades. Still rations:
Two ounces of butter, half an ounce of tea,

Half pound of sugar a week, six of bread.
A big post-war radio forecast crackles
Six weeks of blizzards and drifts ahead.

Mère, madre, mare, maire or *madro*
How we'd guess that *mater* was the source
But since all come from Latin know it's so.

Greek, Germanic, Celtic, Baltic, Indian
Mater, mother, *máthair*, *māte*, *matar*:
A theory's *māter* we call Indo-European.

Baby-talk *mā*, our universal feeding cry,
With *–ter*, one of two, a kinship ending.
Hoagy Carmichael sings *Ole Buttermilk Sky*

In the clothed speaker of an Atwater Kent,
Its orange-dialled cabinet a hive of valves
And condensers someone in America sent.

First son, soon apple of her longing eye.
Thirty-five and matrix of castles in the air.
A flurry of dreams curdles the January sky.

Snows

Here a two-hour train ride north of Oslo
Leaden November flurries usher in
Six insisting months of snow –
Sneachta, sno, nifa, sneg or *nix* –
Swirls and wafts across
Freakish days before it layers and sticks.
Winter's falling over Raufoss.

How I love this sifting time when sap
Sinks to lull the noiseless branches down
Endless dreams that now unmap
Lines and colours autumn took for real.
Nights are ten below.
Stains of rowanberries' blood congeal,
Flaming the early snow.

Snow. Our Indo-European word,
Sniff and snivel noun of crystal flakes,
Sneaking manna blizzard,
Soundless whirlings over our cradle place.
Sneg and *sneachta*. Snow.
All our versions worlds that we retrace
Five thousand years ago.

Yet the need to say exactly where
Hazards lay, describe terrain or how
Best to be aware
Whether it could thaw or maybe slide,
Things a local knows,
Skills passed on or maybe pride,
Sheer delight in naming snows.

Fonn for drift and *gadd* for hardened snow.
Millennia and northern Europeans
Like the Eskimo
Learn to label tiers and densities.
Fluffy, soft as floss,
Crusting now as layers begin to freeze.
Winter's falling over Raufoss.

Raufoss

Foss for 'falls' and *raud* for 'red',
Rapids hued by iron ore,
Traces in a riverbed.

Eas Ruaidh near Ballyshannon,
Red Falls in New York State,
Cascade Rouge in Lebanon.

Rufus, ruds, ruadh, rot,
Longish looping waves of light's
Five thousand years to connote

Leakings from a fountainhead
Into shoots and cataracts,
Rusted veins of minerals bled,

Vehemence of love or blood,
Rouge of cheeks and rowan lips,
Stains of passion understood,

Heartbeats raised, a blaze of fire,
Crimson sign of risk or thrill,
Sudden Niagaras of desire

Colouring this waterway.
Red-lettered tints of fêtes
Leach the falls of everyday.

Time and Tide

Falling through an hourglass waist
Our sifts of time and tide;
The root of both nouns a verb 'to divide'.

Our moments that drop grain by grain
Before the pendulum lock,
Before the shivering quartz or caesium clock.

Days under the sun, nights moon-paced
And measured in ebb and flow,
Gravities of spring or neap, an undertow

In rhythm's rise and cadence. *Tid* for a Dane
Is 'time', like Yuletide,
While *time* is 'hour'. Slowly words glide

On scales of subtlety. In the Italian *tempo*
Or Gaelic *aimsir* together
In one word the sense of 'time' and 'weather'.

Tides and seasons shifting to and fro.
Drifts of thought that grew,
Palette of meaning shaded hue by hue.

Hues

A dancing light, a surface's reflection
Pigment and douse the brain with shafts of colour,
As waves and rays reveal
Hues of a spectrum's schism,
Brilliance diffused in nature's showcase

Delighting in frequencies of perfection,
Green and yellow peppers, arrays of colour,
Black skirts, a red sail,
The rainbow's liquid prism,
Joseph's coat in the common place.

How Irish and Japanese switch direction:
Our *dathúil* 'handsome' derives from colour
Iro can mean sex appeal,
Colour and eroticism
Blur this one semantic space.

I puzzled a while over this connection,
A drift along a scale of meaning from colour
To allure, a peacock's tail,
A shift of sense, a bowdlerism
In reverse I couldn't trace.

But 'hue' is Swedish *hy* for complexion
And Iceland's countenance has a word for colour.
Two meanings dovetail.
Our desire's rouge and chrism,
The glows and glories of a face.

Face

'I'll break your face for you!'
A fist knuckling the tense air,
Angry schoolboy menace

And an ugly set-to
Smouldering that seems to flare
Up in a Japanese

Phrase – *kao o tsubusu* –
Learned three dozen years later
'To crush or squash a face',

Which now has more to do
With ignominy, a slur,
Lost countenance, disgrace

Cradling shame's peekaboo
Behind fingers, bad odour,
An eastern losing face

Our Old Irish knew:
Enech for face or honour,
A good name we abase.

Lives such pride can undo.
East or west same brittle core.
Our schoolboy human race

Still dreams of something new,
Whatever is wanting to dare
Some vulnerable space

Where nothing can subdue
A heart grown beyond such care.
An unloseable face.

Understanding

I imagine the face of some guest
In a strange house standing under
A roof studying the ties and beams
To understand a new design.
Ich verstehe! Germanic
Standing against, around, under,
A fathoming of wonder.

Childhood's soaking up and in –
Nothing arm's length or standoffish –
Quiet osmosis of a gaze
As if the starer and the stared
Once merged in one amazement,
At those things we came alive to,
Awareness that fused and grew.

Yet the urge to figure out
On two islands so far apart:
The Icelandic verb *skilja*
Or the Japanese *wakaru*
Meant 'divide' or 'understand'.
Discernment. An adult mind's gift,
A grown need to screen and sift.

Our *tuigim*, a taking in,
Seizing, a coming to grips with,
Perceive, to grasp thoroughly.
So often a wish to possess.
Je comprends! – comprehensive
Catching on, even clinging to.
Capito! Now I get you!

Again Scandinavian
Skjønne with roots in words 'to view'.
Ageing I gaze and let go.
No need to hold or analyse.
Circles close. Enough to see.
A guest looking to understand.
A return to wonderland.

Triad

Guest

Guest had meant the one
Who stood for common
Pledges of obligation.

Hostis for alien,
Same word in Latin –
Double-edged non-citizen

Shuttling to and fro,
Inside outsider
Comes bit by bit to mean 'foe',

Why invite danger,
Guest or enemy,
The ambivalent stranger?

Host

Host once a compound:
Guest-potentate,
Lord of hospitality,

Russian *gospodin*,
Word to venerate
A foreigner as 'master'.

But treacherous guests,
Judas at the fête,
Some hostile sleepless Macbeth

Betrayed a host's trust.
The face at the gate,
Once a stranger now a foe.

Feast

This word tapping down
Into sacred rites,
Things laid out before our gods.

Against all the odds
Again the stranger
Open to the stranger's face.

A toast and embrace
Repairing two words,
Our glasses raised, our eating

In tents of meeting,
A trust-mended pledge.
The host as guest, the guest host.

Subjectivity

Was the whole world a feast for Japanese?
Europe's 'subjective' and 'objective' adapted
As either the view of host or guest.

A bird-eyed caller observes and leaves the rest
To the work of a busy host laying on a spread.
Together our life all of a piece.

Work

'Work' in English dialects once meant 'pain'.
In sorrow thou shalt bring...
Labours of love. Pangs of childbirth.

French *travail* may be from Latin meaning
'Torture'. Travail of blows.
German *Arbeit* the Icelandic word for 'hard'.

Or Irish *saothar* 'work', 'panting', 'throes'.
The wintery European
Underscores an ardour in all our journeys.

A friend told me once that Thai *ngaan*
Means work or job
But also 'carnival', 'feast', 'party', 'festival'.

Those mangroved islands Europe didn't rob,
The rainforests that blurred
Lines between such sways of duty and delight.

Work parties in every sense of the word.
In bonds of toil or dance
Paradise sweats its stardust in our bones

Across three billion years of dreaming chance
From soup to angel clones.
We carry still our half-imagined Eden.

Labyrinth

After Eden then the years of maze.
Ah, *how beautiful the world would be*
If there were rules for moving in labyrinths.
Umberto Eco, of course, I partly agree
Yet even such bewilderment I need to praise.

A journey of choices with no overview.
Norwegian *irrgang*, Japanese *meiro*
Both name labyrinth 'a road that strays'.
After the garden no one path to go.
No map here. No compass, chalk or clew.

Welsh *drysfa*, 'a thicket', 'a thorny place'
And I know how easily I took a turn
Meaning to remember where but hurried
Down a dead end only again to learn
My slow retreat, forgotten steps I trace.

In labyrinths we only know we never know.
Völundur's saga house that could bewilder
Endless guests in winding rooms or passages,
Dædalus, the highflying labyrinth builder
Still leaves his trademark in Italian *dedalo*.

In tangles of images, my favourite maze;
More bumbling and roaming than astray
I love its hazy echoes of astonishment
At shuffles of choices labyrinths hold in play,
Warrens of turns that baffle and still amaze.

Dead Ends

Blind Alley

The roadway sealed as a sightless eye –
A likeness worked in several tongues,
Uno vicolo cieco, Norway's *blindvei*.

The traveller asks should I have known
To blind is the same as to dazzle
And dazzled was I blind as stone?

Or should, like Auden, this traveller ask
If he himself no longer sees
The light in which he loved to bask?

Strupcelš

In Riga *strupcelš* means a road that's brief.
A wrong exit taken from some roundabout,

Mistaken choices, routes so badly signed
Or in reverie not quite aware how you court

Danger not watching how a road inclined
To narrow till suddenly you're pulled up short,

Another bend and there it has petered out,
An endless dream abruptly come to grief.

行止まり

Ikidomari

In Tokyo the warning is *ikidomari*!
Two characters: a crossroads and footprint;
The one means 'go', the other 'stop dead'.

A going stop! As though someone led
You winkered up this stop–go path
Knowing there was no thoroughfare,

Knowing that this was going nowhere,
While you wove futures in your mind,
Though deeper down something in you

Sensed stalemate, an instinct that knew
What such zigzags could only mean,
You felt this road was running out.

Cul-de-sac

Bottom of a sack! Once French for impasse,
Japan's *fukurokōji* or German *Sackgasse*.

An image to catch my first raging instinct,
Resentment at feeling somehow hoodwinked,

Trapped headlong in a bag and madly flailing
About, glimpsing the light but still just failing

To find the opening and the angrier I grow
The more I'm trapped. O irony of letting go!

The calmer, subtler easing out of a sack.
A courage gathered, the grit for turning back.

Återvändgränd

Swedes the wisest with *återvändgränd*:
'A byway for return',
A compound noun that seems to blend

The dead end with the turning back,
Neither denying an impasse
Or dismissing the grief in this sidetrack

And retrace to where a byroad started
To choose a different way,
Begin again where the fork had parted.

No bag or blindness, no anger or shame
In my doubling back
On roads now richer than the road you came.

So reverse here while the going is good!
How way leads on to way –
It might have been a New England wood.

In dead ends at least there's no mistaking
Advance is by return,
Your journey still a journey in the making.

Journey

Our year's journey etched on a wall –
The apex of a triangle
Inching from December's solstice
Downward allowances of sun
To flood a stone courtyard with warmth.

Une journée, the course of a day,
Latin for 'a daily portion',
A blending of time and motion
Which by Middle English becomes
'A day's travel', 'an excursion'.

Our journey's *per diem* of light.
The root of Latin's day is 'shine',
Likewise found in Jove or Tuesday's
Old sky-god. The way in Japanese
Hi can mean sun or day or light.

It's March of my sixty-first year
And an apex once too acute
Widens, obtuse and generous
Broadcasting on a courtyard wall
Arise, shine, for thy light has come.

A winter's granite at the core
Unchills to glint in the spring-light,
The quartzose grain of a soul
Glitters its stillness towards
A hope of warm-blooded summer.

Like Horace scaling down to now,
An ovened stone I hug this heat,
Storing every moment before
A year's angle lifts and narrows
My journey's geometries of light.

Summer

Fortune owns some, summer belongs to all.
Recollected longing of evenings,
All our waiting as a new year wound up;
Half our memory our expectation,
Counting the swallows to make a summer.

And still across this northern hemisphere
Between the springing and the harvest earned
From when the sun stood still above Cancer
Until day and night again are equal,
A season's names recall the strewn traces.

Germanic 'summer' or our own *samhradh*
Showing up in Old Indian *sámā*
For 'a year' or 'a half-year' or 'season'.
If Vikings reckoned their age in winters,
Old Indians measured theirs in summers.

Natsu Japan's 'summer' a rambling word,
Akin or borrowed Old Turkish *jāz* 'spring',
May carry the memory of a time
When it meant 'the warmer part of the year'
And then diverged as climates demanded.

Warmth beginning our sun already turned.
A wheel moves even while it touches,
In its outset gradual retraction –
Our season arriving in its going.
Summer a word so ripe with remembrance.

Remembrance

Erinnerung

German *Erinnerung*: once 'to interiorise',
Things we've taken up, an inside story
Played again in our remembering eyes,
An archive of images, an inner repository.
Absconded moments leave their trace,
The cortex nicked, niches in our brains,
Thumbprints pressed into a wax of mind,
Whatever stamp or mark that still remains,
Our lifetimes absorbed and learnt by heart
In memories plotting back where we begin
A retrospective line across a chart,
Everything inscribed and logged within;
Etched presence of unshuttered seeing,
Indelible stains on our retina of being.

Ricordo

Latin *recordatio*, act of taking
Again to heart like Japanese *kioku*
'Chronicle of thought lingering at the core'.

Cardiac high fidelity as once more
A reflexive verb snatches up a residue;
Track record of doings, inward note-making.

Souvenir

From Latin 'to relieve' or 'reinforce'
In the sense of 'coming up to aid',
Subvenire now French 'to remember'.

Hard to see how meanings can shade
Into each other and undergo
This shift from 'reinforce' to 'recall',

Unless half-consciously we know
Our stories struggle with forgetfulness,
And every souvenir a self-subvention,

Aide-mémoire for a stumbling psyche,
A keepsake memory we caress,
Another scratch on walls of oblivion.

Remember

Mimir, Norse God and portal keeper,
Guard of wisdom's well,
'memory' and 'remember' double a root
We find in 'mourn'.

Latin through French 'to be again mindful'
A watchfulness grown deeper,
As all too well we know we're born
To weep and so transmute

Things past. We ward off the forgetful,
By rehearsals en route
To wisdom's gate, well-worn
Paths to Mimir's well.

Reminiscence

Deliberate evocation, a thinking of.
This Indo-European men 'to mind',
Long in Irish *cuimhne*, with *'com'* combined,
In *Minnesinger* our minding turns to love.
A root that in its reminding reappears
To build again from swaps and synthesis
Renewed warmth of shared and nested stories
Unfolded out across five thousand years,
As deep within the words 'to reminisce'
We fall into step with common memories.

Recollect

Recollection means a gathering up again
To find some sense among the scattered pieces,
The way we seek motives that might explain
Or more examples to prove a hunch or thesis.
We imagine both what was and will be
In the same magic lantern within a mind;
Yet in the light of slowly conjured memory
What was and now are carefully realigned.
No made-up image we might fancy or forecast
As memory for us must be a kind of work,
Checking every word against the past,
A matching truth and mind we daren't shirk.
Trusting a memory so fickle and protean,
We gather up and sift as best we can.

Words

Word

Word from an Indo-European root
'To say solemnly' or just 'to speak',
Germanic, Baltic, Greek, Latin *verbum*.

Remember school and how a verb describes
A deed or action, the way when parsing
All clauses pivoted on this doing.

Verve and charisma of an utterance,
A psychic energy in what's spoken,
Uncontainable fire in prophets' bones.

Vow, bless, threat, curse, promise or covenant,
The sway of our irrevocable sounds.
O world wanting to be taken at its word!

Focal

Irish *focal* from a root 'to speak'
That comes to mean 'word' or 'noise',
Cognate with Latin *vox* for 'voice'
Or Calliope 'beautiful voice' in Greek.

Hummingbird deep in the larynx,
Words caressed on a tongue's tip
As sweet friction shivers the lip,
Our pleasure's oral high jinks.

Purr of breath still spoilt for choice
As a French kiss of a rising vowel
Shapes and flutters cheek by jowl.
I loved my muses for their voice.

Geir

Welsh *geir* grounded in 'cry' or 'call'
Found in Latin for chatter, hence 'garrulous'
And turning up in Ossetian for 'nightingales'.

Or English 'care' and German *Karfreitag*
'Friday of grief' and here our cry
Itself has named the need it wails.

単語
Tango

Mostly in the land of rising sun
Both language and word are one
But here it's *tan* 'simple' or 'single',
'one unit' of expression *-go*.

Again 'speak' and 'word' mingle:
Go from Chinese *yu* for speech,
Cognate with 'praise', spreads to reach
Burmese as either 'to say' or 'bird'.

What leaps of meaning occurred?
A word breaks its sound barrier
In flight. A soul's pigeon carrier
Taking wing from the word go.

Λογος
Logos

In the fourth Gospel *logos* is the word
That was in the beginning and made flesh
With Yahweh's millennia of pledges
Echoing in one noun for 'what is said',

But laden too with Greek philosophies
Commingling with logic and -ologies,
Rules, laws, argument, reason, measure, worth,
And even for Plato bird of the soul,

Although its root had only meant 'to pluck'
Or 'gather' and then 'to read together',
'To tell', 'to speak', and so to 'the thing said'
Which in turn takes on a life of its own.

Conjure believers reading papyrus
Wondering at a prologue's parallels:
The same was in the beginning with God.
In a word, all and everything that is.

Belief

Creideamh

'Where the heart is placed'.
Irish cognate with *credo*.
Trust in core values.

Trú

Norse, rooted in trees,
Whatever's steadfast and true.
Foliage of trust.

信仰 *Xìnyǎng*
East's 'trust looking up'.
Not seeing but believing.
O doubting Thomas!

אֱמוּנָה *Emunah*

Firm and secure in
Taking Moses's word as true;
Plumb line of a world.

Πιστις *Pistis*

Greek, Latin *fides* too.
Unforgetting confidence
Biding and convinced.

Glaube

Glaube and belief
Both intensifying *leubh*:
'To care',' 'desire,' 'love'.

Forget

Oblivisci

Latin *oblivisci* 'to wipe away'
Slate rubbed clean,
An ironed-out crease.

Some half-conscious overlay,
Slip or psychic caprice
Airbrushes to oblivion.

忘记
Wàngjì

'An account dead in the heart.'
A legend or origin tale?
Maybe. But I'm inclined

To imagine how at the start
Two Chinese lovers pined
For every trembling detail.

Then, years after they part;
Their spoors of memory fail.
O what traces die in the mind.

Oblidar

Mostly we struggle with a maze
Of forgetfulness, to stay
Out of history's oubliette.

Catalan chance to reappraise
Memory's dossier.
Yes, I'm owed so much and yet...

Oblidar: Latin *oblitterare* 'erase',
A letter we take away.
Account closed. A cancelled debt.

Dearmad

Like Welsh, Irish 'disremembers' –
Recalls the given state;
Forgetting a willed leaving behind.

Too easy to rake over embers.
History's bitter freight,
Hurts I wean from my mind.

Forget

Not to apprehend –
'To lose the grip'
We try so hard to hold.

Imagine if we controlled
It all, no godsend
Of amnesia letting slip

Our blundering regret,
Like Borges's hero
Haunted by a full recall?

Give thanks for sleep's zero
When the blinds fall.
Sweet the chagrin we forget.

Gleyma

Nordic 'exult', 'rejoice' that came
To mean 'forget'. Semantic leap.
A going clean out of one's head.

Blotto with joy. An ego shed
The moment my pen ghost-writes,
Such easy, couldn't-care-less

Revelling in self-forgetfulness.
Sweeney swings from birch to birch.
Birds of paradise wing within.

Thanks

Thanks

Thanks and *Danke*, *takk* and *dank*
All over the Germanic world
The same response: to think is to thank.

Indo-European *tong* 'to think
Or feel'. This root that meditates
Keeps lowering its vowel to link

Thought and gratitude, to allow
Us catch what was and is in one,
Taking a past with us into now.

Merci

From Latin for 'hire' or 'fee'
Wage for services rendered
Drifts to 'favour' or 'mercy'.

No longer measure for measure
More a gift bestowed,
A giving at someone's pleasure.

One word to name and bless
A gratuitous *merci*,
Unearned openhandedness.

有難う
Arigatō

This Japanese for 'thanks' is 'grateful';
An adjective that meant 'with difficulty'
Appreciates bother someone incurred.

Such focus on the other and the past
Apologies and gratitude have blurred
So *sumimasen* 'It isn't yet ended'

Blends 'pardon!' and 'thanks' in a word.
Sorry to have troubled you. *Arigatō*.
Deep bowings and an endless closure.

Gracias

Spanish like Italian *grazie*
From the Latin we know in 'grace'
And 'gratitude', which in turn displays

A deeper root that meant 'to praise
Aloud' that shows again in 'bard',
'The one who lauds', 'praise-giver'.

And so I hand it to you. I deliver
My tribute, less *quid pro quo*
Than overflow. Well good for you!

Go raibh maith agat

Longer but to the point
Irish: 'May you have good!'
Our sense of gratitude
Optatives of blessing.
Same not at all the same,

Theme with variations:
Go dtuga Dia do shláinte dhuit!
May God give you your health!
May God compensate you!
A calling down of gifts.

谢谢
Xièxie

End of *gǎnxiè* 'to thank' twice
Gǎn for 'sense', 'feeling' or 'touch',
Its sign hearts in unison.

And *xiè* signals words and shot –
Once an arrow in a bow –
Both to show a parting shot,

A last word of emotion
Fires out a potlatch of thanks.
I'm so grateful. *Xièxie, xièxie.*

Ευχαριστιες
Eucharisties

Again the notion of showing favour,
Charis with its roots in yearning,

A thankfulness crediting generosity
As 'to bid for favour' can mean 'please'.

Daily Greek for 'please' and 'thank you'
Echo that chambered supper we renew

Shedding a cup across the centuries:
This do in remembrance of me.

Desire for what's beyond our earning
A broken bread we long to savour.

Not At All

Not At All!

Oh! the airy dismissiveness in this reply –
No, not at all! Don't even mention it –
A staving off of words that seem to fly
In the face of common years of trust and sit
Uneasily with a careless take-for-grantedness
Which, although it likes to savour such
Utterances of thanks, sometimes none-the-less
Finds digesting it is almost overmuch
As if our daily assumings need a space
Where silence reigns and spares our lungs
All unneeded talk that could undo
The muted promise of any love's embrace,
Sweet nothings murmured in mother tongues:
De nada! De res! Nakas! Pas du tout!

とんでもない *Ton Demo Nai!*

Just *Ie! Ie!*
No! No! Or maybe to use
A *'ton demo nai'*
Meaning 'absurd', 'outrageous'
'What a thing to say!'
Good grief. Nothing of the sort.
Exaggerated
Sweeping to one side, almost
A dutiful disdain
So you start to imagine a Samurai's self-denial:
Service rendered and no nonsense.

Gern Geschehen

You see here how Germans don't shy away,
Or try to brush off terms of gratitude
Denying all as if to underplay
What's done, the service given pooh-poohed;
But rather take this thankfulness for what

It is, a well-meant recognition of gift,
A naming of whatever someone got,
A bid to give the lifter too a lift.
My pleasure! I'd really love to do more,
Surely a favour's nothing to disown.
Then why the would-be bashful need to shun
Whatever grateful words can warm my core?
So I accept with thanks the thanks you've shown.
Gern geschehen! Something 'willingly done'.

Det Skulle Bare Mangle!

Norwegian *Det skulle bare mangle!*
'It would indeed be lacking!' that's to say
What's given's simply a matter of course.

This answer to reassure both parties
To do otherwise would be to betray
A trust, to fail myself as much as you.

Remember we count on each other.
Neither of us could ever walk away
Abandoning a fallen friend to snow.

Verði þér ad góðu!

Iceland's after meals *Verði þér að góðu!*
Like *Go ndéanaí ' mhaith duit* in Donegal
Translates simply as 'May it benefit you!' –
No dismissals here or '*Not* at all!'
Neither overmodestly self-effacing
Waving signs of gratitude aside
Or any thoughts of anxiously erasing
Each excess of thanks with Samurai pride,
More a trust in whatever has begun
Sweeping us with it and out of control
On beyond such dangers of possessing
Any feel or sense of owning favours done
As gifts and thank-yous go on changing role –
Our give and take a ricochet of blessing.

Trusts

Trust

Trust with roots in *deru* meaning 'steadfast',
Through India and Europe words for tree,
Latin *dūrus* for hard, heartwood to last,
Kildare 'Church of Oak' or 'grove' in Derry.
In some Germanic branches 'banking on'
Drifts to 'fellow feeling', 'a standing by' –
A shift of meaning in the lexicon:
Norwegian *trøst* both 'comfort' and 'rely',
As if our minds at rest are minds consoled
By another's word nothing undermines.
As trunk and roots steady and reassure,
The face we count on, the words that uphold
Sinkers and feeders beyond our drip lines;
No matter how long the drought oaks endure.

Confidentia

Confianza, confidència, confidence,
Con and *fidere* 'to trust'
Latin for complete reliance,

Its root 'compel' or 'persuade'
'To be convinced', to count
On what might be betrayed.

A faith whole and entire
Bides its daring time.
You walk this taut high wire.

Hyder

Welsh's old, now slightly literary word
With nuances: 'boldness', 'trust', 'reliance'
Which a century ago was still heard
In *ar i hyder* for 'on the off chance'.

In origin Indo-European
For 'stretching out a hand' that comes to mean
The use of zeal or power and then to span
All the colours of meaning in between
And yet the most generous of its senses
A mark of strength, sign of extravagance
Risks how the other might misunderstand,
Take as weakness the fist that untenses,
The arm begun unfolding trust's off chance.
Panache and daring of an outstretched hand.

Vertrauen

German *Trost* is 'comfort'.
Vertrauen 'to give credence'
'To take at your word'.

Trauen a verb 'to trust'.
Our betrothal over
The odds. Go for bust!

Yes, my belief in you.
Ground of all love. Wager
That a word comes true.

Lit

Mostly now in one or other compound
Scandinavian *lit* for reliance
Based on a verb 'to see' or 'look around',
Then turning noun for 'sight' or 'appearance'
That either tends to mean a 'hue' or 'sheen'
(In Icelandic 'colour' has pride of place)
Or 'sight' becomes how we ourselves are seen
By showing up at times in words for face.
Still in Norway's *Sett din lit til noen*
'Put your trust in someone' two meanings blend,
A match of face and faith that readjust
As thinking through these roots we learn again
The way we turn to countenance a friend,
Our face to face a gazing into trust.

Friend

Amicus

Latin tied to the first verb we conjugated:
Amo, amas, amat
I love, you love...akin to *amicus* and freighted

With our suckling recollection of *amma*
Middle Ages' Latin
'Mother', nursery petname like 'mamma'

We find again in Iceland's *amma* 'Nana'
Or Norway's wet-nurse.
Our once frost-white and honeyed manna.

Amie, amic, amico, amigo
Romance reflexes
Summoning every friendship in embryo,

Our naked cry of milky longing traced
From memory's womb,
Our endless desire embracing and embraced.

Cyfaill

Welsh *cyfaill* 'the co-reared one' –
Our foster-sibling *comhalta* –
A companionship begun

In youth. The sweet risk and fun
Of other friends discovered
And yet all that's said and done

In our knowing inside out,
Long years of coalescence,
Breaking bread for feast or drought.

友

Japan's *tomo*,
Chinese *yǎu* –
As it was on the tortoise shell,
As it is now

Two hands grasped
As friendship's sign
Like a *sean-nós* singer winding
Out a line.

Hand on hand
Thick or thin.
Everything ventured, everything gained.
Win, win.

Vinur

For northmen lust and trouble taken blend:
Iceland's *vinur* or Norway's *venn* for 'friend'

Stems from a root 'to strive' 'to try', 'aspire'
And so 'wish and work to achieve desire'

Both in flower-goddess Venus's sheep's-eyes.
And *fine* in Fine Gael for 'kindred allies'.

Sober northern mixture of lust and rapport,
Some irrefutable call we answer to and for.

No matter what you know I've named you friend.
The garden chosen. The seed and bloom I tend.

Caraid

Kā as in *kamasutra* India's love tract,
An Indo-European verb 'to long'
Ah, when were such borders ever exact,
Our lines between a right and wrong?

694

Our western *caraid*, Welsh *cariad* for 'love'
Same root as 'charity', 'cherish' and 'whore'.
Fond caress we never get enough of
In the pith of friendship's desire for more.

Friend

Grounded in a verb 'to hold dear or please',
Germane to 'free' and words for peace or ease

Found in Old Indian *prīṇāti* 'to rejoice in',
Icelandic *frændi* once 'friend' now 'kith and kin'.

Have we not loved each other as best we could?
Of course such water became thicker than blood.

All secrets confessed under the trusted oak
Our ease and laughter a running inside joke

As rings conspire and years of roots accrue;
My friend! *Mein Freund!* I delight in you.

GRAMMAR

Only in grammar can you be more than perfect.

WILLIAM SAFIRE

Imperative

This inflexible linguistic strut
As speakers ask, demand, insist.
No time for doubt. A minimalist
Approach. Imperious upper hand.
No roundabout or pussyfoot.
Do exactly what I command!

Downright mood of sergeant or lover.
Nothing here but roots of verbs,
No stem or end or person curbs
Or softens. Intimate and peremptory.
Between the sheets or undercover.
Halt. About turn. Kiss me!

Interrogative

Can you hear the courtroom voice of law?
So many ways to shape a leading question.
Weren't you there? Tell us what you saw!

You did see it, didn't you? Answer yes.
But you didn't see it, did you? Answer no.
An interrogative already a second-guess.

The barrister your father dreamt you'd be,
But cross-questions kept on fanning out

Beyond the cut and dry of dock or jury.

So much you ask yet know you can't be sure
In nuanced light and dark of inbetweenness
Your skittish themes and riffs a noodling detour.

All the *blooming buzzing confusion* you've
Called your jazz of open yes or no,
A mood to speak of things you'll never prove.

Indicative

Simple declarative, matter of fact,
A speaker's statement 'this is how it is',
Our pointing out, unmarked modality:
A flower grows in the axil of a bract.

In any utterance no neutrality,
Everything indicative of something;
Mood for ideologue and dogmatist:
'The way I say it how it must be.'

Mood too for chroniclers and glossarists
Not in the humour for command or quiz.
Just *above my lined book birds' chanting.*
The sky is blue. I'm glad that I exist.

Optative

Μη γενοιτο – May it never come about!
Greek inflections of request,
Mode of wishes.
Perish the thought!
Things sought,
Warded off or blessed,
Optings in or out.

Creaking axle shafts of prayer still turn:
May the best man win!
Long may you live!
May they rest in peace!
Desire's grease
An infinite paradigm within.
How endlessly I yearn.

Subjunctive

A Latin term borrowed from Greek grammar
For forms of subordination we'd obey,
Those lists of conjunctions from the crammer:
French phrases with *que*, Caesar's *ut* and *ne*.
Also a stance for what's beyond our ken,
'Uncertain negatives' our rule of thumb:
Mais hélas! je ne crois pas qu'elle vienne –
But I'm afraid I don't believe she'll come.
Mood of but and maybe if I were you,
Tentative just supposings or surmise
And perhaps she was coming all along?
An insubordinate lover's derring-do
Chancing the riffs and pulses of surprise,
I risk what-ifs. So what if I were wrong!

Conditional

A mood known to every Irish classroom,
Modh coinníollach for a hypothesis:
Either 'if I were' or 'if I had been',

A conjecture or supposition seen
From here and now how everything might be
Or might have been, opposed to how it is.

On condition something were such, then this –
A space between a future and our past,
Thought experiment, airbrushed reality.

Dream mode of reconditioned fantasy:
Were I a blackbird I'd whistle and sing,
If wishes were horses, beggars would ride.

Nightmare negatives that set now aside
Ferreting out mistakes we didn't make.
If I hadn't loved you, God alone knows.

Progressive

Are you agoing to Scarborough Fair?
A view of a motion nabbed in full flight,
This song in the course of travelling where

Its love is held for years on end in play,
A balladeer pleading his jilted plight,
On York moors cries an ongoing dismay.

Parsley, sage, rosemary and thyme
where water ne'er sprung nor drop of rain fell
And then she'll be a true love of mine…

Sense of duration, aspect of process,
What the French describe as being in train,
Something on the go, an in-the-actness,

A verb caught up in the flow of living
Dreaming some perfection it can't attain.
Every poem a moment still on the wing.

Habitual

In our home a forbidden paradigm.
Our parents used correct us if we said
'Does be here' to mean 'here many a time'.
Mrs Do-be and her little does-be's
They'd mock, insisting on saying 'is' instead,
'To be polite' just the way we'd use 'please'.

Poor Mrs Do-be didn't fill the bill.
Our habitual now a rural past,
Though some have shown it's echoed even still
In Black 'he be's here', understood as 'daily'
Or 'often' – habit and now in contrast,
Hidden dissonance in jazz or *céilí*.

We learned our Irish endings off by rote:
Éirím, cuirim orm mo chuid éadaí...
I rise, I dress, I eat, I sit and I devote
Whatever allotment of years head bent
Over this page. O does-be monkish me
In love with my habitual present.

Perfective

All those parallel pairs of Slavic verbs:
'I read it' or 'I read it to the end',
One the act, the other its completion.

Less the time than the contours of doing,
A gazing at aspects of the deed itself,
A perfectionist conjuring fulfilment.

So much begun that's still not quite finished,
Learning this and that, never 'having learned',
Same old yearning to say a work is done.

Once more this cluttered table cleared
Believing again hope's guardian angel
And this time I know I will have read...

Flawed stop–start flow. Faultless tomorrow.
Imperfect pasts, dreams of perfect futures.

Recent Perfect

I've just eaten a mango zipped with lime,
So recent and perfect my lips still twang.
Gerade, just now, finished or come from –
Ah! Je viens de manger une grosse mangue –
Only or barely, no mention of time.

On Celtic fringes a like idiom
Conscious of time 'we're after eating'
Reflects an Irish *th'éis* or Welsh *wedi*,
Prepositions that qualify fleeting
Verbal nouns with their temporal aplomb

And hold in suspense the passing heady
Moment to invoke stings of pleasure fresh
In the mouth while still the corrosive lime
Bites slivers of a phantom mango's flesh.
Around my tongue juices whirl and eddy.

Frequentative

Angles of vision that enhance
Heightened eyescape of lovers,
Seeing the parts and whole at once.

Aspect we didn't learn at school,
How *–er* turns a flick to flicker,
How a constant drip is dribble.

O that sudden flare of fancy,
And how at the start you'd startled
Falling for the same frequency.

Weight of any vowel we utter,
Intensity of syllables,
One more sound and chat is chatter.

To dab and dabble and so mate.
Frequentative of *habere* 'have'
In where we dwell, our habitat.

Sparkle of what first sparked us off.
Moist firewood cracked, then crackled
Kindling such inhabitable love.

Future

Futures go back to a fifth form at school.
Amabo, Amabis, 'I'll love', 'you'll love',
Bulldog conducting the air with his rule,
Favourite Latin tense to rattle off.

Then, our Irish future written with *f*s
Molfaidh mé, molfaidh tú, 'I'll praise', 'you'll praise',
These eulogies amid exams and biffs,
Anapaests and dactyls the pulse obeys.

Strange to speak of an English 'future tense',
A term Germanic languages borrow;
Like Japanese, adverbs carry the sense:
We meet today and we part tomorrow.

For most only a present and a past –
Both 'we will' or 'we shall' our current moods –
The things we wish or want or may forecast,
A modal giving up on certitudes.

Here's the tense where a time and fancy cross
In loving and praising beyond our ken;
We wager on tomorrow's pitch and toss,
Our future still a mood of mice and men.

Past

The past a car's rear mirror glanced,
A glimpsed once-off, an aorist dream,
The roadway's cloud of dust behind,
The arrow of now already advanced,
A point in time's reflected gleam
Almost out of my sight and mind.

What is, what was and what's to come
Just one more way of seeing things –
The Hopi split their moods in three:
Timeless truth (like four's the sum
Of three and one), so happenings
(I read), what's still uncertainty.

The pedal down I'm speeding on.
A tense or mood it's all so fast,
So much to say that's still unsaid.
A flickered mirror image gone
As yet another bend slides past
And swallows up the road ahead.

Pluperfect

Here in the Natural History Museum
From Loch Gur, Naglack. Ballebetagh knuckle-necked
Giant Irish deer, a portal-keeping threesome,
Show off their skeleton key to our past perfect.
With Ireland, Britain and mainland Europe still linked
They'd arrived from Asia twelve thousand years ago;
Largest antlers of all deer living or extinct,
Frozen out they'd died like a second-floor dodo.
So strange how a *had* rounds off all halcyon days
Of a perfect past where such specimens had been
One casualty of nature's planned obsolescence;
A *floruit* complete before a climate phase
In their ebony cage of air a long lost gene
Forever exuding its own pluperfect tense.

Causative

The weight of just one syllable,
How even the shapes of a tongue
Make of an intransitive verb
The cause and because of action,

Though often a roundabout way
With another phrase: I'll have you
Know the rain will make the tree grow,
La pluie fait pousser l'arbre,

Some like Japanese or Finnish
Juggle letters, add a suffix,
A self-contained moving spirit
Inflected in the word itself.

But now fossilised in English
Like trees we fell before they fall
Their trunks laid where they lie frozen,
A layer of verbs as 'sit' and 'set',

Where lowered vowels give rise to change,
Raise a forebear's remembered sap
To work such subtle shift in sound,
Ghost in us their shadow patterns.

Potential

Each time I hear a Japanese potential
It brings to mind that nun I never met
Who'd ask her friends to name five unlived dreams,
Then ticking off the list she'd ask why not?

Naru 'become', *nareru* 'can become,
Can grow, emerge, turn out or come to be' –
But 'can' is much too moody and detached,
An auxiliary so like 'may' or 'might'.

Too many pallid years of asking why.
All our endless brief postponements have left
At first a rift and then a cosy gap
Between our modals and infinitive,

So we define ourselves too narrowly,
Saying how we'd love to but never could,
As if we want to make our lack our dream,
Until it seems we'd rather fade than flourish.

But no excuses! Why not? An ending
That binds its potential into the verb.
Saku 'to bloom' and *sakeru* 'can bloom,
Open or blossom or come into flower'.

Active Voice

The mode for inflecting a verb
With subject as action-taker,
The doer of whatever's done.

Endings to indicate the one
Concerned is mover and shaker,
Protagonist of the scene.

For years before St Stephen's Green
Despair forestalled dark with dark,
Gloomy failure in self-defence,

A subject's still verbless sentence.
O resurrection in a park,
Spring and sunlight your leitmotif,

Madness in each unfolded leaf.
Unclenching, another young spark
Dares the inflections of a voice.

Middle Voice

Classic Greek or Icelandic halfway voice,
Subject as gainer, both setter and scene:
Ég gleðst 'I delight myself', 'rejoice',
Not active, not passive, but in between.
Pheromai 'I carry off', on the make
The doers and their benefit cohere,
Sometimes reflexive, others give and take,
þeir heilsast hér, they greet each other here.
Self-possessed verbs for a pivotal time,
Neither old nor young, belonging to each,
The days when still we tuned into both spheres
As two generations bridged in our prime
Were greeting one another within reach.
My middle voice delighted in those years.

Passive Voice

Subjects once the actors and achievers
Learn the lonely voice of ghosts that hover,
The fathers of our youth who slip beyond.

Here we're turned by 'by' into receivers,
In handing and being handed over
The active voice and passive correspond.

Beckoned again, taken and still amazed
Such a range of verbs allow surrender,
Leaving us less the mover than the moved.

Years of action, even attainments praised,
So no need for feats or proofs of gender
Just let one lover enjoy being loved.

Our balance tips and wants to smile and bow
In going with what we must undergo,
Live and let live of things best left unsaid.

Our fathers gone. Are we the fathers now?
Like Rilke's angels we often do not know
If we walk among the living or the dead.

Conjugation

After our meat and wine
Again the time, the voice and mood combine
For conjugation,
Come-hither invitation,
I can't decline.

Latin lover's tense,
Amo, amas, amat – consummate nonsense,
Charms of grammar,
Source of all glamour,
Rhythm's accidence.

A verb to x-rate –
Steady now Bulldog – don't exaggerate –
As we chant
Amamus, amatis, amant.
Let's conjugate.

Imperative but tender
Ama! Single command of either gender.
Love me.
Subject, inflect, perfect me
In my surrender.

Concessive

These clauses begin granting that although
They take subjunctives in many grammars –
Bien que je ne puisse pas réussir,

Even if (it may be) I can't succeed –
They hold concessions somehow in the air,
Let's suppose world of might or might not be

In spite of which still something else is true.
Although we know we've always fallen short
And while this may be the gist of yearning,

As if by laws of increasing returns
Desire expands to meet increased desire,
We keep on conjuring up fulfilments.

Then who under heaven have I but you?
For all my vanities and brokenness,
It's you I've loved all my livelong days.

Infinitive

To wake, to love, to dance, to be, to do –
Unmarked tense or person, unencumbered
English underdetermined point of view,
Non-committal dictionary headword.
Both substantive and verb, a borderland,
For Irish or Turkish only a noun,
In Tokyo the subject hearers understand,
While Portuguese lets pronouns tie it down.
Undefined shifting inbetweenness,
A spirit here and now that yet can soar,
Verbal action and a noun's sereneness,
Movement and stillness at the dance's core.
Beside incarnate person, number, mood,
A silence in the verb to be, infinitude.

Comparative

Were geraniums redder than the rose?
A childhood nagging to like one better.
Odd how I can't remember which I chose,

The roses' flame, the geraniums' flare?
Bit redder, redder, reddest, real reddest,
Lithuanian's five grades to compare.

Upping the pace we're gathering unease,
Fast, faster, big, bigger and biggest,
Worlds haunted by comparative degrees.

Japanese superlatives use *ichiban* –
The number one this, the number one that –
In all comparisons a silent 'than'.

Than you. Than me. Such an urge to compete,
Yet still somehow adequate, unique, whole.
Can anything be more or less complete?

This is my moment, my place in the sun.
Shine the geranium, shine the wild rose.
All incomparable under the One.

Reflexive

'I see myself' – a folding back to where
Subject and object allude to one thing,

'Doer', the patient to whom verbs refer,
Body implied when I say I'm shaving.

This pronoun 'self' reflects long tangled roots:
The *swa* in *swaraj*, the *Féin* in *Sinn Féin*,

'Sib' in sibling, the 'eth' in ethnic roots,
one's own man in King Henry's 'homely swain'.

Reflex that's my own I learned to acquire
In years of overwhelmings I'd withstood,

In ravelled nodes of memory and desire,
Alongside the other, my frail selfhood.

One apprenticeship in our lovely mess
Sui generis of lifelong labour,

Reeled in psychic thread of shifting sameness,
Self I love so I can love my neighbour.

Suppletive

Unknowingly we grow into grammar,
Absorbing freaks in our newfound patterns,
My Daddy goed to his work this morning
As littler, littlest yield to less and least
And learn how fathers went or wended there.

Other words as stopgaps in inflections –
Bon, meilleur, le meilleur, good, better, best;
Tháinig 'came', *tagann* 'comes', *tiocfaidh* 'will come';
Latin's *fero, ferre, tuli, latum,*
Fero 'I bear' mixed with *tollo* 'I lift'.

Evenings we passed swotting principal parts.
Nothing exotic in the abnormal
Come-day, go-day of the commonest things,
The irregular born by frequency,
Strangeness hidden in the ordinary

As it was in the beginning, is now
And ever shall be. Eternal echo.
Is, was that meant 'to stay, dwell, pass a night'
And *be* 'to exist, to grow, to become'
One suppletive. Three verbs interwoven.

Possessive

Word now smeared with green-eyed innuendo –
Desires to keep another under thumb –
Here an older genitive's afterglow
In possessive *s*'s *ad libitum.*
A friend's friend's face I imagine I know,
Germanic *s* links our genitive chain,
Nouns gather up each other as they go,
A network of relations set in train.
But traces of possession elsewhere too:
His and *hers* genitives of *he* and *she* –
These personal pronouns we still decline –
Ours possessive of *we* and *yours* of *you*
Marking what we love grammatically.
I know that I am yours and you are mine.

Consecutive

First a main clause with *such, enough* or *so*
Stating what's true to this or that degree,
A comma, then the consequences flow.

One thing is such, the other follows suit:
Our lives so brief that every moment sings;
Consecutives one statement bearing fruit.

Classic Greek marks off – and German likewise –
Fact from guess, reserving infinitives
Or subjunctive modes to signal surmise.

For most a mood indicative of fact,
Choice by choice we flap our butterfly wings;
Things were such, this is how we had to act.

So far, so good. Judgements made in pauses,
Each choice a breath in our delivery,
Our lives lived in consecutive clauses.

Yet knowing how way leads on to way:
The pulse of words, my birds of paradise
I loved so much, I'm still this child at play.

Relative

A lamp is placed midways on a spaceship
Which moves at a speed relative to Mars,
As the midpoint passes Observer One,
Who stands on the planet, a light flashes
Which another watcher who stands on board –

Lamps, spaceship, observer, light and watcher
All topics to headline our attention
Until they yield to 'which' or 'who' or 'that'
Until their tale unfolds in relatives
Where they move and flash and have their being.

But there are worlds with no relative clause,
Instead, for instance, a longer adjective,
So 'a watcher who stands on board' becomes
'An-on-board-standing watcher' in Japan.
How our relatives are relativised!

– Observer Two, sees at the stern and bow
At once, while for One they are out of sync,
Stern before bow because the ship has moved.
All motion relative to the seer,
The constant that I trust, the speed of light.

Gender

Has gender now taken a carnal turn,
More to do with sex than *der*, *die* and *das*
Or the list of endings we had to learn,
Die See, *der See* mugged up before a class?
For most grammars it meant different things:

Animate or not, the shape of objects;
Indo-European in its beginnings
Must have slowly aligned its nouns with sex.
Those paradigms and gender never squared –
Neuter *Mädchen* a strange anomaly –
Far more than what divides us we'll have shared,
As I'm manning you, you're womaning me.
An inner likeness grows ripe and tender,
Our years flexing towards a common gender.

Subordination

Although for any kite there's wind enough,
Since I can feel a breeze against my cheeks,
As if you'd wafted a Japanese fan,
In order to recall that summer park,
Where father showed me how to fly a kite...

Dreams' unanchored subordinate clauses
Drift through the undergrowth of a psyche;
A complex sentence held in suspension
Like a lengthy learned German sentence,
Patiently waits to find its main clause.

Subordination? A strange word for us
That echoes from father's generation
Parsed and analysed prepositions
Which still govern the accusative case,
The supine or checking the agreement.

My father in the night commanding no.
And so the fancy-led years of freedom,
Moving with one current then the other;
Although for any kite there's wind enough,
Any stringless winged box scuds and plunges.

How many years to learn a discipline
To set 'althoughs' and 'as ifs' in order?
Like a main clause, desire subordinates
Each gentle pulling back to soar again.
My hand holds a kite tense against the wind.

First Person

Singular

The node of all our Western nodes,
Me, me and me of big egos,
Subject of most episodes.

In Japanese 'I' rarely shows –
No need to mention you or me –
From the context everyone knows.

In doubt, a pause for modesty,
Forefinger raised to tip the nose:
Watashi desu ka? Is it me?

Plural

'We' as nominative and 'us' the oblique.
As with 'I' and 'me' no known connection,
A Proto-Indo-European freak.

Insider *wareware*, we the group,
We the company, we the Japanese,
We, we only, dangerously cock-a-hoop.

Of course, Royal We. But some like Malay
Or Oceanic tongues contrast between
'We' as 'you-and-me' and 'I-and-they'.

Gauguin's cherried women in Tahiti
I imagine turning to a lover
Murmuring this sweetest pronoun 'you-and-me'.

Second Person

Singular

Whatever happened to *thee*, *thy* and *thou*
Who art in heaven, hallowed be thy name

Thy kingdom come, thy will be done on earth?
So intimately we speak to our God,

Like Walter Morel's Nottingham lingo
Look thee at it, tha niver wants ter shake.

'You' or 'yer' to priest, 'thou' or 'tha' for friends,
A plural for respect like *vous* or *Sie*,

Until in the end all are speaking proper
With only prayers or traces in England's north.

Plural

Once accusative and dative of 'ye',
'You', old plural of 'thou', a standard use
Blotting out all else, or so it may seem,

But bubbling underground another dream.
The school uproars of 1968
Brought back Europe's youth our *tu* and *Du*.

'Thou' and 'thee' a loss too late to undo,
Instead new plurals in the undergrowth:
America's 'y(ou) all', 'y(ou) ones', 'you guys'.

Given Irish *tú* and *sibh* no surprise
Common Ireland's plurals 'ye', 'yous' and 'yiz'
With 'yous' now striking roots in Liverpool.

A grammar shifts along its sliding rule
As fresh plurals grant a singular 'you'.
A craved intimacy, our need for *thou*.

Third Person

In every utterance a 'you' and 'me',
The third person somehow an afterthought,
Outside our orbit 'they' or 'she' and 'he'

Interlopers in any triangle.
Indo-European fails to tally
Er und Sie, han og hun or *il et elle*,

Cobbled from words for 'that' or 'this' or 'yon',
'This lassie' and 'that one' and 'yon fellow',
Now rooted deeply in our lexicon.

In Japanese for years 'that person there'
Until to translate Europe's novels' 'he',
Kare 'that one' and almost unaware

A language gains *kare* and *kanojo*
For 'he' and 'she' though they still summon up
Other undertones of 'girlfriend' or 'beau'.

Possessive timbres in this 'he' or 'she'
Desire to delight in just their saying.
A lover's name drops between you and me.

Relative Antecedent

A mouthful generations learned in class:
Nouns 'who', 'whose', 'which' or 'that' stand for,
Words so close they're each other's alias,
Two subjects of clauses in full rapport.
Bond both relative and unrelated,
Two parts that both blend and keep a selfhood –
Kinship both embedded and complicated –
Where water's every drop as thick as blood.
One who unknowingly I'd journeyed to,
One for whom it seems my being was meant,

716

One whose time and mine together unfold,
One that I speak of now, of course, is you,
My only relative antecedent,
One whom I promise still to love and hold.

UNDER THE SIGN

Le symbole donne à penser.

The symbol gives rise to thought.

PAUL RICŒUR, *La Symbolique du mal*

心 KOKORO

Heart

A reduced four-stroke pictogram,
Just some vague suggestions,
The subtlest hints or faint outlines,
Traces of ventricles;
A health logo or Valentine,
Metaphor for every
Shaded nuance of heart and mind,
'Spirit', 'thought', 'will' or 'care'.

Pacemaker. Pump-room.
Sign for what we bear in mind,
Things we take to heart.

No longer used alone to mean
The cardiac organ;
Umbrella word for heart and mind
That we've divided up:
Brainbox and sensibility,
Affections and psyche,
A hard-wiring and a software
All under the one sign.

A heart reminded
Heartening its lonely mind.
A mended oneness.

心配 SHINPAI

Worry

1

First left a minimalist stylisation
Of a heart, first organ in our embryo
Blood-pump and relay station.

And next to the left a jar of vino
At the right a figure on his knees
Maybe pouring it out to show

Dispersal. Together 'anxieties',
Shinpai 'worry', to undergo
A divided heart, a mind's unease.

2

Bird of my spirit gone into spin,
Round and round a rim of sanity.
Unnumbered hair. Fallen sparrow.

'Angst' and 'anguish' words for narrow.
The diffuse closes off in anxiety,
A widening out, a shrinking in.

So much caring too diluted, too thin.
This wine jar forever half-empty.
Scattered heart. Sapped marrow.

3

A figure bent and busy at the jar
Pumping adrenalin in a worry gland.
An endless night, closed and circular.

O sandman break the ring of doubt
As surrendering again to the unplanned
A concentration broadens out.

Whole-hearted. All-embracing.
Blake's single grain of sand.
Carefree loving of one thing.

意 ।

Thought

1

The upper portion makes up a sign for sound:
What was a needle shows a passing through
Over a mouth and tongue. The strokes hung

Below, a heart. Thoughts and likings wrung
Out of the core's pump and pulse to imbue
The lonely mind. Our caring's middle ground:

Neither *Rausch* nor Nietzsche's will unbound.
Heart and mind. Needle-sharp. Steel-true.
A heart full of sounds with a ready tongue.

2

Light of reason against the shades of doubt,
A steely dream of certainty we wanted to find.
The pulse was a flirt, the heart a gadabout,

Think and therefore be like René Descartes!
Four strokes out of sight and out of mind,
At bottom a forlorn sound was losing heart.

Top and underside stepping out of line,
Hinted wisdom of a symbol undermined,
Our centuries pass under a fractured sign.

3

Every either–or more our loss than gain.
Stumbling *homo sapiens* divider and tilter
At windmills, trying to draw a perfect line

Between things that willy-nilly still combine.
World of twoness too long out of kilter.
From the heart's safe-deposit a richer vein,

A murmur mouthed in a needle eye of brain,
Currency of give and take; our flow and filter
Safe and sound under one mended sign.

味 AJI

Taste

1

Side by side and here working as a pair:
A mouth and a tree topped with newly sprung
Branches for what's unfinished or left in the air.

Aji (or in compounds *mi*), a shoot twanging
Our taste buds, tang of grape that has clung
To the palate, twinge of pleasure left hanging.

Slack and slop of liquid easing a drouth
A gulp remembering its turn around a tongue,
Something good lingering here in the mouth.

2

Even taste has its roots in a verb 'to touch',
The wine-kissed lips, the tongue caressed,
Of all our five senses this is the apogee.

A foretaste already enjoyed in what we see
Before we relish an aroma along with the zest,
Delighting in the bouquet just as much.

Our savouring hardly just one sense as such
But combining four the most rooted and loftiest,
These taste buds surely at the top of the tree.

3

Our foretaste a tree still about to sprout,
Our aftertaste as much memory as learning,
The sense both recollects and branches out.

A meaning ramifies, growing now to imply
A certain feel for excellence, skill in discerning,
A nose for what's worthwhile, a weather eye.

In gastric juices, in a bud's tangy secretion
A taste for the unfinished business of yearning,
Our growing sense of growing incompletion.

意味　IMI

Meaning

1

So the signs for thought and taste together:
An idea chewed on long enough to find
The pith and gist that seem to linger whether

By choice or dint of whatever tang of hope
Or memory coalesce and shape inside the mind,
A kind of double-think that needs to grope

Behind and beyond a naked present tense
For meaning, first zest and savour combined,
Our double character trying to make sense.

2

Futures grasped too quickly, moves too rash,
All our histories of lust for a simpler sign.
It's brain and body and no overweening

Mind, rather a sense of lives spent gleaning
Mood to mood clues and tokens of design
Caught between the back and forward flash

In day by day of love's unwatched panache,
A career of frames become one storyline,
In flickers of our moments, hints of meaning.

3

Among the five why choose the sense of taste?
Why not the sign for sight or hearing instead
Or even our limbs' recall of loves embraced?

What of Proust's taunting scents that clung
To every bygone Eden? Too much head –
Let the flesh and juices kiss the tongue

Till appetite is both foretaste and residue;
In this sense desire becomes a memory fed,
Feedback of meaning in all we mean to do.

Master

1

This emblem's origin still easily recognised:
In the single slanted stroke above you see
The blaze of a wick wavering just a bit

Above an oil lamp carefully stemmed to sit
Plump upwards, gleaming its own authority,
A simple pictograph only a little stylised,

A Freudian symbol hardly even disguised.
Only the flame shivers in the draft of history
As on a master's orders the lamps are lit.

2

The owner alone decided when at nightfall
To order oil lamps trimmed and lit to shine
Glories of his house and home. A boss's call.

Eyebrows raised to an underling, as if to say
'I hold sway here and all you see is mine',
A gesture of power, an understated display.

And there it stands upright, downright oil lamp,
The leftward skew of its flame a nodding sign
Of power, its master's sanction, seal and stamp.

3

Lord or owner, employer and a whole train
Of meanings: spirit, husband, darling, you,
Prime, head, foremost, chief and main.

Now less a lantern and more like a candlestick
But for five millennia a symbol of overview;
Five brush strokes and one imagined wick,

An icon of mastery for a fourth of humankind
Drifts and gains a nuance or shifts its hue;
An image glows in the lamp-rooms of mind.

注意　CHŪI

Attention

1

Three water drops and the oil lamp that there
Stands for 'column' or 'upright', a long spout
That seems almost to form a shaft in mid-air

As it falls, to show a liquid's downward flow
And give the sense of something pouring out.
Then there's the ideogram for 'thought' to show.

A lavished mind! Two signs mark the need
Of a single-mindedness. No wobble or doubt.
This steady pouring over and taking heed.

2

How so rich a meaning begins to overflow!
'Attention' but as much 'to observe', 'to note' –
Our cooler need to record whatever we know.

Lovely leakage and seeping of each meaning
As nuance after nuance starts to drift and float:
'To care', 'to take an interest' and as if leaning

Over to tend we're watching and watch out for,
So 'to guard' or 'warn' that then may connote
'To caution' or 'advise'. A spillage of rapport.

3

Every shift of meaning yet a tighter bond,
A courtship in some kind of sliding metaphor
Of thoughtfulness splashing from a sign above

And pouring over what we're thinking of.
A logic of attention allows no either/or,
A sense of concentration streaming beyond

Itself as meanings tumble out to correspond.
How this taking care becomes our caring for;
Our daily tendings now tending towards love.

To Show

1

Once a pictograph of a roughly made
Altar with drops of blood on either side
(or splashes of sacred wine?), above laid

Out flat over the top some sacrifice.
And so a verb-ending. Some dove-eyed
Victim on a table or any object of price?

Signs of overflow. A shedding or spill.
Tributes paid trying to bridge the divide
As humans ask the gods to show their will.

2

A hieroglyphic so pared back and stern,
Hiding behind an image hidden away,
Stroke by stroke reveals for us its meaning.

Hints and omens of our gods intervening
To show their will. Drawings by their protégés
Down by the Yellow Riverside still yearn

For a sign on which all other showings turn.
Any action hangs on this divine display,
A holy show making sense of everything.

3

Dreams of five millennia curve and flow
To bend over an altar's unspoken word
Begging moment by moment gods to show

A sign of revelation, any token to appease
Our inborn yearning. O tired heart stirred
By a curtain's twitch or a voice in a warm breeze!

The hints we find or choose to make our own,
Sounds once listened for become what's heard;
The omen sought, the only omen shown.

啓示　KEIJI

Revelation

1

A door on its post, a hand on a cane
(Implying force) and beneath these
An opening as if to underscore

How someone was prepared to ignore
A rebuff and intrude. Then comes a Chinese
Reading for 'show' as *ji*. In vain

The visitor who knocked tries to gain
Entrance. Anything just to squeeze
Past the jamb. A foot in heaven's door.

2

Won't-take-no-for-an-answer guest,
This door-stepper skulking outside
Refuses to settle for second best,

Persists in medleys of praise and grouse
Whose trust in the host is always implied;
Awkward customer, bother-the-house

Who love-bombs or pesters if needs be,
With grit and neck of a psalmist who cried
How long wilt thou hide thy face from me?

3

To haunt a door-sill in heaven's name
As the loyal suitor always on call,
A votary waiting to stake a claim.

No quick come-on or *quid pro quo*.
No cupboard love. The long haul
Of a courtship's slow touch and go

As though even the host is lonely
Those moments before revealing all.
This need to be loved for love only.

聖　HIJIRI

Sage

1

The upper part a conventionalised ear
On the left side, an orifice on the right
(Formerly an open mouth) and here

To denote an attentive ear-hole. Below
A man is standing on the earth, upright
And alert (suggesting clarity) and so

This combination shows us a tableau
Of vigilance, an image used to write
'Sage', 'wise ruler', 'saint' or 'maestro'.

2

Chinese reading *sei* also means 'holy',
A trait seen in such figures long ago
Intent on hearkening to the still unsaid.

Their range of the attentive single-minded:
Sage, wise ruler, saint and maestro
With years of obedience, decades slowly

Tuning in, whole lifetimes spent solely
To pluck from the air a half-heard tremolo,
Upright and up to their ears in the sacred.

3

But what on earth can it be that's clear?
A hint, a whisper, a murmuring which
Will never allow them turn a deaf ear,

A sound more a shiver than any sound,
A tuning fork's discerning twitch,
Upright though with an ear to the ground?

Yet something is clearly to be heard.
The wise man stands there at fever pitch,
Still all ears for some unearthly word.

指導　SHIDŌ

Leading

1　HAND

From the Yellow River to Japan a learning how
Generations of brushstrokes could
Signal 'leadership' in two characters allied.

Shi 'a finger' or 'pointing': a hand alongside
A sign for 'tasty' or simply 'good'
Whose sound may well suggest 'branch' or 'bough'

With *dō*: above a symbol for 'the way' or *tao*,
Below 'a measure' and understood
As a sage or skilful hand to lead or guide.

2　HANDS-ON

Headway of a vessel in rhythm;
Let the sea roar and all that fills it,
Still to tune and trim

And believe a crew's feedback
That feeds forward, a kinship of feeling
When to harden or slack,

Trusting nothing can overwhelm,
Wonder of moving in phase and yet
A lone hand at the helm.

3　HANDOVER

To give it all and still the wisdom to know
How things nurtured steer from inside.
To praise and let go,

A stage well run, to call it then a day
And time a perfect handing over.
At the crux of a relay

One peaks as another hits his stride.
A baton slid from hand to hand.
Glory of standing aside.

經驗　KEIKEN

Experience

1

Beside a generic symbol for any thread
(Tangled skeins) and three warps on a loom
To get the idea of something passing through.

On the right another character with two
Parts: a steed sideways on with a plume
For a tail, a lid (consensus) on a double-head

Of two people talking. A horse inspected
To express 'examine'. Signs for *keiken* assume
We're observing as we go everything we do.

2

Kei a warp or also a line of longitude.
What is, what was, what's yet to come,
The traverse knit of our precious latitude.

Aware or half-aware our interwoven being
Patterns and hues of whatever we become.
A longwise tying down, a sideways freeing.

Lengths of thread spool out our existence.
Over and under of crossed thread and thrum
A daily texture, our weftage of experience.

3

Never seeing both sides of patterns we weave,
Our crossovers a passing through, going under
What's undergone and still not losing the thread.

Lookers in the gift horse's mouth have doubted.
Moment by moment the eternities we plunder,
Given moments rifled and watched as we leave.

Both a letting-go and being on the *qui vive*
As riding a moment's spur we heed the wonder;
An unplanned happening so carefully inspected.

Period

A winnower beside a moon
(Once a sun underneath),
A device to sift chaff by wind
As symbol of harvests
And a pitted oblong crescent.
'Period', 'time', 'date', 'term'
Measured in months and winnowings
To tab season and year.

Reapers marking time.
Husks wafting from the grain
Under August moons.

World of lunar rings and phases –
Not yet the glacial tick
Or the noiseless digital watch
Twitching arrows of time –
Still a dream moving in its seed,
Grain growing out of dark
As generations take their turn,
A blind date with the light.

Chaff riding the wind.
Rhythmic winnowing of time.
Our term's wax and wane.

情　JŌ

Feeling

A form of heart beside what was
A plant over a well
Now modified implies 'blue-green'
Or simply 'fresh' and 'young'.
This combination comes to mean
'Feeling', or just 'passion'.
Renewed springs and stirrings of sap.
A moist and pliant core.

Straight and true-hearted.
Blue-green of plants near water.
A shoot unfolding.

This word for feeling branches out
In lush outgrowths of sense:
'Warmheartedness' or 'affection',
'Sentiment', 'emotion'
And even comes to mean a 'fact',
A 'truth'. Clear-eyed. Hard-nosed.
Things touched. Things palpable and true.
What's tangible and real.

Both feeling and fact.
Fresh and green and tenable.
A heart's roots watered.

Word

1

Over what was once like a grin,
Now this squared-off mouth, four
Strokes piled up on top, a vapour

Of sounds that widen then taper
Off in a shortened stave before
Vanishing; earlier a sign for 'pin'

Or 'needle' to mean a honing in,
A tongue's tip both flap and door,
A breath-stopper and noise-shaper.

2

Mind and tongue's twin thrill
As taste buds wrap around
A vowel, muscling in until

Meaning and voice coincide,
Caressing the right word found.
Inner hum heard on the outside

As messenger and message unite.
Lips pursed for a kiss of sound.
Mouth pleasured. Utter delight.

3

For Greeks a living principle, a force,
A reading of our universe as much
As something said or a message sent.

Here nothing so ample was meant
Or any broader sense as such,
More an articulation than a source,

A noise decoded in due course,
A mouth-music played by touch,
Stave of sound waves in their ascent.

人 ｜ HITO

Human

Side-view of *homo sapiens*
Once bending with arms down
Now matchstick torso striking out,
Stark and upright earthling,
A figure striding, God knows where.
Springy twiglike upside-down Y.
A wishbone. A divining rod.
Hito. Human. *Ein Mensch.*

Naked and maskless.
Here neither female nor male.
A bare-boned biped.

And yet a self-reflecting mind.
At first two downward strokes
Inscribed on bone or tortoise shell,
A bare pictograph.
Bit by bit crisscross of symbols
Living lives of their own,
A pointing out and interplay,
A signal's doubleness.

Grounded sign-maker,
High-minded and down-to-earth.
Our human being.

信　SHIN

Trust

A human body sideways on
With arms and legs aligned;
Two-stroke Picasso matador,
One upright, one tilted,
Beside the character for speech,
A plain symbol for 'trust',
'truth', 'confidence', 'sincerity',
'reliance', 'devotion'.

Homo erectus,
A promiser and truster
Standing by a word.

And for all the Trojan horses,
Pledges kept or broken,
A stranger standing at the gate,
Our fragile city's guest
Barefaced and alone with a sign.
Trust's all or nothingness.
One forlorn figure and a word.
Spoken collateral.

So here then I stand
At least as good as my word.
You can count on me.

Gentle

1

A man walking and a head over a heart
Over an upturned foot that once meant
A dancer performing a slow ritual dance

Until skilfulness tipped a meaning's balance
To 'actor' or 'excellence' which in turn lent
The nuance 'gentle' – mastery's counterpart.

Yasashii: 'kindly', 'with a tender heart',
Its suffixed pot-hanger and ditto of hooks bent
Inward to spell this adjective's loving stance.

2

A friend at four score and ten –
Twenty over the Book's allotment –
Celebrates autumn over again.

Delighted with everything but of late
Paring back to the naked present
Where the head and heart and gait

Of such mastery now move with less
Motion, this gentle dancer intent
On zeroing in on a dance's stillness.

3

A richer twinkling each time we meet,
A dance of stars beyond our ken,
Still with us but glinting stillness.

Deep, deeper, deepest. Endless
Comparative degrees down in a Zen
Of self. *Yasashii* as you greet

Another birthday's bittersweet
When the sumac and maples redden
Gently as a word so full of *s*'s.

火 　HI

Fire

So much more a spark than a blaze,
A glitter of friction.
Earlier a triple-peaked crown
From a story-book king,
A sign on an oven button;
Three jagged tongues of flame
Usurping the blank air.

Suddenly a blitz
As out of rubbed nothingness
Steel and flint spit fire.

Tinderbox of paradox.
Coldest flint, hottest fire,
Riskiest of all elements,
A danger to play with.
Enough to warm not to consume;
A kept fire burns the most.
Still the impromptu blare of tongues,
Quick thrill of a flare-up.

The feared damp fire-stick.
Such flint-eyed moments scraped for.
A bidden spark flies.

Talk

Word and then those two signs for fire
On top of each other
For the most part to indicate
-*itis* 'inflammation',
But here to catch the flash-over,
A wordage set alight,
Instantaneous combustion,
Our talking like blazes.

Flamboyance of speech.
A spirited discussion.
Our words flaring up.

Dan – more often used in compounds:
Sōdan 'mutual talk',
'Consultation', tinder of words,
Sudden kindling of thought,
Poised somewhere in a back-and-forth
Of our inbetweenness.
A speaker and a receiver,
This two-way ignition.

Dialogue. Brainstorm.
Our sparking off each other.
Word-*itis*. Tongues of fire.

Spirit

Raindrops spilling out of the skies,
Below a shamaness
Working into her ecstasy
So the spirit descends:
A 'soul', a 'ghost' or 'memory',
Whatever's wafting above,
A drive, quiver of energy,
A departed essence.

The heavens opened;
An abandon summoning
Downpours of spirit.

Through a rapture or reverie
In soughs of memory
The shade of a forebear conjured
Out of heaven knows where,
A character showing spirit,
Engine, *élan vital*,
Kick-start, quickness, urge to exist,
The bird flying within.

Earthling, skyscraper
In this magical oneness.
Panache of being.

Spirit of a Language

Word-spirit, soul of a language,
Speech-psyche, goblin tongue,
Genius of a past still within,
Old marvels shaping us
In echo chambers of our ghosts,
Distant ventriloquists
Throwing across our centuries
Timbres of their own voice.

Ease and surety
Of our given living room.
Take-for-granted tongue.

All that's familiar and certain
But changing as we speak
Accumulating slippages,
Our half-unconscious shifts,
Patterns slowly rearranging
We mimic and absorb
Passing on such small accruals,
Our mark left unbeknownst.

Elfish go-between.
Spirit-rapping medium.
Brokered gift of tongues.

World

1

A cross means ten and here three
Share a transverse; at the foot of two
A right-angled bar just added on.

Those thirty years before a baton
Passes and creation begins anew:
'Age', 'era', 'world', 'society'.

A downward branch on a family tree.
A lap run. A closure and a début.
Another generation already gone.

2

Ten to soak in life unknowingly,
Ten to unravel all unknowing,
Ten in years you're still fancy-free

To own the globe. Out of the blue
A generation has come tiptoeing,
Stealing gently up behind you.

The way of the world. *Yo no narai.*
A coming that grows into a going.
Then three decades by and by.

3

And suddenly it's your sixtieth year.
A second stroke transverses three
More verticals. Our three score.

The right-angled tails like a semaphore,
Two bars that signal both the memory
Of so much you received and a sheer

Desire for a safe relay as we near
The crossing over. A smooth delivery.
A baton passed that passed before.

森 MORI

Wood

1

This sign can hardly be misunderstood:
Trunks, crosstrees, the weeping shoots,
Three trees to token a forest or wood.

Stare at the middle then let the mind
Wander whichever path best suits,
So it chooses one, leaves two behind.

A dozen strokes conjure the unease,
Confusion of such different routes.
Here we see the wood for the trees.

2

On the edge and a little out of control:
Woodsman, hermit, partisan, rapparee
Flitting moss-footed behind some bole.

Nothing is quite as everything seems.
A track peters out, a futile vagary,
A path trailing off into our dreams

Of routes we once might have gone.
This path or that? Frost's quandary,
Promises you promised to deliver on.

3

Along the shafts of likelihoods
Down corridors of sun we drift,
At every fork still discerning

One way from another, learning
To arrive by whatever makeshift
Path, once we deliver the goods.

Never, never out of the woods.
A wanderlust. Compulsive gift.
Funnel of light in every yearning.

Leaf

1

So intricate! Think with a stroke
Or two how easily you'd outline,
Say, the blade of maple or oak.

Instead to use tokens for 'growth',
'Era' and 'tree', so three combine
To muse on how a leaf is both

Generation and regeneration, a twin
Messenger, a sign and countersign
Of how things both fall and re-begin.

2

Vapour canals, a tissue of doors,
Thermostat, aperture, a steadfast
Network of veins, valve-like pores;

Some evergreen whatever transpires
Lasting as long as they need to last,
Or loose-leafed if their tree desires

As oaks, maples, sumacs or nervous
Aspens nailing their colours to the mast
While eras of leafage fall in service.

3

A leaf's blade with its *bl* sound
Waiting to blossom, to bloom, to blow.
Spans of foliage. Leafings and unleafings,

Unfolded ages of secreted briefings
On how to flourish. A gene flow
And code deciduously onward bound.

An age. A world. A cycle. A round.
An epoch of growth, another O
Curved in a bole's remembered springs.

言葉　KOTOBA

Language

Utterance alongside a leaf
For 'language', 'word' or 'speech'.
Verbal blades, foliage of nouns,
A young bole branching out,
Small subtleties that ramify,
Twigging shade and nuance,
A whole vocabulary of tree
Unfolding its leafage.

From words' roots and stems,
A spring climbing and budding
To breathe in its leaves.

A burgeoning and tapping in.
Mirror world of branches:
One above uttering sunward,
Leaves expressing themselves;
The other one earthward, delving
The darker nourishments,
Keeping the grip, holding its ground.
Opening up. Burrowing below.

Sap quiver in leaves
Fluttering the tips of their tongue.
A flourishing word.

花   HANA

Blossom

1

Firstly the cut-down version of two
Plants growing over a sign for change:
Twin Picasso figures, a side-view

Of someone standing up straight,
A second fallen; our human range
And span to say how flowers mutate.

Like a flower of the field. Upright.
Downfall. An image as lovely as strange.
A blossom revelling in its fragile light.

2

Year after year talk of *hanami*
'Blossom viewing'. No need to cite
Which tree as all over Japan

Friends are making contact to plan
To travel together. What week is right
To catch full bloom? Again to see

In clustered fists of a cherry tree
An aesthetic of all simple and quiet;
Petals flourishing their own lifespan.

3

In every such opening a fall begun,
No wonder within change the fright
Before unfurling towards the sun.

Of course it hurts when buds break
Unwombing what was safe and tight.
Everything gambled, all at stake.

Annual noiseless intensity of seeing
Fists of petals unclenching their light,
One shining out of spanless being.

花火　HANABI

Fireworks

Fire-flower. Beside this, Germanic
Fireworks seem so earnest!
Chrysanthemum and dahlia shells
Burgeoning in the air,
Roman candles shooting their stars,
The blooms of Bengal lights,
Catherine wheels that spin and flourish,
Yellow, orange, green, red.

A Chinese cook's fluke?
Black powder. Chemical fire.
Bamboos detonate.

Roger Bacon the Franciscan
At Oxford feared the mix:
Charcoal, sulphur with saltpetre.
Where would gunpowder lead?
His coded findings hide for years
The shrapnel power behind
Peonies and weeping willows,
The fused cherry bomb.

Shush and hiss explode
Blossoming in the night sky.
A flower takes fire.

Light

Variant of the sign for fire
Above a crouched human,
A bent figure bearing a torch,
Dark-breaker, light-bringer,
Yellow River luminary;
A signal beaconing
Someone's unbushelled light across
These five millennia.

A torch stroke by stroke
Scratched on an animal bone,
A signed tortoise shell.

Light that both reveals and blinds:
Too near, too dazzling,
Lucifer, lured by his brilliance,
Would fall so far from grace.
And yet this token still relayed,
Flambeau from hand to hand;
Light seen only by its own light,
Enough to show a way.

Stooped Olympian
Torch-bearer passing a flame,
A sign travels on.

God

Left a variant of altar
And right what was lightning,
A zigzag flash, a warning sign
Of high voltage, unseen
Voice waggling from a telephone
Across a strip cartoon
But now brought into line can mean
'To state' or 'expound'.

Untamable jag.
In a bolt of forked lightning
A voice from beyond.

Thundercloud's charged separation,
A sudden two-phased flash:
First glittering from cloud to earth,
Second stroke ground to cloud.
Heaven downwards and earth upwards,
Our jagged interplay;
In skies' jerky hieroglyphics
Signs of two-way traffic.

Altars conducting
Their skyline of least resistance.
A lightning grounded.

福 FUKU

Luck

An altar appealing to gods
With a brimful wine jar
To bring down all gifts of well-being,
A drinking vessel blessed
By deities, mediation
Of 'good fortune' or 'luck',
A whole spectrum of 'happiness',
'Thriving', 'prosperity'.

Ancient wine-hued prayer:
That our cup will flow over.
Demons out, luck in!

History of humanity,
Leaking vessels we bring
To lay in hope on an altar,
Crying out for blessings.
Hallowed table and a full pot,
Pictogram and foretaste
Of a wedding feast at Cana
Three thousand years away.

Miraculous sign.
Our stone jars filled to their lips.
A divine vintage.

Collection

Earlier three birds on a tree
But now only the one.
Imagine swoops of homing rooks
As evening tumbles in
Cawing and wheeling to gather
In skeleton branches
With nodes of old nests blackening
Into the roosting night.

Treetop colony.
A rookery congregates.
Dusky assemblage.

Whatever instinct makes us hoard,
A desire to amass,
Toys, dolls, marbles, birds'-nests and eggs
We fondle and brood on
Or how we'd swoop like rooks to nab
Spiky windfalls, stamping
Open their milky husks to touch,
Smooth marvels of chestnut.

The collector's dream
To feel, to caress, to keep.
A bird in the hand.

Medium

Straight downward through a rectangle
A swift bisecting bar,
A stroke that likely started out
An arrow that pierces
Its target's 'medium', 'mid-point', 'midst'.
Definite line between
Refocusing our edge-lured minds.
Golden mean. Middle way.

Shot and follow-through.
A true shaft and singing arc.
Spot on. A bull's-eye.

The sign too for Middle Kingdom.
A centered self-belief:
All else east or west of China.
Assured parishioners.
Poet Kavanagh would have approved
How any dynasty
Knew the axis of everything
Drew a line through their world.

The place where it's at.
Middle of everywhere.
Arrow's *you are here*.

Concentration

Collection at a middle point.
Mindful concentration
As our flights of fancy converge,
Vagaries homing in,
Ruffled feathers of distraction,
Flocks of unruly birds
Beating their wings around the bush
Now gather into one....

A rallied psyche
Nestles down. Zeroing in.
Density of thought.

Statio Benedict once named
The pause between two tasks;
A habit to break a habit,
An action brought to mind,
The moment we collect ourselves
In from the blurred edges.
Patience of filter and focus.
Screening out. Zooming in.

Bird perched and ready.
Concentred and gathered.
Our utmost presence.

ADAGE

Proverbs are the product of daily experience.

Partings

Partire è un po' mourire
To part is to die a little

Even much younger I think I was aware
How in each departure a life has bled,
Another byte deleted in being's software,
A soul-leak, something of our essence shed.
No *forestalling dark with dark*, my friend,
As Herbert knew, love is love's true price
And each separation a trailer for an end,
Our meetings all foretastes of paradise.
Joke me again. I want to remember laughter
Yet each leave-taking now harder than before
As with the years stardust bones grow brittle;
Whatever heaven friendships hanker after
Every parting drains the marrowbone.
Every time we say goodbye, I die a little.

Mødes og skilles er livets gang, skilles og mødes er livets sang
That we meet and part is life's way, that we part and meet life's song

All those encounters down through the years:
Chance meetings, ships passing in the night
Or once sweet sorrowed partings of Shakespeare's
Romeo, old flames long dropped out of sight.
Meetings and partings just the way things are,
No one could keep so many friendships in play,
Still some glimmer of desire in any *au revoir*
Never quite lets go that maybe some day...

Parting and meeting, a hope reversal implies:
Arrivederci! auf Wiedersehen! so long!
Even in our world that changes and drifts
This two-way saying that both accepts and lifts
With bittersweet undertones of a Danish folksong
The doubleness we hide in all goodbyes.

相 見 歡 笑 離 別 憂
Xiāng jiàn huān xiào, lí bié yōu
When meeting happy laughter, when parting grief

The deeper the delight at every re-meeting,
The deeper the transience running parallel;
Our leaving proportionate to our greeting,
Heywood's maxim *such welcome, such farewell.*
Hours of catching up, the days of fun
Relearning each other's common place,
Fluttered tongue of things done and undone,
Our kitchen conversation face to face.
And all those things we say we'll have to do,
Half-knowing how slyly time tiptoes
Already gone while we were only starting
But also more aware in every adieu
How in the light of endings friendship grows.
Laughter echoes even in the grief of parting.

Ge cruaidh sgarachdainn, cha robh dithis gun dealachadh
Though separation be hard, never did two meet but had to part

Severe reminder, a grave rhythm and tone,
In this Scottish proverb no hint of maybe,
More a warning that cuts so near the bone
Saying not just any two but you and me.
A meeting's joy forecasts an equal grief,
Yet Chinese and Italian allow us tomorrow,
In this stark sentence there's no reversal.
You not there for me nor me for you?
Even just at the thought a broken man.
Better that we don't know when or how.
Though separation be hard never did two...
I try to imagine what I know I never can,
Then turn again to now and now and now.

Cheek

Teaching a fish to swim

We who came out of the sea,
We who so soon forget the womb
Hard put to relearn a buoyancy,
That fish out of water should presume
To do the business of those in the swim.
Cheek. The nerve. Such audacity!

Eggið kennir hænunni að verpa
The egg teaches the hen to lay eggs

Hen then egg or the order reversed,
For the old and wiser no backchat,
In Northern Europe hens came first.
A put-down for any young brat.
No doubts. Best seen and not heard.
A snub a proverb has long rehearsed.

Les oisons veulent mener les ois paître
The goslings want to drive the geese to pasture

The kind of cheek no goose should allow
After those weeks of broody caring,
But do geese play along as if somehow
They know youth is always overdaring?
No gosling would dare choose where to graze,
If goslings knew what geese know now.

Teach your grandmother to suck eggs

Did those grandmothers go robbing nests?
Why were they sucking them in any case?
Some secret skill these women possessed
To keep two generations in their place.
Whatever it was, don't teach your betters;
Whatever it was, grandmothers knew best.

Ag múnadh paidreacha don tsagart is iad ar fad aige féin
Teaching prayers to the priest when he knows them all

Wings clipped if anyone dares
Advise those already in the know,
Echo of sharp-tongued forebears,
A double-edged counterblow,
A metaphor half tongue-in-cheek:
As if you'd teach a priest his prayers!

釈迦に説法
Shaka ni seppō
Preaching to Buddha

Further east the meaning gene.
For Japanese losing the run
You preach to Buddha and intervene
Where best left to the serene one,
The Sage of Shakya. A young greenhorn
Upstaging the enlightened go-between.

不要 班門 弄斧
Bù yào Bán mén nòng fǔ
Don't fool around Ban's gate with an axe

A bungler with axe creating a mess,
Some apprentice hopeless effrontery
Determined willy-nilly to impress
Ban Jiang the god of carpentry.
The high sign. A word to the wise.
Wink tipped in transcendent playfulness.

755

Moving On

It's no use crying over spilt milk

Over the world this Sophocles cry
As spilt fluid seeps into clay;
Leaking vessels, a kicked bucket,
Lost milk of our human regret,
Liquid that never returns to its tray.

Ce qui est fait est fait
What's done is done

You can almost hear a Joblike sigh.
French or German or Scandinavian:
The happened can't be made unhappen.
Plain matter of fact. No metaphor.
A mistake it's better to ignore.

Aqua pasada no mueve molino
Water gone by doesn't move a mill

In Spain water, in Holland wind,
What's downstream drives no wheel,
Scruples never moved a sail
To turn the mill and grind to meal,
Flow and whim of all we bewail.

Níl maith sa seanchas nuair atá an anachain déanta
Talk is no good when the harm is done

Sure if only I'd known in time...
All our *ifs* and *ands* but still
Hedging a field already ruined,
Hindsighted babble of goodwill
Binding up another's wound.

Rhy hwyr codi pais ar ôl piso
Too late to lift a petticoat after pissing

Under our tears an earthy humour.
A self-deprecating Welsh laughter
Or Japan's 'tightening buttocks after
Breaking wind'. O smile, Rabelais!
All our thoughts still housed in clay.

Слезами горю не поможешь
Tears don't help trouble

Treeless steppes too harsh for weeping
And an old Cossack within who fears
How clogged self-pity nurtures sloth.
No sobbing. Yet the salt of tears.
Cries and waterings of inner growth.

落花枝に帰らず、破鏡再び照らさず
Rakka eda ni kaerazu, hakyō hutatabi terasazu
Fallen blossoms don't return to branches, a broken mirror doesn't reflect again

A Japanese child mourns blossoms.
A glass once whole, a leafy bough.
Margaret knows what Hopkins meant
When fallen years of mirror fragment.
Memory is then. Life is now.

Aldrei skal gráta gengna stund
Never cry for time gone

Saga of a stable's bolted horse,
Spilt milk and fallen leaves,
Broken mirror and the wind gone.
We cry for what nothing retrieves.
In our weeping we move on.

Unsaid

Toute vérité n'est pas bonne à dire
Not every truth is the right thing to say

Something French and human here:
Thought first filtered through the head,
Gossip others shouldn't know
Things we'd better leave unsaid.
Poised, forgiving, shrewd, urbane,
Why a fuss when there's no gain?
Rise above it unconcerned,
Best not known, a blind eye turned –
Almost careless *bonne à dire*.

Truth is truth. The truth alone.
Fraud unveiled, the trails we'd blaze,
World we'd change, a world our own,
Endless talking student days,
Hard-nosed, certain, fact's a fact,
Age has ripened years of tact.
Subtler now than our first flush,
Sometimes speak and sometimes hush.
Truth is also time and tone.

Friendship's silent idiom
Prudent as a diplomat
Knowing when the word's mum.
Much unsaid but hinted at,
Half in earnest, half jocose
Understood between the close,
All you know you'll never say,
Secrets brought alone to clay,
Songs best sung by singing dumb.

Sanningen är bland det finaste vi har, den skal vi passa på att inte bruka i otid
Truth is one of the finest things we have, we need to watch out not to use it at the
wrong time

A slow rambling Swedish byword.
Someone in low October light
Repeats old prudence.

Who had blurted a confidence
Or some fact when the time was wrong
So all was misheard?

Precept of tact and etiquette:
Proverb's singsong drawl
Finest, nevertheless,

Truth's still truth if told with finesse,
Knowing what's both best to recall
And best to forget.

言わぬは言うにまさる

Iwanu wa iu ni masaru
Non-saying outdoes saying

Come day, go day, ebb and flow,
Just that gaze and still we know

Deep within our unsaid zone
What's unuttered each has known,

One caressing look can glean
All the years of might-have-been

Time now noiselessly atones.
Still as Kyōto's garden stones

Passion's silent interplay,
Eyes that speak what tongues can't say.

Accommodation

柳に風
Yanagi ni kaze
In a willow, wind

Young and full of hungry sap
No one could really understand
Why that pussy willowing,
Weeping while it's billowing,
Flexing as the winds expand
Limbs that dance and overlap,
Boughs that sway but never snap,
Bend, caress and yet withstand.

Better then to bow than break.
Shaking trees are last to fall.
Words that once seemed so fake,
'Bend' like 'bow' had meant to crawl;
Words for fogeys, words for clones,
Old too young and no backbones,
Wily, streetwise, on the make.

Many things we'd thought we'd do.
Time for youth and time to rage,
Time to learn to court a breeze,
Bending with her lure and tease
Root and settle stage by stage.
Wisdom comes when wisdom's due.
Cake that's kept and eaten too,
Reckless youth and rueless age.

Drifting leaves flirt and sough,
Swirl the wind on steady roots,
Shaping futures in each bough,
Cricket bats and sallow flutes,
Cradle boards to crib a daughter.
Dipping low to kiss the water,
Knowing geishas take their bow.

Vannet vet mer enn oss, det finner alltid letteste vei
Water knows more than us, it always finds the easiest way

Can you hear Grieg's *Spring* beginning to spill?
Crusted snow
Or ice floe
Tinkle by tinkle gathering its thaw
Into a rill
That feeds a rush and swirl of water.

Anywhere there's water, there's a way
To go
With a flow
Carving and smoothing its riverbed,
Cantabile,
Oozing around molehills and mountains.

Liquid grace, serial U-turner,
Arpeggio
Of H_2O
That leaps and swerves or changes course,
Curved learner
Shaping and shaped in how it is.

Better to bend the neck than to bruise the forehead

A bowing willow
Or rush and seep of water
But near the bone
Thumps on the front of the skull
Rattling stars in the brainbox.

A medieval house
With a lower stone lintel,
A tall youngster fails
To stoop. A dazed cranium.
A bruise on the memory.

Unbending young man
Banging his head against walls,
Stiff-necked ne'er-do-well
Upsetting portal-keepers
Watching thresholds they can't pass.

If only you'd known.
No need to be a doormat,
Bow and straighten up.
Always a new-brooming youth!
Is this an older man's song?

Confusion

Too many cooks spoil the broth

Who are these cooks? What are they up to?
These broth-makers who keep showing up
And spoiling the kitchens with their brew.

One says a soupçon, another says a cup –
No Indians, everyone the chef in chief –
A third is now pouring one extra sup.

More seasoning. Just another bayleaf.
Were they mischievous then or genuine?
Scandinavia and Italy the same motif.

A spicy tale from Greek or Latin
On through Germany to Budapest?
A boy I imagined salt ladled in

Heap after heap and a droughty guest,
Then how in its telling the gossip grew,
A proverb travelling north and west.

船頭多くして、舟山に登る

Sendō ōku shite, fune yama ni noboru
Skippers increase and the boat climbs a mountain

For French two bosses,
Many steer in Welsh,
In Greek surplus advisers.

Too many skippers,
A boat noses down
To Davy Jones's locker.

But not in Japan.
Here in the scramble
Sailors trip each other up,

Command, countermand,
Topsyturvy world,
Torn masts and a bow ascends

Surreal Mount Fuji;
Nightmare of seascape
Where the boat climbs a mountain.

У семи́ ня́нек дитя́ без гла́зу

U semi nyanek ditya bez glazu
With seven nurses, a child without an eye

East in Europe too many midwives
Spoiling all those deliveries,
But by the time the saying arrives
In Russia it's nurses or nannies

Busy fussing over this and that,
Cross-purposed madams who fly
At each other or absorbed in chat
Fail to keep their weather eye

On an infant now half out of sight
And minds preoccupied with scandal,
The juice and gossip of last night,
Leaving each other a chance to dandle

A child but never quite sure why
It crawled so near a dangerous drop.
Seven nurses. No watchful eye.
Who knows where the buck must stop?

Viele Hirten, übel gehütet
Many shepherds, ill-protected

Right across the ancient Near East
Gods or kings as wise or humble shepherd,
Tender of frail and wayward,
Staff and crook
And priest.
A sadder dictum than sailor, nanny or cook.

Seasoned bonds of nomad sheep and keeper,
The injured carried, the thief warded off,
Daily gathering at the trough
Or watering hole,
The deeper
Their rapport, the steeper now a sudden fall.

What happened once on a German hillside?
Too many shepherds confused or too blasé
To fetch a blundering stray?
A flock nonplussed,
As wall-eyed
Sheep plunge abysses of broken trust.

Obra de común, obra de ningún
A work in common, no one's work

Such strange geographies,
Networks of adage,
Nurse, shepherd, cook or sailor.

But was this once tried?
Line by line by line
Quixotic subcommittee

In monthly meetings
Squabbling out a book,
Sancho Panza consensus

Reducing those giants
To windmills, their arms
Wind-sails to turn the millstones

Grinding to a halt
Our common yearning
Solo dreamers represent.

Hummingbird of love.
Lone can-carrier.
Sí, aquí. The buck stops here.

Praise

> *Mol an óige agus tiocfaidh sí*
> Praise youth and it will prosper

A youngster's smile climbed from the root
Of his being, a blossom so suddenly sprung,
Out of such clay one burgeoning offshoot.

I'd forgotten a friend's father's razor tongue
And how in turn he couldn't praise his son.
A memory stinging again as it was stung.

Everything in him wanted to say 'Well done!
Good on you, my boy! That was flawless!'
No fault to find but why was there always one

To hamper delight he so wanted to express?
For the one stunted tree, an unseen wood.
Too long a longing for his own father's caress.

A friend's son I'd praised in all likelihood
By chance, a small thing I happened to salute
But my words sank deeper than I'd understood.

Down silent wells of generations a chute
Of praise moistened years of childhoods unsung;
A shaft of sap pushing upwards to the fruit.

Sannarlegt lof er ekki um of
Real praise isn't about excess

Nothing on islands of glaciers and volcanoes
Allows for flattery or soft-soaped excess.

No school of blurb and puff or false kudos,
Feelgood factor, success to easy success.

Over the windswept lava a sober tending,
A weighing up. And even so the overflow.

Geysers of warmth, Hekla's cup sending
Again from middle-earth a molten glow,

A crimson boost of praise somehow starker
Against bleak landscapes, as the sudden delight

Of an old teacher brandishing a new marker
To underline in red everything that's right.

Old praise dies unlesse you feede it.

An outlandish proverb Herbert knew,
Long fallen by the wayside;
Instead a hawk-eyed
'Giving credit where credit is due'.

Tame worthiness. No splurge of belief
In an overflowing cup.
A root dries up.
A withered branch, a fallen leaf.

Flare and blaze. The first whirl-about
Of Solomon's poured song,
But unoiled too long
A bridegroom's lamp sputters out.

Teachers in whose inner light we'd grown,
A daily laid hand,
All flaws in sand,
Our wonders etched in red stone.

A mentor's feeding words, a lover's gaze,
Water's lavish spill;
And are we still
Each other's *secretarie of praise*?

Waitings

Þeir få byr sem bíða
Those who wait get a fair wind

A drift of sailors leagues south of Reykjavík
Becalmed and calmly choosing to sit it out
Or maybe even caught in freak
Storms that darken from the north,
Tightening up to go about.

Endless hours of beating, switched tack.
Somehow from these words trust inferred
That out of the blue winds back,
Sails bellying on a beam reach,
Again their bow nosing home.

Whoever makes time has eons up a sleeve.
And so both to abandon and anticipate
In gaining little to achieve
A handing over, a self-surrender.
Is there all the time in the world to wait?

果報は寝て待て
Kahō wa nete mate
Sleep and wait for good fortune

Go and sleep on it!
Do I hear a monk's
Voice in a Kyōto temple

Or a local lord
A shōgun baron
Counselling his samurai

To puzzle deeply,
Or try to work out
Everything as best he can

And then to let go?
With time and patience
A mulberry bush becomes

A silk kimono.
Unravel in sleep
All sleep ravels up again.

Tout vient à point à qui sait attendre
All things come as needed to those who know how to wait

So much doing in our waiting.
Milton serving his light denied,

A Zen master contemplating
Worlds of action turning inside.

The lover who begins as doer
Declaring his hand never knows,

A passive, time-biding wooer
Becalmed until the spirit blows.

The muse resisting any rush,
A scribbler readying at her call,

Around and round a mulberry bush
Tending till the tongues may fall.

Shortfall

Einmal ist keinmal
Once is not at all

For beginners a heartening motto:
Einmal ist keinmal, once won't hurt,
At least give everything one go.

That girl in Hamburg afraid to fall
And her father lifting her into the saddle,
'Come on, once isn't once at all'.

Trusting in motion and a bike's panache,
She shrieks and thrills but losing nerve
Fräulein's wobbles a sideways crash.

And now a soothing tantamount
To saying 'a first try is written off',
Einmal ist keinmal, once doesn't count.

A proverb to brace the faint of heart
And bolster shortfalls in advance;
Our failures forgiven before we start.

Tann sum tíðum rør út, hann fiskar umsíðir
The one who often rows out catches fish in the end

Backbone. Long-haul grit.
Fishermen oaring
Bravely out from the Faroes

And day after day
Facing a knife-edge,
The cliffhangers of failure,

Chance of tides and shoals,
Skill, hunch and hearsay,
Rowing unforgiving seas.

Again and again,
Belief in frequence,
The gleam of tomorrow's catch.

七転び八起き
Nana korobi ya oki
Seven stumbles, eight getting ups

A child learning to ride
Or maybe a sumō apprentice falling
By the ringside?

Again the trawl and line
Laid to trap a moment's wonder,
A trace, a sign,

A perfect mix of thought
And feeling, something wrestled with
And surely caught.

Just as I've written *stet*
The proof of a moment has fled,
Slipped the net.

Tomorrow is keeping faith.
Seven seas. Seven veils. Seven falls.
But, then, the eighth!

Falling

Gutta cavat lapidem non vi sed saepe cadendo
The drop hollows the stone not by force but by often falling

Ovid's droplet on a stone,
A signet ring grown thin,
A plough worn down by soft clay.

The trickle most widely known,
For some a motto to underpin
Where there is a will there is a way.

Persistence. For me an undertone
Of danger. My mother in the kitchen
Warning as we went out to play

'Constant dripping wears a stone'.
Any bad company that we were in
Would whittle and whittle us away.

A ring worn near to the bone,
Ovid's epistle under the skin.
I hear you mother and I obey.

Liten tue velter stort lass
A clump of earth overturns a large load

Ovid took his drip-worn stone from Greek
But here a cart is rattling along fjords

On narrow rutted lanes or winding towards
A forest clearing watching for any freak

Clump or tuft that might upend its freight.
Again the championing of what's small

Or riding a boastful flaw before his fall,
Proud Agamemnon in a low northern light.

朱に交われば赤くなる
Shu ni majiwareba, akaku naru
If you mix with vermilion, you become red

No beat about bush
Or softening clay,
This Japanese straight talking

Allowed in proverbs,
An admonishment
Mother would have understood.

It might be the poured
Voice of Sirach's son
'He that toucheth pitch...'

Who lies down with dogs
Will rise up with fleas.
Earthy images that warn.

But caught red-handed?
Vermilion smeared.
Indelible crimson stain.

Upstream

Hvað ungur nemur, gamall temur
Young should learn if old should know how

Green time of learning
When young we acquired
Knowledge for our doyen days.

Pliant years a mind
Mimicked and sifted
Skills it stowed unconsciously,

But also a sense
How ease and know-how
Travel those generations,

Young to old to young,
Mastered, handed on
Saga of a thousand years,

Current of learning,
Craft riding the flow
Young should learn if old should know.

學如逆水行舟，不進則退

Xué rú nì shuǐ xíng zhōu, bù jìn zé tuì
Learning is like rowing upstream, not to advance is to fall back

Is to live to learn,
Thrill-seeking headway,
Our bending, our stretch, our gain?

Rowing the Yangtse
Someone knew the kick
In the tempo of a stroke,

Surge of hard-won ground,
A fraction of all
We know we can never know

Earned against the flow.
There's no rowing back,
Any resting on our oars.

Catch and pull and drive,
Rhythms of learning.
A blade glints in the water.

Caiff dyn dysg o'i grud i'w fedd
A human learns from cradle to grave

Span of our passage
From eye openings,
And gurglings in the crib's boat.

Two forgotten years
Of absorption – more
Than the whole rest of a life.

A long learning curve
Flattens and stretches
Over ripening decades.

Slow, sweeter strivings,
Aha! of the new
Looming beyond another bend.

Old dog and new tricks;
Livelong making ready,
Striving upstream to the source.

Poise

上手の手から水が漏る
Jōsu no te kara mizu ga moru
Out of skilful hands water leaks

Tight-butted palms with fingers crooked
To scoop water up;
Between the cup and the lip,
A tale of seepage.

So everything attained seems fluked,
Hurried sip and sup,
A cribbed lucky dip,
Digital slippage.

Let off by proverb. Unhooked.
Pardon our clay cup
Its cracks and gaps that drip.
Human leakage.

D'er inkje tre så reint, det ei har ein kvist
There's no wood so perfect it doesn't have a knot

Our time seemed a time of perfect wood,
History's final advance.
I was green in judgment, cold in blood.

God be with the callow days of youth,
Salad days of arrogance,
Sapling dreams of simpler knotless truth.

Year by year loppings of unripe pride.
Pruned back to tolerance,
Trees still earning axioms from inside.

An unforgiven self is a kind of paralysis,
A closing down on chance,
We relearn 'a good marksman can miss'.

For the naïve all but themselves were naïve.
Sap fresh in ascendance,
Has every young man a fool in his sleeve?

Ní bhionn saoi gan locht
No sage is flawless

So many ways to say this:
Monkeys too fall from trees,
Horses with four legs can tumble
And an old woman may blunder.

A smiled compassion. Horace's
'Even Homer nods'. The ease
With which we forgive a stumble.
We're not our mistakes and under

Any guise, leak or marksman's miss,
Message the same in all of these:
At once human, wise and humble,
The poise and not the flaw our wonder.

Once-off

光陰、矢のごとし
Kōin, ya no gotoshi
Light-shadow, like an arrow

A bowstring's taut
Kick and sudden let-go
Pent-up energy
To flee and flee,
Our one-way arrow.

Flight of time caught
In a Japanese compound noun:
Light and shadow,
Chiaroscuro
Of sun-up, sundown.

Sola kjem att men same dagen kjem ikkje
The sun comes back but the same day doesn't.

Think of January in Norway.
Infinities of snow,
A watched pot slow
Thaw of dark towards spring.

Then, imagine a July day
And half-bright night,
As summer's sleight
Of hand draws in its evening.

Fireball of come day go day
Even in its backslide
Seems steady beside
The human arc, an arrow's whizz.

The sun shines. Make hay.
A once-off glow
In light or shadow.
Take time as time is.

Time and tide wait for no man

Someone hurries across the strand
To launch before the high and dry.
The moon's taut bow can't wait.

Mother falters on Douglas beach.
Maybe the afternoon. Late, too late,
The crest has fallen, the sun gone.

Time and tide merge into one
As they recede. So easy to hesitate.
Hair's-breadth moment to wade in.

The waves ebb and underlap.
To stand outside grieving fate
Or plunge into the swim of things?

Time is water and water runs.
Light or shadow. Still to celebrate.
To embrace the flux. To ride the swell.

Mindful

La reconnaissance est la mémoire du cœur
Gratitude is the memory of the heart

A warning menu of forgotten bread
And man's ingratitude. A dearth
Of trust. But this French saying?

Stone-eared and dumb from birth,
A boy at Semens refused
Schooling learns from an Abbé in Paris.

'What is gratitude?' his teacher mused
And deaf-mute Massieu wrote
'Gratitude is *la mémoire du coeur.*'

A soundless byte spreads as a quote,
Blurs into proverb.
An answer stowed in human memory.

饮水思源
Yĭn shuĭ sī yuán
If you drink from the stream, remember the spring

Hunkering low on a bank
To cup handfuls of water,
Where to begin to thank?

Yellow River of a gene
Received, down-draft
Of words passed between

Generations, slow nurture
Of groves holding earth,
Allowing a scoop and curvature,

A brook's scrape and groove,
Communities that nourished,
Gradual shapings of love.

Sudden opened floodgate.
Unstoppable onrush of thanks.
The heart-memory in spate.

This stream takes up everything.
One sweet water.
Drink from a remembered spring.

Calling

Ní féidir leis an ngobadán an dá thrá a fhreastal
A sandpiper cannot tend two shores

Yes, of course, Kierkegaard was right:
Purity of heart is to love one thing.

For twenty helter-skelter years a niggling
Of too little done before the gentle night.

Brown-backed white-bellied wader
Teetering hurriedly between two shores.

Too tired after those day-job chores;
A muse's overwhelmed serenader.

Then the gift and scope of another score
To wade wherever a tidal rip demands.

A bobbing, nodding head in the sands.
A sandpiper busy on a single shore.

If you run after two hares, you will catch neither

My father's whispering I recall
Pity too damned intense, too hyper,
Hunting every hare he can.

On our island once the sandpiper.
But across a landmass to Japan
Deux lièvres, zwei Hasen, Nito.

Lesson one for any huntsman.
Only a fool would ever go
Running after two hares at once.

This easy smiling *bon mot*
Of knowing fathers warning sons
How quickly hares go to ground.

Dream-chaser, I stick to my guns,
Run with hare, hunt with hound.
O no, *mon père,* I'll catch them all.

En kan ikke ri to hester samtidig
One cannot ride two horses at once

To travel overland to Trondheim
Or bring good news
From Ghent one horse at a time.

But yes that red-bloused circus rider
Astride two horses
Reining the gap when it split wider

Over the haltered here and there
Applause endorses
Between the saddle and the giddy air

And fallen for the wonder of a ring
I couldn't choose
Either the moment or its beckoning

When rein and rhythm correspond
In sway and rhyme.
Sweet here. Sweet beyond.

Ease

能ある鷹は爪を隠す
Nō aru taka wa tsume o kakusu
A gifted hawk hides its talons

An air of cunning? A cute hawk
Tucking away its claws
To stalk
Some unsuspecting prey?

But in Japan this is how to say
Gifted have no need
To display
Their wares or flaunt a skill.

Shakespeare's *power to hurt and will*
Do none. The sharpest talons
And still
Hawks lie down with doves.

An dias is troime,'sí is ísle ceann
The heaviest ear of corn bows lowest

I imagine Dvořák's Bohemian tune
Swaying its *largo* in ears of corn
And over horizons of longing,
A New World
Slowly unfurled
Through miles of ripening meadow.

A melody both childlike and endless
Swells in the ears. Yearning beyond
Yearning. A hawk rides
The breeze.
Infinite ease
Of knowing how little I know.

Sunlight hoarded in nodding corn.
Humble hearts, humble desires.
A confidence rich and weighty

Defeatable
By means of the beatable.
Surety of bending low.

Shades

> *Ar scáth a chéile a mhaireas na daoine*
> People live in each other's shade

Here figures walking
Ahead in downpours
Sheltering others behind.

Our way of saying
Two footsteps no path,
One tree can't make a forest.

German *Heute mir,*
Morgen dir reminds
Me today, you tomorrow.

My shade, your shadow.
Zulu's down-to-earth
'One hand washes another

'And both will be clean'
Rubbing together
A mutual becoming.

> 前人種樹，後人乘涼
> *Qián rén zhòng shù, hòu rén chéng liáng*
> One generation plants, another gets the shade

We live in each other's shade
And walk a middle land
Between what was and will be.

Millennia of China expand
A proverb's reach. Shadow relayed
Age to age. A care's extensity.

The signs for before and after,
People, seed, tree and shade;
Limbs stretching out of our past.

A debt prepaid and post-paid.
Plan-receiver, plan-draughter.
A shade taken, a shadow cast.

Abandon

> *Den tid, den sorg*
> That time, that sorrow.

So much caution before you've begun
Insisting you look before you leap,

Reminding you to walk before you run,
How the one you love makes you weep.

But this loophole a let-off and let-go,
A sort of polar grandfather clause.

A spring to sow, a summer to reap
As dragonflies stretch wings of gauze.

High jinks under a midnight sun.
No darkness now and no tomorrow.

Of all our moments this the one.
Hell, high water. That time, that sorrow.

Kümmere dich nicht um ungelegte Eier
Do not worry about eggs not yet laid

Frettings over a morning's eggs?
Further south temperate
Troubles, a tamer climate
Fevers of midnight sun outstrip.

Such a sober letting rip,
Long-headed ecstasy,
Careful strategy
Of crossing only bridges we meet.

Let the morn come with its meat.
An abandon only halfway
Sufficient unto the day;
Tomorrow lurks in the heat of now.

明日は、明日の風が吹く
Ashita wa, ashita no kaze ga fuku
As for tomorrow, tomorrow's wind blows

For the Japanese
Moments we borrow,
Time's arrow on loan for fun.

And so no unease,
No bridge or sorrow,
Sheer lightness of abandon.

Quivers of a breeze
Put off tomorrow,
Trusting to the rising sun.

GRATITUDE

Thou hast giv'n so much to me,
Give one thing more, a gratefull heart.

GEORGE HERBERT

Blaenau Ffestiniog

1

Days of echoed chats. Roberts y Post,
Wil Tattos the potato van man,
Endless teas with dark-haired Mrs Pryce;
I'm nineteen here in Tan y Grisiau
Housed with twice-widowed Mrs Lewis.

At first nervous of her young lodger –
Paddies had built a local power plant,
One fine morning she'd found a navvy
Sleeping it off in her garden shed –
Yet I'd thought she'd begun to settle.

Question by question I gather words
But she hears her second husband's voice
Stumbling and childish after his stroke.
At breakfast pills scattered the table,
My hostess can take no more of me.

Her parting peace offering one husband's
Spurrell's Welsh–English dictionary
Signed August 4th 1966,
Mari Lewis. Demurring mother,
Your dismissed son still remembers you.

2

Like Seth I've fallen on my feet.
Mr and Mrs Owens my foster pair
Who'd lost a son and now find me.

A semi by the end of a terraced street
Jutting off Blaenau Ffestiniog's Square
Out over the lip of a river valley.

12 Bryn Bowydd my Welsh berth.
Mr Owens, chapel elder and slate-cutter,
Tireless after a day at his dressing mill
Pours his tea and talks for all he's worth
Between his hunks of bread and butter.
Dwy galon, he laughs, Two-hearted Phil.

Doris birdlike, good to her marrow,
A country girl from Cwm Nantcol,
She'd fallen for her talking Blaenau beau;
Downright and dutiful house sparrow
She loved to break her daily protocol
With Sunday drives to Chester or Llandudno.

Forty years older a Christmas bulletin
In her headline copy script to say
Ma' Phil wedi marw, out of his pain,
Over ninety his second heart given out.
My mind clouds a 'Stiniog day,
Bryn Bowydd is veiled in slaty rain.

3

Let the resurrection siren sound,
Blink us forth from dusty caverns
Dazzled and gladly over ground
By chapels and diehard taverns
Back through the dove-grey light
Cast from slated streets and waste
Past the Co-'p and Square, then right,
Homeward now the ashen-faced.

Loyal to your prince and crown
Beware hot-headed Papist schemes;
Old Lloyd George's Whiggish town,
No foolishness or 'Welsh Nash' dreams.
Wonder and ask could this be true,
Picture cards from Dublin show a bus?
Sundays at least a chapel or two.
'You see he's speaking just like us!'

4

I don't think R.S. Thomas liked his flock,
Neither Evans nor Prytherch nor Job Davies,
Uneasy fossil in the mind's rock
He feared them all as Kavanagh feared Maguire –
A gofid gwerin gyfan
Yn fy nghri fel taerni tân –
A people's grief my cry's nagging fire.

The grey cramped womb of Blaenau Ffestiniog,
Crimean Pass of Merionethshire,
Cradles memories of dusty fog
Swirling in beams of a slate miner's lantern.
Dai Du gives a mate a lash,
Jim Bach's a 'Welsh Nash'.
Pesychu 'to cough' an important word to learn

When stooping over rubble wagons with grease.
Eisiau seim! We push them round the jagged bends.
In Blaenau Square they sit and wheeze,
The grinder's disease will have them hook or crook.
I'll go with you and be your guide
In thy most need to go by your side
Postman Pierce reads his Everyman book.

Poor R.S. struggling with his own kind.
For me only their warmth and wake through time
Etched against the slate waste tips they'd mined.
O pit-ponies Dai and Jim and Aled,
Stoop to smear the wagon creaking
Noise of small hearts breaking.
I bless a town that gave me all it had.

Homeland

1

Age of open heart and talking soul,
Feverish plans of callow time out,
Suspended time of sixty-eighters

Before the routines of survival,
Our habits of settled common sense,
This aperture for livelong friendships.

Oslo of snow boots and *Pils* and trams,
City of youth and orphan stumblings
I grew up here with sibling students.

All hail those who made me one of you,
You who let me strike these other roots;
I flourish in my second homeland.

2

Bjørn, my proto-Scandanavian,
Long-legged, blond and blue-eyed gleam of charm,
Dreamy mountaineer those years adrift,
Mix of make-believe and action man.

'Noble the human, the earth is rich'
Mood by mood our nightly poems aloud,
Edelt er mennesket, jorden er rik
Nordahl Grieg's *To Youth* at fever pitch.

'Dance my lyric, weep my song'
Skjæraasen and Herman Wildenvey
'Life's desire so strong and near and new'
Danse mi vise, gråte min sang.

Me a poet, you now glacialist,
Every time we meet in two score years,
Quoting Gunnar's words you'd quoted me,
Ghostly Rudin I once more insist:

'Don't forget the one you've never met,
She's the one you love in her you love.'
Action man remember now your dream?
Lines of mine move daily in your debt.

3

Gratitude's language.
For food. For today. For now.
A tongue to thank in.

Edda

1

A fling that ends as quickly as it started
But I'm among Oslo's Iceland crowd;
A few doubtful but mostly open-hearted,
Half-curious about this *Íri*, half-proud.
'Black Death' or beer our nights on the tear,
Sundays Hallgrímur puts me through my paces;
You clearheaded, me the worse for wear,
Busy trying to parse those Eddic phrases.
Maðr er mannz gaman. 'Man's joy man'.
A world cut stone by stone that undergirds
Each noun's monochrome Germanic freight,
A tongue like Hopkins' favoured Anglo-Saxon,
Tee-aitches, *eð*'s, its saga-ness of words
Nearer now than English to Alf the Great.

2

Could I have had a better guide,
Hallgrímur, Magnús góði's son
Who'd over generations taught
Reykjavík's pupils to decline?

En gaman! And all the more fun!
You tell how the skaldic kenning,
A playful and roundabout phrase,
Now too can mean 'a theory'.

Most of all that sense of delight,
Gift of joy. With Laxness we say:
Ég fékk hann til láns af láni
I got as a loan of a loan...

'Often liking with little won,
With loaf half cut, with cup half drained'
A sharp-eyed love of what's simple.
'I find myself a fellow soul.'

3

Two generations on we sit
On a sunny Donnybrook wall
Talking over Gödel's *kenning*.
'Tell me All-Wise thou knowest all?'
'Such my wiles that they seek in vain.'

Our saga unfolds its wisdom.
'Before young, I'd fared all alone.
Then I'd drifted. I know how rich
I struck it, finding another.
Maðr er mannz gaman. Man's joy man.'

Barcelona

1

Strolling la Rambla de les Flors,
Sometimes Spanish, sometimes Catalan.
Franco still can rule his stubborn roost.

1970 and Raimon sings:
Buscant a Déu, al vent de món
'Seeking God, the wind of our world'.

Pablo land, Cassells and Picasso too.
Soon as Montserrat unlocked her door
Here I knew at once I'd struck it rich.

Swarthy, ageless, wealthy draper's wife,
Open-faced, so warm and charged with fun.
Daughter Concha tutored me at home.

Mother like the first who mothered me
Offering now her gifts of praise and tongue.
Yes! *Aixó mateig!* Exactly so!

Slowly born I'm growing here again.
I ja le nèixer és un gran plor
'And our birth already one great cry'.

2

Barcelona days you nourish me,
Role to which you easily revert.
Would this fit I wonder? *Creg que si*
Sending home a leather miniskirt.
All those *v*'s pronounced as if they're *b*'s
J's and *s*'s don't rub the mouth,
Arabs didn't reach as far as these,
Lisps and gutturals still further south.
No flamenco or fiery castanet,
Port of trade and merchant middleman,
Stately as a slow sardana dance,
Brittle Spanish light and somehow yet
Here's this straddling world of Catalan,
Halfway house between Castile and France.

3

Sunday it's a climb to Montserrat.
There an open square for us to dance;
Brass, woodwind and drum the *combla* plays
6/8 rhythm sardanas in the sun,
Down-toned *klezmer* weaves us in.

Named from this serrated pilgrim mount
You're enfolded in that plaza's dance.
Tambourine and bass proclaim *mercès!*
Gràcies! Montserrat Castells,
La meva mama catalana.

Deutsch

1 *Frau*

Ach du lieber Gott! I learn to say,
Words first heard in dingy Dublin rooms
Chatting hours with *Frau* in exile Smith,
Half flirtatious pouring out her past:
Three times wed and now this third time stuck,
Living here for daughter Hildegard.

Ach, she sighs each time she speaks of 'him'.
Once a dancer. Look my photograph!
Aber men no longer double-take.

Say now where all the men are gone.
Ach ja, sag mir, wo die Männer sind.
Always such long-distance happiness,
Here nostalgic, there dissatisfied.
Giving in I slowly draw away.
Then I hear that she's returning there –
Could I maybe even wish her well?
Saddest nurturer I'd ever had.
Unforgiven, still this need for thanks.

2 *Rhythm*

Why I love this *Deutsch* it's hard to say.
Downrightness, some hold on clarity,
German parts I somehow want to play?
Earnest *Doppelgänger* sleep in me?
Concepts seem to grow so sure and clear,
Stark as each staccato idiom,
Doubts or qualms now somehow disappear
Warding off each argument's *warum*?
Loops of iambs persuade now even me –
Raffiniert 'refined' can now mean 'sly' –
Alles muss so klar und deutlich sein!
Plain and straight as everything must be.
Wait and wait the sense comes by and by –
Verbs kept back like Cana's finest wine.

3 *Pfeils*

Strange the hoops of chance that took me here:
Geschwister-Scholl-Straße, Alpirsbach,
Street that's named for student siblings Scholl,
White Rose pamphleteers the Nazis killed,
Apt address for such attentive friends,
Close and open how they welcome me!
Pfeils the gentlest pair I think I've met;
I'm at home and spread my German wings.

Teach me *heute mir* and *morgen dir*
Turned around becomes compassion's core:
'All that's yours today, tomorrow's mine.
Bach's St Matthew and Rilke's Elegies,
Dietrich's *Wann wird man je verstehn?*
Mein Gott! 'When will we ever understand?'
Here the Germany I'll always love.
Pitch my *Heimat* tent at Alpirsbach.

Poitiers

1

For weeks at Poitiers a widow takes me in.
Her husband, then her daughter dead from grief,
Josy Montaigne, proud of Spanish origin
Somehow hangs by threads of her belief.
A life unfurling I attend all ears,
Her memory by memory recall,
We talk and talk unburdening it all
Till slowly an older *joie de vivre* grows.
Chansons. I'm taught Piaf and Barbara:
'When he takes me in his arms,' she sings,
Reminded moments of her *Vie en Rose,*
Quand il me prend dans ses bras...
A touch of joy in Poitiers' late spring.

2

Rev. J.A. Moran SM's
French Grammar and Composition:
No slurred words or syllables
Action of the organs of speech
More vigorous, sharp, than English...
O school *Français!*

All those pursed up haughty vowels,
The huffs and puffs of sullen lips,
Such shrugged shoulders and open palms,
Pouting, sulky, nasal, sultry,

How every word caresses me.
O moody *Français!*

Not just sorry but *désolé*
Or to stop at thanks a million
Merci infiniment!
As meeting you I'm *enchanté.*
Rien. Je ne regrette rien.
O dramatic *Français!*

Sing my Barbara of Nantes,
Tell of your vagabond father
Who dies the night before your smile
Without farewell or 'I love you'
Sans un adieu, sans un 'je t'aime'.
O dolorous *Français!*

No slurring. In those speech organs
Such chic and naughty *savoir faire.*
Loveliest tongue. *La plus belle langue,*
Every sound seems to kiss a nerve,
Each word a bird of paradise.
O sensuous *Français!*

3

A hug as trains approached *un cadeau du ciel,*
Heaven sent. How could she have known at all?
Merci infiniment! Farewell.
Then two days later her unexpected call.
Assigned to Paris, wife in Poitiers,
Of course returning late and tired was rash,
She didn't want to shock but had to say
Her younger son had died in a motor crash.
Any common sense cries out against this fate.
'And all the same I trust.' *Quand même*
Je crois en Dieu. Unbreakable belief.
Was Job so tested – daughter, son and mate?
Sans un adieu, sans un 'je t'aime'.
Our time *à deux* an interlude in grief.

Echo

Into my fifties when I began –
Too late for parent now or lover,
This time around brother or daughter.

First friend Shimizu-san 'Spring Water'
Babytalking me to discover
In myself some *déjà vu* Japan.

Other brothers too but often young
Women daughtering an older man,
Nurturing some new Japanese me.

'Peach-Tail' and 'High-up Mulberry Tree',
Momō-san and Takakuwa-san
Suckle me into another tongue.

Nakamura-san sighing *yoisho*
Or *yokkoisho* as she bent and swung
On her chair to lift a dictionary,

Sound of exertion 'ups-a-daisy',
A straining creak of an effort wrung
Out of the body, a 'yo-heave-ho'.

Yoisho I echo and have begun
As in second childhood to let go.
Brothers and daughters now cradle me.

A tongue-tied me now at last set free.
Dream I'd given up on years ago.
Words take wing into the rising sun.

So

In the beginning
The word. So too in the end.
Birds of paradise.

INDEX

Index of titles

(Poem titles are shown in roman type, book and section titles in italics.)

Index of themes

Index of names

822

CD RUNNING ORDER